A·N·N·U·A·L E·D·

MW01699930

Strategic Management

01/02

First Edition

EDITOR

Dr. Eldon H. Bernstein
Lynn University

Eldon H. Bernstein is professor of business policy and strategy at Lynn University in Boca Raton, Florida. He has more than 20 years of business experience, many of which were as CEO of a small organization. He earned an M.B.A. in marketing and a Ph.D. in business policy, both from the University of Connecticut. His teaching and research interests focus on the history of the development of business, specifically of the modern enterprise in the United States.

McGraw-Hill/Dushkin
530 Old Whitfield Street, Guilford, Connecticut 06437

Visit us on the Internet
http://www.dushkin.com

Credits

1. The Strategic Climate
Unit photo—© 2000 by PhotoDisc, Inc.
2. Elements of Stategic Choices
Unit photo—© 2000 by PhotoDisc, Inc.
3. Formulating Strategies
Unit photo—© 2000 by PhotoDisc, Inc.
4. Organizational Change
Unit photo—© 2000 by PhotoDisc, Inc.
5. Implementing, Measuring, and Controlling Strategy
Unit photo—Courtesy of TRW, Inc.

Copyright

Cataloging in Publication Data
Main entry under title: Annual Editions: Strategic Management. 2001/2002.
1. Management 2. Organizational change—United States. 3. Leadership. I. Bernstein, Eldon H., *comp.* II. Title: Strategic management.
ISBN 0-07-238890-0 658'.2 80-643193 ISSN 1530-583X

First Edition

Cover image © 2001 PhotoDisc, Inc.

Printed in the United States of America 1234567890BAHBAH54321 Printed on Recycled Paper

Editors/Advisory Board Staff

Members of the Advisory Board are instrumental in the final selection of articles for each edition of ANNUAL EDITIONS. Their review of articles for content, level, currentness, and appropriateness provides critical direction to the editor and staff. We think that you will find their careful consideration well reflected in this volume.

To the Reader

In publishing ANNUAL EDITIONS we recognize the enormous role played by the magazines, newspapers, and journals of the public press in providing current, first-rate educational information in a broad spectrum of interest areas. Many of these articles are appropriate for students, researchers, and professionals seeking accurate, current material to help bridge the gap between principles and theories and the real world. These articles, however, become more useful for study when those of lasting value are carefully collected, organized, indexed, and reproduced in a low-cost format, which provides easy and permanent access when the material is needed. That is the role played by ANNUAL EDITIONS.

New to ANNUAL EDITIONS is the inclusion of related World Wide Web sites. These sites have been selected by our editorial staff to represent some of the best resources found on the World Wide Web today. Through our carefully developed topic guide, we have linked these Web resources to the articles covered in this ANNUAL EDITIONS reader. We think that you will find this volume useful, and we hope that you will take a moment to visit us on the Web at ***http://www.dushkin.com*** to tell us what you think.

This is the first edition of *Annual Editions: Strategic Management,* and I hope that it will prove to be a valuable resource for practitioners and students alike. The reader will quickly recognize in my introductions to the five unit sections that I have relied heavily on business history to introduce today's management topics. Rather than glorify the past, I have used this approach to illuminate the future. We must understand that change in the content and the context of strategy has been constant since the founding of the United States. We are all aware of what has happened in the past, but there is nothing that we can do to change it. With that knowledge in hand, we can help shape the future.

Roughly every half century, significant changes have occurred in the United States and in the global economy that have changed the way business has been done. In the early 1800s, the U.S. Post Office and the construction of canals improved the processes of transportation and communication. The result was that an entire new business system emerged. Fifty years later the railroad and the telegraph offered dramatically improved speed and reliability for the movement of information, goods, and people. Once again, marketing and distribution changed significantly. At the beginning of the twentieth century, widespread telephone service and the appearance of motor vehicles facilitated the emergence of the large industrial enterprises as the United States became a true, single national market.

With the development of the large industrial enterprise came the concept of an upper level of manager; a manager to manage managers. Due to the complexity of the large firm, senior managers needed to dedicate their time and energies to the long-term needs of the firm, while salaried hierarchies of professional managers coordinated the functional activities of the firms. Freed from the tasks of daily management, these upper-level managers represent the first generation of strategic planners.

By the 1950s, new communications, such as satellites, and advances in transportation, such as jet aircraft and container shipping, helped lay the foundations for the transformation to a global economy. As we enter the twenty-first century, the Internet seems destined to reshape many business practices.

In examining these dramatic changes, we should recall that the history of American enterprise shows remarkable patterns that have remained constant. The business community has always rewarded speed—speed in delivery, speed in response to consumer needs, or speed in adapting to new technologies. Efficient firms survive; inefficient ones are systematically replaced. No matter how we envision twenty-first century dot.com companies, they will not survive without following one simple constant challenge: a firm must make a profit.

Some strategic concepts have indeed changed along with the environment. Land, captial, and technology were once the original scarce resources. The distribution of land, abundance of capital, and decreasing costs of technology have subordinated them to the value of knowledge.

The task of the strategist, through all these changes, has remained the same. It is not the creation of shareholder wealth, which is often cited as management's responsibility, but the creation of some surplus value. When that value is created, the strategist's task is to apply it effectively to enhance the future performance of the firm. Clearly, the strategies to accomplish those goals have changed, as evidenced by the articles selected for this issue. At the same time, these readings illustrate the similarities between organizations and organisms—how they learn, how they adapt, and how they survive and prosper.

The first edition of *Annual Editions: Strategic Management 01/02* contains a number of features that are designed to make it useful for people interested in the subject. These features include a *topic guide* for locating articles on specific subjects and a *table of contents* with abstracts that summarize each article and draw attention to key words in bold italics. In addition, a list of *World Wide Web* sites, which are cross-referenced by number to the topic guide, is provided for further exploration of the topics. This volume is organized into five units dealing with specific interrelated topics in strategic management. Each unit begins with a unit *overview* that provides the necessary background information to allow the reader to place a selection in the context of the book. Important topics are emphasized, and key points to consider address major themes.

We would like to know what you think about our book. Please take a few minutes to complete and return the postage-paid *article rating form* in the back of the volume. We need your advice and assistance to help improve future editions of *Annual Editions: Strategic Management.*

Eldon H. Bernstein
Editor

Contents

To the Reader iv
Topic Guide 2
Selected World Wide Web Sites 4

Overview 6

A. MACRO ENVIRONMENTS

1. **Danger: Stealth Attack,** Toni Mack and Mary Summers, *Forbes,* January 25, 1999. 8
Many established companies ignored ***innovative threats*** from newcomers with creative ideas. Companies who wish aggressive growth must keep asking, "What ***technology*** could threaten to destroy my company?"

2. **Supersizing the Supermarkets in a Shift of Power; Discounters and Mergers Alter Balance of Power,** Dana Canedy, *New York Times,* November 13, 1998. 12
As ***efficiency-driven consolidation*** has occurred in the ***retail food industry,*** new patterns of competition have arisen and the structure has changed significantly.

3. **Between a Gas Pump and a Hard Place,** Matthew L. Wald, *New York Times,* September 25, 1993. 15
An independent service station operator finds it increasingly difficult to survive as he faces a variety of ***hostile environments.***

B. GLOBAL ENVIRONMENTS

4. **See Jack. See Jack Run Europe,** Thomas A. Stewart, *Fortune,* September 27, 1999. 18
When Jack Welch turns over the leadership of General Electric, he leaves a firm that not only has grown almost fourfold during his tenure, but one that has established itself firmly as a truly ***global organization.***

5. **Nokia: Made in Finland and Sold Just about Everywhere,** Youssef M. Ibrahim, *New York Times,* August 13, 1997. 23
The ***internal environment*** in Finland provides Nokia with the ***technology and culture*** it needs to become a dominant supplier of portable phones in the world market.

6. **Zeneca Buying Astra As Europe Consolidates,** Alan Cowell, *New York Times,* December 10, 1998. 25
To ***compete in a market dominated by giant U.S. firms,*** two European pharmaceutical manufacturers merge. Progress toward an integrated European Community suggests that more ***mergers*** of this type will occur.

7. **China Rolls Out the Red Carpet,** Richard Tomlinson, *Fortune,* May 24, 1999. 27
With partners like Marriott and Hilton, the ***Chinese are building a class-A hotel industry.*** The history of Chinese hotels and hotel managers, however, casts a long shadow over the outlook for the new entrants.

The Strategic Climate

The seven selections in this section look at local and global environments in the management of marketing opportunities.

The concepts in bold italics are developed in the article. For further expansion please refer to the Topic Guide and the Index.

Elements of Strategic Choices

The seven articles in this section consider the relationship between management and leadership in making effective business choices.

Overview 30

A. MANAGEMENT

8. America's Most Admired Companies, Eryn Brown, *Fortune,* March 1, 1999. 32
The largest and most ***powerful corporations*** in the United States are ***ranked*** on several attributes by *Fortune.* Some similarities among the most and least admired companies are identified.

9. Big Kellogg Shareholders Seek More Snap, Crackle and Pop, Dana Canedy and Reed Abelson, *New York Times,* January 24, 1999. 37
A ***flat stock price*** and ***depressed profitability*** have created a high degree of turbulence in Kellogg's management. Family shareholders and foundation interests have a profound effect on the company's operation.

B. LEADERSHIP

10. The Rise of a Star, Anthony Bianco, *Business Week,* December 21, 1998. 40
Following a series of major management changes at American Express, Ken Chenault demonstrates a vision and ***leadership style*** that has ***revitalized*** American Express and challenged some of its traditions.

11. New CEO Preaches Rebellion for P&G's Cult, Tara Parker-Pope, *Wall Street Journal,* December 11, 1998. 48
Durk Jager brings several new dimensions to Procter & Gamble management. His extensive experience in international markets and his dedication to changing the culture at P&G suggest that a much different company will develop under his ***leadership.***

12. The Auctioneer: Margaret Whitman, the CEO of eBay, Talks about the Company's Rapid Growth—and Heady Ambitions, George Anders, *Wall Street Journal,* November 22, 1999. 50
Margaret Whitman, CEO of eBay, personifies the ***new breed of cyber-age manager.*** In an interview she explains her visions for handling the challenges of a rapidly growing company in a world of new technologies.

13. Man on the Spot, *Business Week,* May 3, 1999. 55
When he succeeded to the chairmanship at Coca-Cola, Doug Ivester inherited a company with dominant market share and a significant global presence. A variety of problems exist, but Ivester, with the support of the board of directors, is committed to Coke's long-term ***strategy.***

14. Why CEOs Fail, Ram Charan and Geoffrey Colvin, *Fortune,* June 21, 1999. 62
Most ***CEOs who fail*** seem to do so for one ***fatal shortcoming.*** Those shortcomings, however, may be difficult to identify. Several well-publicized cases of failed leadership illustrate the areas in which they are most likely to occur.

The concepts in bold italics are developed in the article. For further expansion please refer to the Topic Guide and the Index.

Overview 68

A. GROWTH STRATEGIES

15. Evolution and Revolution As Organizations Grow, Larry E. Greiner, *Harvard Business Review,* May/June 1998. 70
In a classic article examining ***growth,*** the author looks at five ***characteristics of organizations*** over a series of five ***growth phases.*** A matrix suggests that different practices are evident over the evolution.

16. The Net-Phone-TV-Cable Monster, *Business Week,* May 10, 1999. 78
The Federal Court forced the breakup of AT&T as a telephone company over a decade ago. Now the new CEO, Michael Armstrong, is rebuilding it into an even ***bigger organization*** through a series of ***acquisitions.***

17. You've Got Time Warner—How the Merger Will Affect Other Big Web and Media Players, David Bank, *Wall Street Journal,* January 11, 2000. 81
In the wake of the monumental ***merger of AOL and Time Warner,*** rival forces are evaluated in terms of their strategic advantages and what their response to this alliance might be.

18. How 2 Executives Pulled Off the Biggest Merger Ever, Allen R. Meyerson, *New York Times,* December 4, 1998. 84
A century after one of the most famous court decisions broke up Standard Oil, two of the main companies that were created have announced a ***merger.*** The merger promises to ***combine the strengths*** of the two to ***offset*** their ***weaknesses*** in a ***global market.***

B. CORPORATE LEVEL STRATEGIES

19. Why Diversify? Four Decades of Management Thinking, Michael Goold and Kathleen Luchs, *Academy of Management Executive,* Volume 7, Number 3, 1993. 86
Understanding what relatedness contributes to a successful diversification strategy remains difficult. The authors present a view of the ***changes in managerial philosophy*** over the last 40 years.

20. A Powerhouse of Technology Decides to Split into 2 Units, Lawrence M. Fisher, *New York Times,* March 3, 1999. 97
Although Hewlett-Packard is generally a highly regarded company, it has lost its focus in recent years. To correct that, management has decided to ***form two separate companies,*** one to focus on computers, printers, and scanners, and the other to concentrate on test equipment and medical technology.

21. How Gillette Wowed Wall Street, *Business Week,* September 30, 1996. 99
An unusually positive response greeted Gillette's ***acquisition*** of Duracell. While the deal makes good sense by providing a genuinely ***synergistic relationship,*** the details of the ***financing*** are ***particularly attractive to investors.***

Formulating Strategies

The nineteen selections in this section examine strategic choices, which include growth dynamics, corporate level decisions, business level strategies, and the importance of building a competitive advantage.

The concepts in bold italics are developed in the article. For further expansion please refer to the Topic Guide and the Index.

22. The New Intel, Andy Reinhardt, *Business Week,* March 13, 2000. **102**
In 1985, under Andrew Grove, Intel changed its focus from a diversified maker of chips to a concentration on one specific area—processors for personal computers. Now, Grove's successor, Craig Barrett, is reversing that ***strategy*** and is ***diversifying*** into a variety of ventures.

23. How Formica Got Burned Out by Buyouts, Debra Sparks, *Business Week,* March 22, 1999. **110**
At one time, Formica owned a commanding market share, and in fact became a generic name for plastic laminates. However, a series of ***buyouts*** and ***leveraged buyouts (LBOs)*** has resulted in a ravaged company.

C. BUSINESS-LEVEL STRATEGIES

24. Prada Goes Shopping, Lauren Goldstein, *Fortune,* September 9, 1999. **114**
Patrizio Bertelli of Prada has ***created a designer empire*** based upon finding the ***"Next Big Thing" in fashion.*** Now he is embarking on a strategy to create a corporate powerhouse.

25. Doc Ebbers' Miracle Diet, *Business Week,* March 1, 1999. **116**
WorldCom Inc. has assembled a communications network based on being the low-cost provider. The recent acquisition of MCI suggests that Bernard Ebbers will ***cut operating expenses*** drastically to support the ***low-cost policy.***

26. Market Place: Midwest Express Profits by Pampering Passengers, Edwin McDowell, *New York Times,* September 23, 1997. **118**
Since deregulation the airline industry has been under constant attack for poor service. Employing a ***focused differentiation strategy,*** Midwest has built a loyal base of customers by catering to all their needs.

27. Specialized Hospitals Taking Over Health-Care Market, Allen R. Myerson, *New York Times,* October 7, 1997. **121**
Private hospital revenues and profits have been constrained by new insurance regulations. To counteract that, many hospitals have developed ***specialized areas of expertise*** that are more profitable to deliver.

D. BUILDING COMPETITIVE ADVANTAGE

28. Predators and Prey: A New Ecology of Competition, James F. Moore, *Harvard Business Review,* May/June 1993. **124**
In an article reminiscent of the approach of renowned economist Joseph Schumpeter, James Moore ***relates the environment to a biological world.*** Moore suggests that the key to survival in this type of ***competition*** is to be ***innovative*** and gives several examples to support his theory.

29. The Changing Art of Becoming Unbeatable, Geoffrey Colvin, *Fortune,* November 24, 1997. **133**
Geoffrey Colvin identifies three critical factors—the ***increased power of customers,*** the ***value of knowledge,*** and the ***importance of speed***—that must be considered if a company is to establish a competitive advantage.

The concepts in bold italics are developed in the article. For further expansion please refer to the Topic Guide and the Index.

30. FedEx CEO Smith Bets His Deal with Cisco Will Recast the Future of Shipping, Douglas A. Blackmon, *Wall Street Journal,* November 4, 1999. **135**

For many years, FedEx crafted a significant ***competitive advantage*** by creating a state-of-the-art technological system that afforded it and its clients a wealth of information. Now that advantage has been neutralized by others, and FedEx needs to react to the ***changes in the distribution processes.***

31. Creating Competitive (Dis)advantage: Learning from Food Lion's Freefall, Gregory G. Dess and Joseph C. Picken, *Academy of Management Executive,* Volume 13, Number 3, 1999. **138**

After building an enviable reputation, Food Lion suffered greatly in the early 1990s. Some problems were attributed to a television exposé, but the authors note that the core problem was that Food Lion's ***competitive advantage*** failed to deliver ***sustainable added customer value.***

32. Six Sigma Enlightenment; Managers Seek Corporate Nirvana through Quality Control, Claudia H. Deutsch, *New York Times,* December 7, 1998. **151**

At General Electric, CEO Jack Welch has invested more than $1 billion in Six Sigma, a process that ***reduces defective products*** to fewer than 3.4 parts per million. The result has been greater customer satisfaction and significantly increased earnings.

33. Inside the Cult of Costco, Shelly Branch, *Fortune,* September 6, 1999. **155**

With 60 percent as many stores as Sam's Club, Costco is outselling the legendary Wal-Mart's entry into warehouse retailing. Costco combines a philosophy of ***driving prices*** down with a customer base of ***uncommonly loyal customers,*** and that turns shopping in their stores into a special experience.

Organizational Change

These seven articles look at the challenges facing today's business organization, and what must be done to make essential changes work.

Overview **158**

A. INDUSTRY AND ORGANIZATIONAL DECLINE

34. Publishers of Paperbacks Are Facing Sliding Sales, Doreen Carvajal, *New York Times,* March 15, 1999. **160**

Doreen Carvajal details the reasons for the serious decline in the sale of paperbacks. With many of its earlier advantages eroded, ***paperback publishing*** is searching for ***ways to reverse the slide.***

35. How Levi's Trashed a Great American Brand, Nina Munk, *Fortune,* April 12, 1999. **163**

For many years, Levi's has been an icon of American business. According to the author, Levi's ***problems*** are a result of management ***concentration on the wrong areas.***

36. How NordicTrack Lost Its Footing, *Business Week,* December 14, 1998. **169**

NordicTrack was a first mover in the field of home exercise equipment. However, changing customer preferences in addition to several ***management errors*** have resulted in the company's declaring ***bankruptcy.***

37. A Makeover for the TV Dinner; Swanson Is Being Upgraded to Restore Market Share, Constance L. Hays, *New York Times,* July 25, 1998. **171**
Swanson, the company that invented the TV dinner, finds itself struggling to regain some of its former market. An analyst charges that "they have ***missed every single trend*** since the Korean War."

B. TURNAROUND AND REENGINEERING

38. Reengineering Work: Don't Automate, Obliterate, Michael Hammer, *Harvard Business Review,* July/August 1990. **174**
Michael Hammer argues that ***reengineering*** is a process that demands drastic changes to discard the outdated rules that governed organizations decades ago. Managers must design entirely ***new procedures based on new principles.***

39. Owens Corning: Back from the Dead, Thomas A. Stewart, *Fortune,* May 26, 1997. **181**
When CEO Glen Hiner came to Owens Corning from GE, the company was deep in debt and sales were declining. A total ***reengineering*** of the company has resulted in a healthy, well-respected organization today.

40. A Close-Up Look at President Rick Wagoner and His Strategy for Reviving GM, *Business Week,* February 1, 1999. **185**
GM has seen its market share plummet from nearly 50 percent to below 30 percent. The new president has made some significant changes to ***reverse the slide,*** but many ***potential obstacles remain*** for GM to overcome.

UNIT 5

Implementing, Measuring, and Controlling Strategy

These ten selections consider what must be done to effectively implement strategies that will guarantee some degree of success in today's fast-paced business climate.

Overview **192**

A. STRATEGY IMPLEMENTATION

41. Why Sizzler Fizzled: As Competition Heated Up, Chain's Concept Went Stale, Glenn Collins, *The Miami Herald,* June 30, 1996. **194**
Aldred Chandler Jr. proposed the ***classic concept*** that a firm's ***structure*** must be designed to ***implement its strategy.*** In the case of Sizzler International Inc., their restaurants' physical structure was not appropriate to their newly designed strategy and therefore failed.

42. Whirlwind on the Web, *Business Week,* April 7, 1997. **196**
In order to function as a low-cost computer producer, it was necessary for Michael Dell to design an ***organization*** that ***responded quickly and operated efficiently.*** The Dell system allows them to do just that.

43. The New VIP Rooms, Lisa Gubernick, *Wall Street Journal,* December 11, 1998. **199**
As the changing composition of the movie theater industry put additional pressure on operating profits, ***theater owners conceived a new, premium-priced offering.*** To do it, however, it was necessary to ***change the structure*** of their theaters.

The concepts in bold italics are developed in the article. For further expansion please refer to the Topic Guide and the Index.

44. Lack of Shopping Carts Impact Sales at Traditional Department Stores, Joseph B. Cahill, *Wall Street Journal,* November 24, 1999. **203**
In the 1930s, the ***invention of the shopping cart*** was essential to implementing the strategy of the ***self-service market.*** Shunned for three generations as degrading to their images, ***department stores*** now find that their ***declining sales*** may be due in part to structural decisions that preclude their use of shopping carts.

45. The Deal Is Done. Now the Work Begins, Claudia H. Deutsch, *New York Times,* April 11, 1999. **205**
Historically, the success of ***mergers and acquisitions*** is less than perfect. If not outright failure, ***unexpected expenses and delays*** may result. The author explains how the process needs to be accomplished to prevent conflict, quarreling, and lack of communications between the parties.

B. MEASUREMENT AND CONTROLLING STRATEGY

46. The Balanced Scorecard—Measures That Drive Performance, Robert S. Kaplan and David P. Norton, *Harvard Business Review,* January/February 1992. **208**
As skills and competencies change, the authors argue, so must the standards by which businesses evaluate performance. They propose ***adding three measures to traditional accounting ratios*** to achieve a more meaningful result.

47. Cendant: Who's to Blame? *Business Week,* August 17, 1998. **216**
The ***merger*** of CUC International and HFS Inc. produced the Cendant Corporation. It also produced a ***tangled web of financial dealings.*** Trying to unravel them has caused great rifts within the company.

48. A Bit of Barnum on Broadway; Livent Drew in a New Team Despite Juggling Expenses, Melody Petersen and Geraldine Fabrikant, *New York Times,* August 21, 1998. **218**
Livent Inc., the corporate theater producer, enjoyed great success producing Broadway shows, spending lavishly to do so. Investigations into their financial affairs, however, have raised questions about their ***financial controls.***

49. The Lesson from Barings' Straits, *Business Week,* March 13, 1995. **221**
Barings was a 233-year-old, major player in international finance. How could one trader, Nick Leeson, lose $1.3 billion and ***bankrupt*** the company? Why were there ***no controls*** in place?

50. How One Firm Tracks Ethics Electronically, Michael J. McCarthy, *Wall Street Journal,* October 21, 1999. **223**
After having been fined $24.8 million for paying an illegal bribe, Lockheed Martin has ***instituted a program to audit, record, and perfect the measurement of employee ethics.***

Index **225**
Article Review Form **228**
Article Rating Form **229**

Topic Guide

This topic guide suggests how the selections and World Wide Web sites found in the next section of this book relate to topics of traditional concern to students and professionals in the study of strategic management. It is useful for locating interrelated articles and Web sites for reading and research. The guide is arranged alphabetically according to topic.

The relevant Web sites, which are numbered and annotated on pages 4 and 5, are easily identified by the Web icon (●) under the topic articles. By linking the articles and the Web sites by topic, this ANNUAL EDITIONS reader becomes a powerful learning and research tool.

TOPIC AREA	TREATED IN
Acquisitions	16. Net-Phone-TV-Cable Monster 21. How Gillette Wowed Wall Street 25. Doc Ebbers' Miracle Diet 45. Deal Is Done. Now the Work Begins ● ***2, 5, 9***
Business Level Competition	24. Prada Goes Shopping 25. Doc Ebbers' Miracle Diet 26. Market Place: Midwest Express Profits by Pampering Passengers 27. Specialized Hospitals Taking Over Health-Care Market ● ***1, 2, 5, 6, 9, 14, 15, 17, 19, 31***
Changes in Structures	2. Supersizing the Supermarkets in a Shift of Power 3. Between a Gas Pump and a Hard Place 38. Reengineering Work: Don't Automate, Obliterate 43. New VIP Rooms 44. Lack of Shopping Carts Impact Sales at Traditional Department Stores ● ***2, 5, 9, 28, 30***
Changing Strategies	18. How 2 Executives Pulled Off the Biggest Merger Ever 19. Why Diversity? Four Decades of Management Thinking 20. Powerhouse of Technology Decides to Split into 2 Units 21. How Gillette Wowed Wall Street 22. New Intel 27. Specialized Hospitals Taking Over Health-Care Market 38. Reengineering Work: Don't Automate, Obliterate 39. Owens Corning: Back from the Dead 40. Close-Up Look at President Rick Wagoner and His Strategy for Reviving GM 43. New VIP Rooms 46. Balanced Scorecard—Measures That Drive Performance ● ***4, 6, 11, 12, 13, 14, 17, 18, 19, 30, 31***
Competitive Advantage	25. Doc Ebbers' Miracle Diet 28. Predators and Prey: A New Ecology of Competition 29. Changing Art of Becoming Unbeatable 30. FedEx CEO Smith Bets His Deal with Cisco Will Recast the Future of Shipping 31. Creating Competitive (Dis)advantage: Learning from Food Lion's Freefall 32. Six Sigma Enlightenment; Managers Seek Corporate Nirvana through Quality Control 33. Inside the Cult of Costco 34. Publishers of Paperbacks Are Facing Sliding Sales ● ***4, 15, 16, 18, 19, 21, 22, 30, 31***
Consolidation	2. Supersizing the Supermarkets in a Shift of Power: Discounters and Mergers Alter Balance of Power 6. Zeneca Buying Astra As Europe Consolidates ● ***2, 5, 9, 14, 21, 28***
Customer Power	26. Market Place: Midwest Express Profits by Pampering Passengers 29. Changing Art of Becoming Unbeatable 31. Creating Competitive (Dis)advantage: Learning from Food Lion's Freefall 33. Inside the Cult of Costco 36. How NordicTrack Lost Its Footing ● ***2, 5, 21, 31, 32***
Diversification	19. Why Diversity? Four Decades of Management Thinking 22. New Intel ● ***1, 6, 9, 14, 17, 21, 28***
Environmental Changes	4. See Jack, See Jack Run Europe 28. Predators and Prey: A New Ecology of Competition ● ***2, 5, 6, 7, 8, 10, 11***
Ethics of Strategy	47. Cendant: Who's to Blame? 48. Bit of Barnum on Broadway—Measures That Drive Performance 49. Lessons from Barings' Straits 50. How One Firm Tracks Ethics Electronically ● ***29, 30, 31, 32***
Global Environments	4. See Jack. See Jack Run Europe 5. Nokia: Made in Finland and Sold Just about Everywhere 6. Zeneca Buying Astra As Europe Consolidates 7. China Rolls Out the Red Carpet ● ***2, 5, 6, 7, 8, 10, 11***
Global Strategies	5. Nokia: Made in Finland and Sold Just about Everywhere 6. Zeneca Buying Astra As Europe Consolidates 13. Man on the Spot ● ***2, 5, 6, 7, 8, 10, 11***
Growth Strategies	4. See Jack. See Jack Run Europe 5. Nokia: Made in Finland and Sold Just about Everywhere 6. Zeneca Buying Astra As Europe Consolidates 7. China Rolls Out the Red Carpet 10. Rise of a Star 11. New CEO Preaches Rebellion 15. Evolution and Revolution As Organizations Grow 16. Net-Phone-TV-Cable Monster 17. You've Got Time Warner—How the Merger Will Affect Other Big Web and Media Players 18. How 2 Executives Pulled Off the Biggest Merger Ever ● ***17, 19, 20, 21, 22, 23***

TOPIC AREA	TREATED IN
Hostile Environments	3. Between a Gas Pump and a Hard Place 34. Publishers of Paperbacks Are Facing Sliding Sales
Innovative Competition	1. Danger: Stealth Attacks 28. Predators and Prey: A New Ecology of Competition 42. Whirlwind on the Web ● ***6, 7, 9, 18, 19, 20, 27, 30, 31***
International Marketing	11. New CEO Preaches Rebellion 24. Prada Goes Shopping ● ***8, 10***
Internet Companies	12. Auctioneer: Margaret Whitman, the CEO of eBay, Talks about the Company's Rapid Growth—and Healthy Ambitions 16. Net-Phone-TV-Cable Monster 25. Doc Ebbers' Miracle Diet 42. Whirlwind on the Web ● ***2, 5, 9, 10, 11, 15, 32***
Leadership	4. See Jack Run. See Jack Run Europe 10. Rise of a Star 11. New CEO Preaches Rebellion 12. Auctioneer: Margaret Whitman, the CEO of eBay, Talks about the Company's Rapid Growth—and Healthy Ambitions 13. Man on the Spot 14. Why CEOs Fail 24. Prada Goes Shopping 40. Close-Up Look at President Rick Wagoner 42. Whirlwind on the Web ● ***1, 2, 5, 10, 13, 14, 15, 31***
Leveraged Buyout	23. How Formica Got Burned Out by Buyouts
Management	8. America's Most Admired Companies 9. Kellogg Shareholders Seek More Snap, Crackle and Pop ● ***10, 13, 14, 15, 16***
Measuring Results	44. Lack of Shopping Carts Impact Sales at Traditional Department Stores 45. Deal Is Done. Now the Work Begins 46. Balanced Scorecard—Measures That Drive Performance 48. Bit of Barnum on Broadway: Livent Drew in a New Team Despite Juggling Expenses ● ***3, 24, 30, 31, 32***
Mergers	2. Supersizing the Supermarkets in a Shift of Power 6. Zeneca Buying Astra As Europe Consolidates 17. You've Got Time Warner—How the Merger Will Affect Other Big Web and Media Players 18. How 2 Executives Pulled Off the Biggest Merger Ever 45. Deal Is Done. Now the Work Begins 47. Cendant: Who's to Blame? ● ***2, 5, 8, 9, 10, 24, 29, 30***
Organizational Failure	34. Publishers of Paperbacks Are Facing Sliding Sales 35. How Levi's Trashed a Great American Brand 36. How NordicTrack Lost Its Footing 37. Makeover for the TV Dinner 41. Why Sizzler Fizzled: As Competition Heated Up, Chain's Concept Went Stale 44. Lack of Shopping Carts Impact Sales at Traditional Department Stores 47. Cendant: Who's to Blame? 49. Lesson from Barings' Straits ● ***5, 17, 18***
Profitability	9. Big Kellog Shareholders Seek More Snap, Crackle and Pop 27. Specialized Hospitals Taking Over Health-Care Market 32. Six Sigma Enlightenment: Managers Seek Corporate Nirvana through Quality Control 43. New VIP Rooms 49. Lessons from Barings' Straits ● ***15, 19, 24, 27, 28, 31, 32***
Reengineering/ Turnaround	38. Reengineering Work: Don't Automate, Obliterate 39. Owens Corning: Back from the Dead 40. Close-Up Look at President Rick Wagoner and His Strategy for Reviving GM ● ***24, 25, 26, 27, 28***
Retailing	2. Supersizing the Supermarkets in a Shift of Power 3. Between a Gas Pump and a Hard Place 31. Creating Competitive (Dis)advantage: Learning from Food Lion's Freefall 33. Inside the Cult of Costco 44. Lack of Shopping Carts Impact Sales at Traditional Department Stores ● ***2, 3, 5, 9, 32***
Strategy Implementation	31. Creating Competitive (Dis)advantage: Learning from Food Lion's Freefall 32. Six Sigma Enlightenment; Managers Seek Nirvana through Quality Control 39. Owens Corning: Back from the Dead 40. Close-Up Look at President Rick Wagoner and His Strategy for Reviving GM 42. Whirlwind on the Web 43. New VIP Rooms 44. Lack of Shopping Carts Impact Sales at Traditional Department Stores ● ***25, 27, 28, 30, 31, 32***
Technology	1. Danger: Stealth Attack 5. Nokia: Made in Finland and Sold Just about Everywhere 20. Powerhouse of Technology Decides to Split into 2 Units ● ***7, 8, 11, 20, 27***
Value of Knowledge	29. Changing Art of Becoming Unbeatable 42. Whirlwind on the Web 44. Lack of Shopping Carts Impact Sales at Traditional Department Stores 46. Balanced Scorecard: Measures That Drive Performance ● ***19, 20, 21, 31, 32***

DUSHKIN ONLINE

AE: Strategic Management

The following World Wide Web sites have been carefully researched and selected to support the articles found in this reader. If you are interested in learning more about specific topics found in this book, these Web sites are a good place to start. The sites are cross-referenced by number and appear in the topic guide on the previous two pages. Also, you can link to these Web sites through our DUSHKIN ONLINE support site at *http://www.dushkin.com/online/*.

The following sites were available at the time of publication. Visit our Web site—we update DUSHKIN ONLINE regularly to reflect any changes.

General Sources

1. Harvard Business School

http://www.hbs.edu/educators.html

Surf through the many valuable links attached to this Educators and Research News site and preview upcoming issues of the *Harvard Business Review*.

2. The New York Times

http://www.nytimes.com

Browsing through the extensive archives of the *New York Times* will provide you with a vast array of articles and information related to strategic management issues. So will the business section, which is available on the Internet daily.

3. STAT-USA

http://www.stat-usa.gov

This site, from the U.S. Department of Commerce, contains Daily Economic News, Frequently Requested Statistical Releases, Information on Export and International Trade, Domestic Economic News and Statistical Series, and Databases.

4. Strategic Management Titles

http://www.blackwellpublishers.co.uk/grant/stratman.htm

Here is a list of titles that includes books and journals in the area of strategic management. A helpful abstract describes each listing.

5. The Wall Street Journal

http://interactive.wsj.com

This is an Internet edition of the *Wall Street Journal*, the august and always interesting newspaper that is used by management the world over.

Strategic Climate

6. Business Policy and Strategy

http://www.aom.pace.edu/bps/bps.html

This site, the home page of the Business Policy and Strategy Division of the U.S. Academy of Management, is packed with information about the theory and practice of international business.

7. CIBERWeb

http://ciber.centers.purdue.edu

The Centers for International Business Education and Research work to increase and promote Americans' capacity for international understanding and economic enterprise. This site is valuable for exploring issues of doing business in a global market.

8. Global Business Network (GBN)

http://www.gbn.org/home.html

Committed to perceiving the present in order to anticipate the future and better manage strategic responses, the GBN's activities and services are designed to think collaboratively about the business environment. GBN originates scenario planning and offers help with the process online.

9. Hoover Online—The Business Network

http://www.hoovers.com

This Internet site offers everything management needs to make business decisions, including news of IPOs, hot companies, snapshots of companies and industries, and links to other business sites on the Web. Check out *http://www.hoovers.com/industry/snapshot/0.2204,19,00.html*, for example, for a snapshot of the food industry.

10. Sales & Marketing Executives International

http://www.smei.org

Visit the home page of SME, a worldwide association of sales and marketing management. Through this "Digital Resource Mall," you can access research and useful articles on sales and management. You can even listen in as marketing leaders discuss their latest strategies and ideas.

11. SMG—Strategic Management Group, Inc.

http://www3.smginc.com/smginc/smg/

This global business learning organization offers high-quality, technology-based performance improvement to companies who need it.

12. SMS—Strategic Management Society

http://www.smsweb.org/Pages/Windows/welcome.html

SMS focuses on the development and dissemination of insights on strategic management process, fostering contacts and interchange among ABCs (academics, business people, and consultants) around the world. The organization holds an annual international conference and smaller special issue conferences.

Elements of Strategic Choices

13. Business Nation

http://www.businessnation.com/library/management.html

This Management section of Business Nation's Library lists many resources about CEOs and other business leaders, as well as articles on management skills.

14. Centre for Strategic Management

http://csmintl.premierdomain.com/menu.htm

This organization consults with and develops senior management using their Systems Thinking Approach to strategic management. Their expertise is in business leadership and strategy, systems thinking and learning, and leadership in facilitating strategic change.

15. Fortune 1000 list

http://www.fortune.com/fortune/fortune500/

Fortune magazine offers many lists concerning the top 1000 companies, as well as the top CEOs and industries. At *http://www.fortune.com/fortune/fortune500/enr.html* read about Enron, the Power Merchant, an excellent example of successful strategic marketing by a utility company.

16. Strategic Management and Michael Porter: A Postmodern Reading

http://www.mngt.waikato.ac.nz/depts/sml/journal/special/harfield.htm

Toby Harfields's academic article explores strategic management from many points of view, and includes its history, Michael Porter's contribution, and a critique of the academic field.

17. Strategic Management Journal

http://www.smsweb.org/Pages/Windows/smj.html

This journal publishes 12 times a year plus occasional special topic issues. Its purpose is to promote the development and dissemination of advances in the field, maintaining high standards of intellectual thought combined with practical relevance.

Formulating Strategies

18. Advances in Strategic Management

http://www.mgmt.utoronto.ca/~baum/asm_index.html

This series of volumes now number 17. Edited by Joel A. Baum, they are dedicated to communicating innovative, new research that advances theory and practice in strategic management. From this page you can dip into the volumes.

19. Design for Competitive Advantage

http://dfca.larc.nasa.gov/dfc/toc.html

Read the many articles, consider the various points of view, and click on the links suggested at this site to explore important business-related theories and issues such as cost management and living systems theory and design.

20. Equifax: Knowledge Engineering

http://www.equifaxknowledge.com

A global company, Equifax offers its services to companies, bringing buyers and sellers together through its information, transaction processing, and customer relationship management businesses.

21. GBN Scenario Planning

http://www.gbn.org/scenPlan.html

Scenario planning is a fundamental tool for thinking strategically about the future. This site, which contains many scenarios, helps organizations to understand the external environment in relation to their own business ideas and competence.

22. High Performance Teams

http://rampages.onramp.net/~bodwell/home.htm

Donald Bodwell's site on high-performance teamwork is filled with valuable information about team concepts, team building, coaching high-performance teams, and the evolving art and science of building teams, one of the newest ways to manage rapid growth and expansion.

23. NBS-Organizationand Management Theory

http://www.nbs.ntu.ac.uk/staff/lyerj/list/hromt.htm

This is part of Ray Lye's Human Resources Management Resources on the Internet. It provides annotated links to an array of documents, studies, and resources on the theory and practice of the learning organization.

Organizational Change

24. Business Forecasting

http://forecasting.cwru.edu

Use this page to access the thinking of business researchers who, using statistics, economics, psychology, and related disciplines, attempt to predict the future.

25. Marketing Energy Services to the Healthcare Segment

http://www.fuld.com/HealthCareReport/index.html

This Fuld & Company study of the healthcare markets is an excellent example of competitive intelligence applied to a specific industry for the purposes of selling a company's services efficiently and effectively.

26. Center for Organizational Theory (COT)

http://socrates.berkeley.edu/~iir/cot/cot.html

COT was founded in 1995 at the Institute of Industrial Relations at the University of California, Berkeley. Its major research project centers on the demography of corporations and industries and organizational processes.

27. Six Sigma for Manufacturing and Non-Manufacturing Processes

http://www.airacad.com/transact.htm

This discussion online by Air Academy Associates describes, using charts and graphs, the quality improvement and business strategy called Six Sigma. Case examples, such as Motorola, Allied Signal, and General Electric, are used to explain the points.

28. Voice of the Shuttle

http://vos.ucsb.edu/shuttle/commerce.html

Information on many subjects includes Restructuring, Reengineering, Downsizing, Flattening, Outsourcing, Human Resources Management, Labor Relations, Learning Organizations, The Team Concept, and Diversity Management.

Implementing, Measuring, and Controlling Strategy

29. Murray G. Bacon Center for Ethics in Business

http://www.public.iastate.edu/~BACON_CENTER/homepage.html

This Iowa State University site was developed to aid businesses to understand and come to grips with ethical dilemmas.

30. Center for Strategic Management

http://www.csmweb.com/body_index.html

Performance management—forcing an organization to achieve the outcomes it must achieve through aggressive planning, thinking, measuring, and acting—is the strength of CSM consulting services. The company offers instructional booklets and pamphlets in addition to professional seminars, academic programs, and personalized consulting and facilitation services.

31. Competitive Intelligence Guide

http://www.fuld.com/index.html

The Strategic Intelligence Organizer offered by Fuld and Company helps an organization to focus intelligence activities to benefit the firm. A game board allows a company to find a matching situation to see the types of intelligence it will require to compete effectively.

32. MELNET

http://www.bradford.ac.uk/acad/mancen/melnet/index0.html

MELNET is a "virtual cooperative" for people looking to improve the way they do business. Through this interactive site, learn about the course of management in the twenty-first century.

We highly recommend that you review our Web site for expanded information and our other product lines. We are continually updating and adding links to our Web site in order to offer you the most usable and useful information that will support and expand the value of your Annual Editions. You can reach us at: *http://www.dushkin.com/annualeditions/*.

Unit 1

Unit Selections

1. **Danger: Stealth Attack,** Toni Mack and Mary Summers
2. **Supersizing the Supermarkets in a Shift of Power; Discounters and Mergers Alter Balance of Power,** Dana Canedy
3. **Between a Gas Pump and a Hard Place,** Matthew L. Wald
4. **See Jack. See Jack Run Europe,** Thomas A. Stewart
5. **Nokia: Made in Finland and Sold Just about Everywhere,** Youssef M. Ibrahim
6. **Zeneca Buying Astra As Europe Consolidates,** Alan Cowell
7. **China Rolls Out the Red Carpet,** Richard Tomlinson

Key Points to Consider

❖ Changes in uncontrollable environments present opportunities to some firms, but they can be devastating to the ones that cannot or do not respond to the challenge.

❖ Access to global markets has produced a host of new rivals and competitors who seek to take advantage of the economies that result.

❖ While crafting global strategies, it is critical to recognize the cultural and structural differences that develop across international economies.

DUSHKINONLINE Links www.dushkin.com/online/

6. **Business Policy and Strategy**
http://www.aom.pace.edu/bps/bps.html
7. **CIBERWeb**
http://ciber.centers.purdue.edu
8. **Global Business Network (GBN)**
http://www.gbn.org/home.html
9. **Hoover Online—The Business Network**
http://www.hoovers.com
10. **Sales & Marketing Executives International**
http://www.smei.org
11. **SMG—Strategic Management Group, Inc.**
http://www3.smginc.com/smginc/smg/
12. **SMS—Strategic Management Society**
http://www.smsweb.org/Pages/Windows/welcome.html

These sites are annotated on pages 4 and 5.

The Strategic Climate

The field of strategic management is relatively new. It owes its existence to research supported by the Ford Foundation and the Carnegie Foundation in the 1950s. The study was in response to a call from the business community to establish a course that would integrate the principles of the functional courses in a business school. This capstone course was usually called Business Policy, and it examined decision making from the perspective of the upper management of a firm. In its original form, it advocated a linear approach to strategy. In that context, organizations assessed their position, weighed the alternatives, chose the course that maximized their shareholder value, and implemented the strategy.

Over the course of time, management thinking has evolved much the same way as organizational forms and individual enterprises have. Now the field is most often called strategic management, and the field offers a variety of insights into the content and the context of managerial decisions.

In what is regarded as the most important building block to understand strategic thought, Alfred D. Chandler Jr. offered a definition of strategy. "Strategy can be defined as the determination of the long-term goals and objectives of an enterprise, and the adoption of courses of action and the allocation of resources necessary for carrying out these goals."[1]

The evolution of strategic thought now encompasses a wide range of philosophies. Diametrically opposed to linear theory are those who equate the existence of organizations to the biological world. In this sense, the organization is subjected to a Darwinian process of natural selection, and the role of management is considered to be subordinated to the forces of natural selection.

Clearly, every organization is forced to react to the set of macro, or uncontrollable environments. How well firms position themselves in relation to these forces explains which ones survive and which do not. We must also recognize that some organizations may be affected positively or negatively through no particular effort of their own. Instead, these strategies may, as Henry Mintzberg suggested, be imposed upon them.[2]

Sweeping changes in the third industrial revolution have produced technologies never before imagined. Demographic shifts in terms of population composition present an entire new array of opportunities and problems. More subtle changes in social and cultural areas quickly make firms obsolete while creating others in their place. As markets become global, the high degree of variation among economies in the world presents another set of challenges to management. Concerns with the preservation of our natural environment mandate strict controls on many firms' activities. New laws and the reinterpretation of existing statues create entire new arenas of competition.

Looking back over the last few decades, one can see that the number of large U.S. corporations that have adapted their strategies to the changing environments is discouragingly small. Of the 65 firms that make up the Dow Jones Industrial average in the year 2000, only a fraction appeared on the list in 1970. Microsoft and Cisco together have market capitalizations greater than General Motors and Ford combined. F. W. Woolworth, Pan American Airways, and The Great Atlantic and Pacific Tea Company (A&P), have all disappeared from the lists of America's largest and most profitable companies.

But many still flourish. General Electric has become a model of effective corporate governance. Some industries have consolidated and radically changed form, due to intense rivalries within them as well as interindustry competition. Petroleum refiners and distributors still dominate the top 10 industries in the United States, although a series of mergers has altered their composition significantly.

The heightened competition of a truly global workplace has mandated many changes in strategies. New rivalries have created new alliances. Strategies to achieve economies of scale and scope are commonplace. As the European Community edges closer to a reality, new strategies are necessary for all countries around the globe. Instead of more than a dozen fragmented markets, the European Community promises one large homogeneous market with a new level of purchasing power. For organizations within Europe, the harmonization process will allow more efficient manufacturing, advertising, inventory, transportation, research and development, and management than ever before. NAFTA (North American Free Trade Agreement) presents a package of opportunities and threats to its member nations. Asian markets loom as attractive growth areas for aggressive organizations, but firms have to learn to deal with an entirely new set of variables.

1. Chandler, Alfred D. Jr., *Strategy and Structure: Chapters in the History of the American Industrial Enterprise,* Cambridge, MA: 1962, The MIT Press.
2. Mintzberg, Henry and J. Waters, "Of Strategies, Deliberate and Emergent," *Strategic Management Journal,* 1985, pp. 257–272.

Danger: stealth attack

By Toni Mack and Mary Summers

Digital Equipment scorned PCs, until they nearly destroyed it. Big steel scorned minimills; utilities sniff at miniturbines. What disruptive technology could destroy your business? What upstart will deliver the blow?

Harvard Business School Professor Clayton Christensen stood before a group of Intel senior managers in September 1997 to tell them how upstarts capture business from established firms. Low-cost steel minimills, he said, stole 40% of the business from stalwarts like Bethlehem Steel and U.S. Steel by starting in the junkiest market segment, reinforcing bar, and working their way up from rebar to sophisticated sheet steel. Christensen showed a slide depicting the trend.

Intel Chairman Andrew Grove listened intently. He'd already begun pointing Intel toward a PC market segment it had previously scorned. "I was looking at his slide," recalls Grove, "and I had this creeping feeling that he was really talking about the introduction of low-cost computers. It is our rebar. It made me resolve that we'd better be very, very serious about this effort or else we will be like the integrated steel producers."

Christensen's ideas framed the after-dinner discussion among Grove and his executives. "Rebar" became Intel's inside slogan for attacking the low-cost PC market.

Grove then used the tale to ignite more than 1,000 Intel salespeople at a January 1998 meeting. Grove told them: "This is what happened to the steel people, and this is what might happen to us unless we are very aggressive in pursuing the low end." Intel's low-end Celeron chip has since taken 35% of the low-cost PC market.

Graveyards are full of firms that ignored a competitive threat like this one. Makers of sailing ships scoffed at steamships. Western Union, once the U.S.' largest company, doubted that AT&T's phone calls could replace its telegrams and even spurned an early chance to buy Alexander Graham Bell's patents. Mighty Sears, Roebuck & Co. laughed at discounters. And let's not forget that utterance from a Baldwin Locomotive Co. executive, just before diesel-electrics swept over the business: "They'll never replace the steam locomotive."

Easy to say that managers grew arrogant and lazy. Easy for managers today to vow: "I won't make that mistake!" Christensen brilliantly shows how they make the mistake anyway, in *The Innovator's Dilemma: When New Technologies Cause Great Firms to Fail* (Harvard Business School Press; $27.50).

This book ought to chill any executive who feels bulletproof—and inspire entrepreneurs aiming their guns. Using industries as chalk-cheese different as computers, motorcycles, earth excavators and accounting software, Christensen shows how often a fatal threat starts as a low-quality, low-margin product that your customers can't use and don't want. Naturally, you shrug—until the new product grows in capability to meet your customers' needs.

The Innovator's Dilemma ought to chill any executive who feels bullet-proof—and inspire entrepreneurs aiming their guns.

Christensen terms a new product that sneaks into an established market a disruptive technology. Grove dubs it "the Christensen effect." We'll call it a stealth attack.

The Internet is the Godzilla of stealth attacks. Once a cumbersome tool wielded only by academics and nerds, today's Web challenges not just retailers but everyone from venerable Merrill Lynch and Aetna Inc. to high-tech Sony Corp. and Microsoft Corp.

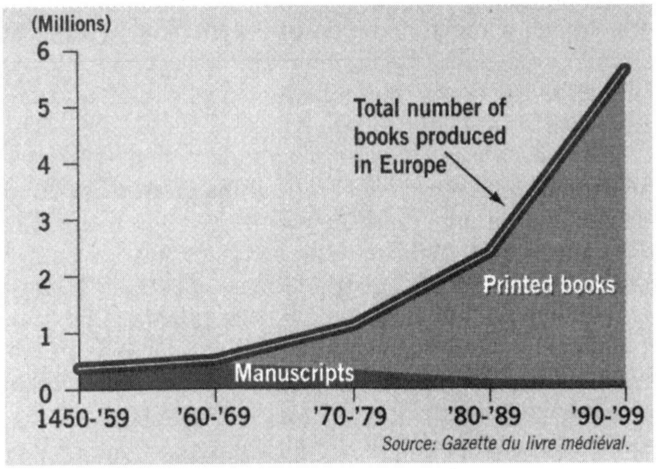

Monks for hire

Stealth attack, 15th-century style: The printing press replaced thousands of manuscript-copying monks and scribes.

Stealth attacks are all around us. Little golf carts are invading the electric-auto market. On-line gossip journals are stealing readers away from august newspapers. Miniature generators are taking electric power business away from giant utilities. Doctors face a stealth attack from nurses. Cost pressures and changes in medical technology have put some of their work in nurses' hands.

Nintendo threatens powerful Eastman Kodak. For a mere toymaker to encroach on classy Kodak's turf seems unthinkable. But as *The Innovator's Dilemma* shows, a disruptive technology alters the marketplace in such a way that low-quality products can migrate overnight into the top drawer.

Kodak's digital cameras employ charge coupled devices and fetch $500 to $30,000. Nintendo's $50 Game Boy cameras use low-tech sensors with so-called CMOS (complementary metal oxide semiconductor) technology borrowed from mass-market computers. Game Boy photos are fuzzy. They make only postage-stamp-size prints. But quality is quickly improving—and Nintendo has already sold more than 1 million cameras.

Terrence Faulkner, who retired last month as a Kodak vice president, read *The Innovator's Dilemma* shortly after it appeared in June 1997 and used it to begin formulating Kodak's counterstrike. He deployed Kodak kiosks in FAO Schwarz toy stores; they make Game Boy-type sticker photos. Faulkner also hints that Kodak will soon introduce a Game Boy-like camera, with quality more acceptable to its mass market, employing CMOS sensors from a Kodak-Intel joint venture.

In October Christensen spent a day and a half explaining to Kodak Chairman George Fisher, Faulkner and other senior executives why stealth attacks are so hard to detect and counter. Successful firms listen well to their customers, who don't want the stealthy product—at first. Middle managers may sense a looming market, but won't bet their careers—and naturally stick to what has worked, explained Christensen.

"His ideas have made us think a little differently," says Fisher. "Even good people get locked into processes that may be totally inappropriate to deal with a new technology attacking from underneath."

"What's valuable about Clayton's ideas is that they give you a framework," notes Andy Grove. "They allow a business to learn from the experience of others. The specifics are different, but you can move the generality over to your business and then go down into your specifics."

Bloomberg Financial Markets attacked from underneath and drove Telerate into a small corner of the market for on-line bond-trading data. Michael Bloomberg started by offering only a smattering of the pricing data the others offered to financial services firms but took advantage of new developments in portfolio theory to offer analytical data that the established vendors did not offer.

Bloomberg now thinks of Christensen when he looks over his shoulder at the Internet and other potential threats. "The easiest thing is to say, 'It's so horrendous to think of going out of business, I won't

Michael Bloomberg now thinks of Christensen when he looks over his shoulder at the Internet and other potential threats.

do anything. I'll pray it goes away.' Christensen gets you to say, 'Which risks do you have to run?' " Bloomberg has sent copies of *The Innovator's Dilemma* to 50 friends.

What to do if you're under fire? Christensen contrasts Digital Equipment Corp.'s and IBM's forays into PCS. DEC tried and failed four times, always from within its mainstream organization. It was a halfhearted effort at first, reflecting the early view of DEC founder Kenneth Olson that the PC was just a toy. IBM put its PC unit in Florida, far from its New York base. There the undistracted IBMers could fit their technology and costs to the smaller-margin PC market. They created a smash hit. IBM's share of the PC business later faded, after it linked the PC unit more closely to the rest of IBM.

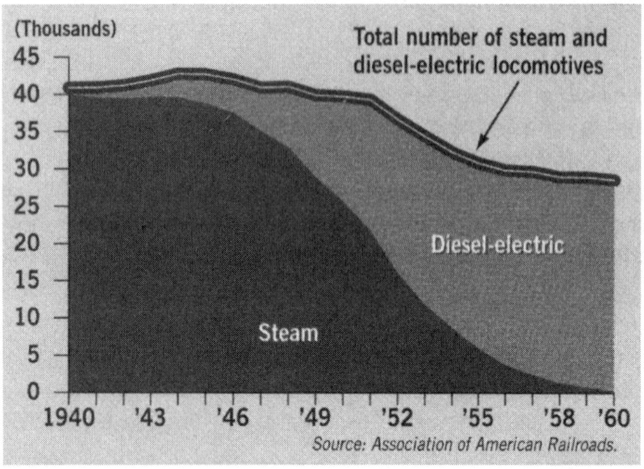

Out of steam

"They'll never replace the steam locomotive," declared a Baldwin Locomotive executive. Diesel-electrics did.

Microsoft is brilliant at detecting new threats, such as the Internet, and reacting to them. Might it nevertheless succumb to a stealth attack? It might. "They've overshot the market in so many products," says Christensen. "Microsoft Excel 2.0 [spreadsheet] used 1.2 megabytes on your hard drive. The latest version takes 36 megabytes just to load. How many of its functions do users even know exist?"

The ascendant attacker: Sun Microsystems' Java software. Many Java applications run slowly. But Java is rapidly improving. Its applications—or even small pieces of applications—run not only on Microsoft-powered machines but also on Apple's Macs and smaller appliances like 3Com's PalmPilot. Users will be able to tap only the features they want, via the Internet. Predicts Christensen: "This will get Microsoft long before the Justice Department does."

Internet telephony is a stealth attack on traditional telcos like AT&T and SBC Corp. and equipment suppliers like Lucent Technologies and Nortel Networks. The established players connect a speaker's voice to the listener's ear in 50 milliseconds. Most people today won't tolerate annoying lags of 300 milliseconds or more on Internet calls. But our ears can't tell the difference between a 50-millisecond gap and a 150-millisecond one. Christensen thinks new technology will shrink the Internet delay to a "good enough" 150 milliseconds as early as next year.

Of course, not all challengers find a market, as Christensen learned firsthand. From 1984 to 1989 he ran a startup company in very high quality ceramics parts. "Whenever we came out with a new product," he says, "the dominant producer, Japan's Kyocera Corp., would counter with its own version." He spreads his fingers in a circle over his heart and concludes ruefully: "You may land ahead of the technology trajectory, but you land there with a big target on your chest." The company nearly sank in the early 1990s, but finally found a niche in cell phones, which didn't exist in the mid-1980s.

The lesson for entrepreneurs: Doing better what a bigger company already does well is risky. Better to start in a neglected market. Honda did that. *The Innovator's Dilemma* tells the tale.

Honda dispatched three executives to Los Angeles in 1959 to sell a bigger, souped-up version of its little Supercub urban motorcycle. Few dealers bit. The Hondas sold were so faulty at highway speeds that warranty costs nearly sank the company.

The Honda execs vented their frustration by dirt-biking on low-tech Supercubs in the hills east of Los Angeles. Neighbors and onlookers clamored for them. Thus was a new strategy born. Honda began hawking its cycles through sporting goods stores. Just a toy? Maybe that's what the big bike makers thought. Honda's sales zoomed. By the 1970s the firm had mastered large-bike engineering and was capturing markets that once belonged to mighty Harley-Davidson, Inc. and BMW AG.

Doing better what a bigger company already does well is risky. Better to start in a neglected market. Honda did that.

Christensen's lesson has already had an impact. For example, Arthur Mannion of Danbury, Conn.'s Sure Power Corp. read an early version of Christensen's work in the *Harvard Business Review.* He realized his fuel cell power systems could

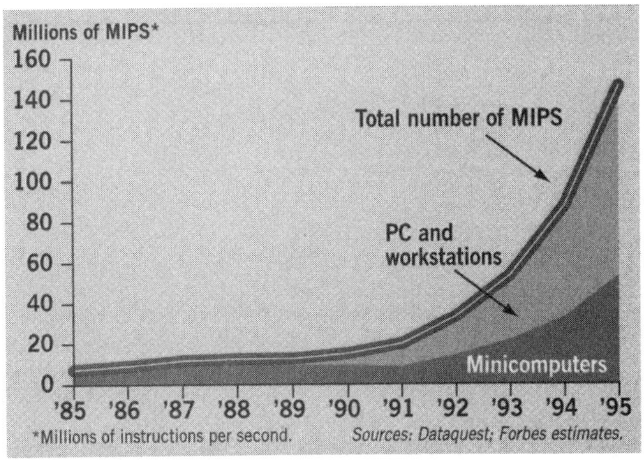

Some toy

Minicomputer-maker Digital Equipment disdained the PC as a toy. Then PCs and workstations took over the industry.

not compete on price with juice from the local utility. So he sought a niche that would value the system's virtue—reliability—more than price. Namely, firms heavily reliant on computers, which can't take even a split-second outage. "One Wall Street investment house told us they'd lose $8 million a minute if their system went down," smiles Mannion. He signed his first deal in July, with the First National Bank of Omaha. If his idea takes off, who knows? Maybe he can get the volume he needs to compete on price.

Electric utilities are already under fire from little turbines that allow customers to produce their own juice, at savings of 10% or more off utility prices (FORBES, *Mar. 9, 1998*). Says Tony Prophet, president of AlliedSignal's power systems subsidiary: "We expect every major fast-food, discount, grocery and department store chain to order at least one of our [75-kilowatt] generators. If it works out, we think they'll order from dozens up to hundreds."

Outfits like Sonat and Unicom will install and maintain the units. "One utility executive told me that his company had 22,000 megawatts on their grid, and the potential for a little 75-kilowatt machine even to show up on his radar screen was unthinkable," reports Unicom Vice President Mark Kuntz. "A lot of utilities view it as a hobbyist kind of thing." Hobby? Sure, just like those Hondas and those Apple IIs.

Might Microsoft succumb to a stealth attack? "They've overshot the market in so many products," says Christensen.

Could golf carts sweep into the automobile industry? Maybe. Look at what happens when big automakers try to tackle the market for electric vehicles. A typically laughable result: A Chrysler minivan bearing at least 1,600 pounds of batteries and a $120,000 price tag. Christensen says that Textron, Yamaha, Bombardier and other golf-cart manufacturers have already sold a reported 400,000 electric carts to people who use them on ordinary city streets. "You can market it as something to drive around the community. Simple, quiet, convenient, stylish."

Christensen chuckles. "The automakers are slaving away in the lab, spending hundreds of millions of dollars to improve battery technology. Meanwhile, the problems will get sorted out by these other folks." Detroit, watch out from below.

Supersizing the Supermarkets in a Shift of Power; Discounters and Mergers Alter Balance of Power

By DANA CANEDY

When the natural order of a food chain is upset, the battle for survival intensifies. Such is the case in the nation's grocery business.

This Darwinian struggle has its roots in two evolutionary shifts. First, discount giants like Wal-Mart have leapfrogged into a powerful position by becoming big sellers of groceries as well as garden hoses. And second, regional supermarket chains like the Kroger Company are in a frenzy of consolidation, merging to create national chains able to compete head to head with the discounters.

As these giants battle it out, manufacturers, wholesalers, distributors and independent grocers risk being trampled if they cannot learn the new rules and adjust to the new order quickly enough. The biggest change? While retailers used to take many of their marching orders from food suppliers, the balance has tilted, with some retailers now so big that they often call the shots.

All these forces converge in the story of James McCoy.

Mr. McCoy is president of the John C. Groub Company, which runs a 30-store grocery chain in southern Indiana that was sold to Kroger earlier this year. In his 33 years at Groub, Mr. McCoy never expected his company to lose its independence.

Then Wal-Mart's Supercenters, which sell food and general merchandise under one roof, moved in.

"They had been coming for five years, and we had been very successful in competing with them in the beginning," recalled Mr. McCoy, whose stores go by the names Jay C Food Stores and Food Plus. "But as time went on, we began to feel the effect because they were going into smaller and smaller towns." And this, he went on, was "the profit lifeblood of our company."

Making matters worse, manufacturers of everything from paper towels to soup began requiring ever-larger orders in return for the best prices. "It was all brought about," Mr. McCoy said, "because of the pressure Wal-Mart brought to bear on P&G, Campbell's, etc., to become more efficient."

So when he was approached by Kroger, the nation's largest food retailer, it was as if a big brother had arrived to stare down a bully.

Kroger, he said, is committed to retaining the stores' small-town flavor. "If you accept the fact that it would only be a matter of time and we would either have closed some stores or laid people off," Mr. McCoy said, "the community is going to benefit."

In Indiana as elsewhere, this power shift is taking place far from shoppers' view, but the impact will be felt from stockroom to checkout counter. Supermarket operators and suppliers insist that customers will be the biggest beneficiaries, and at least in the short term that seems likely, as competitors clamor for consumer loyalty.

Steven A. Burd, chief executive of Safeway Inc., said, "If done well, it lowers the operating expenses for those companies, which allows them to be in a better position to compete with some of the emerging formats out there that typically have lower costs."

If the recent mergers fail to produce cost savings, of course, the long-term benefit will be minimal. The chains, though, are betting big on the power of size.

In addition to buying Groub, Kroger announced plans last month to acquire Fred Meyer in a $13 billion deal that will create the largest supermarket chain in the country, with 2,200 stores in 31 states and combined annual revenue of about $43 billion.

In other recent deals, Albertson's plans to acquire American Stores; Royal Ahold bought Giant Food, Stop and Shop and Bi-Lo chains; and Safeway absorbed Vons and Dominick's.

All of which is not necessarily good news to distributors.

"The retailers are going to be a little stronger and have a little more muscle in the marketplace," said John R. Block, a former Agriculture Secretary who is president of Food Distributors International, a trade group. Already the changes are exacting a toll.

"Twelve years ago we had more than 300 full-line wholesalers," Mr. Block said. "Today we're down to 97, and 12 of them do 80 percent of the business." Though he sees advantages for the most efficient suppliers, "I don't see any end in sight to the consolidation."

What is more, competition from discounters is likely to hit food retailers even harder. Kmart, for example, has said that it is converting nearly 2,000 stores to formats that include grocery sections and is considering a merger with a major supermarket chain or wholesaler. And Wal-Mart, which has almost 500 giant Supercenters—where food accounts for about half the sales—is rapidly expanding their number and geographic reach.

As the market becomes more crowded, small independent grocers will have an even tougher time holding on. Many lack the resources to compete with megastores that sell 20 kinds of olives and practically give away orange juice to lure shoppers.

"The mom and pops, the independent, the life of those people is really very short," Mr. McCoy said.

There was a time when family-owned, one-store grocers were the driving force in the business. Grocers date back to the days of the tea merchants of the late 1800's and came into their own in the 1930's. Over several decades, independents and mostly regional chains filled in the growing suburban landscape. The 1970's and 1980's brought new formats, like convenience stores and warehouse stores. A wave of consolidation hit in the 1980's, when chains became more aggressive about expansion. Now, many of them control entire regions and are seeking to become national in scope.

While some food suppliers are folding under the pressure, others are finding new ways to squeeze profits from, of all things, sardines and cream of asparagus soup.

A wholesale company called One Source, for instance, buys and stocks slow-selling items for chains. The arrangement frees retailers' warehouse space for better-selling products like Tide and Coke and enables One Source to receive volume discounts.

In most stores, "chicken noodle soup and tomato soup fly off the shelf, but cream of asparagus probably doesn't move a case a month," said Jack Haedicke, chief operating officer for One Source, a division of C&S Wholesale Grocers in Brattleboro, Vt. "If you've got a warehouse full of slow movers and grab from enough retailers and put them in one centralized location, they are not slow movers any more."

In fighting back against discounters like Wal-Mart and Costco, supermarket operators have been forced to reduce costs sharply, invest in money-saving technology and remodel or close outdated stores. Then, as leaner, more efficient operators, they have begun to focus on growth, snapping up rivals to expand beyond saturated markets and to benefit from economies of scale.

Now the larger chains have the size to steamroll over weaker competitors and to demand that manufacturers and distributors bend on everything from promotions and product packaging to shipment schedules and fees for shelf space in order to shave costs further.

"There is an entire supply chain out there that talks about all the costs embedded in moving product from the manufacturer's truck to the trunk of the customer's car," said Mr. Burd of Safeway. "We've gotten very good at our element of the food supply chain, and we're looking forward to working with vendors on their side of it."

Of course, the largest manufacturers and wholesalers are the least affected by the new industry demands. After all, even Kroger and Safeway must sell Campbell Soup and Crest. And the makers of these and other top-selling brands were the pioneers of many changes now driving the retail business.

Companies like Procter & Gamble and Colgate-Palmolive were among the first, for instance, to invest in the technology that retailers now use to track product sales by store, manage inventory and billing, and control distribution.

When retailers demanded Colgate's new Total toothpaste as soon as it rolled off production lines last year, the company used technology-driven distribution to get it on store shelves nationwide in less than a month—half the time it would have taken a decade ago.

Backed by a $100 million marketing budget, the largest in the company's history for a new product, "Total was in your face from a consumer point of view, but it was also in your face from a retail point of view," said Ian Cook, president of Colgate U.S.

In four years, the company has cut its shipment time in half—to 6 days from 12—and increased its on-time delivery rate to 97 percent from about 92. This enables it to meet the greater demands from retailers. In the case of Total, it helped catapult the product into a top-selling brand within months.

Manufacturers and retailers that lack the size of a Colgate or Wal-Mart are seeking strength in numbers. The membership of the Independent Grocers Alliance, or I.G.A., has declined to 2,000 from 2,700 over the last decade as more independents have folded into chains or closed altogether. But those grocers that remain are increasing their sales volume, thus swelling the consortium's marketing and purchasing power. The average revenue of an I.G.A. store increased to $5.2 million last year from $3.3 million a decade ago.

Smaller grocers like these are also trying other ways to fight back. They say they are putting renewed emphasis on details that big chains tend to overlook. One scrappy independent, David Skogen, who owns six stores in La Crosse, Wis., says he is going ahead with plans to expand by two stores a year even though Wal-Mart recently said it would build a superstore in his backyard.

Mr. Skogen, who owns two Skogen's supermarkets and four Festival Foods discount grocery stores, said he would beat Wal-Mart and other large chains by continuing to provide "the things they don't mess with."

His stores hold knife-sharpening promotions, for instance, load their parking lots with pumpkins each fall and even provide shoppers locked out of their cars with free locksmith services and a spare set of keys. "People don't forget those things," Mr. Skogen said.

Between a Gas Pump and a Hard Place

Station Owner Grapples With Taxes, Technology and Regulation

By MATTHEW L. WALD
Special to The New York Times

ORANGETOWN, N.Y., Sept. 21— The White House wants a tax increase on gasoline. The Environmental Protection Agency wants gasoline that will pollute less. Paul J. DeMartini wants to pump 1.5 million gallons this year.

Only the first two are going to get their way.

On Oct. 1 the Federal excise tax rises by 4.3 cents a gallon. On the same day New York State says gas stations must make a winter switch to oxygenated fuel, which is supposed to reduce carbon monoxide in cold weather; that will raise the price of gas by one cent to six cents a gallon, depending on who is predicting.

The price increases are but the most recent pressures eating up the profits at Paul's Mobile, the service station that Mr. DeMartini has run for 15 years. Washington raises its taxes. Albany inflicts a new environmental rule. Mobil issues a new decree. One innovation after another requires expensive investments in equipment that seems to become obsolete overnight.

In Mr. DeMartini's tiny office here, he considered these events as if watching the confluence of two evil stars in the heavens.

"My regular customers will come in to the shop and say, 'You don't mind if I got gas in New Jersey for 25 cents less,'" he said. "I'll tell them, 'Of course not, I'd probably do the same thing,'" he said, with a tired smile that said of course he minds.

Mr. DeMartini did sell almost 1.5 million gallons a year during the late 1980's. But since then the tax difference with New Jersey, a mile and a half down Route 303, has grown as New York has increased its taxes. The unleaded regular that he offers for $1.19, full serve, goes for 96 cents in New Jersey. He has probably lost business to self-serve stations in New York, too, often a penny or two cheaper.

The starkest scorecard for Mr. DeMartini, 55 years old, who came to this corner when the station opened in 1966, is on a tattered wall calendar with red circles around the days the tanker delivers its 9,100 gallons. The truck came 8 times this August versus 9 last year, and 8 times in July versus 10 last year. Paul's will end the year under one million gallons.

Not that New Jersey retailers find life any easier.

"I look around and I see gasoline selling for 99 cents in New Jersey, and the dealer is paying 99 cents wholesale," said Jerry M. Ferrara, executive director of the New Jersey Gasoline Retailers. "I'm really worried about them. They're giving the gasoline away."

No station can survive on a markup of less than 15 cents a gallon, he said, to pay rent, insurance and labor, but some are selling gas for much less.

Actually, stations built to minimize labor costs can afford it. The direction of the last few years is like the movement in food retailing, from grocery stores to supermarkets, and stations like Mr. DeMartini's are the equivalent of grocery stores.

Here is how Mr. DeMartini's gallon breaks down at the moment:

61.5 cents for the fuel (43 cents for the crude oil, the rest for refining and transportation);
14.1 cents Federal excise tax (until Oct. 1, when it is 18.4 cents, including on the fuel in his underground tanks);
8 cents New York State tax;
14.04 cents New York gross receipts tax;
7 cents New York sales tax;
.0005 cents New York Motor Fuel Testing tax.

Mr. DeMartini sells the gas for $1.19.9, leaving him a margin of 15.25 cents, from which he pays the rent of $6,000 a month, salaries of the pump attendants, utilities and insurance. He also makes a profit in the shop, but not enough to carry the place. He also gets a rebate of a few cents a gallon from Mobil if he sells enough, and a few other inducements, but they don't help much. Sometimes, he said, there is no money left at the end of the week for himself.

Even with fewer gas stations, the competition is getting stiffer, from multi-island superstations with gleaming retail aisles that resemble miniature supermarkets. His rack of candies and mints, headache remedies and beef jerky are no match for them. These days he also competes with while-you-wait oil change shops, muffler and brake specialists and dealerships that offer extended warranties.

"The business pressures on the gasoline station operator are intense," said Frank Murray, the New York State Energy Commissioner. "And any change whatsoever is not something I think they would particularly welcome."

'The Island Is Dead'

A spokeswoman for Mobil, Susan E. Carter, said she sympathized with the retailers.

"You have to be absolutely as efficient as you can possibly be these days, to make it in this environment," she said.

For Mr. DeMartini, the problem starts with less traffic at the pump and snowballs from there.

"The shop is dead because the island is dead," he said, referring to his row of eight pumps, four regular and four premium. Fewer cars stopping for gas means fewer for attendants to scan for an expired inspection certificate, a bald tire or a frayed hose. Even if he can keep up business in the shop, he said, gasoline sales are the bottom line, the reason he works six and a half days a week.

"Mobil would close this place in a heartbeat If I didn't make quota," he said. His complaint is common to retailers, who say that the oil companies try harder and harder to make them sell more gasoline, a challenge that leads them into selling newspapers, coffee, doughnuts and anything else they think will pull in customers.

There is another problem with the shop: like thousands of others, it is one step away from being a museum. The tow truck and air-conditioning repair equipment are already antiques, and the computer for emissions inspections, only three years old, will soon be obsolete, too.

The tow truck is an old-fashioned wrecker. It runs as well as it ever did but new cars have so much plastic skirting on them, he said, that they can be safely moved only with a flat bed, which costs $40,000 to $50,000. That only makes sense for a station with a 24-hour mechanical shop, he said. Mr. DeMartini is on the Job only from 6 each morning til 4 each afternoon six days a week, though he makes a point of dropping by on Sundays, too.

New Rules on Coolant

He used to refill air-conditioners that had leaked their coolant, some times bleeding refrigerant into the air in the course of repair. But as part of a worldwide effort to cut down on chlorofluorocarbons, which destroy ozone in the stratosphere, gas stations are now required to plug all leaks and to use machines that suck the refrigerant out of air-conditioners and purify it for re-use. The machine would have cost $3,000 and will be obsolete in a few years when the car industry switches to a new refrigerant. So he gave up servicing air-conditioners.

Then there is the $15,000 computer for emission inspections. New York State made him install it two years ago, to improve his inspections, he said, but it will be obsolete in two or three years, when the state moves to more advanced tests.

In the old days he dumped used antifreeze into a floor drain, along with used oil, used solvents and other chemicals. Now his drain is sealed, to keep those chemicals out of the environment, a move that Mr. DeMartini, who drinks well water at home, applauds. The station now pays to have waste oil taken away. A machine could clean up and recycle the anti-freeze, but servicing 8 or 10 cars a day, six days a week is not enough business to support one.

Battling the Specialists

Every year the cars have more electronic parts, and sometimes it is hard to determine just which one has gone bad. A dealer can use trial and error, taking a part from stock and installing it to see if it solves the problem; if it doesn't, he tries another. But if Mr. DeMartini orders a part, he is stuck with it.

Then there is specialization. Old customers come in for repairs and he sees reminder stickers on their windshields from quick-change oil places, whose prices he cannot quite match. Other companies aggressively advertise muffler and brake work. New cars increasingly come with 50,000 mile warranties. A few years ago, Mr. DeMartini's adult daughter bought a Jeep Eagle, he said, and he, acutely aware of what it can cost to fix a car's electronics, advised her to pay $700 for an extended warranty.

He considered closing his two service bays and asking Mobil to "turn it all into a big candy store, selling nothing but soda and potato chips." But Mobil told him that he had to sell two million gallons a year to justify the company's investment, he said.

At one point, he said, Mobil scheduled a $1 million renovation, to install electronically controlled pumps in separate lanes, replacing his dented mechanical pumps, which are laid out in a row so that self-serve is impossible. But the company later decided it had no money for the project.

From 20 to 12

Twenty Mobil stations served Rockland County In 1978 when Paul's Mobil began, he said. Now there are 12. Two of those are owned by Mobil itself, and of the other 10, half are for sale. On the four-mile drive from the New York Thruway to Paul's Mobil three gas stations are defunct Two of those have been put to other uses and one is boarded up.

At Paul's Mobil, Mr. DeMartini is not the only one concerned about the station's future.

Chuck Massey opens the place at 5 each morning and pumps gas until early afternoon. Mr. Massey is 44 and he was laid off three years ago from a middle-management position at a company that handled billing for cable television companies.

He sees his new role as providing customer satisfaction, and he chats about something with almost every one who pulls in. A Plymouth Voyager with two broken taillights pulled up to the pump, but then the driver pulled away again as he. fished through his wallet "Maybe your wife's got the credit card?" said Mr. Massey, affably. The man eventually found a $5 bill, knocking another four gallons off Paul's Mobil's million-gallon challenge.

See Jack. See Jack run Europe.

The globalization of General Electric may be the greatest legacy of Jack Welch's 19 years as CEO. An incomparable management tool kit and a passion for growing leaders made it possible. **by Thomas A. Stewart**

You don't become head of General Electric by being a scaredy-cat, but one thing frightens Jack Welch, even after 18 years in the job: the sheer size of the company. "Don't talk to me about how big this place is," he says, nearly shouting. "I hate it." Size means sloth, systems, and smugness rather than speed, simplicity, and self-confidence. Over and over, Welch urges people to "tear this place apart."

At the same time, of course, he has grown GE so much it's, well, scary. GE is the ninth-biggest and second most profitable company in the world. Since Welch took over in 1981, GE's sales have risen 3.7 times (from $27.2 billion to $100.5 billion), and profits have grown 5.7 times (from $1.6 billion to $9.2 billion). Size is a burden if you try to lug it around, but it's an advantage if you can make it work for you. "Jack always says, 'You can't manage a company the size of GE. You leverage it,' " says Claudio Santiago. Spanish-born Santiago, 42, works in Florence, Italy, as CEO of one of GE's bigger divisions, a $2.1-billion-in-sales compressor and turbine manufacturer, Nuovo Pignone.

Welcome to global GE. Businesses like Nuovo Pignone symbolize one of the biggest stories of Welch's storied career: how America's most admired company, and a very American one, has become a truly global corporation. It is the story of how GE leveraged its businesses to buy and build, in just over a decade, a European business nearly as large as all GE was when Welch became CEO, and now intends to do the same in Asia, only faster. It is the story of how GE leverages its intellectual capital—an incomparable management tool kit that has turned a bunch of state-run sinecures and niche businesses into a powerhouse whose net income, now a fifth of the company's, is compounding at 34% a year. And it's the story of the lever itself, the reason this Gargantua can be as agile as Nijinksy: a leadership-development system that won't let GE stop improving.

As Welch prepares to retire next year, much attention has focused on the race to succeed him. He'll be a tough act to follow: If the creek don't rise, Welch will have created more shareholder wealth than any CEO in history. But his real legacy is the tools and leaders he has helped to forge, and nothing displays it better than GE's globalization.

Until a decade ago, GE treated the world as an export market. The company had some European operations, notably its aircraft-engine manufacturing joint venture with Snecma of France, formed in 1974, and a greenfield plastics operation begun in 1970 when Welch ran that business. But in 1987, 44% of GE's overseas sales were exports from the U.S. That year Welch gained a European base for GE Medical Systems by swapping his consumer electronics business for Thomson-CGR, the medical equipment division of France's Thomson, then state owned. Two years later, as the Iron Curtain rang down, GE landed another government-owned business, Hungary's lighting manufacturer, Tungsram. Since 1990, GE has paid nearly $30 billion for 133 European acquisitions; some 90,000 people are on GE's payroll there, about as many as Euro-giants Axa and BP Amoco employ worldwide. Europe accounted for $24.4 billion of 1998 revenue, of which only $2.7 billion, or 11%, came from exports from America. Inflation-adjusted, that's less than at the start of the decade.

GE's first buys were anything but aggressive. In lighting, "we were on the defensive," John Opie, now vice chairman, recalled in 1994. Dutch giant Philips bought Westinghouse's U.S. business in 1983; Germany's Siemens was making goo-goo eyes at GTE Sylvania (buying it in 1993). Tungsram was a mess—good lamps hidden under a bushel of communist mismanagement—but had 7% of the European market. If it fell into other hands, Thomas Edison's lighting business would be trapped, with strong rivals on its home turf and no way to counterattack on theirs.

Those early buys were stubbornly unprofitable, partly because they were defensive, partly because GE was still unsure how to export management know-how. Says Mike Zafirovski, a Macedonian who in July was named CEO of GE Lighting worldwide: "From '92 to '94 almost no one could convince Jack to buy in Europe. He was losing money at Tungsram, Capital, everywhere—Europe was a dirty word." GE turned to the attack only when signs of a turnaround came and a European recession made assets cheap. Between 1994 and 1995, European revenues jumped from $9.1 billion to $14.1 billion as GE made big buys in everything from reinsurance to power controls.

When you do a lot of deals—GE made 108 acquisitions worldwide last year—you get good at it. One secret is an "integration model" developed chiefly at deal-hungry GE Capital Services. It rests on an obvious fact, but one many companies fudge: There are no "mergers of equals" here; there are acquisitions. "If you won't want to change, don't be acquired," says Norris Woodruff, a general manager in Industrial Systems and an in-house expert on the subject. Sure, GE wants to inspire change rather than compel it, to learn as well as teach, but GE is boss.

A second key point: Integration begins before the deal, with a due-diligence team that's not just financial but includes human resources and general management. They draft a plan to take effect the instant the pens are capped. Says James Conheady, an unsentimental Irishman who runs HR for GE Power Controls, which makes circuit breakers and the like and is based in Barcelona: "You have to move very, very quickly. There's a window of opportunity—an expectation of change—so you must deliver it fast."

First to arrive is someone from finance who is expected, literally on day one, to take control of the books, with the general ledger set up in the format GE uses worldwide. An "integration manager" is a half-step behind—usually a high-potential youngster brevetted into the acquired company. The integration manager doesn't supplant the people running the business. He works full-time on integration; the general manager runs the shop and owns the P&L.

Splitting the roles speeds up integration, and "Do it faster next time" is the conclusion of every postmortem at GE. Many of GE's early European buys—the French medical business (1987), Tungsram (1989), an aircraft-engine repair facility in Wales (1991)—went through two or three general managers before being fully integrated. Leery of Europe's unions and wary of riling host governments, GE had "a certain view that the walk had to be slow, in all the European countries," says Zafirovski, who ran lighting's European operations from 1996 till this summer. Integration plans now run about 100 days. When time's up, basic operational fixes will be under way—like reducing inventory or cutting sourcing costs. Restructuring will be planned, probably begun. Sales forces will have been unified. If the company had a matrix or geographical organization, it will be gone, together with a layer or two of management. It will be replaced by a functional organization—marketing, sales, manufacturing, etc. "Soft-side" initiatives in GE values, expectations, and management methods will have begun.

Most important, leaders will have taken stock of the people to identify "blockers"—who are removed because they impede change—and key people GE wants to keep. To the latter, GE hands out big jobs or glamorous training slots. Says Rino Piazzolla, HR head of Nuovo Pignone: "You have to get rid of blockers and identify high-pots simultaneously. Otherwise you lose the high-pots. You need to show people the future."

There's nothing special about these changes except the speed with which GE does them. But they're worth two to eight percentage points of operating margin, says Joaquim Agut, the Catalonian CEO of GE Power Controls, an $800 million operation composed of ten acquisitions in eight countries, including his family-owned company, sold in 1993.

After generic change comes GEneric change. Agut ticks off a list of GE tools—CAP, CMS, MGPD, bullet trains, QMI, Six Sigma, and more—and says they're worth another eight points of margin. That's an astonishing number, but you can make the case: Ten businesses that today represent about half of GE's European revenues had a combined operating margin of 5% in their first year of GE ownership, vs. an expected 13% margin for 1999.

Says Welch: "These companies have nothing in common except leadership and best practices," but that's not chopped liver. In the view of Merrill Lynch analyst Jeanne Terrile, GE is not so much a collection of businesses as it is "a repository of information and expertise that can be leveraged over a huge installed base." The ability to leverage expertise is why GE's globalization works.

Among GE management tools, several are particularly powerful aids to globalization. One of them, Work-Out, is so fundamental that GE trademarked the term and in its values statement says, "GE leaders . . .are committed to Work-Out." Work-Outs, begun in 1989, are meetings that can be called by anybody to address any problem, from niggling to humongous, with no boss in the room. When the participants have a plan—kill that stupid form, replace that balky pump—the boss must say yes or no on the spot, no haggling, no waffling. Work-Outs have become so common that there's probably one every day in each sizable GE facility, without management's knowing about it till someone pops in saying "We had a Work-Out and need to talk to you."

Its simplicity is deceptive. Piazzolla says, "We saw 'committed to Work-Out' and asked, 'What's Work-Out? A meeting? Why should we spend time in meetings?' " But Work-Out's few rules totally subvert traditional executive power, and that's radical, especially in Europe.

Says Welch: "Getting a company to be informal is a huge deal, and no one ever talks about it." Informality is the key to GE's in-your-face, just-do-it culture. It allows the other tools to work. QMI, for example, is "quick market intelligence," a tool adapted from Wal-Mart. A regularly scheduled, intense meeting where managers, salespeople, and others pore over data and share anecdotes to get a pulse of the market, QMI can't succeed if people are afraid to tell the boss he's all wet.

In a classic GE twist, the idea that subordinates should push back at their bosses allows bosses to demand more. Magnus Beer, who runs GE's consumer finance business in Scandinavia, vividly recalls his first lesson in "stretch." As head of GE Capital's fleet services business in Sweden, leasing vehicles to corporate customers, Beer made his first presentation to his then-boss, Mike Zafirovski. When he was finished, Zafirovski said, "Nice try. You've done a very professional job. Now try something else." Rather than the 13% growth Beer foresaw, Zafirovski challenged him to imagine 25% growth, "then come back to me and tell me what resources you would need to make it happen." That, Beer exclaims, "is a very different discussion!"

GE's European work force has taken to its style with surprising ease. Says Anneliese Monden, who runs GE's leadership-development programs in Europe: "Respect for titles isn't what GE is about, and it's a little strange in the beginning. Once people understand it's safe to think, they love it." According to Kary Wright, an American who is site manager of the aircraft-engine repair facility in Wales, "Personal contact is the key. You need it to share best practices." The plant had belonged to British Airways; it was a cost center servicing BA's engines. GE bought it at a time when the airline wanted cash for new aircraft. That helped GE expand its services business and earned some good will that didn't hurt GE's successful bid later to sell GE-90 engines to BA.

The plant has become Rumpelstiltskin, a cash spinner in a business that's more profitable than selling new engines. Shop-floor workers credit some of the turnaround to GE's wallet—when it was a cost center, management naturally avoided putting money into it—but give equal or greater weight to informality, stretch, and know-how. Says Wayne Glanville, deputy leader of the plant union: "GE's investment speaks for itself. What you can't see is, before, management sat on one side and we sat on the other. Now we have a round table." In the test area, Neil Saxby says, "Teamwork is the key, not authority. All the best ideas come from teams." Almost every GE factory, in every business, uses manufacturing cells where teams share work, rather than assembly lines, which isolate workers. Result: "Information flows so quickly it's almost frightening," says an obviously unintimidated Matthew Gray, who works on Rolls-Royce engines. Color-coded bins and charts—the same around the world—allow workers to monitor stock and see the day's scheduling just by looking at what's in each bin. One area of the plant, which handles accessories such as hydraulic controls and fuel pumps from 70 different suppliers, has just one manager for 130 workers.

Some myths about European labor turn out to be just that, myths. Says William Conaty, GE's senior HR officer: "What I heard six or seven years ago was, You can't restructure; European labor unions are impossible to deal with." Easy they're not, of course. In France, Medical Systems weathered a 55-day strike in 1997. Says European CEO Larry Johnston, who came

Now It's Electron Jack

"THIS IS CLEARLY THE BIGGEST revolution in business in our lifetimes—and I've got all the tools to go after it." Jack Welch is talking about electronic commerce, the passion of his final year as CEO of General Electric.

Welch used GE's annual top executive meeting at Boca Raton, Fla., in January—the meeting where he is likely to name his successor next year—to order a major companywide e-commerce initiative. Welch had been skeptical about the power of the Internet, but there's no zealot like a convert; these days people at headquarters in Fairfield, Conn., call him e-Jack.

Welch himself is not skilled on the computer—his assistant Rosanne Badowski is used to his hollering for help when he accidentally closes an application on the Dell PC in his office. But if Welch is no power user, no one is a quicker student of power. Welch sees the Web changing everything:

"It will change relationships with employees. We will never again have discussions where knowledge is hidden in somebody's pocket. You will have to lead with ideas, not by controlling information."

"It will change relationships with customers. Customers will see everything. Nothing will be hidden in paperwork. Where is the inventory? Where is that part? They will see it all. Execution is very important. Look what quality will do to the Internet, and vice versa. Every error you make is transparent on the Web, so without Six Sigma quality you can't win."

"It will change relationships with suppliers. Within 18 months, all our suppliers will supply us on the Internet or they won't do business with us."

Welch won't give companywide targets for the e-commerce initiative. Instead, he says, "I've got to go crazy over the next months to make e-commerce happen." He can't imagine being better equipped. At Crotonville, GE's corporate university, every business management course—a four-week, action-learning program offered to 50 high-potential managers each quarter—will do an e-commerce project. Every GE business is appointing a maverick, an e-commerce fanatic, who reports to the business' CEO and is empowered to break every GE rule except the company's values.

His one worry: "Do we have the right gene pool—do people who join big companies want to break glass? We've got to break this company to do this—there's no discussion, we've just got to break it."

Characteristically, Welch wants in on the brick-throwing. To that end, he's sponsoring his own e-commerce blitzkrieg: a 90-day, all-company Work-Out, which will run through December. The Work-Out will take place on the company intranet; its subject is how to use the Web to eliminate bureaucracy and move to electronic commerce.

"The attic's getting full again," Welch says. "This way we'll get an Internet focus and clear out some crap," handing his successor a wired company newly scoured of administrivia. E-Jack is ionized: "I just wish we were faster—I never move fast enough."

to France from GE Appliances in Kentucky: "I'd dealt with the union in Louisville, but here it's something else. The three unions are the communists, the socialists, and the anarchists." GE prevailed by being as punctilious about work rules as the strikers were, having a notary record questionable union behavior, storing finished goods at the airport to keep shipments going, and hiding parts on-site so that work went on when deliveries couldn't get through. And by talking: Johnston never let a day go by without meeting with the strikers to tell GE's side of the story.

Clearly it helps that GE is probably harder on management than it is on labor—at Tungsram, for example, some 10,000 people were let go, but about 40% were salaried. Helpful, too, are gestures like one GE made in Wales, where workers had received air-travel perks from British Airways: Unable to do that, GE gave them its highflying stock instead.

"GE is a language—it is a world—and at the beginning it is difficult," says Pier Luigi Ferrara, 62, Nuovo Pignone's chairman. Ferrara knows pressure—he is a famous engineer who designed compressors that deliver ten million pounds of thrust per square inch, 100 times more than the GE 90 engine. He chose to see pressure from GE as a source of new power for a company he loved. Nuovo Pignone didn't understand the value of keeping inventories low, for example; on Welch's first visit there, managers boasted that they never needed to fear a break in production because they had so much extra stock.

More and more, the language of GE is the language of Six Sigma, the quality initiative begun in late 1995. It has become central to GE's ability to operate as a global whole. "Six Sigma" refers to a standard of excellence defined as having no more than 3.4 defects per million—in anything, whether it's manufacturing, billing, or loan processing. GE says it will spend $500 million on Six Sigma projects this year and will get more than $2 billion in benefits. Many are the things quality programs have always delivered—in lighting, for example, reductions in shrinkage (the amount of raw material that doesn't make its way into a lamp) and increases in fill rates (the percentage of a customer's order delivered on schedule), up from 78% in 1996 to 93% today. GE, however, is pushing quality into new realms.

One is asset utilization. Using capital efficiently has always been one of Welch's goals, and Six Sigma gives him new ways to pursue it. For example, GE businesses have long been expected to track productivity gains. (GE measures productivity the right way: Rather than measure output per unit of labor, it measures output per unit of all inputs, whether labor, materials, or capital.) Using Six Sigma data, GE can go further: The company tracks how much of a productivity gain came from new equipment—that is, spending money—vs. from new ideas—that is, from thinking. In Euro lighting, according to Zafirovski, more than half the productivity gains now come from thinking. A big gain: using process improvements to increase output from old plants, thereby avoiding new spending. Says Zafirovski: "The rule of thumb for capacity additions used to be that we needed a dollar of investment to get a dollar of capacity. Now we need 12 1/2 cents." Companywide, Welch watches the ratio of plant and equipment spending to depreciation. It fell from 1.5 in 1996 to 1.2 in 1998; his goal is to get below 0.8. To Welch, this shows Six Sigma's ability to find "hidden factories" built of brainpower.

GE Medical Systems, whose European operations are based near Paris, is leading another advanced Six Sigma effort: using its methodologies to design new products from the customer's point of view. Says Larry Johnston: "Each GE business has taken on a Six Sigma challenge. Design for Six Sigma was ours." GE Medical Europe's contribution: an all-digital mammography system—now in use in Europe but not yet approved in the U.S.—that eliminates film, provides clearer imaging, and allows images to be copied without loss of detail; they can also be manipulated (rotated in 3-D, for example, so surgeons can plan their work better) and shipped over a hospital network.

The new process begins not with prototypes but with a series of Work-Outs with customers. For the mammography system, 16 "luminaries"—top oncologists and surgeons, along with hospital technicians and officials—sat through long sessions with GE experts discussing machine uptime and ergonomics, etc. Customers, in effect, wrote the specifications, working with GE to translate their requirements into technical terms.

A global company needs a common language. Six Sigma is it, more than English. The shared grammar makes it easier to swap ideas around GE. Before, two plant managers, even making the same product, probably had different performance measures. Says Piet van Abeelen, vice president for Six Sigma: "Without Six Sigma, if you run a plant and I run a plant, it's tough to understand your numbers. Then you can say, 'Your ideas won't work, because I'm different.' Well, cry me a river. The commonalities are what matter. If you make the metrics the same, we can talk."

And they talk: Never in business history have so many people talked so much to so many other people as they do at GE. In 1988, when GE started benchmarking other companies and sharing best practices internally, people embraced the notion, but with reluctance, as one might embrace a loved one who had come in from a hard run on a hot day.

It's obvious to anyone who spends time in GE that hesitation has turned to obsession. Says Welch: "This is all about moving intellectual capital—taking ideas and moving them around faster and faster and faster." There is no "GE Europe" per se—no Rome to which all roads lead; the businesses report in to Schenectady, Cincinnati, Milwaukee, Kansas City, etc. But there are dozens of councils: In Europe alone, a Corporate Executive Council for the pooh-bahs, a Marketing Council, Technical Council, Sourcing Council, Finance Council, Human Resources Council, Sales Council, Manufacturing Council, Quality Council, and more. Each business operates similar cross-business or cross-functional networks, which meet for a day or two every few months. Probably every professional in the company—tens of thousands of people—sits on at least one cross-business council. At meetings, everybody is expected to bring something—an idea that made a few bucks, a process that's quicker than the old one. "Go to the European Corporate Executive Council," says Larry Johnston, just named to head it, "and you see 30 people writing all day long."

GE's culture is both deeply competitive and furiously collaborative. It's a company joke that within minutes of Welch's leaving a site, the phone starts ringing as other businesses ask, "What's this thing you told Jack about?" More and more best practices flow both ways across the Atlantic. A system for managing sales forces developed in Barcelona is spreading worldwide. In May 1998, in Florence, Welch heard how a Six Sigma team making turbine packages had cut the total cost 30%. Show me, Welch demanded, and spent an hour grilling the team so he could, when he left, tell everybody else in GE to call Nuovo Pignone.

Ultimately people, not money or tools, make the global GE work. From the beginning, Welch has poured money and energy into creating a massive iceberg of leadership ability. The tip is Crotonville, the company's spiffy executive development campus in New York State; it was a "hovel" when Welch took over, according to one GE executive. What's beneath Crotonville is more important—a passion for leadership development everywhere in the company. The heads of GE's European businesses, asked how much of their time is spent on HR subjects, give answers ranging from 30% to 50%.

There's nothing egalitarian about GE's HR philosophy. It finds the best and culls the rest—period. It can be a cultural shock. Says Tone Rongstand, 32, who has been promoted twice in 1999 and now heads risk management for GE Consumer Finance in Norway: "When I was young I went to a ski competition, and the winner was the one who went in the average time. This is not like GE!"

Leadership development ranks with Work-Out, Six Sigma, and idea swapping as GE's best tools for globalization. It starts with new hires—or people at newly acquired companies. Engineers might get into TLP, a tough, two-year technical leadership program that involves three eight-month projects interwoven with classroom work in project management, process-improvement methods, and so on. Similar courses exist in every functional discipline from finance to information management, as well as Six Sigma training leading to "black belt" and "master black belt" status. Still more courses are offered at intermediate and advanced levels, always with lots of time in the field.

The training unleashes a number of forces, of which content is least important. It creates networks that unify the company and leverage its diversity. It's impossible to exploit GE's size if people don't know one another. Second, lavish investment in high-pots sparks ambition. Says Danielli Schenarelli, a sourcing expert at Nuovo Pignone: "The American idea of the self-made man translates into a management style of self-selected leadership." When someone at GE feels the urge to lead, he just starts leading, regardless of age or title—and has almost infinite running room. Raf Jansen, an electrical engineer, joined GE from college in 1994. In March 1998, Joaquim Agut spotted him and asked him to lead Power Controls operations in Poland. The project involved converting a joint venture into a 100% GE-owned operation, building (in six months) a greenfield factory in Klodzko, and moving production of small circuit breakers there from high-wage Western European countries. Jansen is 30 years old.

Sophisticated HR systems make sure that no sharp knife stays in a drawer. These include annual self-evaluations and feedback as well as a yearly, companywide review of talent. Welch himself reviews some 3,000 people. Top managers pursue top people like kids chasing an ice cream truck. At the Hotel Gellert in Budapest one spring morning, Mike Zafirovski bought breakfast for a 30-year-old hot-shot high-pot from Medical Systems, whom he wanted for lighting's operations in Istanbul. Said Zafirovski: "Larry Johnston wants to keep him. He has sexier technology, but I can offer P&L responsibility." (Zafirovski won.) Leaders also compete to see who shares talent best. When Nils Albert, who runs a leasing business for GE Capital in England, needed a salesperson in Spain, he called Agut in Barcelona, who leaped at the chance to give him one. Says Agut: "Now everyone in Europe knows that Nils got someone from Power Controls, so we get a reputation for developing people—which helps me."

Leadership Darwinism cuts both ways. Since the beginning of 1999, GE has been pushing a harsh forced ranking of employees. For years, GE has divided salaried employees into A, B, and C players—with pay and promotions disproportionately given to A players, and C players left back. Now an "organizational vitality" measurement requires every manager to rank his staff—even if they're all A players—into a "top" ten, "strong" 15, "highly valued" 50, "borderline" 15, and "least effective" ten. "It's wild," says Welch: "You send your top ten on, and see how many of them get into the top ten for the whole business. Or you look at what functions are represented. If there are no tens or 15s from finance, it means the whole function is stuck in the middle." It's not pretty, but Welch thinks a merciless push to upgrade human capital is vital.

There are, Welch says, three stages of globalization. First is globalization of markets—acquiring the assets to sell in any market you choose. Second is globalization of sources—becoming able to buy or build wherever it's most advantageous.

Welch sees GE entering phase three: "Globalizing the intellect of the company"—going wherever the best brains are. Says Welch: "It means using Russian engineering and Indian software—not to arbitrage labor costs, but because these are the best people you can find." GE gives stock options as generously to Europeans as it does to Americans. As a result, there are two dozen dollar millionaires at GE Medical in Europe. Non-Americans fill Crotonville's top classes in rough proportion to their numbers in GE's total employee base. The head of GE's corporate audit staff is French, Six Sigma's leader is Dutch, and now a European leads one of GE's core businesses. But, Welch says, to globalize intellect deep into the organization, "is the hardest thing a company can do, because no one is safe then."

Nokia: Made in Finland and Sold Just About Everywhere

By YOUSSEF M. IBRAHIM

HELSINKI, Finland—About five years ago, Nokia hatched a telecommunications project with the code name "Responder" and formed a secretive unit to carry it out. Some 25 researchers, managers and scientists gathered discreetly in Tampere, a bastion of high-technology research in Finland, and were given this broad mission: "Look at the next challenge" in tapping the exploding world of wireless communications.

That challenge, they decided, was to combine Internet, computer and phone technologies to produce a portable machine that could use all of them equally. When presented with the idea, Nokia's top management pressed their engineers to move quickly to outflank the company's two giant competitors, Motorola of the United States and Ericsson of Sweden. And sure enough, the Nokia 9000, or Communicator, will hit American stores this fall.

It is a risky move. For with mobile phones everywhere, only the most innovative ones will turn a decent profit, but it fits Nokia's aggressive strategy.

The company has not only transformed the portable phone—with five factories around the globe turning out some 1.5 million phones a month, it is the world's No. 2 producer, after Motorola—but has also transformed itself from an old-line paper company into a leading technology company.

Along the way, it has also helped transform the Finnish economy. "We used to have two clusters of strength in the Finnish economy: Wood and paper, and metals. Now we have a third: it's called Nokia," notes Kurt Nordman, chairman of Helsinki Telephone Co., a private telecommunications company that is a big client of Nokia.

How could tiny Finland give birth to such a company? Simple. Though its population is only five million, Finland is by all accounts the world's most wired country, with a highly educated and technologically savvy population.

Nokia, with an ever-growing staff of 34,000 scientists, researchers, salespeople and other employees peppered around 45 countries—6,000 of whom joined last year alone—is rapidly joining the ranks of international household names like Sony and Microsoft.

Inside Nokia House, the new Helsinki headquarters, a growing sense of confidence is palpable. This "ecologically sensitive" building, an architectural marvel set on the shore of the Baltic Sea, is encased with 26,000 glass plates flooding its eight-story atriums and offices with the light of Finland's long summer days.

As the Communicator project progressed, the focus became to create, essentially, the world's first movable, pocket-sized office. The device would allow conference calls, receive and send faxes, handle e-mail and cruise the Internet—all from a moving car, train or sidewalk cafe. It would, says Yrjo Neuvo, senior vice president for product creation, "turn one-plus-one into more than two," which he calls a creed of Nokia's corporate culture.

The culture must work. Revenues hit $8.5 billion last year, and Nokia's share price went from $35 in January 1996 to $56.50 a year later and now stands at $85.75. Its price-earnings ratio of 26 exceeds the 23.5 of the Standard & Poor's 500.

It is an article of faith in Finland that by 2002 well over half the world's data, voice and images will travel without wires, which is why Nokia is heavily focused on what its vice president for communications, Arva Suominen, calls the manufacture of "mobile phones and everything you have in between."

Long gone are the days when Nokia was known for its paper-processing mills nestled by the Nokia River. Nokia executives calculate that by 2000 the world will have 500 million mobile phones, up from 135 million today. And 60 percent of them, they predict, will use a technology supported by Nokia called Global System for Mobile Communications.

Nokia's upbeat mood is enhanced by a widely shared conviction among its executives that new markets in Asia, Latin America and the Middle East will ensure growth well into the next century.

"Our objective is to continue to grow annually by 25 to 35 percent a year," says Pu Kotilainen, vice president for human resources, and Nokia employees have a clear incentive to meet those targets. Every worker gets a bonus of 5 percent of salary if profit growth beats 35 percent, and some 2,000 top executives also get lucrative stock options.

Such growth, though, is by no means guaranteed. Luke Szymczak, a telecommunications analyst at

Prudential Securities in New York, agrees that "if you looked at Nokia 10 years ago, you would have never predicted they'd be where they are today." But he cautions that the company may be putting too many eggs in one basket. "I mean 55 percent of their mix is into handsets. This is a very favorable thing right now, but could be a risk sometime in the future."

For one thing, Szymczak says, Motorola is catching up quickly in Nokia's specialty, "smart" mobile phones. And other analysts note that many other companies, like Phillips, Lucent and Sony, are also set to produce mobile phones. The risk is that what happened with color televisions could happen to portable phones—with rising volumes but falling profits on each phone.

To Nokia executives, the immediate risk lies in failing to meet demand for smart phones like the Communicator, those with added features that they believe consumers will pay more for.

"Handsets will increasingly enable the use of advanced digital services which can be loaded with all kind of services to consumers," says Pekka Ala Pietila, president of the mobile telephone division.

For Nokia, the challenge is to keep its enormous research and development staff—8,000 employees—focused on the cutting edge of smart, user-friendly products.

This year, Nokia is marketing set-top boxes that turn televisions into Internet terminals, mobile pay phones that can be placed in taxis or restaurants, and credit card-size inserts that turn portable computers into phones.

Then there is the Nokia 8110 phone line, with a single key that opens a menu of options allowing a user to track a stock, a news item, a ballgame and send and receive written and audio messages. Or Nokia Cellular Data Suite, which allows the use of Windows 95 with a digital portable.

And Nokia just introduced the 2180 portable, its first foray into the competitive digital standard growing in the United States.

"They put quite a big emphasis on the 'music' part of their business, so to speak," said Risto Linturi, technology multimedia director of Helsinki Telecom Co., a large private concern. "Take the Communicator, for example. It has all the components necessary for hand-held communications. It's pragmatic, easy to use and a simple touch-button proposition."

True. But the failure of competitors to match the Communicator, noted an executive at a competing company who insisted on anonymity, could be their belief that "the market is not ready" for such sophisticated gimmicks. Sales of the Communicator, with an initial cost of about $1,000, have been sluggish in Europe, but Nokia insists it is too early to gauge demand.

"It will be interesting to see how it will do in the U.S.," said Neuvo, the Nokia vice president. "It takes some time before people realize how convenient some services are."

Meanwhile, Nokia's chief competitor, Motorola, thinks it is on the verge of surpassing the Finnish company's technological lead. Margaret Rice-Jones, Motorola's product marketing director for Europe, says her company has its own smart phone, to be released around the end of the year, with "capabilities that go beyond those of the Communicator."

When Nokia began to emerge as a telecommunications phenomenon, one company executive said its success was founded on "enthusiasm and madness." Today, the focus in collegiality. Its core is held together by several common denominators: a requirement that all employees speak English; a younger crowd, with a median age of 31, and a hiring policy marked by extensive interviews designed to ensure a staff with the ability to get along with others.

"No politics, a lot of trust, realism with equality between people, titles are not important—teamwork with openness is," explains Matti Alahuhta, president of Nokia Telecom, who has worked for the company for two decades. "There is a Finnish word, Noyrwws, which means humility, humbleness, that you take pride in the past but don't project it into the future."

To workers this seems attractive enough. "They understand what you need," said Siberg Jukka-Pekka, an engineer who joined Nokia a year and half ago. "It is the same pay, but what attracts here is being on the cutting edge."

Much of the success has to do with Nokia's being a Scandinavian company born in Finland. Scandinavia took a giant leap into deregulating telecommunications in the late '80s. That gave Nokia and Ericsson free rein to learn how to operate in a competitive environment and establish a lead over others in Europe and surpass the technology then in place in the United States.

Nokia has also forged strong ties with many of Finland's 20 universities. At Tampere, about 100 miles north of Helsinki, Nokia's research laboratories are next to Tampere University's media lab, and professors regularly stroll over to the labs for lunch.

"It guarantees the universities know where the business is and where the business is going and Nokia knows what the scientists are doing and thinking," Pietila notes.

"It means that many more researchers are finding killer applications," says Markku Laukkanen, chairman of the administrative council of Finnish Broadcasting, which does business with Nokia.

But what if the world eventually heads for satellite-driven communications, not earth-based switches and relay stations. Indeed, satellites are being deployed by rivals like Motorola, at great expense.

"Satellites will have two million subscribers after the year 2000," Neuvo predicts. "Cellular phones will have nearly 400 million, at a much lower cost for use. In my opinion, satellites are a niche market—certainly a big niche, but still a niche, for places like the Gobi desert, the Atlantic Ocean or the Sahara."

But just in case, Nokia is also coming out with a phone for anyone stuck in the Gobi desert. It is a new solar-powered model, the Nokia 1610.

Zeneca Buying Astra As Europe Consolidates

By ALAN COWELL

In one of Europe's biggest mergers, the Zeneca Group P.L.C. of Britain announced a stock deal valued around $35 billion today to buy Astra A.B. of Sweden, creating a pharmaceutical giant.

The deal, which had been expected, was the latest in a series of cross-border mergers and acquisitions in the European pharmaceutical industry. These deals reflect a quest for size to pursue costly research into new drugs and to compete in a market dominated by United States corporations.

The new company, to be called AstraZeneca, will be the world's fourth-largest pharmaceutical concern, with a market value of $67 billion. It will also represent the 10th-largest of all mergers and acquisitions.

Under the deal, Zeneca will offer 0.5045 share for every Astra A-series or B-series share. Zeneca stockholders will control 53.5 percent of the combined company, which will have corporate headquarters in London and research headquarters in Sweden. AstraZeneca plans to cut 6,000 jobs, or about one-ninth of the work force, to save $1.1 billion.

"Astra and Zeneca are a perfect fit," said Thomas McKillop, head of pharmaceutical business at Zeneca—which was spun off from Imperial Chemical Industries in 1993 and has since increased its market value to seven times that of its onetime parent.

The new company will combine the manufacturers of two well-known medications—Astra's ulcer drug Prilosec and the Zeneca cancer treatment Nolvadex, or tamoxifen generically—and will, according to Mr. McKillop, represent a great leap in global sales and marketing power. The companies had combined sales in 1997 of $15.9 billion and combined drug sales of $11.5 billion. Their combined pretax profit was $3.5 billion, and the combined research and development budget was $1.9 billion, the world's third largest.

Mr. McKillop was named chief executive of the combined company today. Contrary to analysts' expectations, the chairman of new company will not be Astra's chairman, Haaken Mogren, but Percy Barnevik, one of Sweden's best-known industrialists. Mr. Barnevik is chairman of Investor A.B., a holding company that is the investment arm of the Wallenberg family, which owns about 12 percent of Astra's stock. Mr. Mogren, who will be one of two deputy chairmen, had reportedly been under pressure from the Wallenbergs to improve the company's return. The other deputy chairman will be Sir David Barnes, chief executive of Zeneca.

Mr. Barnevik is also chairman of Asea Brown Boveri, the world's largest electrical engineering company, and has a reputation as a no-frills manager with a history of fusing corporate cultures, a matter particularly relevant to the drug business. Only this year a planned merger between Britain's two biggest pharmaceutical companies, Glaxo Wellcome and SmithKline Beecham, fell apart largely because the companies could not agree on who would run the merged businesses.

People close to the deal said that in discussions lasting several months, a central issue had been selecting the lineup of top management to try to avoid the divisions that torpedoed other drug industry deals after they were announced. "This was gone through thoroughly to avoid that happening," one person said.

Today's deal prompted speculation about a counterbid from other companies, perhaps Glaxo Wellcome. But Mr. McKillop said in a conference call with reporters: "We have had overtures from quite a number of parties on a number of occasions. We did not feel they would be the right combination."

Analysts were divided, with some arguing that sharp increases today in the share prices of both companies were driven by the possibility of a counterbid. In London, shares of Zeneca rose 6.9 percent while Astra's A shares climbed 10.6 percent in Stockholm.

The deal closely followed an agreement by Hoechst of Germany and Rhone-Poulenc of France to merge their drug and agricultural products operations and a $10.4 billion stock swap between Sanofi and Synthelabo, two French drug companies. The proposed AstraZeneca deal would be the largest drug merger, surpassing the $28 billion combination of Ciba-Geigy and Sandoz, two Swiss producers, to create

Novartis in 1996, according to the Securities Data Company. Under British accounting rules, the newest deal is classified as a merger of equals.

It also coincided with expectations among some American investment bankers that Europe's move toward mergers of equals would increase as the single European currency, to be introduced on Jan. 1, spurs cross-border deal-making.

"There is massive potential for this kind of deal, especially in Continental Europe," said Paul Gibbs, head of analytical policy in the European advisory department at J.P. Morgan. He spoke on Tuesday at a year-end briefing—before details of the Zeneca-Astra deal became known—and underlined a European trend toward mergers of equals that avoid paying a premium to the shareholders to companies being acquired.

According to figures he presented, European mergers and acquisitions so far this year—before the Zeneca-Astra deal—totaled $643 billion, $214 billion of that in deals between companies of similar size. That represented a marked increase from $490 billion in 1997, with $51 billion in mergers of equals.

"This year for me was the year of mergers of equals," said Klaus Diederichs, co-head of Global Advisory business at J.P. Morgan, saying at the same briefing that the wave of deals had been driven both by corporate revamping and by increasing pressure on executives and directors to create shareholder value. "We believe there's much more to come," he said.

Within Europe, the merger frenzy has been led by British companies, with 39 percent of the business, Mr. Gibbs said. But, with 11 countries joining in the euro next month, many analysts say that Continental European companies—with their shares denominated in euros—will find themselves pressed toward cross-border deals free of currency-exchange problems.

Mergers were bound to be explored in the European pharmaceutical industry anyway, some analysts said, because of the escalating cost of research as patents on existing drugs expire. For example, the patent on Astra's Priloseec ulcer medication—sold outside the United States as Losec—expires in 2001.

"Astra has not felt strong enough to go it alone in this fierce competition," said Sigfrid Leijonhufvud, economic columnist at the newspaper Svenska Dagbladet in Stockholm. "They need to put a lot of money into future research."

China Rolls Out the Red Carpet

Richard Tomlinson

With partners like Marriott and Hilton, the Chinese are building a class-A hotel industry. The surprise: Some companies are already making money.

Here's a hotel manager's nightmare: You're standing by the front desk when a huge marble slab comes loose from the atrium wall and crashes to the ground. Your staff freeze for an instant, then return to their business as if nothing has happened. When a worried guest suggests they might want to check the rest of the wall for loose tiles, he's firmly told there's "no problem." The scene, however, isn't a bad dream. It happened last year at a hotel in China managed by a FORTUNE 500 global chain.

Hell is a Chinese hotel. The toilets leak, the staff are brain dead, and room service has a built-in time-delay switch. At least that's the caricature passed around by long-suffering diplomats, tourists, and corporate China hands. So who would want to get into this game? The answer: just about everyone. Most major hotel players are currently engaged in what seems at first glance like a reckless scramble for mainland venues. Until the mid-1990s few big-name hotels were found outside Beijing, Shanghai, and Guangzhou. Today around 80 hotels are being managed or launched across China by a roster of leading operators: Marriott, Hilton, Hyatt, Starwood (owner of Westin and Sheraton), Shangri-La, and Bass (British owners of Holiday Inn). Foreigners are the initial target clientele, but Chinese travelers are the ultimate prize.

In Mao's time the masses stayed at home, except when dispatched to the countryside to help build communism. Not anymore. Last year, according to government statistics, a staggering 659 million domestic tourist and business trips were made in China. It all adds up to an industry that China claims was worth $28 billion in 1998. If the global hotel chains can unlock this market, the rewards for them could be just as mind-boggling.

When international hoteliers talk about the China market, they roll out the same cliches as most foreign investors. The potential is huge. We can't afford not to be here. We're here for the long term. But there's a crucial difference. Most big hotel chains can plausibly claim to turn a profit in China while they wait for the market to grow. That's because groups like Hilton and Marriott don't risk capital in real estate but earn their income from hotel-management contracts, which reduce overhead and liabilities to a minimum. What the hotel industry illustrates is the value of not getting sucked in. Call it constructive but limited engagement.

That's not, of course, how it appears on the surface. In Beijing, Shanghai, and Guangzhou, and increasingly in secondary cities such as Chengdu and Wuhan, the hotel heavyweights have embarked on what looks like an insane dash for mainland growth at the worst moment in the economic cycle. Take Starwood, which now operates ten mainland hotels. Within a year, three more will be added to the list, and by 2005, if Starwood's Asia-Pacific president, Ted Teng, keeps his China strategy on track, the portfolio will have swollen to 30 establishments. Says Teng, a former refugee who checked out of China in 1959: "My dream is that there will be more Starwood hotels in China than anywhere else outside the U.S."

Starwood's chief mainland competitors are singing the same groundbreaking tune. "All our current expansion is in China," reports Joanne Watkins, spokeswoman for Shangri-La, the Asian luxury chain controlled by Malaysian billionaire Robert Kuok. In June 1989, Kuok's commitment to the mainland was sorely tested during the Beijing crackdown, as tanks passed by the nearly completed China World Center—a glitzy hotel and commercial project developed by Shangri-La and China's Trade Ministry. A decade after that unnerving welcome, the complex includes a second, less expensive hotel at the rear (managed under Shangri-La's Traders brand), and another luxury venue is set to open across the road. By year-end two more hotels will be launched in Harbin and Wuhan, boosting Shangri-La's mainland portfolio to 12.

But if any hotel epitomizes the current mood of the big chains, it's the Grand Hyatt in Shanghai. Opened in March, the hotel occupies the top 34 stories of the brand-new Jinmao Tower—an astonishing 414-meter skyscraper designed with Shanghai's art deco heritage in mind at a total cost of $540 million. Hyatt can now claim to operate the world's tallest hotel. The group plans to expand its mainland network from three venues to ten.

So how's the view? Not good. Business and tourist traffic to Shanghai has been badly hit by the regional crisis, with total visitor arrivals down 7.6% in 1998. Hotel occupancy rates fell from 69% to 61%. Predicts Nigel Summers, a travel industry consultant at Horwath Asia Pacific in Hong Kong: "For

WHY CHINA'S HIGHFLYING AIR INDUSTRY HIT TURBULENCE

So dire is the current condition of China's aviation industry that in February the government decreed that CEOs of domestic carriers would be fired if their companies lost money for two consecutive years. Don't count on any of them keeping their jobs.

The state-owned sector is currently carved up between four main carriers (China Southern, Eastern, and Northern, and Air China), which operate half the domestic fleet. At least two dozen smaller airlines share the rest of the market. Combined losses for domestic carriers in 1998 were officially around $725 million. "They're getting absolutely killed," says David Strine, an aviation analyst at Bear Stearns Asia.

In the mid-1990s domestic demand was increasing at 30%-plus annual rates, but last year's growth declined to just 6.3%, as the mainland economy slowed and the regional crisis continued to bite. Slower growth means that the airlines are now encumbered with far too many planes, forcing the government to react. In February, China's Civil Aviation Administration, the industry regulator, imposed a moratorium on commercial aircraft purchases until 2002 and instructed manufacturers to postpone delivery of an unspecified number of planes ordered for 2000 and 2001. That's unwelcome news for Boeing and Airbus, which were banking on China to fill their order books. Only two years ago Boeing predicted that China would spend $140 billion on more than 2,000 aircraft by 2014.

What's bad for the plane manufacturers is also bad for the international carriers. In January, Qantas Airways announced it was suspending service on the Beijing-Shanghai leg of its China-Australia route, citing "commercial reasons" (read: falling demand). Qantas is not abandoning the route altogether. The Australian group is negotiating a linkup with Shanghai-based China Eastern to cover the Beijing run and is publicly confident that traffic will recover.

That view is shared by most foreign airlines. One example: Richard Branson's British-based Virgin group. In May the effervescent Branson—whose last excursion into Chinese air space was onboard a balloon—will launch a twice-weekly service between Shanghai and London. British Airways also bid for the route, and Virgin is predictably puffed up about beating its rival. Says Virgin spokesman Paul Moore: "It should be, and probably will be, one of the big business routes of the next millennium."

If that sounds like hot air, it's still true that major airlines are much less worried by the present China downturn than by the prospect of losing out when the mainland market picks up. The dilemma is especially acute for U.S. carriers. Despite an aviation pact in April that will double U.S.-China flights, only United and Northwest are permitted to operate passenger routes (FedEx flies cargo planes).

Grudgingly, China will allow another U.S. carrier in 2001. Beijing's concern: The addition will further undermine the competitiveness of Air China, China Eastern, and China Southern, the three domestic airlines authorized to fly to America.

hotels, the next three years are going to be tough." The picture looks even worse in the secondary cities, where the big hotel chains have started to plant their flags.

Hence the need to secure risk-insulated management contracts. Consider a standard, renewable ten-year contract to run a top-tier hotel in Beijing's international district, where you'll find Hilton, Marriott, Starwood, and a clutch of other leading names. According to Summers, the management company typically claims 2% to 3% of total revenues, plus up to 10% of the operating profit. That can yield annual profits of between $500,000 and $1 million per property.

Since this is China, there has to be a downside. It begins for any overseas player that sinks capital into the mainland's overstocked hotel property market—a legacy of the mid-1990s construction boom. Shangri-La, which builds its own hotels, has put several China projects on hold because of the economic slowdown. In March, Hong Kong & Shanghai Hotels announced a $42 million provision against losses at the top-tier—and underperforming—Palace Hotel in Beijing, in which it has a 20% joint venture stake.

At times even management groups that don't normally risk their own equity are persuaded to take minority holdings by owners that need cash to finish the projects. Starwood, for instance, took the unusual step of taking a 31% stake in Beijing's New International Club Hotel, for which it paid $54 million to the developer, Beijing's Diplomatic Services Bureau (DSB). Part of China's Ministry of State Security, the DSB isn't the most obvious candidate for the luxury-hotel game: It is the monopoly provider of cooks, cleaners, and drivers (and some would say spies) to the capital's foreign embassies. Starwood, plus the other leading foreign players, claims to be comfortable with such state-backed owners. But it can't be easy to work with entities with no track record in hotel development.

Is dealing with shadowy, frequently incompetent local owners worth the hassle? To understand why it might be, consider the series of bets the hotel chains have made on the market's future growth. First, they're assuming that inbound business and tourist traffic to China will pick up. Second, that sooner or later a critical mass of mainlanders will tire of Chinese hotels—think bath stains, cockroaches, and dingy karaoke bars—and opt for something a little more salubrious. In anticipation, big names such as Marriott and Holiday Inn are signing deals in smaller cities like Wuxi, Jiangsu province, and Hefei, Anhui province—the Chinese equivalents of Dayton or Fresno—with a view to building a local customer base.

But given China's modest per capita income—at most $800 a year—finding customers won't be easy. So the hotels have their sights set on mainland business travelers—a huge emerging customer class of joint venture executives, state enterprise managers, and party officials whose defining feature is an expense account.

Already these people are generating enough demand to whet the appetite of hotel strategists like Daniel Lai, sales and marketing director for Marriott in China. Room charges at provincial Chinese hotels can sink as low as $10 (with service to match); not even a budget chain can work at those rates. What can be built are $50-per-night (or a little more) venues, in the hope that China's corporate man can be persuaded to kiss the cockroaches goodbye and move up-market. Marriott, says Lai, aims to be operating seven Courtyard hotels in this price range by the end of the year. Hilton, too, is pondering whether to launch the group's economy Garden Inn brand. Says Koos Klein, Hilton's Asia-Pacific president: "The gut feeling is that a serious market will develop over the next decade."

It won't be an easy market to enter, though. Downtown land prices in Chinese cities remain way too high for economy hotels, while cheaper suburban sites are too inaccessible to make commercial sense. Add the crippling cost of expatriate managers—essential for such a specialized business—and it's hardly surprising that Hilton's Klein is treading cautiously in this niche of the market. His downbeat view: "There've been many gung-ho statements by other companies about the economy market, but most of them haven't operated in China yet."

That leaves the top end of the market—a five-star world of sleek doormen, plush carpets, and $200-plus room rates. No mainlander can afford those prices, right? Well, not exactly. All big chains offer heavy, undisclosed discounts to local guests. A mainlander can usually expect to knock at least 50% off the room rate, and sometimes much more. Nobody's pretending that such a custom generates riches, but with occupancy levels in a trough, it's better than leaving the rooms empty. And although we're talking about only a tiny customer sliver—supremely well-connected types like senior party officials and big-shot businessmen—the cut rates help to build brand awareness for the day when locals can afford full fare.

Meanwhile, there are the foreign guests, who pay international rates and often receive lousy service in return. The leading chains would like you to believe that in China they deliver the same quality of service as they would in, say, Hong Kong or Switzerland. It isn't true, principally because Chinese staff are still prone to some distinctly communist work habits—chief among them a tendency to do nothing unless issued extremely specific orders. Starwood's Teng has introduced "attitude training" for the staff at the group's Beijing flagship, aimed at teaching them how to anticipate customer needs. He ruefully notes, "That's not easy to do in a structured society like China, where most people aren't keen to take on responsibilities." To be fair, Starwood's personnel blitz seems to be taking effect at the New International Club, whose reprogrammed staff are noticeably eager to please. Elsewhere it's a different story, with many five-star hotels in China still woefully short of international standards.

Which raises the question: Is the global hotel industry's current breakneck expansion in China really worth the effort? Maybe it is—but only if such teething troubles as overcooked food, undercleaned rooms, and yes, the occasional flying tile are fixed before too many more stories are added to China's hotel horror anthology.

Unit 2

Unit Selections

8. **America's Most Admired Companies,** Eryn Brown
9. **Big Kellogg Shareholders Seek More Snap, Crackle and Pop,** Dana Canedy and Reed Abelson
10. **The Rise of a Star,** Anthony Bianco
11. **New CEO Preaches Rebellion,** Tara Parker-Pope
12. **The Auctioneer: Margaret Whitman, the CEO of eBay, Talks about the Company's Rapid Growth—and Heady Ambitions,** George Anders
13. **Man on the Spot**, *Business Week*
14. **Why CEOs Fail,** Ram Charan and Geoffrey Colvin

Key Points to Consider

- Effective management involves some basic principles. While many remain unchanged, some need to be refined to fit into twenty-first century businesses.

- Successful companies share many common characteristics in their management practices, and they generally outperform the general population of firms.

- Effective leaders have a vision, a clear understanding of their firm's mission. They also have an interpersonal style that keeps their firms at the forefront of the competition.

DUSHKINONLINE Links

www.dushkin.com/online/

13. **Business Nation**
    http://www.businessnation.com/library/management.html
14. **Centre for Strategic Management**
    http://csmintl.premierdomain.com/menu.htm
15. **Fortune 1000 list**
    http://www.fortune.com/fortune/fortune500/
16. **Strategic Management and Michael Porter: A Postmodern Reading**
    http://www.mngt.waikato.ac.nz/depts/sml/journal/special/harfield.htm
17. **Strategic Management Journal**
    http://www.smsweb.org/Pages/Windows/smj.html

These sites are annotated on pages 4 and 5.

Management is responsible for identifying the strengths and weaknesses of the firm and crafting a strategy that fits the opportunities and minimizes the threats of the environment. In this sense, the critical element of a company is how well management discharges those duties.

A major change in the role of management occurred in the early part of the twentieth century as very large, integrated organizations began to dominate the U.S. industrial scene. These organizations combined diverse functions such as mining, manufacturing, marketing, and service. Few owners had the managerial talent needed to lead these complex firms, and a new class of professional managers emerged. At the same time, the financial resources necessary to operate these firms was rarely available to trained managers. As access to capital markets and debt financing became available, firms started to grow with funds from outside sources. The result, known as agency, theoretically meant, in effect, that owners no longer managed, and managers no longer owned. The establishment of an upper level of management allowed middle-level managers to concentrate on coordinating the activities of the firm, while the upper-level managers were able to devote their attention to long-range planning, the beginning of the modern strategic process.

Now, a new set of stakeholders has emerged, each with its own goals and objectives. As a result, management must satisfy the needs of stockholders, bankers, suppliers, unions, customers, and the rules of numerous public agencies.

In that context, the question of effective and ethical corporate governance becomes a critical measure of the strategic management process. To represent the diverse interests of stakeholders, companies are required to elect a board of directors whose responsibility is to advise, direct, and monitor the corporation but not to manage it on a daily basis. How members of a board are selected and the degree of influence that they have in the long-term direction of their company is often a key to understanding how the company is being managed.

Strategists recognize that effective leadership and management must be carefully cultivated, constantly nourished, and adapted to the business climate. Automotive entrepreneur Henry Ford's management style was eclipsed by General Motors' president Alfred Sloan. Within two decades, that style proved to be ineffective. As management consultant Peter Drucker argues, management styles need to be flexible. Some tried and tested axioms remain critical, while others need to be discarded and adjusted to current conditions.

At the close of World War II, technology and economics produced an organizational form that worked best when a hierarchy of management supervised a pyramidal form of workers. The emphasis was on the control and organization of subordinates. Information was generally guarded by

management to ensure the preservation of company processes and secrets.

As we enter the "information age," it becomes increasingly evident that the scarce resources today are considerably different from those of previous times. Knowledge becomes the defining factor in organizational success. Flexible conditions to accommodate the most capable workers replace rigid workplace rules. The role of women as active members of upper management is increasing dramatically. Managers are more likely to be drawn from a variety of minority groups than ever before.

Surely the destruction of old firms and the creation of new, more efficient, and more responsive ones are testimony to economist and educator Joseph Schumpeter's concept of a business world characterized by "perennial gales of creative destruction." In his writings, he illustrated how the new organizations ruthlessly replace the less efficient ones through a process of entrepreneurial activity. These entrepreneurs, he explained, were innovators who found new and better means of production and distribution. Some introduced ideas that resulted in the restructuring of entire industries. These leaders who are identified as the innovators are often the target of severe criticism because some of their decisions may have unpleasant social costs that are associated with the changes.

Those who lead the new organizations are also significantly different from their predecessors. New skills, new techniques, and new styles characterize the new leaders. They have learned to adapt to the global economy, to a changing workforce, and to a set of technologies and processes that place extraordinary demands on leaders.

What can be learned from the most successful managers and companies? We see a set of common values that becomes evident. Obviously, no two managers have the same personalities, but the most successful display talents and capabilities that focus their organizations on providing superior customer value while addressing the particular needs of their employees and all of the other stakeholder groups.

America's Most Admired Companies

by Eryn Brown

We tell you why the two new companies in the top ten, Dell and Wal-Mart, are just alike—sort of.

EVERY YEAR WE SURVEY THOUSANDS of business people to compile our list of America's Most Admired Companies. And every year the companies that rise to the top exemplify precisely the qualities that people have come to admire in business: Ingenuity. Profitability. Laserlike focus. The willingness to work hard, work harder, and then work just a little bit harder.

Many of the survey's perennial favorites seem to dig in as they age. For the second year in a row, General Electric is FORTUNE's most admired company, winning praise for its value as a long-term investment and, naturally, for the quality of its management under CEO Jack Welch. No. 2 Coca-Cola and No. 3 Microsoft continue to amaze competitors with their financial stability, their use of corporate assets, and their ability to attract capable employees. Only two companies dropped out of the top ten. Hewlett-Packard, No. 5 last year, fell to No. 18, and Johnson & Johnson went from No. 9 to No. 12. Their replacements, Dell and Wal-Mart, have achieved impressive growth and killer shareholder returns through the expert use of technology.

the top ten

1	General Electric
2	Coca-Cola
3	Microsoft
4	Dell Computer
5	Berkshire Hathaway
6	Wal-Mart Stores
7	Southwest Airlines
8	Intel
9	Merck
10	Walt Disney

the bottom ten

460	Foundation Health
461	Fruit of the Loom
462	Viad
463	Olsten
464	U.S. Industries
465	Stone Container
466	Oxford Health Plans
467	MedPartners
468	Shoney's
469	Trump Hotels & Casinos

In the industry rankings, companies that stand to profit from the Internet scored especially well. America Online, which has solidified its position as the preeminent power on the Net, moved up four places, to No. 2, in the computer and data-services group. Sprint, the new No. 1 among telecommunications companies, was the first major long-distance player to announce it would combine voice and data services on the same network. Equipment maker Lucent Technologies landed with a splash in its industry rankings, debuting at No. 2.

In the financial sector, "merger" is still the magic word. J.P. Morgan, the No. 1 commercial bank every year since FORTUNE began its Most Admired survey in 1982, finally lost its title this year to Citicorp, which merged with Travelers Group. And Travelers itself moved up three slots within the securities industry. The No. 2 commercial bank, Chase Manhattan, has been advancing steadily over the past five years, in part because of its successful combination with Chemical Bank; it also came through the Asian financial crises relatively unscathed. Morgan Stanley Dean Witter, another merger winner, jumped four places in the securities group. NationsBank advanced this year, although its new sibling, BankAmerica, took a hit, the result of significant losses overseas and the messy dismissal of CEO David Coulter.

Getting to the customer on time: Dell can make and deliver a computer within 24 hours of receiving the order.

Companies that made news—good or bad—made waves in the rankings. Viagra propelled Pfizer to the No. 1 pharmaceuticals spot, where it unseated Merck, the long-time category leader. Apple, with Steve Jobs at the helm and candy-colored iMacs flying off shelves, greatly improved its score, though it still lags behind IBM and Dell. Northwest Airlines, hurt by a pilots' strike, fell from No. 5 to No. 8. Boeing, long king of its category, plunged in the wake of massive layoffs.

Among the losers, a physicians' practice management company, MedPartners, saw its score fall 40.53%, more than any other. Trump Hotels & Casinos, Oxford Health Plans, and Shoney's joined it in the basement, scoring poorly on financial soundness, use of corporate assets, keeping talent, and community and environmental responsibility.

Predictable? Sure. But the companies that lead our list really do have the sharpest managers, the best-run operations, the coolest products, the happiest shareholders. They remind us that doing things

eight key attributes of reputation

Cisco ranked 14th overall, yet it appears more often than any other top-ranked company in the categories below. Repeat winners this year include Du Pont and Herman Miller (social responsibility) and Enron (innovation).

INNOVATIVENESS		QUALITY OF MANAGEMENT		EMPLOYEE TALENT		QUALITY OF PRODUCTS/SERVICES	
MOST ADMIRED	SCORE	MOST ADMIRED	SCORE	MOST ADMIRED	SCORE	MOST ADMIRED	SCORE
Enron	9.18	Philip Morris	9.12	Microsoft	8.59	Mirage Resorts	8.84
Mirage Resorts	8.50	General Electric	9.09	Cisco Systems	8.58	Corning	8.78
Herman Miller	8.43	Cisco Systems	8.89	Coca-Cola	8.33	Toyota Motor Sales U.S.A.	8.72
LEAST ADMIRED	SCORE	LEAST ADMIRED	SCORE	LEAST ADMIRED	SCORE	LEAST ADMIRED	SCORE
Trump Hotels & Casinos	3.83	Oxford Health Plans	3.92	MedPartners	3.41	Viad	4.31
Fruit of the Loom	3.81	Cabletron Systems	3.42	Shoney's	3.40	U.S. Industries	4.24
Shoney's	3.51	Trump Hotels & Casinos	3.25	Trump Hotels & Casinos	2.87	Shoney's	3.99

LONG-TERM INVESTMENT VALUE		FINANCIAL SOUNDNESS		SOCIAL RESPONSIBILITY		USE OF CORPORATE ASSSETS	
MOST ADMIRED	SCORE	MOST ADMIRED	SCORE	MOST ADMIRED	SCORE	MOST ADMIRED	SCORE
General Electric	8.79	Microsoft	9.56	Corning	8.56	Cisco Systems	8.63
Coca-Cola	8.77	Intel	9.46	Du Pont	8.09	Berkshire Hathaway	8.45
Cisco Systems	8.63	Cisco Systems	9.42	Herman Miller	8.04	Coca-Cola	8.34
LEAST ADMIRED	SCORE	LEAST ADMIRED	SCORE	LEAST ADMIRED	SCORE	LEAST ADMIRED	SCORE
Shoney's	3.16	MedPartners	2.60	Shoney's	3.76	MedPartners	3.41
MedPartners	3.07	Trump Hotels & Casinos	2.40	MedPartners	3.74	Oxford Health Plans	3.15
Trump Hotels & Casinos	2.42	Oxford Health Plans	2.19	Trump Hotels & Casinos	3.50	Trump Hotels & Casinos	2.75

FORTUNE TABLE

well does reap rewards. Who would want it any other way?

This year's newcomers don't appear to have much in common. No. 4 Dell manufactures a limited number of customized products to sell online and over the phone, mostly to large companies. Dell is sleek, high tech, and virtual, with no stores. You can't see it when you drive down the street.

No. 6 Wal-Mart, on the other hand, sells millions of items to millions of people: everything from African violets to zippers, everywhere from California to Germany. With more than 3,000 stores, it's literally, physically, everywhere. There's nothing spare about it. Folksy to the core, Wal-Mart executives are as likely to lead employees in the company cheer as they are to cite sales figures or operational details.

how they do for shareholders

Dell turned in an amazing year; Cola-Cola and Disney disappointed with meager returns, but still get plenty of admiration.

THE MOST ADMIRED

COMPANY	TOTAL RETURN 1998	TOTAL RETURN 1993–98*
General Electric	41.0%	34.2%
Coca-Cola	1.3%	26.1%
Microsoft	114.6%	68.9%
Dell Computer	248.5%	152.9%
Berkshire Hathaway	52.2%	33.8%
Wal-Mart Stores	107.6%	27.6%
Southwest Airlines	38.4%	6.6%
Intel	69.0%	50.6%
Merck	41.3	37.0%
Walt Disney	–8.5%	16.9%
Top ten average	70.5%	45.4%
S&P 500	27.1%	23.5%

THE LEAST ADMIRED

COMPANY	TOTAL RETURN 1998	TOTAL RETURN 1993–98*
Trump Hotels & Casinos	–43.9%	N.A.
Shoney's	–57.7%	–43.1%
MedPartners	–76.5%	N.A.
Oxford Health Plans	–4.4%	2.3%
Stone Container**	36.2%	5.8%
U.S. Industries	–38.4%	N.A.
Olsten	–49.9%	–16.7%
Viad	59.4%	27.0%
Fruit of the Loom	–46.1%	–10.6%
Foundation Health Systems	–46.6%	N.A.
Bottom ten average	–25.8%	–5.9%
S&P 500	27.1%	23.5%

FORTUNE TABLE

N.A. Not avaliable. *Compound annual rate.**Company was acquired Nov. 18, 1998; returns are calculated through that data.

But a closer look at the two companies reveals similarities. Both have famous CEO-founders. Both have killer stocks. Dell, which has gained 87,000% since 1990, is already legendary. Wal-Mart has rebounded nicely from an early '90s slowdown, adding 290% to its stock price over the past two years. Most of all, both companies are operational superstars, obsessed with quick product delivery. Keenly focused on their customers, they measure performance in minutes and seconds, rather than days and hours. And they force suppliers to keep pace. By maintaining low inventories and streamlining processes, they cut costs and pass the savings along to customers. Both companies steep employees in this philosophy. Dell bases bonuses largely on the company's return on invested capital—that is, how efficiently it operates. At Wal-Mart, every employee is expected to read and understand endless printouts of sales and inventory data.

Technology makes all this possible. But while Dell and Wal-Mart spend scads on computers and do amazing things with them, their executives bristle when asked to talk tech. All those fancy systems are just tools, they say. The means to an end. It's that attitude—unwillingness to get mired in technology for technology's sake—that keeps both companies ahead of the pack.

At Dell everyone talks about the direct model, the company's practice of eliminating middlemen and selling PCs directly to customers. "Our only religion is the direct model," says vice chairman Kevin Rollins. CEO Michael Dell's new book is called *Direct From Dell;* a company-customer powwow scheduled for this summer will be called Direct to Dell. Ask an executive what it's like working with the Chinese government, one of Dell's newest customers, and he says approvingly, "They really understand the direct model." Everything is direct, direct, direct. "Analysts complain that we say the same thing over and over," says vice chairman Mort Topfer. The repetition may grate, but being direct has made Dell a powerhouse by putting it in constant touch with customers, enabling it to respond almost immediately to problems, and giving it constant, actionable feedback.

In the 15 years since Michael Dell began selling computers from his University of Texas dorm room, his company has grown into an $18-billion-a-year business that sells more PCs to medium-sized and large U.S. companies than giants like IBM, Hewlett-Packard, and Compaq. Dell is gunning for other parts of its rivals' business too, such as servers and high-margin storage products; it now sells almost 20% of the PC servers bought in the U.S., according to Roger Kay, an analyst at International Data Corp. Dell is also expanding internationally. Michael Dell says he eventually hopes to control 20% to 25% of the global PC market and aims to unseat leader Compaq (which has a 14.8% market share worldwide) in every region it serves.

Dell executives are confident that technology will help them capture those new customers. "We're always looking to see what we can do to make our customers' lives easier or save them money," says Michael Dell. "It pervades every part of the company. It might be a design challenge; it might be a manufacturing and distribution challenge." Take manufacturing. Dell makes its OptiPlex desktop computers at a 250,000-square-foot facility called Metric 12 in Austin, Texas. Bar-code readers flicker incessantly as they follow each PC on its journey down the line. A steady stream of trucks drops off raw materials from suppliers and picks up finished computers.

A Dell employee walks along the production line to show where the company's engineers have sped up production, bit by tiny bit (collectively, Dell engineers have more than 200 process-related patents). Workers used to touch a computer 130 times in the process of assembling it; that number is down to 60. At one station near the beginning of the line, workers attach motherboards and power-supply units to a computer's chassis. This effort, which once required six screws, now takes one. Farther down, a forklift-like tool called the stacker moves piled PCs in groups of five; workers used to move them one at a time. Near the end of the line, almost-finished computers sit on racks, ready for software installation. Employees plug the computers in to special adapters to download the software, which takes 45 to 90 minutes. Dell engineers are working on an automatic installation system that will reduce that time to 20 minutes. Even now, Dell can assemble OptiPlex computers in five hours or less.

Dell is equally single-minded about electronic commerce, which causes so much confusion for so many companies. Dell does about 20% of its business online ($10 million a day) and expects that eventually half its sales will be through the Internet. "Michael says the Internet is the ultimate direct model," explains Topfer. In 1997 the company created Premier Pages, Websites that enable a customer's authorized employees to research, configure, and price the PCs they plan to buy. To minimize processing errors, all information specific to the customer—system preferences, support details, inventory management policies—is included on the Web page. Like the manufacturing improvements in Metric 12, Premier Pages save money. Ford Motor cut procurement costs by $2 million when it moved its Dell business online. Dell saved money on the Ford deal too, because it didn't have to hire as many order-entry people.

The Net is transforming Dell's sales to small businesses as well. It used to be that the small fry couldn't dream of getting the sort of service Dell gave its FORTUNE 500 customers. Now they (almost) can. "Our goal is to take all the expensive things we do for large accounts and make them happen for small ones," says senior vice president Paul Bell. Michael Dell isn't likely to drop in on a customer who works from home, but he might talk to her through one of the "Breakfast with Dell" seminars broadcast over the Net. "We stand to benefit quite a bit from [the Internet]," says Dell. "A lot of our competitors are going to be challenged, because they're stuck with an old model." Direct from Austin, Dell has loudly proclaimed itself the new model.

Five hundred miles north, at Wal-Mart Store No. 1 in Rogers, Ark., a man leans over a freezer full of boneless, skinless chicken breasts. He swipes a hand-held computer over a bar code near the freezer. Within seconds, computers in the home office download a pile of statistics: how much the Rogers store makes selling chicken breasts, how many packages it has on hand, how many are on their way to the store, how many are sitting in freezers within a 150-mile radius.

Wal-Mart's computers track everything there is to know about everything the company sells. They know how much an item costs; the time a checkout person needs to scan it at the register; other items customers tend to buy along with it; and how many more the supplier has on hand. And Wal-Mart's executives know exactly how to use that data to keep the company's merchandisers in sync with its stores, its stores in sync with its distribution centers, its distribution centers in sync with its suppliers. If Dell is all about being direct, Wal-Mart is all about being exact.

Wal-Mart made its first top-ten appearance on FORTUNE's Most Admired list in 1987, when it had revenues of $12 billion. Then as now, the world's largest mass-market retailer was admired for its relentless customer focus, its sophisticated distribution, and its superior information systems. But Wal-Mart fell out of the top ten in 1993, shortly after Sam Walton's death from bone cancer. While sales remained strong, executives had begun to believe that sustaining consistent earnings growth year over year depended on developing new markets. "It had become clear that we needed to reposition ourselves," says CEO David Glass. Wal-Mart began investing what would eventually become nearly $20 billion to open new stores abroad and to build Supercenters, combined grocery and general merchandise stores. Wall Street began to wonder if the company had lost its focus; the stock languished. Wal-Mart insisted it would post $100 billion in annual revenues by the end of the decade, just as Mr. Sam had promised. But observers—including FORTUNE—were skeptical.

They—and we—were wrong. Wal-Mart will soon report fiscal 1999 revenues of $137 billion. Its stock is back too; investors got a return of 107.6% last year.

The Bentonville, Ark., headquarters has a low-tech ambiance. Wal-Mart lore has it that Walton used to print out computerized reports, copy them in longhand, and tack them to a wall in his office. CEO Glass doesn't even have a computer in his office; neither does senior vice chairman Don Soderquist. "Sam never liked technology," Glass says. "He thought 'damn computer' was one word."

Yet Walton allowed Glass to computerize Wal-Mart. In 1976, Glass supervised construction of a satellite network that enabled stores to communicate with the central office (think of it as a proto-intranet). He also computerized the company's distribution systems, which he says were shockingly antiquated in 1978: "We were way behind. But being way behind was the best thing that ever happened to us." Because of its isolation from most technology and distribution centers, Glass explains, Wal-Mart was able to design and build its systems from the ground up.

Most companies these days are discarding homegrown computer systems in favor of cheaper, prewritten programs they buy off the shelf. But more than 90% of Wal-Mart's software is still written in-house by 1,000 full-time developers. Explains CIO Randy Mott, who as a young programmer helped write the 1978 distribution software: "We study off-the-shelf software to make sure we're not missing anything. But those programs tend to be very broad. We try to make our software very specific to our business. With the volume we're dealing with, it makes sense for us to know how to do this."

In other words, aw-shucks mythology notwithstanding, Wal-Mart has made technology a core competency. At the same time, the company spends less on technology, as a percentage of sales, than other retailers—0.5% last year, vs. 1.43% for the industry. Wal-Mart can do this because of its size. "They reap economies of scale from being so large," says Kurt Potter, a research analyst with the Gartner Group. Wal-Mart's computer centers in Bentonville and Tulsa can store 43 terabytes of data—more than any other corporation's. In an interesting turnabout, Amazon.com has hired away several Wal-Mart IT executives, and Wal-Mart is now suing the online book company for stealing its intellectual property and trade secrets. "What we've built here doesn't exist anywhere else," says Mott. "They've replicated things that are proprietary. All their ideas about retail distribution come from here. It's targeted raiding." (Wal-Mart, by the way, sells hardly anything online. "We'll be there to take advantage at the right time, and in the right way," says Mott. "First, we need to find a profitable business model. A legitimate retailer makes a profit," he adds, in another dig at Amazon.com.)

Wal-Mart is nothing if not legitimate and profitable. Even its big-ticket investments are beginning to pay off. The company has more than 500 Supercenters, and Glass plans to open 150 new ones every year. Wal-Mart is also introducing smaller grocery stores it calls Neighborhood Markets, aimed at shoppers who don't have the time (or the inclination) to wander through 200,000 square feet looking for peanut butter.

Abroad, a Wal-Mart outpost opens every week. Point-of-sale data flowing back to Bentonville reveal unexpected market trends. Mexicans, it turns out, love bagels. "We can't make enough of them!" says Bobby Martin, who runs Wal-Mart's international business. Smoke detectors are a surprise hit in Brazil. Puerto Ricans buy house paints in the winter. Even the corny Wal-Mart culture seems to be a successful export. Police dispatched to check out a racket behind a Frankfurt-area Wal-Mart found 35 employees practicing the company cheer. "Everyone said there was no way we'd get people in Germany to do the cheer," says Martin. "Honest story."

CEO Glass, at age 63, says he will now work to "really develop the next generation of management." He and the board of directors recently promoted Lee Scott, 49, to COO. That makes Scott, a distribution and logistics expert, Glass' heir apparent. "I like things that challenge conventional thinking," says Scott. Like damncomputers? Scott, a reader of *Wired* magazine, points to a monitor in the corner. "Well," he grins, "you've got to have a PC."

All ten companies at the top of our list have a single-minded focus. Wal-Mart is intent on quickly moving merchandise to 3,000 stores. GE homes in on shareholder value to create strategies for growth. Microsoft hires brilliant workers—and uses incentives to keep them—to create and market its software. Southwest Airlines promotes a culture that impels employees to deliver topnotch service on the ground and in the air. In every case, it's a matter of nurturing that unique, essential core.

REPORTER ASSOCIATE *Len A. Costa*

Big Kellogg Shareholders Seek More Snap, Crackle and Pop

By DANA CANEDY and REED ABELSON

BATTLE CREEK, Mich.—The Kellogg Co. has been scrambling to revive its stagnant breakfast business, but its approach so far has been about as successful as trying to freshen soggy cereal by pouring on more milk.

Now, key investors seem to have run out of patience, some senior executives have left in frustration and major shareholders and analysts wonder how long the company can remain independent.

"I'd hate to see a takeover, but I don't know if that would not be better all around," Agnes Gund, the president of the Museum of Modern Art in New York, whose family is Kellogg's second-largest shareholder, said earlier this month.

Her brother, Gordon Gund, a Kellogg board member who owns the Cleveland Cavaliers basketball team, said he, too, had been concerned about the company's performance. But he insisted on Friday that Kellogg has a strategy that will lead to a turnaround.

Even so, Kellogg's missteps in the marketplace—its slow response to changing eating habits and overestimation of what shoppers would pay for flakes of wheat and corn—are well known. The stock is now trading no higher than it did in 1995, and the company has warned investors that 1998 profits may be as much as 20 percent lower than in 1997. The company is expected to report its annual results on Friday.

Amid mounting displeasure among shareholders, Kellogg's board—after years of watching people eat less and less of the company's Corn Flakes, Frosted Flakes and Raisin Bran—announced earlier this month that it would replace Arnold G. Langbo, the chief executive for the last seven years.

"There is no secret that the numbers have not been good," said Dorothy A. Johnson, president and chief executive of the Council of Michigan Foundations, who joined the Kellogg board last year.

Ms. Johnson, who has been a trustee since 1980 of the W. K. Kellogg Foundation, Kellogg's largest shareholder, acknowledged that she was aware of the frustration felt by many of the company's investors. The board has "devoted numerous extra hours to it," she said.

Still, Gund said the decision to replace Langbo was prompted by his own desire to speed his retirement. "This is a very orderly transition and is a good one," Gund said. "I feel very confident, as do the other board members."

But it remains to be seen whether the appointment of Carlos M. Gutierrez, a long-time Kellogg manager, as chief executive is just another example the company's inability to think outside the proverbial box. While current Kellogg executives and most board members declined repeated requests for interviews, discussions with several former senior executives as well as analysts and money managers paint a portrait of a proud, insular organization that has long relied on tradition and shopworn tactics to solve its problems.

"Kellogg is a funny company," explained one former executive who became so disillusioned with Kellogg that he sold his shares. Like all the executives interviewed, he would speak only on the condition of anonymity. "As recently as the mid-90's, we were still asking what Kellogg would have done," he said.

Kellogg, of course, was Will Keith Kellogg, the visionary business manager who along with his brother, Dr. John Harvey Kellogg, invented flaked cereal in 1894 at the Battle Creek Sanitarium, where they offered rich and famous patients a regimen of exercise, fresh air and strict diet. The flakes spawned what in 1922 became the Kellogg Company and established Battle Creek as the cereal capital of the world.

For decades, falling back on the Kellogg heritage served the corporation well, as it capitalized on its wholesome reputation for nutritious products at a fair price. But in recent years, the company has found it hard to react to the pressures of the modern marketplace.

Now the question is whether Gutierrez, who has been at Kellogg 23 years, and its board, heavily influenced by its two largest shareholders and a former chief executive, are willing to break with tradition to turn around the company and prevent it from being sold. If so, the fire will have to come from within:

Those shareholders, which together own nearly half of the company's shares outstanding, make it possible for Kellogg's management to ignore the rumblings of all but a few investors.

"For Carlos to succeed, he has to operate very different from the past," said another former executive. "If he becomes another Arnie, I don't think he can turn it around."

There certainly are striking parallels in the backgrounds of Carlos Gutierrez and Arnold Langbo. Both started their careers as sales representatives and have never worked anywhere else. Both have extensive experience in virtually all aspects of the company's management structure. Neither has a college degree.

But there also are important differences. Gutierrez, a native of Cuba who was raised in Mexico, has far more international experience, having run Kellogg's Mexican and Asia-Pacific divisions. He is also expected to focus more than his predecessor on expanding sales, rather than cutting costs, although last week the company announced it would slash a fifth of its European salaried workforce.

What is clear is that Gutierrez, who is to take over as chief executive in April, may not have nearly as much time as Langbo did. If the company's results do not soon improve, Kellogg may explore other options, including a possible merger, several analysts said.

"Kellogg looks like an attractive candidate," said Jaine I. Mehring, an analyst at Salomon Smith Barney. "It has a leadership position in what is a very large category that is important to retailers and has something that really few other companies have, and that is truly global brand equity."

One name frequently mentioned as a merger partner is the much larger Unilever, whose international distribution network would help push Kellogg's strong global brand name into more households abroad.

Ms. Gund, saying on Friday that she did not want to foster conflict within her family, emphasized that she and her siblings did not favor a sale of the business.

Kellogg has been unable in recent years to capitalize on the power of its brand. While it remains the nation's top-selling cereal maker, it lost more than two percentage points in market share from 1994 to 1997, according to Information Resources Inc., a research firm in Chicago. Competitors, like General Mills Inc., that lost share in that period rebounded last year. But Kellogg lost nearly another two percentage points.

Critics say that Langbo, who joined Kellogg in 1956 and will remain chairman until next year, has lacked creativity in solving Kellogg's problems. He has tried to cut costs by slashing jobs, to lure back customers by throwing money at advertising and promotion and to restore profits by raising prices. The last few years have been difficult for all cereal makers, as companies that offer cheaper supermarket or other private-label brands have taken an increasing share of the market. Consumers also have favored bagels and other convenience foods to a bowl of cereal in the morning.

Still, Langbo seemed unable to rise to the challenge. Hand-picked by his predecessor, William E. LaMothe, who remains on the Kellogg board, Langbo is described by former colleagues as unwilling to delegate, choosing for years not to appoint a chief operating officer, for example.

Kellogg has been unable to get a grip on just how much people are willing pay for its cereals, especially when other boxes of corn flakes seem more like its brand than ever before. A few years ago, the company set off a price war, hoping to make up the lost profits through volume, but then struggled to raise prices again. In the end, the approach gave consumers sticker shock at grocery checkout lanes and benefited competitors like General Mills, whose strategy depended less on its pricing.

"There has been so much discounting and repricing going on that it is very confusing to consumers, and General Mills seems to have taken advantage of that," said Timothy Ghriskey, a senior portfolio manager at the Dreyfus Corp., which sold its 540,000 shares of Kellogg months ago. General Mills also has benefited from marketing that stressed nutrition even as it promoted the addition of frosting and honey flavor to old-line cereals like its Cheerios, he said.

A Kellogg spokesman insisted that Langbo has positioned the company for future growth. The company has added an advertising agency to push its nutrition message more aggressively. Kellogg has also purchased several factories to produce convenience foods. It is rolling out a product line it calls Ensemble—frozen entrees, cookies, muffins, and other foods, for both breakfast and other meals, that the company will promote as being healthful. And it is adding 200,000 distribution points in places like convenience stores to increase sales of single-serving snacks, like Rice Krispies Treats.

In Langbo's defense, Gund also was quick to blame industry trends, like people eating on the run, for the company's troubles. While he said the change in leadership "was appropriate" he added that he would not "speculate on the past."

The stock market, nonetheless, has judged Langbo harshly. During his tenure, the stock significantly underperformed other food stocks, returning an average 3 percent a year, compared with 13 percent for the Standard & Poor's index of food stocks. While the board stood by, many investors abandoned the company, selling their shares.

"You either expect to get change or go onto something else," said Charles Mayer, a portfolio manager with Invesco Funds in Denver, which continues to own stock in Kellogg. Even steadfast investors, he said, had made their feelings known to the company. At its closing price Friday of $38.125, Kellogg has a market value of $15.5 billion.

What has protected the company for so long from investors' wrath is its domination by two friendly shareholders. The W. K. Kellogg Foundation, created in 1930 by Will Keith Kellogg, owns about a third of the company. The Gund family received shares in 1928 after selling what is now known as Sanka, the decaffeinated coffee brand, to Kellogg; the Gunds now control about 12 percent of the shares outstanding, worth about $2 billion.

The foundation and Kellogg continue to be closely tied, and many directors sit on both boards. Langbo, for example, serves as co-trustee of the foundation's trust, which controls its Kellogg shares and whose bylaws require a company representative on the trust board.

Three foundation trustees are also company directors: LaMothe, the former chief executive of Kellogg; Ms. Johnson, the head of the Council of Michigan Foundations, and Dr. William C. Richardson, the chief executive of the Kellogg Foundation.

Here are other ties as well. Donald H. Rumsfeld, the former Defense Secretary, for example, used to serve on the board of Sears, Roebuck with LaMothe.

"The cozy relationship between the company and the foundation and Battle Creek made it difficult for the board to see the forest for the trees," said one of the former executives.

By way of contrast, the Lilly Endowment, which owns 16 percent of Eli Lilly, has no representatives on the drug maker's board.

What is also striking is the presence of LaMothe—who presided over the company in its heyday—on Kellogg's board. He is viewed by outsiders as having considerable sway over other board members. "He is so tied up in the corporate history that they don't know how to make an independent decision," said one former executive.

The challenge will be compounded for Gutierrez, who will be looking at two ex-chief executives when he sits down for board meetings.

Gund insisted that Gutierrez "is going to express his own views and not be influenced by anyone else." What is more, Gund said, both former chief executives are likely to step down from the board next year.

He also took issue with criticism of the board, saying that "there is no insular issue here."

The directors, he said, were independent: "We want to do the very best we can for this business and shareholders."

Shareholders are restless. Ms. Gund says her family became increasingly concerned about the stock's performance because it threatened to hamper their philanthropic activities. Ms. Gund said that she and other family members had expressed their concerns to Gund several months ago.

In its latest annual report, the foundation made reference to the stock's volatility and said that it "has a significant impact on the foundation's grant-making capacity."

While the foundation—which supports numerous causes, including those related to health, education and youth—has been able to increase the amount it gives, the value of its assets has declined.

The appointment of Gutierrez represents the potential for a new direction. He is described by colleagues and others who have met him as a driven and intelligent executive who was clearly the best choice among the inside candidates.

One colleague recalls Gutierrez's spending an hour on Sundays, after buying his children dessert at McDonald's, watching consumers buy cereal at a supermarket. "There were people running the company the last five years who didn't understand why that was important," this person said. Gutierrez, he said, realized that adding frosting to flakes or spending more on Tony the Tiger commercials was futile unless the company figured out why once-loyal shoppers were switching to its competitors' products.

Gutierrez also seems decisive. Money managers and analysts credit him with being the force behind a shake-up at Kellogg's headquarters in September, in which all managers were forced to justify their jobs and hundreds were subsequently dismissed.

In his first significant management appointment, Gutierrez took the step—unusual at Kellogg—of naming an outsider to a top job, bringing in a Procter & Gamble manager whom the company found through a search firm to oversee the company's Asia-Pacific operations. He is expected to hire another outsider, possibly later this month, to run the company's all-important North American division.

"That is revolutionary for this company," said Ghriskey of Dreyfus.

One reason, as even Battle Creek community leaders acknowledge, is that it is a challenge to lure executives to this sleepy town tucked beside the Battle Creek River, 113 miles west of Detroit and 170 miles northeast of Chicago. It is a community where nearly every resident either works for Kellogg or knows someone who does, and where schools, auditoriums and museums are named for the company.

It is against this backdrop that Gutierrez, who himself was anointed by Langbo, will soon reign. That is why some people are skeptical about how hard he is likely to push for change. Beyond wooing executives from other companies and expanding lines of noncereal foods, "I really doubt he will significantly rock the boat," Ghriskey said. "He's someone from inside, he's a longtime crown prince, and he pretty much toes the company line."

While the company insists that this year will be a turning point and Gutierrez "is not looking for a honeymoon period," investors are waiting to see the tangible results of any new strategies.

One advantage Gutierrez has is that there now appears to be no one else at Kellogg prepared to run the company. Describing him as the last inside hope, one former colleague remarked, "Carlos knows he is holding the cards right now."

THE RISE OF A STAR

Ken Chenault helped bring AmEx back from the brink. Now, he may be on the brink of even bigger things

At Bowdoin College in the early 1970s, Ken Chenault spent endless hours at the Afro-American Center debating the great issues of the era with his classmates. That his peers often chose Chenault to represent them in negotiations with school administrators had everything to do with his character and abilities and little to do with his views. Unlike most other "Afro-Am" activists, Chenault argued that the cause was best served in the long run by rising to power within the Establishment instead of assailing it from without. "We all thought he'd rise to high position on the inside," says George Khaldun, Chenault's roommate. "The joke was that when we all had to go to jail for our radicalism, at least we knew Ken would be there to bail us out."

As it happened, no one needed bailing out, but Kenneth Irvine Chenault has met his classmates' lofty expectations and then some. Today, he is president and chief operating officer of American Express Co., a $19 billion pillar of corporate respectability and possessor of one of the world's premier consumer brands. Chenault, 47, has held American Express' second-highest executive post since February, 1997, and also sits on its board of directors. Early this year, his authority was enlarged to include the only two operating divisions not already reporting to him. He moved even higher into the corporate stratosphere on Oct. 27, when IBM elected him to its board.

An elegant, quietly charismatic man of even temper and unrelenting drive, Chenault tends to inspire his admirers to extravagant praise. "Ken radiates such a depth of belief that people would do anything for him," says Rochelle Lazarus, chairman and CEO of Ogilvy & Mather Worldwide Inc., AmEx' lead advertising agency. "He is a true leader." Adds Amy DiGeso, a former AmEx executive who is chief executive of Mary Kay Inc.: "I can say unequivocally that I admire Ken more than anyone else I've ever worked with. I think he will be our generation's Jack Welch."

Still an up-and-comer in the corporate world, Chenault is an established star in what his friend Richard D. Parsons, president of Time Warner Inc., calls "the circle of African American professionals who have achieved." Denzel Washington was dining in a Manhattan restaurant recently when he spied Chenault across the room. The actor asked the proprietor to introduce him and followed her to Chenault's table. "My mouth was hanging open, but it seemed like Denzel knew all about Ken," recalls Geoffrey Canada, a longtime friend (and Bowdoin classmate), who was sitting with Chenault. Says basketball legend Julius Erving, who has known Chenault since boyhood: "He is a man of destiny—and a really good person besides."

Chenault worked his way up through the huge card and travel unit known as Travel Related Services Co., which generates two-thirds of AmEx' revenues and most of its profit, too. He was instrumental in not only reviving but reinventing TRS, which nearly collapsed in the early 1990s under the weight of its own hidebound complacency. "It would be hyperbole to say that we were in danger of going out of business, but I did fear that we were running out of time to turn things around," says Chenault. AmEx' stock, which scraped bottom at 17 in 1991, hit a high of 118 earlier this year and now trades at about 100.

Harvey Golub, whose 1993 appointment as AmEx chairman and chief executive was the key event in the company's comeback, has rewarded Chenault with a series of promotions and pay hikes. In elevating him to president and the newly created position of chief operating officer in February, 1997, Golub dubbed Chenault "the primary internal candidate to succeed me when the time comes." Golub, 58 at the time, hastened to add that he was not planning to retire early. He still isn't. For his part, Chenault declines to speculate on his prospects of making CEO at AmEx, or anywhere else, insisting that he is wholly focused on the job at hand—and a demanding job it is.

ROOM FOR IMPROVEMENT. AmEx has three overriding financial goals: to boost earnings per share by 12% to 15% annually, to maintain a return on equity of 20%, and to increase revenues by at least 8% a year. The first two objectives have been met handily, but the team of Golub and Chenault has proven far more adept at creating cost efficiencies than at spurring revenue growth. For the first three quarters of 1998, AmEx posted a revenue gain of 7.5%, pulling its three-year average up to 6.4%. "The company has come a long way, but our performance has been mixed," Chenault concedes. "We need to improve it dramatically."

Golub's predecessor, James D. Robinson III, spent the 1980s diversifying AmEx through a series of bold but disruptive acquisitions of other financial-services firms. With a big assist from Chenault, Golub took AmEx back to basics, jettisoning many of the acquired assets and thoroughly restructuring those that remained. But now that AmEx has been restored to solid profitability, Golub and Chenault face the same question that sent Robinson on his shopping spree: Can AmEx develop the heft and global reach it needs to remain self-sufficient, or will it have to seek a merger partner?

Golub says he promoted Chenault to president because he found this challenge too daunting to tackle alone. "I could not get done all the things I needed to do," he says. "I needed help." He says he took the added step of identifying Chenault as his successor to buttress the new president's authority. In fact, it was his hope that Chenault would be seen less as his subordinate and more as a collaborator and alter ego: "What I sought was a horizontal relationship with Ken that would enable him to do more and more of what I was doing."

Golub's hope has been realized. Both he and Chenault say they have built an unusually symbiotic partnership. "If Ken and I went separately to 10 different meetings at which a decision was needed, my guess is that 9 times out of 10 he and I make the same decision, and the 10th would involve just a nuance of difference," Golub says.

The effectiveness of the Golub-Chenault combo is surprising only in that AmEx' CEO has never been considered an easy man to work with. A cerebral sort who spent nearly 15 years as a McKinsey & Co. consultant before joining AmEx, Golub takes a blunt, uncompromisingly analytical approach to business that tends to inspire respect and fear in roughly equal measure. He made his mark running AmEx' Minneapolis-based money-management arm, acquired in 1984 and now known as American Express Financial Advisors. His ascent to chairman and CEO of the parent company was followed by a sizable exodus of senior executives, especially from TRS.

A former management consultant himself, Chenault is said to be as hard-driving and pragmatic as his boss. Unlike Golub, though, he has always been able to engage the emotions of his colleagues as well as their intellects. "Harvey is a brilliant man, but Ken has the hearts and minds of the people at the TRS company," says Thomas O. Ryder, a longtime AmEx exec who recently became CEO of Reader's Digest Assn.

OPEN DOOR. An extensive survey of current and former colleagues suggests that the Chenault personality is mercifully free of the rough edges that usually accompany vaulting ambition. Not one could recall him losing his temper or even raising his voice. He makes time to chitchat with secretaries when he telephones their bosses and has taken it upon himself to mentor dozens upon dozens of promising AmEx managers. A methodical, inclusive decisionmaker, he leaves his door open to subordinates and encourages them to speak their minds. "With Ken, there is no game-playing, no politics whatsoever," says Norma Arnold, a 23-year AmEx vet who joined Prudential Insurance Co. last year.

It must be said that Chenault has been conspicuous at AmEx not only for his accomplishments but for the color of his skin. Like many large corporations, AmEx has made a belated effort to make its workforce more racially diverse. Minorities now make up 17% of the company's managers—a figure that was much lower when Chenault began his rise through the ranks. While Chenault supports AmEx' remedial campaign, he is loath to be seen as its product, friends say. "Ken wants one day to be known as the best CEO, not the best African American CEO," says John Utendahl, founder and CEO of Utendahl Capital Partners, Wall Street's largest black-owned investment bank.

In fact, Chenault's career does not give off the slightest whiff of racial preference. He entered AmEx with sterling credentials and, by all accounts, rose on the strength of talent and hard work. The real issue is the opposite one: To what extent was his rise made more arduous by race? This is a question given added

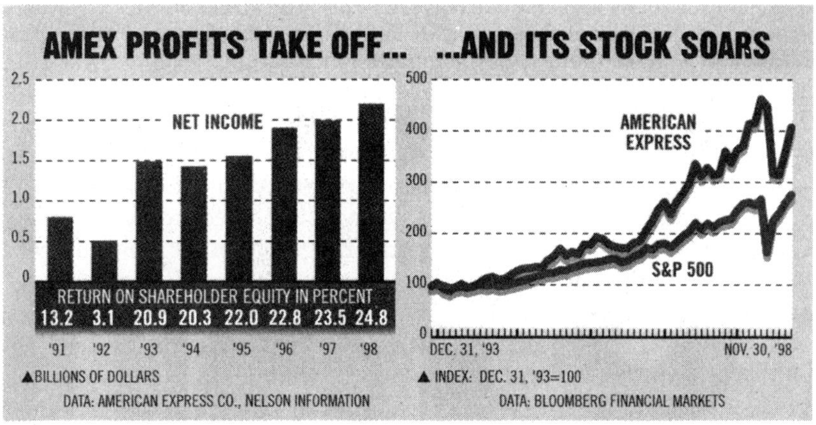

CHARTS BY RAY VELLA/BW

meaning by AmEx' identity as an icon of upper-class affluence. In America, membership does indeed have its privileges, and they have never been evenly distributed between black and white.

The question of how race has factored into his corporate career is not one Chenault cares to address. But even some of his closest chums wonder to what extent his extraordinary self-composure is a product of bias-hardened stoicism. "There has to be struggle within Ken—he's only human—but I have never seen it," says Khaldun, who has maintained close contact with Chenault ever since college. "Even in our most vicious debates at school, he never lost it. It's just unreal. I don't know where he gets it."

Like father, like son. Ken revered his father, Dr. Hortenius Chenault, who died in 1990 at age 80. Not long after his father's death, Ken told *Newsday* that he was the most determined person he had ever known. "He overcame every possible type of obstacle," he said.

"USEFUL BALANCE." The son of a butler and a maidservant, Hortenius Chenault grew up in a small, mostly white town in Ohio and graduated from Morehouse College with honors. In 1939, he earned a degree in dentistry from Howard University and passed the New York state dental licensing exam with the highest score recorded to date. During World War II, Chenault enlisted in the Army, but segregation blocked his path into the multinational Allied Dental Corps. Undaunted, he befriended a group of foreign officers and entered the corps through an international arm.

Chenault married an African-American dental hygienist, Anne N. Quick, who hailed from an affluent and accomplished South Carolina family that had founded a cargo-shipping business in the early 1900s. In 1947, Hortenius and Anne Chenault settled in Hempstead, N.Y., where they raised four children. Born in 1951, Ken was the second of three brothers and a sister.

Ken's boyhood coincided with the peak of civil rights activism on Long Island, and the movement was a frequent topic of conversation at the dinner table. "My father's basic view was that you really needed to concentrate on the things you can control," Ken recalls, "and what you can control is your own performance." Unimpressed with the education afforded blacks in Hempstead's nominally integrated public schools, the Chenaults sent their kids to a small private school, the Waldorf School of Garden City, N. Y. "It created a useful balance for me," Chenault says. "In Hempstead, my environment was predominantly black, while the school was predominantly white."

PICK A CARD

Chenault directed the effort to expand AmEx' lineup of credit cards. Today, the company offers dozens of "co-branded" cards

Chenault attended Waldorf from kindergarten through 12th grade. "As early as middle school, real qualities of leadership became obvious in Ken," recalls George Rose, one of his teachers. "But at the same time, there was a certain quiet within him that won everyone's respect." Chenault was elected class president in each of his last four years, and as a senior captained the basketball, soccer, and track teams.

FAST TRACK. After a year at Springfield College, Chenault transferred to Bowdoin College in Brunswick, Me., at the urging of a Waldorf teacher who had gone there. It was 1970, and America's college campuses were seething with protest. Chenault added his voice to demands that Bowdoin recruit more black students and professors but took issue with the militant black nationalism of his fellow Afro-Am activists. "I never saw Ken falter in the belief that he would get the chance to show his skill and scholarship to the world, which was aggravating, I admit," says Canada, now the president and CEO of Rheedien Centers for Children, which fights truancy among Manhattan's minority schoolchildren.

After graduating magna cum laude with honors in history, Chenault enrolled at Harvard Law School. He got his law degree in 1976 and landed a job at the tony Wall Street firm of Rogers & Wells. Three years later, he moved back to Boston to join some of his Harvard classmates at management consultancy Bain & Co. "I wasn't bored or disappointed by law," recalls Chenault. "I wanted to try something new: business."

At 28, Chenault had found his métier. At Bain, he quickly was promoted to manager and was put on a fast track to partnership, though co-founder Ralph R. Willard doubted that he would be able to hang on to Chenault for long. "Ken had CEO written all over him," Willard says.

In 1981, Chenault accepted a job offer from American Express. At the time, TRS was headed by Louis V. Gerstner Jr., now chairman and CEO of IBM. Gerstner had joined AmEx a few years earlier from McKinsey & Co. and was looking for four or five young hotshots capable of rising to the top while acting as "change agents."

Chenault started in the strategic planning department. His first assignment involved TRS's merchandiseservices division, which sold jewelry, stereo equipment, and a wide range of other gear to cardholders by direct mail. Run by a former R. H. Macy & Co. buyer named Robert Myers, "merch services was a poorly organized, foundering stepchild of the card business. However, its potential intrigued Chenault,

KENNETH IRVINE CHENAULT

BORN 1951, New York City.

EDUCATION BA 1973, Bowdoin College; JD 1976, Harvard University.

FAMILY Married to Kathryn Cassell Chenault, a nonpracticing lawyer. Two sons, Kenneth Jr., 9, and Kevin, 7.

FATHER'S ADVICE ON COPING WITH DISCRIMINATION "You need to really concentrate on the things you can control, and what you can control is your own performance."

CONFESSIONS OF A LATE BLOOMER "It was not until I was 13 or 14 that I began to focus on academics, and not until my 20s did I think about going into business."

AMEX CARD MEMBER SINCE 1976, his last year at Harvard Law School. His first card was gold.

HOBBIES Skiing, tennis, golf, swimming, reading biographies.

LEAST USED TALENT Excellent baritone singing voice.

who, to Gerstner's dismay, joined the unit as vice-president for marketing when his obligatory two-year stint in planning ended. "It was a rather high-risk opportunity for him in that I had guaranteed him a line job in the heart of the business," recalls Gerstner.

A few months later, Gerstner stunned Chenault and his new colleagues by declaring during a budget review that he did not think merch services had a future at AmEx. Myers was present, but it was Chenault who broke the uneasy silence, asking Gerstner to reserve final judgment for 45 days. Led by Chenault, merch services put together a strategic plan and won a stay of execution. Myers was fired soon afterward, and Chenault replaced him. Says DiGeso, the unit's personnel director: "Not only did Ken not scheme against Bob, he did everything he could to help him." Once he was in charge, though, Chenault sacked a half-dozen managers and made wholesale revisions in product line and sales methods.

In the two years that Chenault ran merch services, its revenues soared from about $150 million to $500 million a year. If anything, he was too successful, for many mail-order merchants began threatening to stop accepting AmEx cards. To his dismay, Chenault then had to dismantle much of what he had built to appease the custodians of AmEx' card business. After unsuccessfully proposing that AmEx spin off the merch-services division as a standalone business, Chenault recalls that he was issued new marching orders by Gerstner: "Lou said, 'You're going into cards.' "

From 1986 to 1989, Chenault was promoted three times, managing in succession the gold card/platinum division, the green card division, and the entire consumer card group. Even so, these were frustrating years for Chenault, whose proposals for new marketing initiatives generally fell on deaf ears. AmEx was an old-line company (founded in 1850) that had ruled its lucrative niches in traveler's checks and travel-and-entertainment charge cards for so long that its top management saw no need to innovate. "It was hard even to engage people in a discussion of who our competitors were," Chenault recalls. "The attitude was: 'We really don't have a competitor. We are unique.'"

Chenault belonged to a rising generation of AmEx managers who saw MasterCard International and especially Visa USA as a dire competitive threat. By the late 1980s, the bank-card associations were flooding the market with a myriad of low-fee cards offering frequent-flier miles, shoppers' discounts, and other benefits. Not only was American Express finding it harder to sign up new accounts, but its existing members were using their cards less and less.

HIGH GROUND. Within AmEx, a great debate raged over the issue of how to restore growth to the card business. Chenault and his pro-change peers made some headway as AmEx introduced a revolving credit card, Optima, and began broadening its merchant base by adding mass-market retailers. But they were opposed by higher-ranking traditionalists who argued that AmEx should retreat to its T&E niche and hunker down. While Chenault was steadfast in his advocacy, he made his case judiciously. AmEx was not a place where even someone at his level could vehemently dissent without risking retaliation from above. "Ken clearly was among the group pushing for change, but he wasn't the most radical of us," says Roger H. Ballou, a former colleague who is now CEO of Global Vacation Group.

In mid-1989, Gerstner abruptly resigned to head RJR Nabisco Inc. and was replaced at TRS's helm by three co-CEOs—a stopgap measure that only exacerbated the unit's woes. Amid the disorder, Chenault captured the conceptual high ground by sponsoring a series of studies that represented the first real attempt to gauge TRS's performance by such external measures as market share of total plastic spending. To Chenault, anyway, the evidence was clear: The AmEx brand was fading fast.

In 1991, a gradual decline in TRS's profits accelerated into a rout as AmEx had to write off $265 million in bad loans made to Optima cardholders. Worse, merchants' long-smoldering resentment at AmEx' high-handed treatment and steep transaction fees flamed into open revolt in Boston, where a group of 100 restaurants captured front-page attention by threatening to boycott AmEx. Soon, angry merchants all across the country were hurling ultimatums at AmEx, which faced the corporate equivalent of a run on the bank.

Robinson summoned Golub from Minneapolis and made him president of AmEx and CEO of TRS. Golub emerged from a hurried round of meetings at headquarters with new respect for Chenault. "It was his courage I noticed first," Golub says. "He was the only one at TRS who was standing up and saying, 'Here is the problem.'" Chenault was no less impressed, finding Golub's incisiveness liberating after his years of trying to "penetrate the wall of arrogance" within TRS. "Harvey is a fact-based person," he says. "With him, I could sit down and give it to him straight."

Golub added to Chenault's duties by putting him over the Establishment Services Div., which managed TRS's fraying merchant relationships and was far and away AmEx' largest source of revenue and operating income. At the time, the typical merchant was paying back to AmEx 3.5¢ of every dollar charged on one of its cards, compared with 2¢ for Visa and MasterCard. AmEx' premium 3.5% "discount rate" was a product of the upscale image it had cultivated and the fact that its typical member outspent his or her bank-card counterpart by a margin of nearly 3 to 1.

GAME MASTER. Chenault made Tom Ryder the new general manager of Establishment Services. Ryder immediately imposed a moratorium on the signing of new accounts (eliminating what had been a key bonus criterion) and insisted that salespeople bend over backward to cater to the existing clientele. A group of 16 sales managers went to Chenault with an ultimatum: Lose Ryder or you will lose us. Chenault explained the need for fundamental change and then delivered his own ultimatum: Get with the pro-

THE OTHER SIDE OF KEN CHENAULT

As a child, Ken Chenault dreamed of becoming a professional athlete. It was not until age 13 or 14 that a grander ambition kicked in, inspiring him to apply himself to his studies for the first time. "I started to think in terms of wanting to make a difference, of bringing about change in society," Chenault says. He certainly changed American Express Co., helping to create billions of dollars of wealth and thousands of new jobs. That is social impact of a high order, but what young Chenault had in mind was something else: righting the wrongs of race discrimination—or at least helping to blunt its effects.

While attending Bowdoin College in Brunswick, Me., Chenault made frequent trips to New York City to help organize the American Council for Drug Education, which eventually was merged into Phoenix House. Even so, some of Chenault's activist friends wondered whether someone so obviously destined for high-level professional success would retain his idealism. "The question we left open regarding Ken was if and when he got to where he wanted to be, would he still care about the kind of people we work with here?" says former Bowdoin classmate Geoffrey Canada of Rheedlen Centers for Children & Families, which combats truancy among minority schoolchildren in Manhattan.

This question was answered to Canada's satisfaction long ago. Chenault ranks among Rheedlen's largest donors—as does American Express—and is one of Canada's most valued advisers. "I try to be respectful of his time," Canada says. "But when I do call to bat around an idea, I always get to talk to Ken." Chenault also is active on the board of Columbia University's drug research center, the National Center on Addiction & Substance Abuse, and makes frequent inspirational speeches at black colleges, high schools, and grade schools. Even so, he feels he has fallen short of his youthful aspirations. "On a social basis, I have not been as front and center involved as on the business side," he says. "I feel strongly that I have a responsibility to do more over time."

Time has been the problem. About 8 o'clock one night during AmEx' crisis year of 1992, CEO Harvey Golub dropped by Chenault's office to suggest that he should spend more time relaxing. "A lot of us were working very hard," Golub says, "but Ken was working the hardest." Ignoring the boss's advice, Chenault continued to work most every evening and weekend until mid-1996, when he took advantage of AmEx' much-improved performance to spend more time with his family. He and his wife, Kathryn, a former Wall Street lawyer who once worked for the United Negro College Fund, live outside New York City in suburban New Rochelle. They have two sons, Kenneth Jr., 9, and Kevin, 7.

At the same time, Chenault has taken up golf—one of the few sports he did not master as a boy. He started a couple years back, when Golub invited him along on a golf trip to Florida. "I didn't play much over the next six months," Chenault says, "but then it finally hit me." Many lessons later, he's got his handicap down to 19 and is part of a foursome that regularly golfs at such exclusive Long Island clubs as Shinnecock Hills and the National Golf Links. "If you'd asked me two years ago, I would have said it will take Ken 10 years to improve his game to where it is now," says friend and foursome member John Utendahl. "But when Ken commits, he really commits." No kidding.

By Anthony Bianco in New York

Chenault once flew from New York to San Francisco on a few hours' notice to take an unhappy client to dinner

gram or find a new job. All but a few of the 16 remain at AmEx today.

To placate the angriest and most important merchants, Ryder often turned to Chenault. He went to great lengths to smooth ruffled feathers, once flying from New York to San Francisco on a few hours' notice to take a client to dinner. Still, he made only nominal cuts in discount rates. His resolve was tested by many of AmEx' biggest customers, including United Airlines Inc. CEO Stephen M. Wolf, who threatened to stop accepting AmEx cards unless United's discount rate was slashed, according to Adam Aaron, then United's marketing chief. "Ken told him, 'It will be interesting to watch you try to survive without American Express,'" Aaron says. "It was a game of chicken, and United backed down."

CHENAULT'S ACCOMPLISHMENTS

- ➤Led a restructuring drive that redeployed $3 billion in spending
- ➤Increased the number of cards AmEx offers to 60 from 4
- ➤Defused a merchant rebellion without a big cut in fees

KEY CHALLENGES

- ➤Accelerate revenue growth to build the scale needed to remain independent
- ➤Reclaim market share lost to Visa and MasterCard by enticing their members into the AmEx network

At a TRS management meeting in March, 1992, Golub warned that if the division did not cut its annual operating costs by $1 billion over the next three years, AmEx "would be out of business." Golub says he arrived at $1 billion "arbitrarily" but fostered the impression that it was the product of painstaking analysis. "The figure was roughly what I thought it would take for us to match Visa's discount rate if we had to," Golub says. "But I had no idea how we were going to do that. None."

The burden of identifying and implementing cuts fell mainly to Chenault as the senior card executive. Each of TRS's four main lines—green card, gold card, platinum card, and traveler's checks—had its own sales, marketing, and processing staffs. In mid-1992, Chenault started the daunting task of collapsing these four principalities into a single, leanly staffed unit. TRS promptly took a $342 million restructuring charge and eliminated 4,800 jobs. This amounted to fully 9% of AmEx' workforce, but the pain was just beginning.

NEW FOCUS. In early 1993, AmEx' board ousted Jim Robinson and moved Golub up to chairman and CEO. Promoted to president of TRS, Chenault put the card business into high gear at last. Under his direction, the type of cards AmEx issues soared from 4 to 60 in a few years' time. The vast majority of AmEx' new offerings were "co-branded" cards bearing not only the familiar blue box but the logos of such joint issuers as Delta Air Lines, Peugeot Motors, and the New York Knicks. At Establishment Services, meanwhile, the focus shifted from damage control to expansion. The number of new merchant accounts doubled to 60,000 in 1993 from 30,000 the previous year and is now running above 400,000 a year. Although AmEx' discount rate has fallen to about 2.7%, it remains considerably higher than Visa's or MasterCard's.

After Chenault's 1995 promotion to vice-chairman of American Express, the restructuring drive that he led broadened beyond TRS to encompass every part of the company and deepened to include every managerial system and work process. At its peak, 300 of AmEx' most talented managers were assigned to the project, and Chenault frequently had to exert his authority to overcome grassroots opposition to particular reforms. In the end, not $1 billion but $3 billion in cost was eliminated, along with 15,800 jobs. "Ken took the reengineering bit in his teeth and really made it happen," says Philip J. Riese, who succeeded Chenault as president of the consumer-card group. "And yet people really don't recognize reducing headcount as a Ken-like activity."

Partly this is because of the way he handled the layoffs. Chenault personally visited each of TRS's nine operating centers and explained at length why cutbacks had to be made. Employees slated to lose their jobs were notified as soon as the decision was made—resulting in advance notice of as much as 18 months. What is more, AmEx continued to grow on balance as the $3 billion in savings was wholly reinvested within the company. In fact, total employment rose to 73,620 in 1997 from 61,108 in 1991.

Although AmEx is again a formidable competitor in the credit-card wars, its brand position remains fundamentally tenuous. As measured by the value of purchases made, Visa commands 53.9% of the worldwide card market, vs. 49.2% in 1994, according to *The Nilson Report*, a credit-card industry newsletter. Visa's gains have come at the ex-

INVISIBLE IN THE EXECUTIVE SUITE

In *An American Dilemma,* his classic 1944 study of race relations in the U.S., sociologist Gunnar Myradal revealed the plight of aspiring black "managers of industry" who "have to work in the white economy which does not want Negros in such positions."

Half a century later, African Americans have gained scattered footholds in Corporate America—but the corner office remains an exclusively white preserve. And executives of Kenneth Chenault's stature, with the clout and connections to take on big-time CEO jobs soon, remain very much the exception.

True, Franklin D. Raines will become Fannie Mae's CEO on Jan. 1 after two years at the Office of Management & Budget. Richard D. Nanula, who left a soaring career at Walt Disney Co. to join Starwood Hotels & Resorts Worldwide Inc., is prime CEO timber. Lloyd Ward is expected to land the CEO job at Maytag Corp. next summer.

NEAR MISSES. Beyond that intimate fraternity, though, there's a stark void. The federal Glass Ceiling Commission reported in a 1995 study that blacks held just 0.6% of senior executive posts. Membership of the Executive Leadership Council, composed of big-company black managers within three reporting levels of the CEO, has boomed in the 12 years since its founding—but only to a total of 193. Black representation on corporate boards, the council says, has expanded modestly, but not on key committees.

In the past decade, moreover, CEO hopefuls such as McDonald's Robert M. Beavers Jr., Corning's Hayward R. Gipson Jr., and Montgomery Ward's Roland C. Baker have, one by one, faded. On Nov 14, A. Barry Rand, a highly regarded executive vice-president, announced he would leave Xerox Corp., having made clear his disenchantment when the company hired IBM marketer G. Richard Thoman last year as Paul A. Allaire's heir apparent.

Why are the ranks still so thin at the top? Some advocates argue that the old white boy's club isn't yet comfortable enough with minorities to include them in critical mentoring relationships. "The pipelines to promote African Americans are not in place," says Ella L. J. Edmondson Bell, professor at the University of North Carolina at Charlotte.

Explicit racial bias likely impedes progress, too. More than half of senior minority executives surveyed by recruiter Korn/Ferry International and Columbia Business school reported observing "a double standard in the delegation of assignments" or "harsh or unfair treatment of minorities by whites."

Still, there is cause for hope. The number of black college graduates and MBA's has swelled over the past two decades, and increasingly vigorous networks "offer tremendous opportunities for insight and advancement," says Curtis J. Crawford, who left a senior post at Lucent Technologies Inc. last year to take charge at chipmaker Zilog Inc. David Thomas, a professor at Harvard business school, argues that compared with their predecessors, today's top black managers are more often in core operating roles and so on a true "CEO trajectory."

Yet in most industries, blacks remain invisible. That's business' loss. "There is a wealth of capability and experience that is not being utilized to its fullest in Corporate America," says Adriane M. Brown, 40, who was promoted on Dec. 3 to run Corning Inc.'s $400 million environmental products division. "I still look for a day when you will not consider [my promotion] a news story."

By Keith H. Hammonds in New York, with bureau reports

CEO MATERIAL

Leading black executives and their career prospects

ANN FUDGE The first black woman to crack the top corporate ranks, she heads Philip Morris' Maxwell House Coffee Unit. **PROSPECTS:** Very strong candidate.

RICHARD NANULA After starring at Disney, he joined Starwood Hotels this year as president. **PROSPECTS:** He's young (37), but he's top-notch.

FRANKLIN RAINES Will get the CEO post at Fannie Mae on January 1 after two years heading the Office of Management & Budget. **PROSPECTS:** He's cracked the ceiling.

A. BARRY RAND Top sales exec quit Xerox on Nov. 14, a year after the company hired Richard Thoman as CEO-in-waiting. **PROSPECTS:** He'll find a great job—but maybe not as CEO.

ROY ROBERTS Heads General Motors' North American sales and marketing. **PROSPECTS:** The best of any black in the industry, but still not great.

LLOYD WARD Former Pepsi exec was named Maytag's president last February. **PROSPECTS:** The CEO job is his to lose.

pense of MasterCard, which now has 28.3% of the market. AmEx ranks third, holding steady at 13.7%.

AmEx could add handsomely to its share by deluging the market with cut-rate cards. But rather than sacrifice AmEx' profit margins on the altar of transaction volume, Golub and Chenault are doggedly implementing a strategy they call "opening the network." Essentially, it is an attempt to entice the very banks that are members of the Visa and MasterCard networks to issue cards in partnership with AmEx, and it may be the company's last best hope to substantially narrow the market-share gap.

TIES THAT BIND. From a standing start two years ago, AmEx has struck up card-issuing alliances with 38 foreign partners, including such banking giants as Crédit Suisse and National Westminster Bank. However, in the U.S. it has been thwarted by Visa and MasterCard bylaws that prohibit member institutions from participating in any other card networks. In October, the Justice Dept. filed an antitrust suit against Visa and MasterCard, alleging, among other things, that their exclusionary rules have unfairly stifled competition. Visa and MasterCard are contesting the allegations.

If the open network strategy fails to add handsomely to AmEx' revenues over the next few years, the company likely will seek a merger partner well before Golub turns 65 in 2004. In 1996, Golub instigated merger talks with Citicorp, the world's largest Visa and MasterCard issuer. Unwilling to pay the premium price that Golub sought, Citicorp merged with Travelers Group Inc. instead. How Chenault might fare in a future megamerger is anybody's guess. He is well aware of the fate of Travelers wunderkind James Dimon, who was considered a lock to run Citigroup until the very day he was let go in October.

Over the years, Chenault has been besieged with calls from executive recruiters representing one corporate giant or another. His commitment to AmEx will be tested again and again in the coming years, but it would take a breathtaking offer to break the ties that now bind Chenault to AmEx. "I have a psychic investment in its success," he says. Patience and persistence have been hallmarks of Chenault's career. That's not likely to change now that he is one step from the top of the mountain.

By Anthony Bianco in New York

New CEO Preaches Rebellion for P&G's 'Cult'

By Tara Parker-Pope
Staff Reporter of The Wall Street Journal

Durk I. Jager, the man about to become chief executive of Procter & Gamble Co., keeps an editorial cartoon on display in his office. It shows him smashing a shopper in the face with a box of detergent. "Hmmm . . . P&G is changing their marketing approach," another shopper deadpans.

Mr. Jager won't ascend to the CEO seat until Jan. 1. But already, the 55-year-old Dutchman is assailing the cult-like corporate culture at P&G, the maker of Tide, Crest, Pampers, and other big brands.

Having recently completed a three month tour of P&G sites in nearly two dozen cities around the world, Mr. Jager, a 28-year P&G veteran, has a major complaint: The company recruits job candidates from a variety of backgrounds, yet once they get inside the company, they begin to sound alike, think alike—even look alike, he says.

The company has a tendency to "Procter-ize" people, says Mr. Jager (pronounced YAH-ger). "It can become a cult in its own right."

Mr. Jager's attack on one of the most insular corporate cultures in America is jangling some nerves inside P&G's fortress-like twin-towers in Cincinnati. At a company where managers have a passion for memo-writing and dissent is rarely tolerated, the blunt talk about reform is nothing short of revolutionary.

Mr. Jager is a large man who tends to look rumpled and liberally pour Tabasco sauce at meals. In speeches to employees, he often opens with a "capability check," asking how many speak Dutch, then promising Dutch lessons will soon become corporate policy. When asked whether he's really as mean as his reputation, he answers, with a smile, "A lot worse."

Back in 1997, P&G promised to double sales to $70 billion by 2005. But following a period of lethargic sales, reaching that goal will require annual growth of 9%. Last year, sales rose just 4%.

Mr. Jager hopes to boost sales by speeding up decision making and getting new products out faster. Employees may be wasting up to half their time on "nonvalue added work," such as memo writing, he says. During a recent talk with employees in Kobe, Japan, one worker complained to Mr. Jager that he had to continually create new management-review charts, often with the same information in several different forms. "No new charts," Mr. Jager told him. "If you get in trouble with your boss, let me know."

It may not be easy for P&G to weather the transition from its current chief executive, John Pepper. The affable, refined Mr. Pepper, who will retain the chairman's title until Sept. 1, is popular with P&G employees and a consensus-builder. Mr. Jager, on the other hand, is a self-described loner. A protege of Ed Artzt, P&G's legendary chief executive from the early 1990s, Mr. Jager is known as a hard-driving manager. One reason George Fisher, chairman and chief executive of Eastman Kodak Co., says he recruited Mr. Jager to his board is the P&G man's reputation as a "tough" manager who doesn't mince words.

Wall Street is giddy with the prospect of Mr. Jager at the helm. "He has a reputation for shaking up the organization, and that's what the organization needs," says PaineWebber Securities Inc. analyst Andrew Shore.

Mr. Jager's career path is unusual for a P&G CEO. He spent most of his time outside Cincinnati. After a stint in the Dutch air force, Mr. Jager joined P&G as an assistant brand manager in 1970. He was transferred to Japan 12 years later as an advertising manager and was later named general manager. "He grew up totally removed from the central bureaucracy," says his former mentor, Mr. Artzt. "Durk had a view of the company and its strengths and some of its weaknesses from outside the infrastructure."

Japan proved to be a turning point in Mr. Jager's career. In the early 1980s, P&G's Japan operation was struggling; the company even mulled shutting it down. Mr. Jager, who speaks seven languages, quickly learned to speak Japanese, immersed himself in local customs and penetrated the closed ranks of Japanese wholesalers. "It was a very personal kind of relationship he was able to strike up with our wholesalers," says John Smale, P&G's CEO from 1981 to 1990. "He went to their weddings and funerals."

Mr. Jager soon noticed that some of P&G's American merchandising traditions—heavy store promotion of Cheer detergent, for example—weren't working. In Japan's convoluted chain of wholesale distributors, some retailers were selling Cheer for less than what some wholesalers were paying for it.

He bucked P&G traditions. In one instance, P&G wanted to fire a handful of Japanese managers. Mr. Jager realized that causing the men to "lose face" would demoralize the entire operation. After studying up on Japanese management traditions, he announced to the staff that every P&G manager in the country would offer their resignations; the company would decide which ones it would accept. A few of the resignations were accepted, and the managers left with dignity, according to Mr. Artzt.

P&G's turnaround in Japan solidly behind him, he moved to Cincinnati in 1989 and two years later was assigned to run the company's U.S. business. He led an overhaul of P&G's domestic sales and marketing—one of the most sweeping changes in the company's history. The company culled the number of brand extensions and product promotions and began sharing sales data with retailers. As a result, today P&G uses checkout data to deliver only as much soap or toilet paper as stores need—rather than forcing retailers to accept truckloads of merchandise, only to have it gather dust in a warehouse. All told, P&G says, the overhaul saved about $1.4 billion over four years.

Colleagues and analysts describe Mr. Jager as a gifted strategic thinker who has a knack for zeroing in on significant issues. During a board meeting of the United Negro College Fund, on which Mr. Jager sits, fellow board members responded with surprised silence when, moments before the vote on a new program, Mr. Jager interjected a question: How would the fund measure whether the new program was successful?

"Everybody just stopped because nobody had thought about that question," said Bill Gray, president and chief executive of the Fund. "He'll get right to the point immediately."

Today, Mr. Jager is preaching "stretch, innovation and speed." He says he wants P&G to take more risks and wants to put more of his executives' pay at risk. The company also needs to look outside its core business more often for inspiration, he says. On a recent visit to an Atlanta photography store, he watched as consumers, with some help, were allowed to crop photos themselves. The visit prompted Mr. Jager to wonder about the potential for a more "interactive" environment in mass-market retailing. Shoppers, for example, could design a broad skin-care regimen with P&G's Oil of Olay products.

"You learn more from the things that are not in the area where you normally operate." he says. "Don't go to a Kroger. . . . Maybe you should get to an outlet that sells furniture."

Unconventional thinking also applies to organizational issues, he says. "Great ideas generally come from conflict—a dissatisfaction with the status quo," he adds. "I'd like to have an organization where there are rebels."

The Auctioneer: Margaret Whitman, the CEO of eBay, talks about the company's rapid growth—and heady ambitions

By George Anders

Of all the new companies spawned by the Internet, few have made as big—or rapid—a splash as eBay Inc., the industry leader in online auctions. After going public in September 1998 at a split-adjusted $9 a share, eBay's stock rocketed ahead so fast that a mere 10 weeks later, it was trading at 10 times that level. (By contrast, it took Microsoft Corp. four years to achieve a similar gain after its initial public offering in 1986.)

For more than 5.6 million registered users, eBay is the ultimate flea market: a place where they can buy or sell everything from Beanie Babies to rare books and antique lamps. With Internet connections bringing countless strangers together, buyers no longer need to comb through dozens of curio shops and regional fairs, looking for that special item. Sellers needn't worry that their best customers are two time zones away, and almost impossible to locate by traditional means. Instead, thousands of times an hour, eBay users type new bids into their computers, chasing after whatever listings strike their fancy.

Over the past year, eBay has been repeatedly held up as an example of both the cleverest and the most worrisome aspects of Internet commerce. The company remains a Wall Street darling, in large part because its business model has almost no variable costs, and thus enormous profit margins. The company doesn't hold any inventory, doesn't run a shipping department and doesn't even typeset listings. Users do all that themselves, even as they pay eBay commissions for the privilege of using its service.

But eBay has had its bumpy moments, too. Computer problems led to repeated site outages earlier this year, including a 22-hour shutdown in June that infuriated many users. Meanwhile, eBay's original freewheeling approach—in which it permitted listings of almost anything—has come under fire as the site grows bigger. Alcohol, tobacco and firearms all had their own spots on eBay a year ago. Now all have been delisted amid concern about possible criminal conduct or regulatory snags.

Since early 1998, eBay's chief executive officer has been Margaret Whitman, a longtime consumer-products executive who had worked at Stride-Rite Corp., Walt Disney Co., FTD Inc. and Hasbro Corp., where, among other things, she oversaw the Mr. Potato Head brand. That background makes her part of a new breed in Silicon Valley—a seasoned general manager whose mission is to ensure that a young company with promising technology can master all the classic challenges of strategy, marketing and finance that are necessary to succeed at a higher level.

In late September, Ms. Whitman sat down with Wall Street Journal reporter George Anders for an extended chat at this newspaper's Technology Summit conference in Washington, D.C. In that session, Ms. Whitman explained how eBay is handling its growth challenges, why it can recruit new customers so quickly and cheaply, and how a new eBay initiative might send shudders through the newspaper industry. Here are excerpts from that session.

Rivals to eBay

The Wall Street Journal: Your marketplace is getting more competitive all the time. Recently, an alliance of other companies—including Microsoft Corp. and Excite At Home Corp.—announced plans to enter the online auction business. And Amazon.com Inc. has opened zShops, which let small businesses sell directly to consumers via the Amazon Web site. As you look at these rivals, do you see anyone that could take away 20% or 40% of your business? Or is eBay just too far ahead to be vulnerable?

Ms. Whitman: We always look at these competitors very carefully. The minute Microsoft decides to come after you, I think you need to be careful. I particularly like that the press characterizes Microsoft as the underdog in this battle. But I think we have a number of competitive advantages that will stand us in very good stead. First, we built our brand in record time. The brand eBay does stand for person-to-person trading on the Internet in an auction format. Second, we have the largest marketplace by far. That does matter because the sellers want to be where the buyers are and the buyers want to be where the sellers are.

But we have got to continue to deliver a fabulous customer experience. Customer support matters a lot in our space. We have to continue to do a great job at that as our community grows. We had 300,000 users when I got to eBay 18 months ago. At the end of the second quarter, we had more than 5.6 million. I feel pretty good about where we are today, but we are always extremely vigilant about the competition.

WSJ: You mentioned eBay's rapid growth. I would think that must be a business challenge. How do you get all your new users to get the hang of eBay—so they don't behave like first-time motorists on the highway, driving everyone crazy?

Ms. Whitman: It is a challenge. We have very experienced users, and we also have 20,000 to 30,000 brand-new registered users every day at eBay. One thing that really is true about eBay is it is a community-commerce model, with users who help one another. Even though sellers might view one another as competitors, they in fact are pretty good about helping new people get started. A lot of our new users now are coming from America Online Inc. We now have something called the AOL cafe where new users congregate together and try to understand what works and what doesn't. But it is a process.

When I came to eBay, only 30% of the listings had photos. Today, 80% of the listings have photos. People learn to be more effective merchants—and that happens over time.

WSJ: I see more and more services on the Internet becoming free. But you've gone counter to the trend, taking a small fee on every listing and a fee on every completed transaction. Has that been the right call, and if so, why?

Ms. Whitman: I think it's been absolutely the right decision. We have faced free competitors from the beginning. Onsale Exchange launched as a free service, which later morphed into Yahoo Auctions, which is free today. We've done a good job of winning against free competitors. I'll tell you why I think that is. Our listing fee, even though it's small on eBay, 25 cents to $2, does keep the junk off the site. If you just have to think a little bit—do I want to pay 50 cents to put this up?—it keeps the dust bunnies off.

WSJ: Help me understand your definition of junk. As much as eBay is packed with cool listings, you do have a lot of stuff that might strike people as just a bit on the junky side.

Ms. Whitman: Well there is junk, but there would be even more if we didn't have a listing fee. As for our final-value fee, people only pay it if they sell their items. Users think that is entirely fair in terms of getting access to the biggest marketplace. So we think it's been the right thing. In this environment, free is not necessarily a good thing.

Managing the Community

WSJ: It has always struck me that eBay's center of gravity isn't so much at your San Jose, Calif., headquarters as it is in your wider community of 5.6 million users. Tell us how you manage a company like that. You don't have a lot of subordinates on the payroll who will snap to attention when you want something done. Instead, you've got this broad network of users—many of whom you've never met—who are your core asset.

Ms. Whitman: We like to say that our community has actually built eBay. Without the sellers selling merchandise and the buyers buying, we would not have been able to be as successful as the company has been. And so, we view ourselves as a marketplace manager. The challenge is, how do you manage a marketplace that is growing this fast? As recently as 18 months ago, our membership was equivalent to the population of Gilroy, Calif. Everyone pretty much knew each other. It was a small-town feel. Now it's almost the size of New York City. That has some real challenges.

As we have grown bigger, we have worked hard on communicating with the community. We'll put things up on the bulletin board and say: "We're going to have a discussion about this particular item Tuesday from 2 p.m to 4 p.m. Come and tell us what you think." I'll tell you, we have not been flawless at this. We have made unilateral decisions that probably shouldn't have been made the way we did. Still, we're better now at communicating with the customer.

Most relationships are based on good, open communication. When we remember that and are good at that, we tend to come out to the right answer in a way that our community feels pretty good about.

WSJ: I've also seen some friction. When you stopped listing guns, the people selling antique firearms were upset and said you were taking away their livelihood. Is that a complaint you've got much time for? Or in the end, is the Internet simply moving away from its original laissez-faire culture to something that's a bit more controlled, especially as sites like yours become bigger and more important?

Ms. Whitman: It's an issue that we think about a lot. As you know, in February of last year we did eliminate the entire firearms category. Two weeks ago or 10 days ago we eliminated the alcohol category and the tobacco category. There are items in those categories that are absolutely perfectly legal, such as antique firearms. Obviously assault weapons and bazookas and rocket launchers are not. But all of those have appeared on eBay at one time or another.

With firearms, we felt the Internet was not an appropriate venue, because you could never be completely sure about who the purchaser of that firearm was. That was a very unpopular decision with our 2,000 firearms dealers. Yet we felt we had to make the decision in favor of the entire community. Had a gun been bought through eBay—and been used in a very visible killing or shooting—that would have been a horrible thing for eBay and for the entire community.

With alcohol and tobacco, there's myriad complex governmental rules and regulations surrounding those two categories. We felt it was almost impossible to deal with all that on the site. It was the easiest and cleanest thing to do. Again, there are a number of sellers of those categories who are not happy with eBay. But we felt the risk to the community was higher in allowing those categories than to take them down.

WSJ: So you're willing to let someone else take over the rights to booze.com and see where they can go with it?

Ms. Whitman: Yes. Maybe someone else would like alcohol.com and tobacco.com.

Regional Auctions

WSJ: You've got a really interesting experiment going on called eBayLA. Get us up-to-date on what you're finding there. It's a very regional targeted site just for people in Southern California. What's being sold, and how are people using it?

Ms. Whitman: We began this experiment in regional auctions at the behest of our community. Our members said: "We would like to trade items that are fundamentally not shippable either because they're too bulky or it costs too much to ship that item." That would include items like boats, cars, recreational vehicles, bedroom-furniture sets, motorcycles and refrigerators. Think about the things that are largely in the classified ads in the newspapers.

So we launched a test market called eBayLA where you can list an item for sale in Los Angeles and certain suburbs. As a buyer, you can view items for sale only in the L.A. area. As a seller, you have the option of putting up a listing that can appear in the big eBay database as well, for viewing around the country.

This new service has had a couple of really interesting effects. We're seeing higher sales in new categories, particularly used automobiles, as well as boats and RVs and furniture. In fact, the auto category has actually grown much faster than we had anticipated.

The average selling price of everything at eBayLA is 22% higher than on regular eBay. The new service also has increased the velocity of trade in the more typical eBay items. So if you're interested in buying a Beanie Baby and you see three Princess Diana Beanie Babies, one of which is near you in L.A., you tend to pick that one. As a result, people are coming back faster to do more business with us, because we shrink the delivery time between when you see an item and when you can actually get it.

WSJ: What are your expansion plans beyond Los Angeles?

Ms. Whitman: By the end of the year, our regional service will be operating in 50 metropolitan areas. It's a classic case of test-market it, get it right and then replicate rapidly. So stay tuned.

WSJ: Will you enter each market solo? Or at some point does it make sense to team up with local media or other groups?

Ms. Whitman: At the moment we are anticipating going solo. One of the real advantages that eBay has, because we have so many users on a national basis, we have critical mass in almost every single metropolitan area. For example, in L.A., we have over 250,000 registered eBay users who form the nucleus for a vibrant local market. That is a huge advantage. I think it's a lot harder to start a regional business without national scale than the other way around. We want to do some small-scale partnering with radio stations and other local charity organizations so that each of these sites takes on a local flavor. But at the moment, we look at this essentially as going on our own.

WSJ: If I'm, say, a newspaper publisher with a big classified ad section, and I see eBayLA growing, should I be getting nervous? Should I be partnering with you? Should I be letting go of my classified ad section? What's the big impact here?

Ms. Whitman: Well, we expect that there will be some impact. Interestingly, one of the founders of eBay, Jeff Skoll, came to eBay from Knight-Ridder Inc. His original idea was to partner with the newspapers. In 1996 he went out and sought every major newspaper chain in the country. All of them said: "Absolutely not. We don't want to do this. We wouldn't want to partner with you if our life depended on it."

So that was actually the way we first approached this business. We remain interested in partnering with newspapers. The difficulty is that we do move on Internet time. We have had difficulty getting newspaper partners that think about this the same way that we do and move at the same pace that we do. So we remain open to it. There have been a couple of things that are kind of interesting, but nothing that is hot at the moment.

Upscale Moves

WSJ: You made an interesting acquisition earlier this year, buying Butterfield & Butterfield. It's a venerable San Francisco auction house that sells rare books, paintings and other classic collectibles. Tell us a bit about how you want to integrate your two businesses. And if I'm a high-end collector, why should I feel comfortable spending more than $10,000 for something I saw on an Internet site?

Ms. Whitman: If you think about our core markets before eBay, they amounted to fragmented groups of buyers and fragmented groups of sellers who couldn't get together in any meaningful way. By creating eBay we enabled a forum that allowed them to get together. About six to eight months ago, we identified the high-end auction market as another very inefficient, fragmented market. If you're in Chicago interested in Remington paintings and the auction is in New York, chances are you're not going to go to that auction. You might phone in, but it's difficult. We also found a significant group of people who would like to buy higher-end items, but who feel a little intimidated about going to an auction. You know, maybe they are going to bid on something they didn't really want, or maybe they feel a little bit uncomfortable in that melee. We said we think that this new area is very interesting for us, but we don't have the expertise.

So we bought Butterfield & Butterfield for their expertise in these fine-art categories and decorative collectibles, as well as their relationships with dealers and auction houses around the world. This autumn, we launched eBay Great Collections, which aggregates auction houses and high-end art dealers who can sell on eBay. We then marry them with our top-end eBay buyers.

You should feel comfortable because all the parties we work with are very well-known and vetted auction houses and dealers. They stand behind their product for three years. So if you buy something and it turns out not to be what you had hoped, they will take it back for three years. We also are letting eBay sellers sell on this site if they meet certain criteria in terms of the feedback score and reputation within the eBay community.

WSJ: Now when we say the fine-art auction market, we always think of Monet and Renoir paintings. But in fact that's 5% or 10% of the classic auction houses' business. Do you really expect to be active in making a market for such paintings? Or will you make a bigger mark in some other, nontraditional collectibles?

Ms. Whitman: We think the core audience for our service involves items between $250 and $10,000. The little-known fact about auction houses like Christie's International PLC and Sotheby's Holdings Inc. is that their average selling price for many items is about $500 to $750. So if you look at the Whitney estate, for example, you might see seven or 10 fabulous paintings. But there would also be a lot of china dogs and other modest items that filled these estates. I think those will be incredibly apropos for this site.

Do I think we're actually going to be selling Monets? I don't think so—although we have sold items on eBay well over $100,000. So you never can tell.

WSJ: Whose commission structure are you going to use? Yours is pretty lean. Your top rate is 5%, and theirs is much plumper, say 15% or so. Will you switch the high-end art world to your kind of commissions? Or will you come up with some sort of compromise?

Ms. Whitman: Our take today on eBay is about 5% to 6% of the value of the item, when you include the listing fee and the final-value fee. The high-end auction houses today typically have a 15% to 20% seller's premium. They may also have a buyer's premium of 10%. EBay Great Collections will not have a buyer's premium. So our site should become a far more efficient and cost-effective venue for sellers and buyers.

I think it will grow the market, too. There are a lot of people who want to buy these kinds of items who just don't feel comfortable in a land-based traditional auction environment. Additionally, the auction season usually runs only in the fall and the spring. Our service will run 24 hours a day, seven days a week, 365 days a year. In that respect, it will be just like eBay.

WSJ: So if an item is available for market in August, you can sell it in August.

Ms. Whitman: That's exactly right.

WSJ: Something that's made headlines in the past six months—which you probably wish hadn't happened—is the recurring pattern of outages at eBay's site. As you look back at how technology was built at eBay, what did the company do wrong? If you had it over again, what should you have done to build a more enduring, robust system?

Ms. Whitman: The biggest difficulty we have is that eBay has been growing between 40% and 70%, quarter over quarter, for the past eight quarters. There is this constant roar in the background. If I had it to do over again, I would bring in more senior management talent sooner than I did. We have a fabulous head of technology who is now our chief scientist, Mike Wilson. He had the genius and foresight to build a system that scaled far beyond what it was designed to do 2u, three years ago.

What I didn't do soon enough is say: "You know what? To go from a little company to a big company, you need not a developer mentality but a mission-critical-system mentality."

Expansion Capacity

WSJ: Come back to that point about growth. In the telephone industry, long-distance carriers build systems that can handle five times their regular traffic and about 30% more than peak volume. That's enough to tide them over for several years before they need extra capacity. In your business, how much capacity above current levels do you need so that you don't outgrow it within a year?

Ms. Whitman: We try to [plan for] anywhere between five times and 10 times the anticipated demand. We've become pretty good at forecasting demand on the system. Now, we are adding complexity as we add regional auctions, international services and Great Collections. It's a classic production system for us because our service breaks down into many sub-tasks, including listing items, bidding and feedback. So you're only as good as your weakest link. We are trying to build fivefold to 10-fold capacity on each of those links.

WSJ: We talked a bit about what you did wrong in terms of the outages. Now tell me what you did right. You had about 2.2 million listings when your site went down for 22 hours in June. Right after that, your listings dropped to just 1.7 million. There was a lot of news coverage suggesting that other online-auction rivals such as Yahoo and Amazon had a golden opportunity to gain ground on eBay. And now you've got about three million listings—putting eBay farther ahead than ever. How did you keep your members' loyalty?

Ms. Whitman: I think we did a couple of things right. We communicated very clearly with our customer base, almost on a quarter-hour basis as to what the status was. We had this constant communication with current information. Our announcement board is actually on a separate server, so that is always up. Good communication really, really helps in these situations.

Second, we decided to refund all fees for all auctions on the site during the outage. So 2.2 million items got a refund of their final-value fee and a refund of their listing fee and any other features they had chosen. A lot of folks said: "You don't have to go that far. All you need to do is extend people's auctions. They still have a chance to sell those items. It's not really a hardship."

But we felt it was really the right thing to do, even though it meant a $4.6 million charge against earnings in the second quarter. Our community depends on this service. And you're right, the items being listed jumped back.

WSJ: What sort of e-mail were you getting during the time?

Ms. Whitman: Hundreds of items, every day. On the Web, everyone figures out that I'm reachable at mwhitman @eBay.com or meg@eBay.com. Users tell one another what the e-mail address is. In fact, the e-mail address was posted on our "discuss new features" board. So the second day of the outage, I came in and there were about 570 e-mails. So the good news is that people care a lot about eBay.

WSJ: If they cared any more, would you have to hire a bodyguard?

Ms. Whitman: Yes. [Laughter.] The only thing I think I'll rue is the day when they actually stop writing. We have become so much a part of our community's lives that people do let us know what they think. It's very similar to the role that AOL plays in people's lives. As you recall, when AOL had its big downtime episode a few years ago, you would have thought it was a national emergency. With us, people get so used to their eBay friends, their eBay selling and their eBay buying that when it is interrupted, they feel very strongly about it.

WSJ: Would you send personal e-mail answers to your users? Or did you have some more automated way to respond?

Ms: Whitman: I answered the first few, and then I realized this was going to be a problem. So we had a couple of assistants and some customer-support people help reply to all the messages. But we answered every single e-mail that I got.

WSJ: How about on a continuing basis? You came out of the traditional, land-based economy. At Hasbro or Disney, I assume, the main ways of keeping up with customers involved written surveys, research summaries or other more distilled, remote techniques. Now that you do business on the Internet, how do you gauge the pulse of the outside world? How do you like the tools available to you, compared with what you had before?

Ms. Whitman: What we have now is so far superior I can't even describe it to you. We get instant feedback on eBay about almost everything that we do. You know instantly. You can put up a new feature, and within 20 minutes you will have a very good sense of what the adoption rate is going to be. It's also far easier to survey the user base. In the land-based world, you had to typically do focus groups, or send people a mail survey or contract for phone surveys. In this regard, we'll put a survey up on eBay, and within an hour we'll have 4,000 responses. It's terrific. You really can do polling and surveying and try to see what needs are not being met far faster.

WSJ: What does that do to your speed of innovation?

Ms. Whitman: It's much faster. The time-to-launch is no longer limited by this formal review process, where people have to ask: "Is it a good business idea? What are the consumers going to think? What is the adoption rate?" Our limitation is sheer technology now. "How fast can we develop the product, do the quality assurance and get something into the system?" So the cycles here are far shorter. We've probably introduced 50 major new features to the site this year and six new major lines of business, if you count each country as a line of business. That would have taken years in the land-based world.

WSJ: We're hearing a lot about business-to-business e-commerce. Is that a market that looks like a natural extension for you? Are there ways you want to play there, or is that off limits for you?

Ms. Whitman: It is not on the near-term list of things to do. It sounds much more complicated than our business. We are really trying to run a very focused and disciplined company, and our plate is full. We have our consumer-to-consumer and small-dealer-to-consumer business—both in the U.S. and internationally. We also have eBay Great Collections. And we have our whole end-to-end trading-services business, where we help users with shipping, insurance, escrow, credit-card payment and posting photos with their listings.

In most of these areas, the devil is in the details. You've got to push things to closure. If you keep starting new things and don't get them to closure, I think you do the company a disservice in the long run. So I will say we remain interested in business-to-business, but in the near term will not be playing there ourselves. We may make some investments in some b-to-b companies so that we have a pole position there, but we will not be entering it on our own.

WSJ: And your market capitalization at this point is how much?

Ms. Whitman: About $15 billion.

WSJ: So price is not a problem. You've got some liquidity.

Ms. Whitman: Yes.

Marketing on the Cheap

WSJ: One of the unusual things about eBay is how quickly you pick up new customers at low cost. You do have a big marketing alliance with AOL. But otherwise, you aren't doing a lot of expensive advertising to recruit new customers. They just seem to keep coming. Explain how that works.

Ms. Whitman: If you just do the math off our sales and marketing line in our quarterly financial filings, we're spending less than $10 to acquire each new customer. Even that number includes our product-marketing staff and a lot of things that you wouldn't necessarily term the cost of customer acquisition. So the true cost is decidedly sub-$10 per customer.

The reason for that is that we are still being driven by word-of-mouth. Consider every new customer that we get through the AOL relationship. Our estimate is that they tell seven other people about eBay. That has always been the main driver of eBay's customer acquisition. When we ask new users: "How did you find out about eBay?" more than half the people say: "I heard about it from a friend," or relative, or colleague.

That, of course, is the best kind of advertising on two dimensions. It's the lowest cost. In addition, if you told me about eBay and I get on eBay and I can't figure out what to do, I call you.

WSJ: So your existing members aren't just your hidden marketing force—they also do double or triple duty as your unofficial tech-support team.

Ms. Whitman: We have found that to be incredibly valuable. People who are referred by a friend tend to do better faster than someone who was not referred by a friend.

WSJ: One closing topic that's always interested me: You were a pioneering executive, leaving a comfortable East Coast executive job with a big company so you could join a Silicon Valley start-up with a completely uncertain value. Things have worked out pretty well for you. Now I see a whole second wave of westward-bound executives leaving the AlliedSignals and the Pepsis of the world to make a new career at an Internet company. What advice would you have for someone making that switch?

Ms. Whitman: It's probably the best move that I ever made and the best move that a lot of these kind of executives can make. I think the Internet is the most exciting sector of this economy, where we have a chance to make fundamental change to how people across the globe actually do business with one another.

My main advice is: Fasten your seatbelt. This is a far faster world. You have to be far more nimble and far more willing to make decisions without nearly the kind of data and analysis that I used to have at a Hasbro or a Disney or a P&G. You've got to let go of some old notions pretty quick. You have to use your instincts and learn from the right folks. I really learned a great deal from the folks at eBay who were the early denizens of the Net. They truly understood what the Net was about and what it could be used for.

MAN ON THE SPOT AT COCA-COLA

Nowadays, things go tougher at Coke. But Doug Ivester has his eye on the long term

The CEO of Coca-Cola Co., M. Douglas Ivester, believes in digging into the details of all his company's far-flung operations. When an executive from Coca-Cola Femsa, Coke's biggest Mexican bottler, mentioned his country's tens of thousands of mom-and-pop retailers at a presentation last year, Ivester cut him short, saying: "So which are they—moms or pops?" John Santa Maria Otazúa, Femsa's chief operating officer, stammered back: "I think it's more moms than pops, Doug, but I'm not sure."

This wasn't just a tough leader trying to throw a manager off balance. Ivester was dead serious, a fact that speaks volumes about the CEO—and the state of Coke's business around the globe. These days, some of the soft-drink maker's biggest investments aren't in markets dominated by giant retail chains where customers buy in bulk. They're in Brazil, Russia, and Indonesia, where the local economies have been ravaged and soda is sold a few ounces at a time. Many of the store owners in Mexico, Coke's second-biggest market, turned out to be single mothers and retirees who couldn't afford health insurance. Armed with that intelligence, Femsa was able to create an incentive program that rewards shopkeepers who sell enough Cokes with access to group insurance—a move that helped boost Coke's sales volume in Mexico 13% last year.

The emphasis on nitty-gritty details and creative solutions is vintage Ivester. And it's a sharp departure from the arm's-length, patrician style of his predecessor, the legendary Roberto C. Goizueta. Now, 18 months into his tenure, Ivester's style and substance are being tested in ways he never could have anticipated. Although he took over one of America's most admired companies after spending years preparing for the role, the soft-spoken ex-accountant is steering a company that faces a world of trouble.

TRICKLE. Over the past 12 months, Ivester has watched the global crisis leave the mighty Coke machine sputtering—its sales and profits battered by the turmoil abroad. In Brazil and Japan, two of Coke's biggest overseas markets, flattened consumer buying power left growth last year almost nonexistent. In Russia, where Coke has invested more than

$700 million over the past eight years, the collapse of the economy has left the Coke system operating at 50% capacity.

Things are not much better back at home. At the very moment he can least afford it, Ivester is being forced to expend precious resources to fight off a reinvigorated PepsiCo Inc. (PEP), which is aggressively trying to win back the market share it lost to Coke earlier this decade. Suddenly, Pepsi is fighting tooth and nail for every restaurant chain, every supermarket display, and every vending machine opportunity that comes up. That new sense of purpose has forced Coke to make much costlier concessions to retain its biggest customers. Unlike past skirmishes, this Cola War is shaping up to be a war of attrition, in which the market-share winner may turn out to be the earnings loser. "The gloves are off again," says consultant Stanley Makadok, a former Pepsi executive.

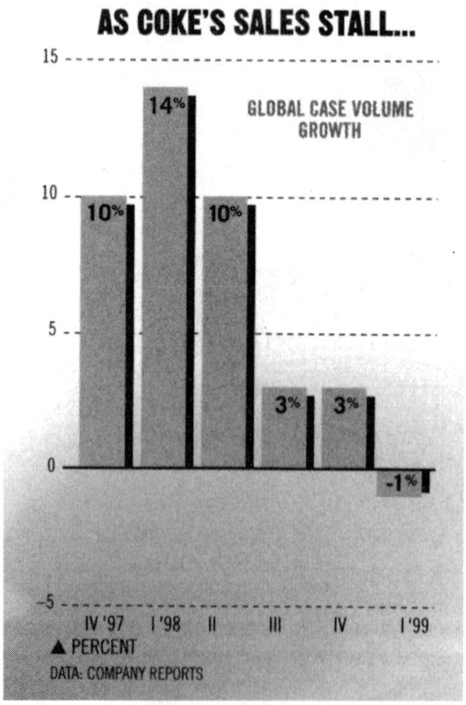

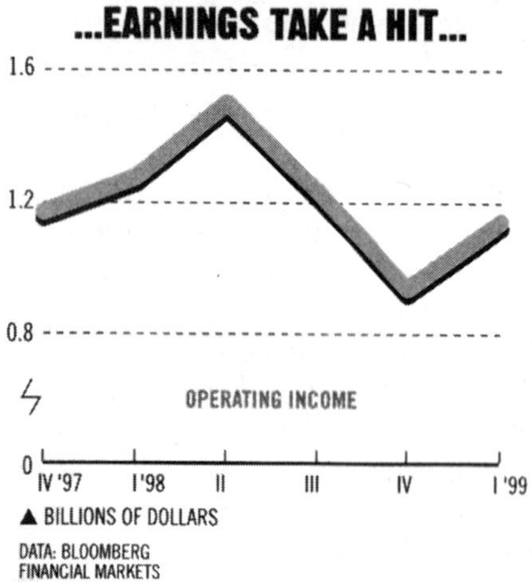

For Atlanta-based Coca-Cola, which rode the wave of global capitalism further than almost any other U.S. multinational, the recent turbulence strikes at the core of its being. After years of solid 15% or better annual earnings gains, Coke surprised Wall Street in the third quarter last year with weak results. That was followed by a fourth quarter in which earnings plunged 27% from 1997. For the year, Coke registered a 1% drop in operating income, to $4.97 billion on $18.8 billion in revenues—and is likely to be flat again this year. To a company that has long been considered one of America's premier growth stocks, that's akin to falling off a cliff.

Indeed, the reaction on Wall Street has been humbling. During Goizueta's 16-year reign, Coke shares rose a breathtaking 3,500%. But after the bad news began to pile up last summer, Coke's stock fell by nearly a third, from 88 to around 59 in early April. Some investors have questioned whether Coke's days of outsize returns are gone forever. "I think it's up to Coke to prove they can get back on the growth track," says Ned Riley, chief investment officer for BankBoston, who started paring back his Coke holdings last summer. Still, there are some who believe the worst may be over. Despite a dismal first quarter in which operating profits fell by 9%, Coke shares climbed in recent weeks to 66.

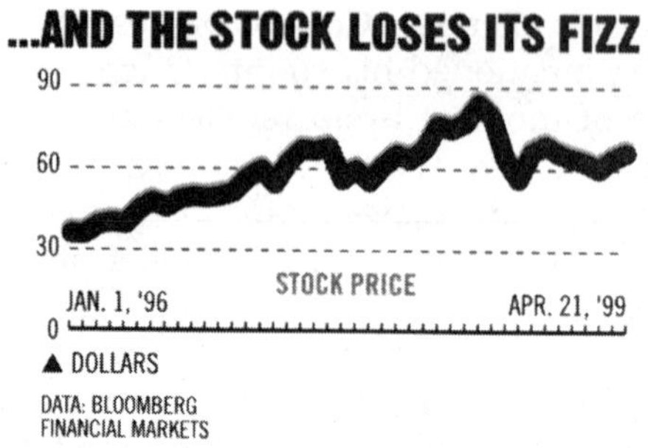

ON THE OFFENSE. So far, Ivester's response to his company's myriad problems has been remarkably consistent. Rather than pulling back as the going got rough, Ivester has repeatedly doubled his bets—spending lavishly in order to win an ever-bigger slice of the global market. Overseas, where Coke derives more than three-quarters of its profits and

71% of its growth, that has meant using the downturn as a chance to buy bottlers, distribution, and even rival brands cheap. In the U.S. it has meant spending whatever it takes to hold on to key customers or sign up new ones.

Ivester argues that the investments will allow Coke to emerge from this period stronger than ever. "My view is that in any crisis there's opportunity," he says. In effect, he is betting that the big investments made today will buy Coke market share and growth opportunities in the future. It's a risky bet. In the short term, the spending spree has added to the pressure on Coke's bottom line and hammered operating margins down from historical levels of 26% and better to 21% by the end of last year. Even at its current depressed stock price, Coke trades at a price-earnings ratio of 45—a number that will surely decline if Ivester's strategy falls short. Already, Wall Street is becoming more skittish. Salomon Smith Barney analyst Jennifer Solomon recently advised clients that "this may be the end of giving Coca-Cola the benefit of the doubt."

The barrage of bad news catches Coke at a ticklish time. Managing a downdraft is tough for anyone, but Ivester, 52, had barely moved into the corner office when the numbers began to fall apart last summer. On top of that, he follows one of the most successful and revered CEOs in corporate history. For all their mutual respect and long working relationship, the two men couldn't have been more different: Goizueta, the Cuban aristocrat, and Ivester, the first in his family to attend college. The cerebral Goizueta fancied himself the master strategist who ruled at one remove. His pupil, who puts in 14-hour days and stays in contact with managers worldwide through E-mail, voice mail, and alphanumeric pager, doesn't hesitate to get involved at street level, whether it's monitoring a minor acquisition in Peru or a bottler's complaint in South Africa.

RIGHT STUFF. If Ivester is nervous about the challenges he faces, he doesn't show it. The son of a textile-mill supervisor, he gave up the partner track at accountants Ernst & Whinney to join Coke's finance staff in 1979 and has since worked in nearly every corner of the Coke empire. Under Goizueta, he executed many of the tactics that have won Coke a 50% share of the worldwide soda market. In 1986, Ivester engineered the ingenious spin-off of Coke's bottling operations. As European chief later in the decade, he led the push into Eastern Europe by driving a trunkful of Coke into East Germany even as the Berlin Wall was falling. And as head of Coca-Cola USA from 1991 to 1994, he introduced a plastic version of Coke's contour bottle that helped lift Coke's U.S. market share two percentage points.

THEY'D LIKE TO SELL THE WORLD A COKE

Sales are sagging both at home and abroad, where Coke derives nearly three-fourths of its earnings. Here are the challenges—and Coke's solutions:

SATURATED U.S. MARKET

Americans already drink more than two helpings of soft drinks a day on average. To grab share, Coke is striving to make its drinks available everywhere people gather—from the post office to the school cafeteria.

ROUGH WATERS ABROAD

Coke has bet on emerging markets from Asia to South America. But with those economies devastated, getting consumers to trade cash for a soda pop is a tough sell. Coke's answer: cheaper packaging and smaller savings.

STYMIED ACQUISITIONS

Attempts to snare big overseas brands such as Orangina, or the foreign rights to Cadbury Schweppes's soft drinks and mixers have been blocked by regulators. But observers expect Coke to eventually make concessions and close the deals.

RESURGENT PEPSI

Coke still dominates, but its nemesis Pepsi is suddenly richer and more focused. To fight back, Coke is taking the long view, paying big bucks for the chance to bond with consumers through exclusive sales deals.

Inside the Coke camp, few question that Ivester has the right stuff to take Big Red back to its glory days. Coke's board has made it clear that Ivester has its undiluted confidence. "I can't think of anyone better suited to lead Coca-Cola through its current situation," says director Herbert A. Allen, president of Allen & Co. And Warren E. Buffett, a director and Coke's largest shareholder, with 200 million shares, or 8% of the company's stock, tells BUSINESS WEEK: "Doug is as good as they've ever had. If I owned the whole company, Doug Ivester would still be running it."

Even as the economic winds battering Coke reach gale force, Ivester has remained unflappable. In a pep talk to employees in February, Ivester was resolute that the business hadn't fundamentally changed, noting that Coke had weathered countless economic crises in its 113 years. "We're dealing with human thirst," Ivester tells employees in his gentle Georgia accent. "There's nothing about economic change that is going to change people's thirst."

Still, the global crisis has left many thirsty people in Asia, Russia, and Latin America unable to afford a Coke. In Brazil, its third-largest market, Coke has lost more than one-tenth of its 54% market share to low-cost local drinks produced by family-owned bottlers exempt from that country's punitive soft-drink taxes. And in Japan, Coke's fourth-largest market, sales have been flattened both by economic turmoil and an emboldened Pepsi, which last year signed up beverage giant Suntory as its new Japanese distributor.

In the short run, Ivester is doing whatever it takes to keep the syrup flowing. To make drinks more affordable, Coke has switched from plastic to refundable glass packaging and introduced cheaper 6.5-oz. bottles. It has scaled back ad campaigns in favor of in-store "instant win" promotions. In Poland, Coke bundled free candy bars with its half-liter bottles—one of several moves that have helped boost first-quarter sales there 17%. And costs are being cut, too: Coke's Indonesian officials, for instance, relinquished their downtown office space and moved into a bottling plant.

But Ivester doesn't manage just for the short term. By investing in new capacity around the world, he's making a bet that the global economy recovers swiftly. On a recent swing through Brazil, he announced that despite the 40% devaluation of the real—or maybe because of it—Coke will boost its investment in Brazil by 10%, to $366 million, this year. In October, he vowed to plow more than $1 billion into Africa over the next three to five years, doubling Coke's investment there. And in China, where Coke volume grew 20% last year, Coke managers are taking the ultimate long-term view, putting together a 100-year plan at Ivester's request. "I think we'll look back and view the coming 10 years as one of the greatest periods of market-share gains in the company's history," says director Allen.

Ivester insists in some cases that prices now are just too low to pass up. Last summer, Coke offered $187 million to Britain's Inchcape PLC for four bottling plants in Russia. But as the economy continued to sour, Coke eventually got them in October for just $87 million. Still, critics such as Schroder & Co. analyst Caroline Levy, warn that it could be 15 years before Coke gets a return on its Russian investments. "Coke is overcapitalized relative to the growth rates of many emerging economies it operates in," she says. Coke Chief Financial Officer James E. Chesnut says investments in Russia will pay off much faster than analysts think.

Coke points to Mexico as an example of the strength of its long-term strategy. Mexican managers boosted market share in their coun-

HARD ACT TO FOLLOW

Ivester's style differs completely from that of late CEO Goizueta. Like Goizueta, however, he has the board's total confidence

A CASE OF DEJA VU

Doug Ivester isn't the first Coke CEO to face big challenges. His predecessor, Roberto Goizueta, also became a "Man on the Spot" after his ill-fated 1985 decision to replace Coke's transitional secret formula with a sweeter New Coke. But just like Ivester today, Goizueta took a long view. He quickly cut his New Coke losses, ended Coke's foray into film-making, and refocused on the core brand. A reinvigorated Coke went on to become an earnings phenomenon.

try from 53% to 68% by investing in new plants during the peso crisis. Coke doesn't break out earnings by country but says the market is "very profitable" and that volume rose 13% last year.

BIGGER GULPS. Ivester isn't betting just on his ability to get more people around the world to drink more Coke. Having spent the past decade building a worldwide bottling system, he intends to use it to deliver any beverage that can find a big following. His boldest gambit yet is his $1.85 billion deal to acquire rights in 120 markets outside the U.S. to Canada Dry, Dr Pepper, and the rest of Cadbury Schweppes PLC's soft drinks and mixers—a deal that would give Coke two more percentage points of global market share, and probably more than that in time.

That's a big if. The deal is facing stiff resistance from regulators in such countries as Mexico and Australia, where Coke already has 65% market share. "Out of sheer stupidity, they're tying the rope around their own necks—it's like Microsoft," says Enrique Molina, chairman and CEO of Pepsi-Gemex, Pepsi's largest bottler in Mexico. Some analysts and rivals say the problem stems as much from Coke's intransigence as its size. In France, Coke's proposed takeover of the Orangina brand has been blocked by regulators for 16 months, though analysts believe Coke will make concessions and end the impasse soon. "Coca-Cola counted a lot on its size and reputation, and in fact, things didn't turn out the way they wanted," says one Paris analyst.

Back at home, where Coke derives one-fifth of its profits, it faces an entirely different order of problems. Consumers here already drink more soft drinks than in any other country outside of Mexico—45% of it from the Coca-Cola Co. Combine that with a reinvigorated Pepsi fighting for every scrap of market share (See box: Now That's a Pepsi Challenge), and Coke is left with less room to maneuver. Almost anywhere it turns it faces the prospect of having to sacrifice profitability to increase sales.

Far from shrinking from the challenges, Ivester has set a goal of increasing per capita U.S. consumption of all Coke products by 25% a year, to 500 eight-oz. servings. Yes, that does mean he thinks every American, on average, should be drinking close to two cups of Coke's products every day. To get there, he's looking for new ways and new places to sell a thirsty public a Coke—or a Coke product.

If Ivester has his way, consumers will soon find Coke's red-and-white machines everywhere from the local post office to the school cafeteria. Although they account for an estimated one-tenth of Coke's systemwide sales, vending machines carry rich margins, and Ivester thinks there's room for a lot more. A couple of years ago, he asked execs at Coca-Cola Consolidated—his second-largest U.S. bottler—to try an experiment. He wanted them to double the number of vending machines in Salisbury, N.C., a small city that had been budgeted for a modest 4% increase in capital spending. The result: Each machine generated a 30%-to-50% annual return. Coke Consolidated is now adding 25,000 new vending machines. "I'll spend capital all day long if it generates a return like that," says Consolidated CEO Frank Harrison III. Now, Coke is testing a hybrid gas pump/vending machine in Pennsylvania and is working on a similar stamp/beverage machines for post offices.

WATER, WATER. But not all of Coke's U.S. marketing expenditures are likely to be that lucrative. With Pepsi upping the ante, Coke must pay more to keep its most important fountain contracts. Consider the heated bidding over the 10,000-store chain of Burger King Corp., which recently came up for renewal. Burger King pays Coke about $220 million a year for 40 million gallons of soda syrup, according to people close to the deal. Under the old contract, they say, Coke gave back about $25 million of that in rebates to the food chain. After Pepsi pitched Burger King for the business, Coke ended up winning, but only by doubling its rebate. Says consultant Tom Pirko, president of Bevmark Inc.: "That has to do a real number on Coke's margins." Worse, the Burger King rebates will likely jack up the price for many of Coke's remaining contracts.

Increasingly, Coke is also having to pay top dollar to sign smaller, less traditional deals. In April, a Coke bottler agreed to pay $28.5 million over ten years for sales rights across a single Michigan school district, twice what Pepsi offered. Coke thinks the hefty fee, which works out to an annual $28 per student, will pay off, since soda loyalties are often established in the teen years. Meanwhile, in the supermarket aisles, where margins are a paltry 3%, Coke's attempts to raise prices have hurt sales.

Still, with the average American already swilling more than 800 servings of soda a year, skeptics wonder how much growth can be wrung out of the U.S. The flagship brands, Coke Classic and Diet Coke, are still growing roughly 4% a year, but they may be approaching the limit. In recent years, consumers' appetite for colas overall has flattened—and diet has actually lost ground to bottled water. That's why Coke has added a host of new products in the U.S.—from other soft drinks,

NOW THAT'S A PEPSI CHALLENGE

NEXT STOP, McDONALDS?

Pepsi's renewed assault on Coke's lead focuses on fountain and vending-machine outlets and, above all, fast-food chains

The Cola Wars used to be a walkover for Coke. As relentless as a Roman legion, it regularly humbled a distracted Pepsi, widening its market-share lead. But Coco-Cola Co.'s easy victories are history. A newly invigorated Pepsi has launched a hellacious assault on its archrival that has forced Coke, already struggling with international woes, to expend huge chunks of money and time to defend its 44%-to-31% U.S. lead.

Whipping No. 2 PepsiCo Inc. into fighting trim has been the mission of Chairman and CEO Roger A. Enrico since he took over in 1996. Enrico has made Pepsi a leaner, feistier foe by spinning off capital-intensive distractions such as restaurants and bottling. Now, with revved-up marketing, price wars in the stores, and an assault on Coke's lead in fountain and vending-machine sales, he is going after Coke with a vengeance. Says Philip a Marineau, Pepsi's head of beverage operations: "We've reenergized our system."

KUDOS. Nowhere is the change more visible than in Pepsi's marketing. After years in which it pumped out glitzy ads that didn't sell much, Pepsi is doubling spending—to $300 million a year—to launch a fusillade of new initiatives that are finally winning kudos from marketing experts. In March, Pepsi rolled out a splashy new campaign for its flagship Pepsi-Cola brand. And to hype its new Pepsi One diet drink, the cheeky No.2 is even dusting off its old "Pepsi Challenge" gambit from the 1970s—the last time it made gains on Coke. But perhaps its biggest move will come starting in May with the release of *Star Wars: Episode I—The Phantom Menace.* With plans to spend up to an estimated $2 billion over the six-year, three-film deal, Pepsi has scored a big piece of what should be one of the hottest promotional opportunities around. Look for Pepsi to exploit the films with toys, ads, and co-branded soft-drink cans.

Out in the real world, the newly pugnacious company's chief avenue of attack is fast-food chains. Now accounting for one-quarter of all beverage sales, such chains are the fastest-growing distribution channel—and, with margins of 15%, one of the most lucrative. Coke, with 8 of the 10 largest fast-food chains in its pocket, has a commanding 65%-to-25% market-share advantage. But Pepsi has scored some minor victories, stealing seven smallish fast-food accounts from Coke, including Pizza Inn Inc. (525 outlets) and Bojangles' Restaurants Inc. (257). And its biggest victory may have come simply from being a contender when Coke recently renewed its contract with Burger King. Pepsi's competing bid forced Coke to spend a boatload to keep the contract. "The fact is, we put a scare into Coke," says a Pepsi exec. "Wait till we go after McDonald's."

Coke must also worry about Pepsi's bid to plant more of its blue vending machines around the landscape. Since 1997, Pepsi has added 170,000 machines nationwide, for a total of about 1 million. Today, Coke remains far ahead, with roughly 1.4 million machines. But Pepsi's push has made the battle to place the machines —which boast margins of more than 30%—far more competitive.

SNACK TIME. Enrico also wants Pepsi to do better at exploiting the one edge it enjoys: the combined strength of its soft drinks, its new Tropicana juice unit, and Frito-Lay, the world's largest salted-snack provided. After all, people heading to the store for a snack often pick up soft drinks at the same time. So far, the "Power of One" campaign has consisted of a few joint promotions. But Enrico is making sales calls on supermarket-chain CEOs with the heads of Frito-Lay, Pepsi, and Tropicana. Their pitch: Increase your sales by moving soft drinks next to snacks. Count on Coke, which would be at a disadvantage because it doesn't sell chips or pretzels, to resist Pepsi's aisle-placement plans.

The reality remains that Coke can no longer coast. "Pepsi has changed the rules," says William W. Wilson, CEO of independent Pepsi-Cola Bottling Co. of New York. "It's finally willing and able to spend big-time on catching Coke." No wonder Coke is looking over its shoulder.

By Larry Light in New York

such as citrus-flavored Surge, to juices, teas, and now water.

Yet even as he moves to capture a larger share of those side markets, Ivester emphatically rejects the notion that Coke has hit a permanent plateau in the U.S. He says that pundits have predicted the passing of colas ever since the 1930s. During lunch in his executive dining room, Ivester jumps up and quickly returns with a color-coded U.S. map comparing consumption per capita for each city or region with that of another country. The per-person consumption of Coke in Lubbock, Tex., for instance, is no higher than in Chile; Knoxville, Tenn., the same as Mexico. And consumers in Phoenix and Los Angeles—two of the lowest in soft-drink consumption—drink no more Coke than people in Hungary. "Why am I so optimistic about the future? Look at this map," he says.

Ivester insists that his strategy includes nothing that his mentor, Goizueta, wouldn't have done. But although Ivester may have held to his original vow of "no left turns, no right turns" after Goizueta's death from cancer in late 1997, there have been some subtle changes in the Coke culture and style.

"DOWN TO EARTH." While Goizueta kept constant watch on Coke's stock and the analysts who followed it—sometimes critiquing their reports with handwritten notes—Ivester pours his energies instead into Coke's customers, no matter how small. J.L. "Sonny" Williams, president of Minyard Food Stores in Coppell, Tex., still recalls how Ivester sent a red wagon after the birth of his first child last year, and then took time during a recent stop in the Lone Star State to chat over barbecue and tour one of Minyard's 85 stores. "It was nice to see a CEO who was so down to earth," recalls Williams, who says he's never met anyone from Pepsi headquarters. Says Ivester: "If you focus on the customers, the business will prosper, and if the business prospers, the stock will eventually be priced right."

Ivester has also begun the delicate task of shifting Coke's corporate culture, which had developed a reputation in some quarters for arrogance and stodginess. To speed the decision-making process, Ivester has cut several layers out of Coke's organizational hierarchy. Under Goizueta he began scrapping Coke's grueling December planning marathons with managers in favor of real-time budgeting—giving his field generals more freedom to respond to any opportunities that may arise. And he has tried to soften Coke's old "tough-love" style of management. "Many employees today did not grow up with authoritarian fathers, did not grow up in traditional households," Ivester says. "You've got to transition to a modern style of motivating people."

As a part of that strategic effort, Ivester has encouraged more of his troops to think boldly, to take more risk—even encouraging one manager who schemed up an idea to use a laser to beam Coke's trademark off the moon to "go for it." ("It actually would have worked," assures the manager, Steve Koonin. "But the FAA was worried about the risk of us slicing airplanes in half.")

In the end, Ivester's biggest obstacle may be Coke's tremendous size and success. The bigger Coke gets, the harder it is to reproduce the earnings record set by Goizueta—and demanded by Wall Street. The bets Ivester has placed around the globe have added to Coke's immediate pain. But if he's right, the current crisis will not turn out to be the end of an era—simply the pause that refreshes.

By Dean Foust in Atlanta and Buenos Aires, with Geri Smith in Mexico City, David Rocks in Prague, and bureau reports

Why CEOs Fail

By Ram Charan and Geoffrey Colvin

It's rarely for lack of smarts or vision. Most unsuccessful CEOs stumble because of one simple, fatal shortcoming.

What got Eckhard Pfeiffer fired? What fault did in Bob Allen? Or Gil Amelio, Bob Stempel, John Akers, or any of the dozens of other chief executives who took public pratfalls in this unforgiving decade? Suppose what brought down all these powerful and undeniably talented executives was just one common failing? It's an intriguing question and one of deep importance not just to CEOs and their boards, but also to investors, customers, suppliers, alliance partners, employees, and the many others who suffer when the top man stumbles. The answer even matters to the country; America is the world's most competitive nation, thanks in large part to the overall high quality of its CEOs. If people knew how to spot CEOs headed for failure—even if the company's results still looked fine—they could save themselves much pain. Trouble is, they usually look in the wrong place.

Consider the Pfeiffer episode. The pundits opined, as they usually do in these cases, that his problem was with grand-scale vision and strategy. Compaq's board removed the CEO for lack of "an Internet vision," said USA Today. Yep, agreed the New York Times, Pfeiffer had to go because of "a strategy that appeared to pull the company in opposite directions."

But was flawed strategy really Pfeiffer's sin? Not according to the man who led the coup, Compaq Chairman Benjamin Rosen. "The change [will not be in] our fundamental strategy—we think that strategy is sound—but in execution," Rosen said. "Our plans are to speed up decision-making and make the company more efficient."

You'd never guess it from reading the papers or talking to your broker or studying most business books, but what's true at Compaq is true at most companies where the CEO fails. In the majority of cases—we estimate 70%—the real problem isn't the high-concept boners the boffins love to talk about.

It's bad execution. As simple as that: not getting things done, being indecisive, not delivering on commitments. We base our conclusions on careful study of several dozen CEO failures we've observed over the decades—through our respective work as a consultant to major corporations and a journalist covering them. The results are beyond doubt.

Here's what we aren't saying: That failed CEOs are dumb or evil. In fact they tend to be highly intelligent, articulate, dedicated, and accomplished. They worked hard, made sacrifices, and may have performed terrifically for years; Pfeiffer, for example, transformed the company more than once and multiplied Compaq's revenues, profits, and market values, a remarkable achievement. And failure as a CEO is never final. These are strong people who can come back successfully in other roles.

Nor are we saying execution is the only reason CEOs falter. Sometimes they adopt a strategy so flawed that it's doomed, or they refuse to confront reality in their markets, or they antagonize their board. And when a CEO really goes down in flames, there's almost always more than one reason. But business people learn to focus on the main thing, the explanation that accounts for most of what they're worried about, and in the realm of CEO failures that explanation is clear.

It's clear, as well, that getting execution right will only become more crucial. The worldwide revolution of free markets, open economies, and lowered trade barriers and the advent of e-commerce has made virtually every business far more brutally competitive. The frantic spread of information through technology is making customers everywhere more powerful and pushing toward the commoditization of everything. Institutional investors now own more than half the equities in U.S. corporations and relentlessly demand results. Indeed, two of the nation's preeminent headhunters, Tom Neff and Dayton Ogden of Spencer Stuart, calculated recently that while average CEO tenure in the biggest companies has remained fairly steady at seven to eight years, those who don't deliver are getting pushed out quicker. (See the graph later in the article.) A new academic study reaches the same conclusion—poorly performing CEOs are three times more likely to get booted than they were a generation ago. Even if their boards spare them, their companies often get taken over, like Digital Equipment under Robert Palmer and Rubbermaid under Wolfgang Schmitt. Bottom line: whatever cover CEOs used to hide behind has been blasted away. Either they deliver, soon, or they're gone.

So how do CEOs blow it? More than any other way, by failure to put the right people in the right jobs—and the related failure to fix people problems in time. Specifically, failed CEOs are often unable to deal with a few key subordinates whose sustained poor performance deeply harms the company. What is striking, as many CEOs told us, is that they usually know there's a problem; their inner voice is telling them, but they suppress it. Those around the CEO often recognize the problem first, but he isn't seeking information from multiple sources. As one CEO says, "It was staring me in the face, but I refused to see it." The failure is one of emotional strength.

The excuses and rationalizations that CEOs concoct are largely unconscious, a mechanism for avoidance. They make an impressive list; six cover most cases:

"He has to succeed." The CEO may become a victim of "intellectual seduction," installing a subordinate so talented that the CEO persuades himself failure is impossible. If the protege then fails to deliver, the CEO can't come to terms with it, especially if the protege is a succession candidate. Often these subordinates have been promoted into line jobs from staff positions or consulting firms, with their high-level executional abilities untested.

"He's my guy!" The problem of blind loyalty shows up more often than you may suspect. The boss and the subordinate may have worked together a long time; in some cases their families vacationed together. Judgment becomes blurred. Mention this to people who were around General Motors in the early '90s and they tend to nod vigorously and say, "Lloyd Reuss!" He became president when Robert Stempel became CEO, and many GM managers considered him a smooth talker who belonged nowhere near the company's pinnacle. Stempel emphatically disagreed, often putting his arm around Reuss' shoulders and exclaiming, "Lloyd's my guy!" Not anymore, said the board, as GM's losses sank to historic depths. When the directors took the chairman's title away from Stempel, they also demoted Reuss, and when they fired Stempel six months later, they booted Reuss too.

"I can coach him." The CEO of a FORTUNE 500 manufacturer brought in an outsider a few years ago to run North American operations and eventually become the next CEO. The executive missed his commitment the first year, then missed it again the second, causing the whole company to fall short of its publicly stated promises to Wall Street. The CEO decided he wasn't giving the subordinate enough coaching and resolved to help more. He was human. But was this response humane? It wasn't. Results continued to decline, the stock collapsed, and the company was taken over. Both executives are gone, later joined by several thousand employees deemed unneeded by the new owner. It isn't uncommon for a strong CEO, otherwise decisive, to be blind to this fatal flaw.

"Wall Street and the press like him—I'd better keep him around." When a failing subordinate forms strong links with these important constituencies—sometimes through his own public relations efforts—the CEO faces a dilemma. Poor performance hurts the company's results, but taking out the subordinate may hurt its image. Typically the CEO doesn't act until the problem is acute, and by then it's sometimes too late.

"I've fired a lot of people lately. The board won't like it if I sack another." Specifically, the board may begin to worry that the CEO isn't developing the company's leadership. But if the subordinate is failing, delaying action just makes the problem worse.

"He's in the job, and I'll take the devil I know over the devil I don't." The CEO may be insecure about his ability to hire an outsider, especially someone from outside the industry. If the company has a strong, insular culture, he may rationalize that the culture wouldn't accept an outsider.

We've heard all these statements, and they're virtually always a sign of trouble ahead. Quick action on problems in the top team is simply imperative. Bob Allen of AT&T deserves credit for trying to break company (and Bell System) tradition by concluding that his successor had to come from outside. He recruited four candidates—most notably President John Walter—but none worked out. When Walter got fired, the board seized control of the process, and the company took

FIVE SIGNS OF FAILURE: A SELF-TEST FOR CEOs

1. How's your performance—and your performance credibility?	Of course you have to deliver results, but you're unlikely to do so if you haven't developed performance forecasts for the next eight quarters, not just the usual four. You should have ideas now for changes you may have to make six to eight quarters out.
2. Are you focused on the basics of execution?	You should feel connected to the flow of information about your company and its markets; that includes regular, direct interaction with customers and front-line employees. Are you following through on all major commitments from your direct reports? Are you listening to the inner voice telling you whether these things are going well or badly?
3. Is bad news coming to you regularly?	Every company, even the most successful, has bad news, usually lots of it. If you're not hearing it, are you letting the trouble build? The information you get should force you to take competitors seriously.
4. Is your board doing what it should?	That means evaluating you and your direct reports, asking for information about your markets, and demanding a succession plan—but not formulating strategy (your job) or trying to manage operations.
5. Is your own team discontented?	Top subordinates often start bailing out before a CEO goes down.

SIX HABITS OF HIGHLY INEFFECTIVE CEOS

How did these chief executives come up short? Count the ways.

Not all would agree that these CEOs, chosen solely by FORTUNE, failed. Those who returned calls vigorously disputed it. All here were pushed, saw their company bought, or left a company that had lost its way.

[1] People Problems
[2] Decision Gridlock
[3] Lifer Syndrome
[4] Bad Earnings News
[5] Missing in Action
[6] Off-the-Deep-End Financials

CEO Name	COMPANY	TENURE	[1]	[2]	[3]	[4]	[5]	[6]
William Agee	MORRISON KNUDSEN	1988–95	X			X	X	
John Akers	IBM	1985-93		X	X	X		
Les Alberthal	EDS	1986–98	X	X	X	X		
Robert Allen	AT&T	1988–97	X	X				
Ron Allen	DELTA AIR LINES	1987–97	X		X			
Gil Amelio	APPLE COMPUTER	1996–97	X	X		X		
Joseph Antonini	KMART	1987–95	X	X	X	X		
Tom Barrett	GOODYEAR	1989–91		X	X	X		
Dean Buntrock	WASTE MANAGEMENT	1968–96	X		X			X
Mathis Cabiallavetta	UBS	1998			X			X
Al Dunlap	SUNBEAM	1996–98	X			X		X
Jeffrey Erickson	TWA	1994–96				X		
William Fields	BLOCKBUSTER	1996–97						
	HUDSON BAY	1997–99			X	X		
Walter Forbes	CUC	1976–97						X
Robert Ferguson	CONTINENTAL AIRLINES	1991–94	X			X		
Carl Hahn	VOLKSWAGEN	1982–92			X	X		
Robert Horton	BP	1990–92	X	X	X	X		
Arnold Langbo	KELLOGG	1992–99		X	X			
Paul Lego	WESTINGHOUSE	1990–93			X	X		
Philip Lippincott	SCOTT PAPER	1982–94			X	X		
Frank Lorenzo	CONTINENTAL AIRLINES	1972–90	X			X		
Michael Miles	PHILIP MORRIS	1991–94	X					
Robert Palmer	DIGITAL EQUIPMENT	1992–98		X		X		
Eckhard Pfeiffer	COMPAQ COMPUTER	1991–99	X	X		X		
Michael Quinlan	MCDONALD'S	1987–98		X	X	X		
James Robinson	AMERICAN EXPRESS	1977–93	X		X	X		
Charles Sanford	BANKERS TRUST	1987–96			X	X		X
Heinz Schimmelbusch	METALLGESELLSCHAFT	1988–93			X	X		X
Wolfgang Schmitt	RUBBERMAID	1993–98	X	X	X	X		
John Sculley	APPLE COMPUTER	1983–93				X	X	
William Smithburg	QUAKER OATS	1981–97			X	X		
Michael Spindler	APPLE COMPUTER	1993–96		X		X		
Robert Stempel	GENERAL MOTORS	1990–92	X	X	X	X		
Cornelis van der Klugt	PHILIPS	1986–90			X	X		
Kay Whitmore	KODAK	1990–93		X	X	X		
Stephen Wiggins	OXFORD HEALTH PLANS	1984–97			X	X		
Walter Williams	RUBBERMAID	1991–92	X					
John Zabriskie	PHARMACIA & UPJOHN	1994–97	X	X	X			

THE SUPERIOR CEO: A PROFILE

Our study of scores of CEOs, successful and otherwise, yields eight qualities that characterize the champs.

• Integrity, maturity, and energy.	The foundation on which everything else is built.
• Business acumen.	A deep understanding of the business and a strong profit orientation–an almost instinctive feel for how the company makes money.
• People acumen.	Judging, leading teams, growing and coaching people; cutting losses where necessary.
• Organizational acumen.	Engendering trust, sharing information, and listening expertly; diagnosing whether the organization is performing at full potential; delivering on commitments; changing, not just running, the business; being decisive and incisive.
• Curiosity, intellectual capacity, and a global mindset.	Being externally oriented and hungry for knowledge of the world; adept at connecting developments and spotting patterns.
• Superior judgment.	
• An insatiable appetite for accomplishment and results.	
• Powerful motivation to grow and convert learning into practice.	

considerable heat from Wall Street and the press. "If you have three or four people in the mill and some run short along the way, you can't wait," says Larry Bossidy of AlliedSignal, one of America's most successful CEOs. "You've got to make a change right then."

Yet you needn't be ruthless to get things done. Ron Allen's willingness to swing the ax so antagonized Delta's work force that the board asked him to leave. When Lou Gerstner parachuted in to fix the shambles John Akers had left of IBM, famously declaring that "the last thing IBM needs right now is a vision," he focused on execution, decisiveness, simplifying the organization for speed, and breaking the gridlock. Many expected heads to roll, yet initially Gerstner changed only the CFO, the HR chief, and three key line executives—and he has multiplied the stock's value tenfold. The best CEOs never hesitate to fire when they must, but the larger point is that they're deeply interested in people—far more so than failed CEOs are.

GE's Jack Welch loves to spot people early, follow them, grow them, and stretch them in jobs of increasing complexity. "We spend all our time on people," he says. "The day we screw up the people thing, this company is over." He receives volumes of information—good and bad, from multiple sources—and he and his senior team track executives' progress in detail through a system of regular reviews. His written feedback to subordinates is legendary: specific, constructive, to the point. Of course some come up short. When Welch committed the company to achieving six-sigma quality a few years ago, he evaluated how the beliefs of high-level executives aligned with six-sigma values. He confronted those who weren't on board and told them GE was not the place for them.

This continual pruning and nurturing gives GE a powerful competitive advantage few companies understand and even fewer achieve—extraordinary longevity in top executives. Consider: Robert Wright is in his 13th year running NBC; vice chairman Dennis Dammerman was CFO for 14 years; Gary Wendt ran GE Capital for 12 years; John Trani ran GE Medical for 11 years; vice chairman Eugene Murphy has been in top positions for 13 years, plastics chief Gary Rogers for 13 years, vice chairman John Opie for 16 years. Because Welch has the right people in the right jobs, he can leave them there and things tend to get better, not worse.

The motto of the successful CEO, worthy of inscription on his or her office wall, is "People first, strategy second."

Regular review of subordinates is a vital process, but every process carries a mortal danger—that the CEO will forget its purpose and begin to think that the process itself is what matters. It happens all the time. A CEO becomes committed to an organizational model. Maybe he insists on 100% consensus. Middle managers resort to informal networks to get things done. Cliques form. Indecisiveness takes over, and a fast-moving competitor grabs the advantage. Decision gridlock can happen to anyone, but it happens most often to CEOs who've spent a career with one company, especially a successful one. The processes have worked, they're part of the company's day-to-day life—so it takes real courage to blow them up.

Listen to Elmer Johnson, a top GM executive, describe this problem to the executive committee: "The meetings of our many committees and policy groups have become little more than time-consuming formalities. The outcomes are almost never in doubt. . . . There is a dearth of discussion, and almost never anything amounting to lively consideration. . . . It is a system that results in lengthy delays and faulty decisions by paralyzing the operating people. . . ." That was in 1988, during Roger Smith's troubled tenure, and the problem persisted through Stempel's brief reign. Neither man could break the process machine, and both must be considered failed CEOs.

Process gridlock is never good, but in the unforgivingly fast Internet age it's the way to catastrophe. It was a major problem during Gil Amelio's short time atop Apple Computer. Roger Siboni, who spent 20 years as a KPMG consultant, now runs a Silicon Valley startup called Epiphany and says the differences in process are stark: "You can't imagine the contrast here with the cordialness of corporate America. That whole world—meetings, facilitators . . . facilitators? Out here that would be ludicrous." There's just no time.

Effective CEOs use processes to drive decisions, not delay them. They start by focusing on initiatives that are clear, specific, and few, and they don't launch a new one until those in progress are embedded in the company's DNA. We've heard many employees, and so have you, speak witheringly about their CEO's flavor of the month—vision statements, quality, empowerment, leadership, all of which beget process and apparatus. By contrast, Welch has introduced just five major initiatives in 18 years as CEO (the most recent is e-commerce).

With their initiatives firm, effective CEOs implement them through a process that seems simple, even obvious, but has profound effects. Watch the likes of Welch or EDS's Richard Brown or Bossidy or any other proven implementer in a meeting. Near the end he'll grab a pen and start writing: He's noting exactly what is supposed to be done by whom, by when. He'll go over this with everyone before the meeting closes, and he'll probably send each one a reminder afterward.

It's fascinating to watch what happens when a CEO who executes well brings these habits into a company where they didn't exist. The whole tone changes. People prepare for meetings differently. They interact differently. They begin to see a fundamental distinction between failed CEOs and effective ones: For many failures, process is everything; for the great ones, commitments are everything. As Dick Brown says, "Delivering on commitments is the most important thing." Great CEOs hold people accountable, always.

Keeping track of all critical assignments, following up on them, evaluating them—isn't that kind of . . . boring? We may as well say it: Yes. It's boring. It's a grind. At least, plenty of really intelligent, accomplished, failed CEOs have found it so, and you can't blame them. They just shouldn't have been CEOs.

The big problem for them is not brains or even ability to identify the key problems or objectives of the company. When Kodak ousted Kay Whitmore, conventional wisdom said it was because he hadn't answered the big strategic questions about Kodak's role in a digital world. In fact, Kodak had created, though not publicized, a remarkably aggressive plan to remake itself as a digital imaging company. Whitmore reportedly embraced it. But he couldn't even begin to make it happen. Same story with William Agee at Morrison Knudsen—plausible strategy, no execution.

The problem for these CEOs is in the psyche. They find no reward in continually improving operations. Failing CEOs ask, "Why can't people do it themselves?" They're afraid of being seen as too controlling. The winners have what Bossidy calls "a drive to be competitive all the time—competitive in the operational sense." They get a charge out of pushing, pushing, pushing to make change happen.

That's why they're also constantly hungry for information from the battlefield. Effective CEOs have a strong external focus and get stimulated by details of what's happening in their markets, details that others might find boring. They're haunted by a familiar warning: "The CEO is always the last to know." They pull in loads of data from diverse sources. Then, as Welch says, you don't do what you want to do, you do what must be done—what reality demands.

Failed CEOs, by contrast, avoid facing market realities in all sorts of inventive ways. They remain in denial. They may become prisoners of one or two executives or of a guru or consulting firm, looking nowhere else for advice. Or they may look outward—but not at their markets.

Some CEOs get distracted by serving on too many boards. Others, like former American Express CEO James Robinson, see themselves as global ambassadors and lose focus. John Sculley became enamored of politics—he was a vocal supporter of Bill Clinton. By the final months of his tenure, the board realized he "was not focused on the day-to-day operations of Apple, other than on its technology," said former inside director Albert Eisenstat in a lawsuit. When profits deteriorated, the board asked him to leave.

But wait. In all this talk about CEOs and execution, aren't we forgetting someone? What about the COO? If operating the company isn't the job of the chief operating officer, whose is it?

Good question, but it doesn't get the CEO off the hook. Certainly some CEO-COO partnerships have been terrifically successful. Look at Tom Murphy and Dan Burke at Capital Cities/ABC or Roberto Goizueta and Don Keough at Coke. Today, Steve Case and Bob Pittman at AOL could be a winning team.

But be careful—these partnerships depend on a rare chemistry that's hard to predict, and the stakes are high. If it doesn't work, the resulting trouble is worse than most. Compounding it, the CEO must then fire the COO fast, which is often a problem.

Note how many of today's best CEOs, the master executors, don't even have a COO: Craig Barrett of Intel, Bossidy, John Chambers of Cisco, Michael Dell of Dell, Gerstner of IBM, Ray Gilmartin of Merck, Herb Kelleher of Southwest Airlines, Jacques Nasser of Ford, and Welch, among others. That's a multi-industry all-star team of CEOs who've put themselves squarely in charge of meeting their commitments and getting things done. Of America's ten most admired companies, as determined in FORTUNE's latest survey, eight don't have COOs (Microsoft and Wal-Mart are the exceptions). Most of the best CEOs seem to agree with Bossidy, who acknowledges that COOs can work but believes that someone needs to "know in total what's going on." His view: "It's best to have that responsibility invested in one as opposed to two people."

Any way you look at it, mastering execution turns out to be the odds-on best way for a CEO to keep his job. So what's the right way to think about that sexier obsession, strategy? It's vitally important—obviously. The problem is that our age's fascination with strategy and vision feeds the mistaken belief

I'LL EVEN PAY YA TO LEAVE

Why failed CEOs take so much of their shareholders' wealth with them.

It makes shareholders steam: When a CEO gets shoved out for poor performance, why does the board so often reward him with a mammoth severance package? EDS fires Les Alberthal and announces that his exit pay will knock down the quarter's earnings 12%. Waste Management crashes, and former CEO Dean Buntrock gets a $14 million goodbye. What's going on?

In this, as in most matters of CEO pay, there's more happening than meets the eye. Yes, the boards may have been profligate—but then again, maybe not.

In many of the highest-profile cases, directors were simply abiding by contracts negotiated months or years earlier. That was the case with John Walter at AT&T (who left with $25 million) and Michael Ovitz at Disney ($100 million), both of whom were hired as president and lasted less than a year. Attorney Joe Bachelder, America's No. 1 negotiator of top CEO employment deals, estimates that most FORTUNE 500 CEOs now have contracts, and many have learned that the time to negotiate severance is when the board still loves you and divorce seems unthinkable.

When a divorce does happen, much of what a CEO gets is what he would have received upon ordinary retirement. In Buntrock's case, most of that $14 million was a garden-variety supplemental retirement plan that had been building for 30 years. Even so, some Waste Management board members believe that Buntrock ought to contribute at least some of his pension toward the settlement of lawsuits stemming from accounting irregularities during his tenure.

With a contract, whether the booted boss gets a lot or a whole lot depends on whether he was fired "for cause." If so, he'll probably have to forfeit his unvested restricted stock and options and be forced to exercise vested options almost immediately, a penalty that could cost him tens of millions of dollars. Directors may believe they had ample cause for firing the S.O.B., but proving it is tough, so they often give him the big money and get it over with.

The stock holds a going-away party

Indeed, getting it over with—whatever the price—is sometimes the best thing for shareholders. Look what happened when Joe Antonini left Kmart, EDS fired Les Alberthal, Bill Smithburg departed Quaker Oats, and GM booted Bob Stempel. In each case the stock jumped immediately after the change at the top was announced—even though no successor had been named. That is a pretty clear indication that investors had already made up their minds that the CEO had to go, even if the board hadn't. And the severance package was worth every penny. —G.C.

that developing exactly the right strategy will enable a company to rocket past competitors. In reality, that's less than half the battle.

This shouldn't be surprising. Strategies quickly become public property. Ask Michael Dell the source of his competitive advantage, and he replies, "Our direct business model." Okay, Michael, but that's not exactly a secret. Everyone has known about it for years. How can it be a competitive advantage? His answer: "We execute it. It's all about knowledge and execution." Toyota offers anyone, including competitors, free, in-depth tours of its main U.S. operations—including product development and distributor relations. Why? The company knows visitors will never figure out its real advantage, the way it executes. Southwest Airlines is the only airline that has made money every year for the past 27 years. Everyone knows its strategy, yet no company has successfully copied its execution.

Yes, strategy matters. A good, clear strategy is necessary for success—but not sufficient for survival. So look again at all those derailed CEOs on the cover. They're smart people who worried deeply about a lot of things. They just weren't worrying enough about the right things: execution, decisiveness, follow-through, delivering on commitments.

Are you?

Dallas-based RAM CHARAN advises many FORTUNE 500 CEOs and is author of an acclaimed book on corporate governance, Boards at Work.

Unit 3

Unit Selections

15. **Evolution and Revolution As Organizations Grow,** Larry E. Greiner
16. **The Net-Phone-TV-Cable Monster,** *Business Week*
17. **You've Got Time Warner—How the Merger Will Affect Other Big Web and Media Players,** David Bank
18. **How 2 Executives Pulled Off the Biggest Merger Ever,** Allen R. Meyerson
19. **Why Diversify? Four Decades of Management Thinking,** Michael Goold and Kathleen Luchs
20. **A Powerhouse of Technology Decides to Split into 2 Units,** Lawrence M. Fisher
21. **How Gillette Wowed Wall Street,** *Business Week*
22. **The New Intel,** Andy Reinhardt
23. **How Formica Got Burned Out by Buyouts,** Debra Sparks
24. **Prada Goes Shopping,** Lauren Goldstein
25. **Doc Ebbers' Miracle Diet,** *Business Week*
26. **Market Place: Midwest Express Profits by Pampering Passengers,** Edwin McDowell
27. **Specialized Hospitals Taking Over Health-Care Market,** Allen R. Myerson
28. **Predators and Prey: A New Ecology of Competition,** James F. Moore
29. **The Changing Art of Becoming Unbeatable,** Geoffrey Colvin
30. **FedEx CEO Smith Bets His Deal with Cisco Will Recast the Future of Shipping,** Douglas A. Blackmon
31. **Creating Competitive (Dis)advantage: Learning from Food Lion's Freefall,** Gregory G. Dess and Joseph C. Picken
32. **Six Sigma Enlightenment; Managers Seek Corporate Nirvana through Quality Control,** Claudia H. Deutsch
33. **Inside the Cult of Costco,** Shelly Branch

Key Points to Consider

- The choice of corporate strategy rests on a firm's capabilities as well as on market conditions. As firms grow, the demands that are placed on management change. Managers must choose between diversification and concentration strategies.
- At the business level, firms must choose to compete on the basis of a differentiated product or service that supports a premium price, or they must provide the product or service at a price lower than that of their rivals.
- Firms that create some unique feature, or that offer superior service that their rivals cannot copy easily, create an advantage for themselves in their market.
- Lack of a coherent strategy can result in the ruination of an organization.

DUSHKINONLINE Links — www.dushkin.com/online/

18. **Advances in Strategic Management**
    http://www.mgmt.utoronto.ca/~baum/asm_index.html
19. **Design for Competitive Advantage**
    http://dfca.larc.nasa.gov/dfc/toc.html
20. **Equifax: Knowledge Engineering**
    http://www.equifaxknowledge.com
21. **GBN Scenario Planning**
    http://www.gbn.org/scenPlan.html
22. **High Performance Teams**
    http://rampages.onramp.net/~bodwell/home.htm
23. **NBS-Organizationand Management Theory**
    http://www.nbs.ntu.ac.uk/staff/lyerj/list/hromt.htm

These sites are annotated on pages 4 and 5.

Formulating Strategies

Strategy formulation is the art of designing the appropriate course of action to attain the goals of an organization. The first step is to define the mission of the firm. A firm's mission should not be confused with its goals. A firm's primary goal is to survive; if the firm does survive, its next goal is to be profitable. A mission statement, sometimes called a vision statement, explains the organization's reason for existing. A clear, concise mission statement should define what business the firm is in, and what customer it serves. Further elements may include such areas as technologies employed, ethical standards, and community service goals.

Most organizations hope to grow larger over time. Growth has many benefits, as well as a positive image. Organizations may grow internally, by reinvesting their retained earnings, by selling shares to others, or by taking on debt. They may grow externally by merger, acquisition, or vertical integration. As they grow, like any other human organism, however, they must constantly monitor the changes within and outside of the firm. In the most common growth scenario, a firm begins very small and is managed by a single owner. As it grows, it divides the workload into separate functional departments. Further growth involves increasing the width of the product line, then expanding geographically. In the last stage, firms integrate vertically, reducing their dependence on outside forces and internalizing whatever activities they can perform more efficiently than can outsiders.

The fundamental question facing the decision makers is whether to channel the resources for growth into a concentrated area or to engage in a variety of businesses. A concentration strategy, relying on a single, dominant product or service, offers a firm the possibility of dominating its marketplace. However, it increases their exposure to environmental changes if the firm has no alternative avenues. Some firms choose to limit their market to small segments. These niche marketers often serve markets that are highly specialized, too small for larger suppliers to serve, or require products or services that are not profitable for larger rivals.

Corporations commonly practice a diversification strategy to reduce risks of economic downturns or seasonal fluctuations. The individual companies may produce seemingly unrelated products or services. Common technologies, shared resources, and the use of the same distribution channels produce cost savings and marketing efficiencies. Some organizations, however, find that a diversification strategy eventually may lead to a loss of focus.

The ultimate unrelated diversification is the conglomerate form, a truly innovative form of corporate structure. In a conglomerate, large corporations acquire firms solely on their potential financial contribution. The basic assumption was that financing would be more efficient than through traditional capital markets. Because of the diversity of their component businesses, conglomerate managers were forced to rely on financial and statistical measures only to evaluate performance. Few true conglomerates exist today.

The final word on corporate growth may be supplied by the government. Antitrust laws mandate that combinations that have the effect of restraining competition are illegal. The Sherman Antitrust Act, passed in 1890, was a response to the public's perception that the popular organizational form at that time, the trust, served the owners' interests at the expense of those of the consumers. Over time, different court interpretations cast a varying light over what exactly constitutes restraint.

While corporate strategies define what business the company is in, the strategic question at the individual business level is how to compete. Firms compete for customers by providing some specific value. This can be accomplished by offering a more attractive price, or by differentiating the product or service in some way that customers see as worthy of a premium price. Cost leaders constantly seek ways to drive prices down. They reward cost-cutting measures, rely on high volume and low per-unit cost production, advertising, and distribution. Those who differentiate their product do so by innovating continually and building networks of loyal customers and dedicated distributors.

How can the strategies of successful high-growth organizations be explained? The underlying theme is the establishment of some competitive advantage. That advantage affords the firm a dominant position that rivals cannot easily duplicate. Competitive advantage may be the result of a patent, an improved process, a superior image, better workmanship, quicker response, more innovate design, or a variety of other sources that separate the firm from its rivals. Successful firms realize that some advantages are fleeting. Companies that built what appeared to be an advantage based on their early adoption of sophisticated computerization found that as computer prices fell, others were able to neutralize their hard-fought position.

Often competitive advantage is a result of being the first entrant into a market. While this has a high degree of risk, the first entrant is likely to attract the most capable employees, the best outlets and customers, and the most customer loyalty. Those first entrants must recognize the importance of sustaining that advantage.

The importance of luck merits serious consideration. Luck, both good and bad, has played a very important part in the success or demise of many organizations. Standard Oil Company's John D. Rockefeller was "lucky" when the automobile emerged and used petroleum as its fuel. The major use of petroleum up until that time had been for street and residential lighting, and the advent of electric power had destroyed that market.

Some will argue that good luck played a part in Microsoft's rise to dominance. Several events suggest that IBM's decision to outsource their operating system and the resulting language of the contract were "lucky" breaks for Microsoft.

Management practices that work well in one phase may bring on a crisis in another.

EVOLUTION AND REVOLUTION AS ORGANIZATIONS GROW

BY LARRY E. GREINER

KEY EXECUTIVES of a retail store chain hold on to an organizational structure long after it has served its purpose because the structure is the source of their power. The company eventually goes into bankruptcy.

A large bank disciplines a "rebellious" manager who is blamed for current control problems, when the underlying causes are centralized procedures that are holding back expansion into new markets. Many young managers subsequently leave the bank, competition moves in, and profits decline.

The problems at these companies are rooted more in past decisions than in present events or market dynamics. Yet management, in its haste to grow, often overlooks such critical developmental questions as, Where has our organization been? Where is it now? and What do the answers to these questions mean for where it is going? Instead, management fixes its gaze outward on the environment and toward the future, as if more precise market projections will provide the organization with a new identity.

In stressing the force of history on an organization, I have drawn from the legacies of European psychologists who argue that the behavior of individuals is determined primarily by past events and experiences, rather than by what lies ahead. Extending that thesis to problems of organizational development, we can identify a series of developmental phases through which companies tend to pass as they grow. Each phase begins with a period of evolution, with steady growth and stability, and ends with a revolutionary period of substantial organizational turmoil and change—for instance, when centralized practices eventually lead to demands for decentralization. The reso-

This article originally appeared in the JulyAugust 1972 issue of HBR. For the article's republication as a Classic, the author has removed some outdated material from the opening sections. He has also written a commentary, 'Revolution Is Still Inevitable," to update his observations.

Larry E. Greiner is a professor of management and organization at the University of Southern California's Marshall School of Business in Los Angeles.

lution of each revolutionary period determines whether or not a company will move forward into its next stage of evolutionary growth.

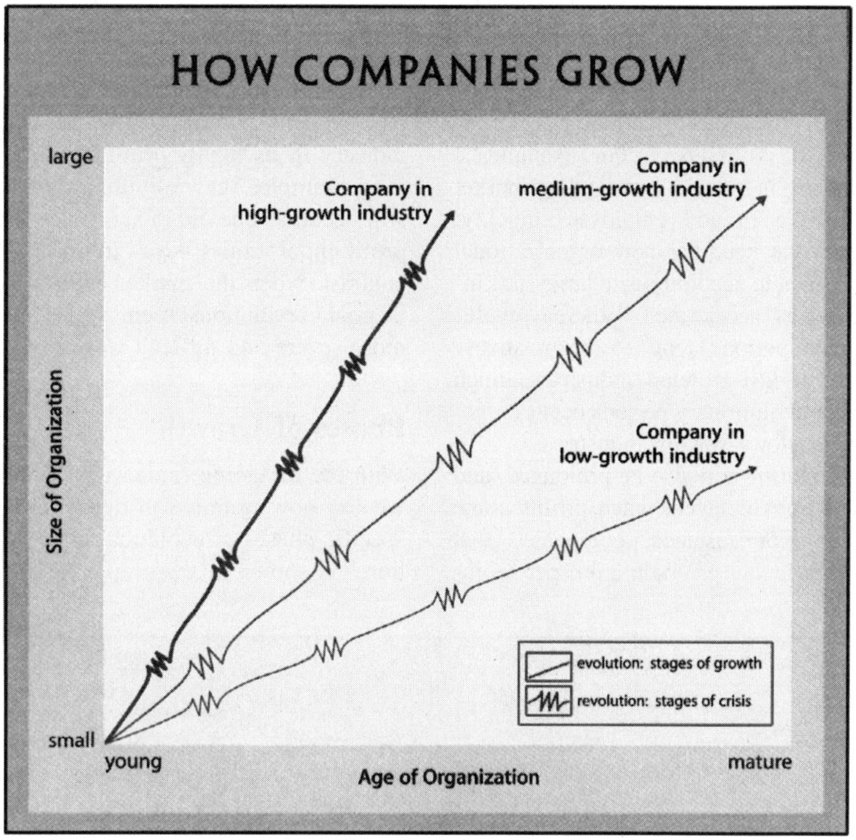

A Model of How Organizations Develop

To date, research on organizational development has been largely empirical, and scholars have not attempted to create a model of the overall process. When we analyze the research, however, five key dimensions emerge: an organization's age and size, its stages of evolution and revolution, and the growth rate of its industry. The graph "How Companies Grow" shows how these elements interact to shape an organization's development.

Age of the Organization. The most obvious and essential dimension for any model of development is the life span of an organization (represented on the graph as the horizontal axis). History shows that the same organizational practices are not maintained throughout a long life span. This demonstrates a most basic point: management problems and principles are rooted in time. The concept of decentralization, for example, can describe corporate practices at one period but can lose its descriptive power at another.

Managerial problems and practices are rooted in time. They do not last throughout the life of an organization.

The passage of time also contributes to the institutionalization of managerial attitudes. As these attitudes become rigid and eventually outdated, the behavior of employees becomes not only more predictable but also more difficult to change.

Size of the Organization. This dimension is depicted on the chart as the vertical axis. A company's problems and solutions tend to change markedly as the number of its employees and its sales volume increase. Problems of coordination and communication magnify, new functions emerge, levels in the management hierarchy multiply, and jobs become more interrelated. Thus, time is not the only determinant of structure; in fact, organizations that do not become larger can retain many of the same management issues and practices over long periods.

Stages of Evolution. As organizations age and grow, another phenomenon emerges: prolonged growth that we can term the *evolutionary period.* Most growing organizations do not expand for two years and then contract for one; rather, those that survive a crisis usually enjoy four to eight years of continuous growth without a major economic setback or severe internal disruption. The term evolution seems appropriate for describing these quiet periods because only modest adjustments appear to be necessary for maintaining growth under the same overall pattern of management.

Stages of Revolution. Smooth evolution is not inevitable or indefinitely sustainable; it cannot be assumed that organizational growth is linear. Fortune's "500" list, for example, has had considerable turnover during the last 50 years. In fact, evidence from numerous case histories reveals periods of substantial turbulence interspersed between smoother periods of evolution.

We can term the turbulent times *periods of revolution* because they typically exhibit a serious upheaval of management practices. Traditional management practices that were appropriate for a smaller size and earlier time no longer work and are brought under scrutiny by frustrated top-level managers and disillusioned lower-level managers. During such periods of crisis, a number of companies fall short. Those that are unable to abandon past practices and effect major organizational changes are likely either to fold or to level off in their growth rates.

The critical task for management in each revolutionary period is to find a new set of organizational practices that will become the basis for managing the next period of evolutionary growth. Interestingly enough, those new practices eventually sow the seeds of their own decay and lead to another period of revolution. Managers therefore experience the irony of seeing a major solution in one period become a major problem in a later period.

Growth Rate of the Industry. The speed at which an organization experiences phases of evolution and revolution is closely related to the market environment of its industry. For example, a company in a rapidly expanding market will have to add employees quickly; hence, the need for new organizational structures to accommodate large staff increases is accelerated. Whereas evolutionary periods tend to be relatively short in fast-growing industries, much longer evolutionary periods occur in mature or slow-growing industries.

Evolution can also be prolonged, and revolutions delayed, when profits come easily. For instance, companies that make grievous errors in a prosperous industry can still look good on their profit-and-loss statements; thus, they can buy time before a crisis forces changes in management practices. The aerospace industry in its highly profitable infancy is an example. Yet revolutionary periods still occur, as one did in aerospace when profit opportunities began to dry up. By contrast, when the market environment is poor, revolutions seem to be much more severe and difficult to resolve.

Phases of Growth

With the foregoing framework in mind, we can now examine in depth the five specific phases of evolution and revolution. As shown in the graph "The Five Phases of Growth," each evolutionary period is characterized by the dominant management style used to achieve growth; each revolutionary period is characterized by the dominant management problem that must be solved before growth can continue. The pattern presented in the chart seems to be typical for companies in industries with moderate growth over a long period; companies in faster-growing industries tend to experience all five phases more rapidly, whereas those in slower-growing industries encounter only two or three phases over many years.

It is important to note that each phase is at once a result of the previous phase and a cause for the next phase. For ex-

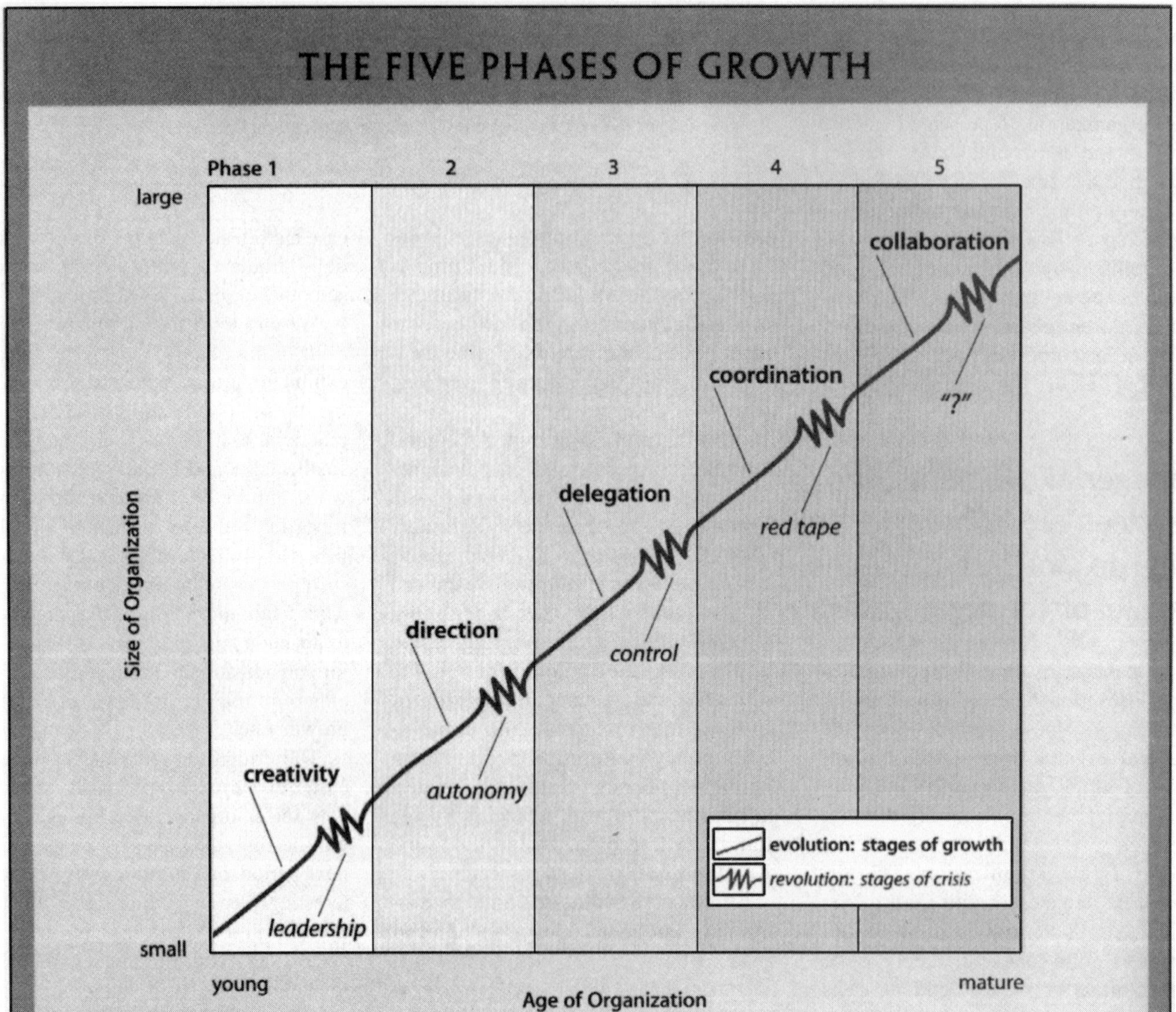

ample, the evolutionary management style in Phase 3 is delegation, which grows out of and becomes the solution to demands for greater autonomy in the preceding Phase 2 revolution. The style of delegation used in Phase 3, however, eventually provokes a revolutionary crisis that is characterized by attempts to regain control over the diversity created through increased delegation.

Creative activities are essential for a company to get off the ground. But as the company grows, those very activities become the problem.

For each phase, managers are limited in what they can do if growth is to occur. For example, a company experiencing an autonomy crisis in Phase 2 cannot return to directive management for a solution; it must adopt a new style—delegation—in order to move forward.

Phase 1: Creativity. In the birth stage of an organization, the emphasis is on creating both a product and a market. The following are the characteristics of the period of creative evolution:

- The founders of the company are usually technically or entrepreneurially oriented, and they generally disdain management activities; their physical and mental energies are absorbed entirely by making and selling a new product.
- Communication among employees is frequent and informal.
- Long hours of work are rewarded by modest salaries and the promise of ownership benefits.
- Decisions and motivation are highly sensitive to marketplace feedback; management acts as customers react.

All the foregoing individualistic and creative activities are essential for a company to get off the ground. But as the company grows, those very activities become the problem. Larger production runs require knowledge about the efficiencies of manufacturing. Increased numbers of employees cannot be managed exclusively through informal communication, and new employees are not motivated by an intense dedication to the product or organization. Additional capital must be secured, and new accounting procedures are needed for financial control. The company's founders find themselves burdened with unwanted management responsibilities. They long for the "good old days" and try to act as they did in the past. Conflicts among harried leaders emerge and grow more intense.

At this point, a *crisis of leadership* occurs, which is the onset of the first revolution. Who will lead the company out of confusion and solve the managerial problems confronting it? Obviously, a strong manager is needed—one who has the necessary knowledge and skills to introduce new business techniques. But finding that manager is easier said than done. The founders often resist stepping aside, even though they are probably temperamentally unsuited to the job. So here is the first critical choice in an organization's development: to locate and install a strong business manager who is acceptable to the founders and who can pull the organization together.

Phase 2: Direction. Those companies that survive the first phase by installing a capable business manager usually embark on a period of sustained growth under able, directive leadership. Here are the characteristics of this evolutionary period:

- A functional organizational structure is introduced to separate manufacturing from marketing activities, and job assignments become increasingly specialized.
- Accounting systems for inventory and purchasing are introduced.
- Incentives, budgets, and work standards are adopted.
- Communication becomes more formal and impersonal as a hierarchy of titles and positions grows.
- The new manager and his or her key supervisors assume most of the responsibility for instituting direction; lower-level supervisors are treated more as functional specialists than as autonomous decision-making managers.

Although the new directive techniques channel employees' energy more efficiently into growth, they eventually become inappropriate for controlling a more diverse and complex organization. Lower-level employees find themselves restricted by a cumbersome and centralized hierarchy. They have come to possess more direct knowledge about markets and machinery than do their leaders at the top; consequently, they feel torn between following procedures and taking initiative on their own.

Thus, the second revolution emerges from a *crisis of autonomy*. The solution adopted by most companies is to move toward more delegation. Yet it is difficult for top-level managers who previously were successful at being directive to give up responsibility to lower-level managers. Moreover, the lower-level managers are not accustomed to making decisions for themselves. As a result, numerous companies founder during this revolutionary period by adhering to centralized methods, while lower-level employees become disenchanted and leave the organization.

Phase 3: Delegation. The next era of growth evolves from the successful application of a decentralized organizational structure. It exhibits these characteristics:

- Much greater responsibility is given to the managers of plants and market territories.
- Profit centers and bonuses are used to motivate employees.
- Top-level executives at headquarters limit themselves to managing by exception based on periodic reports from the field.
- Management often concentrates on acquiring outside enterprises that can be lined up with other decentralized units.
- Communication from the top is infrequent and usually occurs by correspondence, telephone, or brief visits to field locations.

The delegation phase allows companies to expand by means of the heightened motivation of managers at lower levels. Managers in decentralized organizations, who have greater authority and incentives, are able to penetrate larger markets, respond faster to customers, and develop new products.

A serious problem eventually emerges, however, as top-level executives sense that they are losing control over a highly diversified field operation. Autonomous field managers prefer to run their own shows without coordinating plans, money, technology, and personnel with the rest of the organization. Freedom breeds a parochial attitude.

Soon, the organization falls into a *crisis of control.* The Phase 3 revolution is under way when top management seeks to regain control over the company as a whole. Some top-management teams attempt a return to centralized management, which usually fails because of the organization's newly vast scope of operations. Those companies that move ahead find a new solution in the use of special coordination techniques.

Phase 4: Coordination. The evolutionary period of the coordination phase is characterized by the use of formal systems for achieving greater coordination and by top-level executives taking responsibility for the initiation and administration of these new systems. For example:

The delegation phase brings a new period of growth, but freedom eventually breeds a parochial attitude.

- Decentralized units are merged into product groups.
- Formal planning procedures are established and intensively reviewed.
- Numerous staff members are hired and located at headquarters to initiate companywide programs of control and review for line managers.
- Capital expenditures are carefully weighed and parceled out across the organization.
- Each product group is treated as an investment center where return on invested capital is an important criterion used in allocating funds.
- Certain technical functions, such as data processing, are centralized at headquarters, while daily operating decisions remain decentralized.
- Stock options and companywide profit sharing are used to encourage employees to identify with the organization as a whole.

All these new coordination systems prove useful for achieving growth through the more efficient allocation of a company's limited resources. The systems prompt field managers to look beyond the needs of their local units. Although these managers still have a great deal of decision-making responsibility, they learn to justify their actions more carefully to a watchdog audience at headquarters.

A lack of confidence, however, gradually builds between line and staff, and between headquarters and the field. The many systems and programs introduced begin to exceed their usefulness. A *red-tape crisis* is in full swing. Line managers, for example, increasingly resent direction from those who are not familiar with local conditions. And staff people, for their part, complain about uncooperative and uninformed line managers. Together, both groups criticize the bureaucratic system that has evolved. Procedures take precedence over problem solving, and innovation dims. In short, the organization has become too large and complex to be managed through formal programs and rigid systems. The Phase 4 revolution is under way.

Phase 5: Collaboration. The last observable phase emphasizes strong interpersonal collaboration in an attempt to overcome the red-tape crisis. Where Phase 4 was managed through formal systems and procedures, Phase 5 emphasizes spontaneity in management action through teams and the skillful confrontation of interpersonal differences. Social control and self-discipline replace formal control. This transition is especially difficult for the experts who created the coordination systems as well as for the line managers who relied on formal methods for answers.

The Phase 5 evolution, then, builds around a more flexible and behavioral approach to management. Here are its characteristics:

- The focus is on solving problems quickly through team action.
- Teams are combined across functions to handle specific tasks.
- Staff experts at headquarters are reduced in number, reassigned, and combined into interdisciplinary teams that consult with, not direct, field units.
- A matrix-type structure is frequently used to assemble the right teams for the appropriate problems.
- Formal control systems are simplified and combined into single multipurpose systems.
- Conferences of key managers are held frequently to focus on major problems.
- Educational programs are used to train managers in behavioral skills for achieving better teamwork and conflict resolution.
- Real-time information systems are integrated into daily decision-making processes.
- Economic rewards are geared more to team performance than to individual achievement.
- Experimenting with new practices is encouraged throughout the organization.

What will be the revolution in response to this stage of evolution? Many large U.S. companies are now in the Phase 5 evolutionary stage, so the answer is critical. Although there is little clear evidence regarding the outcome, I imagine that the revolution arising from the *"?" crisis* will center around the psychological saturation of employees who grow emotionally and physically exhausted from the intensity of teamwork and the heavy pressure for innovative solutions.

My hunch is that the Phase 5 revolution will be solved through new structures and programs that allow employees to periodically rest, reflect, and revitalize themselves. We may even see companies with dual organizational structures: a habit structure for getting the daily work done and a *reflective structure* for stimulating new perspective and personal enrichment. Employees could move back and forth between the two structures as their energies dissipate and are refueled.

One European organization has implemented just such a structure. Five reflective groups have been established outside the company's usual structure for the purpose of continuously evaluating five task activities basic to the organization. The groups report directly to

REVOLUTION IS STILL INEVITABLE

I wrote the first draft of this article while I was felled by a bad leg during a ski vacation in Switzerland. At the time, the business world was buzzing with numerous faddish techniques. Perhaps it was the size and height of the mountains that made me feel that there were deeper and more powerful forces at work in organizations.

Four basic points still seem valid about the model. First, we continue to observe major phases of development in the life of growing companies, lasting anywhere from 3 to 15 years each. Although scholars debate the precise length and nature of these phases, everyone agrees that each phase contains its own unique structure, systems, and leadership. The growth rate of the industry seems to determine the phases' length.

Second, transitions between developmental phases still do not occur naturally or smoothly, regardless of the strength of top management. All organizations appear to experience revolutionary difficulty and upheaval, and many of these organizations falter, plateau, fail, or get acquired rather than grow further. IBM before Lou Gerstner and General Electric before Jack Welch both suffered badly at the end of the fourth phase of coordination, when sophisticated management systems evolved into rigid bureaucracies.

Third, the logic of paradox underlying the model continues to ring true, although it often haunts and confuses the managerial psyche. Managers have difficulty in understanding that an organizational solution introduced by them personally in one phase eventually sows the seeds of revolution.

Fourth, the greatest resistance to change appears at the top because revolution often means that units under each senior executive will be eliminated or transformed. That is why we so often see new chief executives recruited from the outside and why senior managers frequently leave companies. Executives depart not because they are "bad" managers but because they just don't fit with where the company needs to go.

As for the differences that I have observed since the article's original publication, there is obviously much more "death" in the life of organizations today. Few organizations make it through all the phases of growth. If they don't fail, as most do in the initial phase of creativity and entrepreneurship, they often get acquired by companies that are in a later phase.

The phases are not as cleanly marked off as I depicted them. The vestiges of one phase remain as new approaches are introduced. Such overlaps are most notable in the case of the first-phase entrepreneur hanging on when professional management is added in the second phase of direction.

There are also miniphases within each evolutionary stage. The delegation phase, for example, does not typically begin with the complete decentralization of the entire organization into multiple product units, as the article implies. Usually one product group is launched, and then others are added over time. Also, as delegation—or *decentralization,* as I now prefer to call this phase—advances, senior managers at the corporate office are not as hands-off as I depicted them. The addition of multiple product or geographic units over time requires a sophisticated level of involvement by senior management to review strategies, evaluate results, and communicate the organization's values—but not to micromanage the units under them.

I would change some of the things I said about the fifth phase of collaboration. My original description of this phase suggests that the entire organization is turned into a matrix of teams. I now see the matrix as confined largely to senior management, where the heads of geographic areas, product lines, and functional disciplines collaborate as a team in order to ensure that their decisions are coordinated and implemented across global markets. The most significant change in phase occurs when the previously bureaucratic Phase 4 control-oriented staff and systems are replaced by a smaller number of consulting staff experts who help facilitate, rather than control, decisions.

My speculation that "psychological saturation" is the crisis ending Phase 5 now seems wrong. Instead, I think the crisis is one of realizing that there is no internal solution, such as new products, for stimulating further growth. Rather, the organization begins to look outside for partners or for opportunities to sell itself to a bigger company.

A sixth phase may be evolving in which growth depends on the design of extra-organizational solutions, such as creating a holding company or a network organization composed of alliances and cross-ownership. GE may have developed a similar model in which a periphery of companies is built around a core "money" company or bank (GE Capital) that attracts capital, earns high returns, and feeds the growth of other units.

I doubt that the advancement of information technology has made much of a difference in the basic aspects of the model. Information technology appears useful as a tool that evolves in different forms to fit each phase. For example, the Phase 2 functional organizational structure requires data that reflect revenue and cost centers, whereas Phase 3 decentralization needs data that measure profit center performance.

I wrote the article mainly about industrial and consumer goods companies, not about knowledge organizations or service businesses, which had yet to come into prominence. After recently studying a number of consulting, law, and investment firms, our research team found that those organizations also experience evolution and revolution as they grow.

In the first, entrepreneurial phase, the professional service firm pursues and tests a variety of market paths. The phase ends with the partners arguing about whether or not to stay together to concentrate on one partner's vision for the future. In the second phase, the firm focuses on one major service and eventually finds itself with a debate among the partners about whether to continue focusing on the current practice or to open another office or add additional services. A third phase of geographic or service expansion typically ends with a struggle over ownership: how much equity are the original partners willing to share with the younger partners who led the expansion and brought in new clients? The fourth phase involves institutionalizing the firm's name, reputation, and its standard way of operating, and ends in a crisis of cultural conformity in the face of which the firm must restore innovation and flexibility.

Finally, as a strong caveat, I always remind myself and others that the "ev and rev" model depicted in this article provides only a simple outline of the broad challenges facing a management concerned with growth. It is not a cookie-cutter solution or panacea. The rate of growth, the effective resolution of revolutions, and the performance of the company within phases still depend on the fundamentals of good management: skillful leadership, a winning strategy, the heightened motivation of employees, and a deep concern for customers.

ORGANIZATIONAL PRACTICES IN THE FIVE PHASES OF GROWTH

CATEGORY	PHASE 1	PHASE 2	PHASE 3	PHASE 4	PHASE 5
Management Focus	Make and sell	Efficiency of operations	Expansion of market	Consolidation of organization	Problem solving and innovation
Organizational Structure	Informal	Centralized and functional	Decentralized and geographical	Line staff and product groups	Matrix of teams
Top-Management Style	Individualistic and entrepreneurial	Directive	Delegative	Watchdog	Participative
Control System	Market results	Standards and cost centers	Reports and profit centers	Plans and investment centers	Mutual goal setting
Management Reward Emphasis	Ownership	Salary and merit increases	Individual bonus	Profit sharing and stock options	Team bonus

the managing director, although their findings are made public throughout the organization. Membership in each group includes all levels and functions in the company, and employees are rotated through the groups every six months.

Other concrete examples now in practice include providing sabbaticals for employees, moving managers in and out of hot-spot jobs, establishing a four-day workweek, ensuring job security, building physical facilities for relaxation during the workday, making jobs more interchangeable, creating an extra team on the assembly line so that one team is always off for reeducation, and switching to longer vacations and more flexible work hours.

The Chinese practice of requiring executives to spend time periodically on lower-level jobs may also be worth a nonideological evaluation. For too long, U.S. management has assumed that career progress should be equated with an upward path toward title, salary, and power. Could it be that some vice presidents of marketing might just long for, and even benefit from, temporary duty in field sales?

Implications of History

Let me now summarize some important implications for practicing managers. The main features of this discussion are depicted in the table "Organizational Practices in the Five Phases of Growth," which shows the specific management actions that characterize each growth phase. These actions are also the solutions that ended each preceding revolutionary period.

In one sense, I hope that many readers will react to my model by seeing it as obvious and natural for depicting the growth of an organization. To me, this type of reaction is a useful test of the model's validity.

But at a more reflective level, I imagine some of these reactions come more from hindsight than from foresight. Experienced managers who have been through a developmental sequence can identify that sequence now, but how did they react when in the midst of a stage of evolution or revolution? They can probably recall the limits of their own developmental understanding at that time. Perhaps they resisted desirable changes or were even swept emotionally into a revolution without being able to propose constructive solutions. So let me offer some explicit guidelines for managers of growing organizations to keep in mind.

Know where you are in the developmental sequence. Every organization and its component parts are at different stages of development. The task of top management is to be aware of the stages; otherwise, it may not recognize when the time for change has come, or it may act to impose the wrong solution.

Too often, it is tempting to choose solutions that were tried before but that actually make it impossible for the new phase to emerge.

Leaders at the top should be ready to work with the flow of the tide rather than against it; yet they should be cautious because it is tempting to skip phases out of impatience. Each phase produces certain strengths and learning experiences in the organization that will be essential for success in subsequent phases. A child prodigy, for example, may be able to read like a teenager, but he cannot behave like one until he matures through a sequence of experiences.

I also doubt that managers can or should act to avoid revolutions. Rather, these periods of tension provide the pressure, ideas, and awareness that afford a platform for change and the introduction of new practices.

Recognize the limited range of solutions. In each revolutionary stage, it becomes evident that the stage can come to a close only by means of certain specific solutions; moreover, these solutions are different from those that were applied to the problems of the preceding revolution. Too often, it is tempting to choose solutions that were tried before but that actually make it impossible for the new phase of growth to evolve.

Management must be prepared to dismantle current structures before the revolutionary stage becomes too turbulent. Top-level managers, realizing that their own managerial styles are no longer appropriate, may even have to take themselves out of leadership positions. A good Phase 2 manager facing Phase 3 might be wise to find a position at another Phase 2 organization that better fits his or her talents, either outside the company or with one of its newer subsidiaries.

Finally, evolution is not an automatic affair; it is a contest for survival. To move ahead, companies must consciously introduce planned structures that not only solve a current crisis but also fit the next phase of growth. That requires considerable self-awareness on the part of top management as well as great interpersonal skills in persuading other managers that change is needed.

Realize that solutions breed new problems. Managers often fail to recognize that organizational solutions create problems for the future, such as when a decision to delegate eventually causes a problem of control. Actions in the past determine much of what will happen to a company in the future.

An awareness of this effect should help managers evaluate company problems with a historical understanding instead of pinning the blame on a current development. Better yet, it should place managers in a position to predict problems and thereby to prepare solutions and coping strategies before a revolution gets out of hand.

Top management that is aware of the problems ahead could well decide not to expand the organization. Managers may, for instance, prefer to retain the informal practices of a small company, knowing that this way of life is inherent in the organization's limited size, not in their congenial personalities. If they choose to grow, they may actually grow themselves out of a job and a way of life they enjoy.

And what about very large organizations? Can they find new solutions for continued evolution? Or are they reaching a stage when the government will act to break them up because they are too large?

Clearly, there is still much to learn about processes of development in organizations. The phases outlined here are merely five in number and are still only approximations. Researchers are just beginning to study the specific developmental problems of structure, control, rewards, and management style in different industries and in a variety of cultures.

One should not, however, wait for conclusive evidence before educating managers to think and act from a developmental perspective. The critical dimension of time has been missing for too long from our management theories and practices. The intriguing paradox is that by learning more about history, we may do a better job in the future.

THE NET-PHONE-TV-CABLE MONSTER

AT&T grabs for an all-in-one pipeline into millions of homes

You'd think he was running a hot Internet startup, not big old AT&T. Just six weeks after completing the $54 billion acquisition of cable giant Tele-Communications Inc., AT&T CEO C. Michael Armstrong on Apr. 22 announced an audacious $54 billion bid for MediaOne Group, trumping an earlier offer for the 5-million subscriber cable operator by Comcast Corp. If he pulls it off, Armstrong will make AT&T the biggest player in cable, with systems reaching no less than 60% of U.S. cable households—if you count all TCI's and MediaOne's wholly owned systems and various partnerships.

And Armstrong isn't fazed by the prospect of a counterbid by Comcast—even if the Philadelphia-based cable operator manages to enlist mighty backers like Microsoft Corp., or America Online Inc. to boost its standing $48 billion offer for MediaOne. "Since this is of such value to us," Armstrong says, "I'm not prepared to do anything but win."

WIRELESS, TOO. Why? Because the MediaOne deal is more than simply the next step in AT&T's strategy to offer local phone service via cable. The back-to-back cable deals would transform AT&T into a digital leviathan with high-speed "broadband" pipes into millions of homes over which to offer bundles of voice,

SHAKING UP THE INDUSTRY

How AT&T's MediaOne bid changes the landscape:

AT&T

The phone company transforms into a broadband juggernaut reaching 60% of U.S. cabled households. But AT&T's buying binge is making shareholders jittery.

MICROSOFT

With $1 billion already invested in Comcast, Microsoft may want to limit AT&T's control of broadband software and technology by helping a Comcast counterbid.

BABY BELLS

If the new millennium's preferred telecom provider must offer telephony, cable, and Internet access, then the Bells must play catch-up to AT&T, which is almost there.

COMCAST

If it doesn't counterbid, it and other big cable operators may be forced to consolidate to create clusters big enough to deliver broadband competitively.

AMERICA ONLINE

Since cable-modem services At Home and Road Runner could end up under AT&T's roof, AOL might back Comcast to ensure itself a seat at the high-speed access table.

TIME WARNER

The media giant is close to finalizing a local phone deal with AT&T and stands to benefit from unwinding strained partnerships with MediaOne in cable and Road Runner.

video, and Internet services. With MediaOne, AT&T would have the leading Net-over-cable services: At Home, which it controls, and Road Runner, in which MediaOne is the co-controlling shareholder. And, just to make the bundle complete, AT&T can throw its wireless service in, too.

Nobody else even comes close in terms of being able to deliver the long-prophesied convergence of telecom, media, and Internet access. That alone virtually guarantees a flurry of dealmaking as everyone from Microsoft to the Baby Bells to AOL tries to keep up. "You don't have clearly defined lines anymore—everyone's in competition with everyone to become the living-room brand of the future," says Francis O. McInerney, principal of communications consultant North River Ventures Inc. in New York. "All of a sudden, AT&T has become a real contender for living-room dominance.

The Baby Bells are already crying foul—pointing out that they still have to jump through regulatory hoops to compete with AT&T in its core long-distance business. "I think it's grossly unfair," says Edward E. Whitacre Jr., CEO of SBC Communications Inc. "They're just running around gobbling up companies. We are being held to a terrible double standard." Baby Bell executives fear that if AT&T—or somebody else—can offer their customers a bundle of communications and media services first, they'll never win those ratepayers back. "If the Bells wait until AT&T is punching them in the nose," warns Atlanta-based independent telecommunications analyst Jeffrey Kagan, "they are going to be losing a lot of market share."

To get to where AT&T is headed, the Bells will have to come up with video service and accelerate the rollout of broadband technology for high-speed Internet access over phone lines. One likely shortcut, say Wall Street and industry analysts: team up with direct satellite operators. This could come about either through acquisitions or alliances. Bell Atlantic—which backed out of a merger deal with TCI in 1994—already offers DirecTV in some cities. "I would bet that you are going to see Bell operating companies buy EchoStar and DirecTV," says one top media exec.

AT&T's long-distance rivals also have to make some strategic adjustments. Sprint, for instance, has been gearing up a broadband strategy with multiple options. Its customers can connect via ADSL, which allows high-speed connections over copper

AOL EYES A HOT NEW MEDIUM: RADIO

What's the next medium that America Online Inc. hopes to conquer? Try radio. The online giant, BUSINESS WEEK has learned, is negotiating to buy an equity stake in Dallas-based Chancellor Media Corp. and gain rights to broadcast Chancellor programming across the AOL system on the Internet. The talks come just weeks after AOL's main Internet portal rival, Yahoo! Inc., agreed to pay $5.6 billion for Broadcast.com Inc., the top provider of audio and video programming over the Internet.

Media industry insiders say that America Online is expected to invest a relatively modest amount—$250 million or so—in Chancellor in exchange for exclusive rights to feature the company's radio stations on the Internet. Following Chancellor's acquisition of San Antonio-based Capstar Broadcasting Corp. this summer, it will be the nation's largest radio chain, with 469 stations in 106 markets. The talks, which a source close to Chancellor say began in early April, could result in a deal by late May.

MULTIMEDIA HOOK. For AOL, which has long been searching for a broadcast strategy, linking up with Chancellor could be an important step. Like Broadcast.com, a new AOL/Chancellor service could offer "streaming" programming, which allows PC users to view and/or hear content as it is broadcast. Streaming also makes it possible to use the Net for services such as teleconferencing. At a minimum, it would give AOL a stronger multimedia hook to keep its 17 million customers online. AOL declined comment on any potential deal.

The investment could be a boon to Chancellor, which has suffered through management turmoil and sluggish stock performance during the past year. Since Chancellor underwent a major restructuring in March that included ousting its chief executive and scrapping lofty plans to turn it into a multimedia giant, investors have been warily awaiting the next big move.

While declining to comment on AOL or any other potential Internet deals, Chancellor Chairman and Chief Executive Thomas O. Hicks says his company plans to become a major Internet player by getting Chancellor stations onto local Web portals and by creating new Internet-based radio stations. Then, Chancellor's sales staff could sell Internet advertising along with radio air time. "We have more than 65 million listeners around the country. That gives us a tremendous ability to help drive listeners to Internet portals," says Hicks, who is also chairman and CEO of the Dallas-based investment firm Hicks, Muse, Tate & Furst Inc., Chancellor's founder and controlling shareholder. "We see the Internet as a major growth opportunity."

STERN STUFF? Chancellor is far from the only radio player looking for new growth on the Web. CBS Corp.'s Infinity Broadcasting Corp., for one, is laying plans for an independently run Web site that will feature its 160 radio stations as well as additional content from such syndicated stars as Howard Stern and Don Imus.

"No one knows what the commercial viability of this is really going to be," says J. T. Anderton of radio consultancy Duncan's American Radio. "But the Internet offers the prospect of doing some very specific, very targeted programming for a very specific, very targeted advertising customer." That seems to be what AOL and Chancellor are banking on.

By Stephanie Anderson Forest in Dallas and Richard Siklos in New York, with Catherine Yang in Washington

wire. And recently it bought two "wireless" cable systems that can reach 18 million households via radio waves in such markets as Chicago and Denver. Wireless cable could also support broadband services.

For the rest of the cable industry, the immediate result of AT&T's deals may be more consolidation. For example, if Comcast can't or won't beat the AT&T bid, cable execs say it's likely to seek another merger, perhaps with Cox Communications Inc. Similarly, billionaire Paul Allen, who has spent $6 billion buying up cable systems, is said to be considering backing a MediaOne bid.

The wild cards are Microsoft and AOL. Microsoft has a $1 billion stake in Comcast, and a source close to the cable company confirms that both the software giant and AOL are considering backing a counteroffer for MediaOne. Neither company nor Comcast would comment on a possible MediaOne bidding alliance. But AOL CEO Stephen M. Case said in the company's Apr. 27 earnings announcement: "We want to embrace every broadband technology, certainly including cable."

FCC'S DREAM? Even before AT&T made its play for MediaOne, though, AOL and other Internet companies were raising concerns at the Federal Communications Commission about creating a level playing field in broadband. They want the FCC to ensure equal access to cable customers, rather than letting AT&T give At Home or Road Runner an edge.

But the agency has not granted that request. Nor is it voicing concern yet over AT&T's new cable prowess. It may figure that competitors will respond by building new broadband capabilities that will benefit consumers. "The goal is to get the infrastructure deployed as quickly as we can," says FCC Chairman William E. Kennard. Indeed, former FCC Chairman Reed Hundt hails the AT&T/MediaOne deal as exactly what the 1996 Telecommunications Act called for. "AT&T is putting its money where the government has asked the bets be placed," says Hundt, now a McKinsey & Co. consultant.

Even if the Feds give the deal a thumbs up and no counteroffers materialize, there are still obstacles to AT&T's deal. For one, Armstrong's shareholders may question his huge bet on an unproven strategy of selling local phone service over cable. Also unclear is how the deal will affect the media world's shifting, often conflicting alliances.

On that score, Time Warner Inc. may welcome the AT&T deal. MediaOne owns 25% of a Time Warner subsidiary that houses much of its cable holdings, and the two companies also co-control Road Runner. While Time Warner officials say they are not taking sides in the battle, Time Warner recently drew closer to AT&T by agreeing to offer AT&T's phone service over its cable lines. But media observers say that if Time Warner threatens to back a new Comcast bid, it could benefit both from unwinding the MediaOne partnership and extracting better terms from AT&T.

Already, closing the Time Warner/AT&T local phone deal has taken longer than expected. Although the companies deny it, analysts are speculating that the difficulty of defining which services AT&T can offer and which would remain solely Time Warner's has led to the delay. Striking similar deals with cable operators "has been harder than they thought," says a top executive at another cable operator.

Indeed, AT&T had put similar talks with Comcast, MediaOne, and Cox on hold earlier this year, until it worked out the Time Warner deal as amended. Armstrong says it was a combination of the difficulty in securing deals with other operators and the help of cable pioneer and dissident MediaOne shareholder Amos B. Hostetter Jr. that led to AT&T's unsolicited bid.

Another risk of Armstrong's offensive strategy: He could end up alienating other cable companies that he wants to use to sell phone service. Says Armstrong: "If you don't control the asset, I don't know how you control the destiny." Everyone from Comcast to Microsoft to AOL is wondering the same thing.

By Richard Siklos in New York, and Amy Barrett in Philadelphia, with Catherine Yang in Washington and Roger Crockett in Chicago

You've Got Time Warner!

How the Merger Will Affect Other Big Web and Media Players

By David Bank

WALT DISNEY

Strategic Advantages: Disney acquired Infoseek and created the Go Network Internet portal to try to turn itself into an online competitor of AOL, Yahoo and other Web titans. The Go Network includes key Disney properties like ESPN.com, Disney.com and ABC NEWS.com. Go.com's advantage is the strength of its individual sites. ESPN.com, for example, is the longtime leader in online sports news.

Disney has also jumped into e-commerce with an online version of its Disney Stores unit and a majority stake in retailer Toysmart.com. Last year, it issued a new class of stock, called Go.com, to track all its Internet properties.

Disney has also been aggressive in trying to foster the convergence between television and the Internet.

What Now: Disney will be cited as a possible merger partner for any number of concerns. That probably doesn't jibe with CEO Michael Eisner's vision, but Disney's ability to continue on its own may hinge on shoring up weaknesses. While some individual Disney sites have done well, the Go Network portal hasn't yet challenged Yahoo and the others.

The talk about Disney is likely to focus on whether it can partner or merge with Web concerns like Yahoo! and/or cable companies like AT&T. Opportunities for such alliances may grow if AOL's existing partners begin to feel like outsiders.

NEWS CORP.

Strategic Advantages: News Corp. is one of the few media giants that can truly call themselves global.

The Australian-based owner of the Fox TV network and Fox movie studio controls a ring of satellite channels around the world that are upgrading to digital platforms. These platforms—BskyB in the U.K., Star TV in Asia and Sky Latin America—can essentially act like a broadband pipeline to distribute both video channels and Internet services to subscribers.

The company's chief executive, Rupert Murdoch, is the only media company head who acts like a head of state: He is chummy with presidents and prime ministers. And in recent years he has spent time in China hoping to establish a foothold when, and if, it opens its market to outsiders.

What Now: After a late start, News Corp. woke up to the reality of the Internet and the digital economy two years ago. Since then it has made a rapid-fire series of investments in various dot-com companies, including TheStreet.com, free Internet service and e-mail provider Juno, Spanish-language portal Yupi and medical information service Healtheon/WebMD, among others.

Its challenge is marketing its sprawling satellite system into actual subscriptions on the ground. The company is betting that satellites will be the preferred broadband distribution pipeline outside the U.S., but it isn't clear there is a market to support its billion-dollar-plus investment to date.

EXCITE AT HOME

Strategic Advantages: Working in partnership with many of the biggest cable-TV companies, Excite At Home has built an Internet-access network that offers remarkably fast online connections—at least when everything works. Web surfers can zip from one page to another as quickly as if they were switching TV channels. Even online video, which doesn't really transport well with phone-line modems, becomes an option.

As of Dec. 31, analysts estimate, At Home had about 1.1 million users of its high-speed service. Its cable partners include AT&T, Comcast, Cox Communications, Cablevision Systems and Rogers-Cablesystems.

What Now: Even before the AOL-Time Warner announcement, there was plenty of debate about whether At Home could keep its preferred position with cable-company partners, or whether other Internet service providers might gain equal access.

So far, that battle has been fought mostly in regulatory and lobbying circles. But with the sudden prospect that AOL will gain access to Time Warner's vast cable network, competition for At Home's leading position clearly is heating up.

At Home stock climbed about 3% yesterday, amid speculation that the company might itself become a merger candidate. A substantial block of At Home's stock is controlled by AT&T, which could probably block any deal it didn't like.

MICROSOFT

Strategic Advantages: AOL has risen in recent years to the top of Microsoft's list of most-feared competitors, but the two now appear to be pursuing different strategies. Having dabbled in media, Microsoft has reverted to being primarily a software-technology company.

In that effort, Microsoft's major advantage is still its Windows operating system, which will be installed on more than 100 million PCs this year, allowing the company to influence Internet-technology standards to its own advantage.

Microsoft also has influence over a slew of cable operators. Last year's $5 billion investment in AT&T Corp. was the biggest in a string of deals that have given Microsoft minority shares in cable companies in Europe, Latin America and Asia. All told, Microsoft has commitments to deploy its software on more than 10 million interactive-television set-top boxes.

Microsoft is also making a renewed push to gain subscribers for its MSN Internet-access service.

What Now: The AOL-Time Warner deal is likely to push Microsoft even closer to AT&T and other owners of "broadband" pipes. The goal: become the dominant provider of system software and Internet services for all digital devices. The company will also have an uneasy partnership with AOL as a minority investor in RoadRunner, a provider of high-speed Internet access over cable lines partly owned by Time Warner.

Microsoft commands the world's highest market value and lots of cash. But its ability to pursue major acquisitions is hampered by its antitrust troubles.

VIACOM

Strategic Advantages: Viacom Inc. has been looking to transfer its dominance in cable through its MTV, VH1 and Nickelodeon franchises to the Internet.

MTVi, the Internet arm of MTV Networks, is preparing an IPO with an expected market valuation of several billion dollars. Like most content providers, Viacom uses the Web to promote its programming assets. It has created Web sites for Nickelodeon and TV Land.

What Now: Viacom's acquisition of CBS gives it more content to play with, both from the CBS network, its cable holdings including Nashville Network, and CBS's Internet investments.

CBS has been taking a relatively low-risk approach to acquiring stakes in content providers while also steering clear of Internet service providers. CBS's investments have mostly come in the form of ad time in return for ownership stakes. CBS now has ownership positions in more than a dozen public and private new media companies, including iWon.com, CBS MarketWatch and CBS Sports-Line. It also has stakes in Hollywood.Com and MVP.Com. But Viacom's Internet plans could supersede CBS's Internet strategies.

The combined entities of CBS and Viacom make it a true powerhouse in traditional media such as television and film, but the Time Warner-AOL marriage may have it wondering if it needs to get even bigger. Viacom may rethink its content-only Internet strategy if it means that reaching consumers on the Web will get tougher.

SONY

Strategic Advantages: The same problems that handicap Sony in the television business in the U.S.—it doesn't own a broadcast network and has a very small presence in cable—haven't completely hampered the company from building a brand presence on the Internet through Sony.com.

In particular, through Sony Music Entertainment, the company has been very aggressive in its Internet strategies. It is a founding member of the Madison Project, a trial of IBM's systems for the digital download of music content with the five major music companies, and it's a member of the Secure Digital Music Initiative.

Sony Music Entertainment also has investments in Launch Media, Listen.com, OnRadio and AOL-owned Spinner.Com. It also owns Yupi.com, a portal for Latino users of the Internet that complements the company's Spanish TV network Telemundo and draws six million visitors a month.

The company also has a strong presence in games. Everquest, an Internet subscription game, has 40,000 users every night, according to Sony. Its interactive versions of "Wheel of Fortune" and "Jeopardy," which are produced by Sony's TV arm, are among the most popular on the Internet.

What Now: While the company has numerous investments and entertainment-related Web sites as well as its hardware and consumer electronic operations, it doesn't have the cachet of MTV or ESPN to package its content holdings around. It seems a candidate for a partnership down the road with an Internet service provider to ensure its content has distribution. Its ability to make such alliances may hinge on how the new Time Warner-AOL partnership treats other content providers.

AT&T

Strategic Advantages: The nation's largest long-distance company is also the biggest cable operator, with access to some 25 million customers following its pending acquisition of MediaOne. The company also aspires to bundle local, long-distance, Internet and entertainment services for delivery over its cable lines, not just the Internet and movies as AOL and Time Warner are expected to do.

Finally, AT&T still boasts perhaps the best-known brand in the communications industry. And its 63 million long-distance customers dwarf AOL's 20 million subscribers.

What Now: Suddenly, AT&T's acquisition of Tele-Communications Inc. and its ownership stake in Internet provider Excite At Home are dwarfed by AOL and Time Warner's proposed merger.

That hookup could push Excite At Home to the sidelines, exacerbating tensions between AT&T and its Internet partner, which apparently hasn't performed to AT&T's satisfaction.

Meanwhile, watch to see if AOL now cuts a deal with AT&T on the issue of "open access." AOL had been fighting with AT&T over access to AT&T's cable lines; now that AOL is seeking to become a big cable company, it may make nice in a bid to distribute its content to AT&T customers.

YAHOO!

Strategic Advantages: For the past few years, Yahoo's Web site has resembled an incredibly busy airport hub. Everyone passes through it, even if they really want to head somewhere else. That allowed the five-year-old company to amass an estimated $128 million in ad revenue last quarter as swarms of old-line and "dot-com" businesses paid to put their messages in front of people using Yahoo's popular—and free—Internet directories.

In recent months, Yahoo has also become a serious force in electronic commerce. It doesn't run any sizable online stores itself, but people wanting to buy books, humidifiers or almost anything else start their shopping journey at Yahoo, where search engines and ads help them find the right online stores.

Yahoo has also become one of the few new Internet companies to report consistent profits before acquisition charges. That has made it a darling among stock-market investors.

What Now: So far, Yahoo has chosen to line up most of its content from dozens of independent sources. That has kept costs down and has given Yahoo maximum flexibility to add whatever services users want.

But it means Yahoo doesn't have anything quite like the high-powered marketing pipeline that AOL and Time Warner could create for movies, music and magazines if their proposed merger is completed.

How 2 Executives Pulled Off the Biggest Merger Ever

By ALLEN R. MYERSON

NEW YORK—The Tiger and the Flying Horse would have been too obvious.

Instead, Lee Raymond, chairman and chief executive of the Exxon Corp., and Lucio Noto, his counterpart at the Mobil Corp. decided to refer to the companies they run by the code names Lion and Moose.

Thus began Lee and Lucio's intensely personal quest to pull off the world's largest corporate merger, a deal between two companies that were once part of a monolithic whole but which, during 87 years apart, had grown as proud and self-sufficient as sovereign empires.

For years, Raymond had insisted that others might seek alliances and mergers, but that Exxon could only be weakened by taking on a partner. Meanwhile, Noto had been looking for a huge acquisition or at least a merger of equals to lift his oil company, already the nation's second-largest, into Exxon's league.

Some of their board members were skeptical. Others were incredulous.

Even as Raymond and Noto negotiated in secret, the lawyers for both companies continued battling in court over Exxon's accusation that Mobil had infringed on a patent worth hundreds of millions of dollars. And even after they had summoned their respective directors to gather in New York on Tuesday morning to ratify the deal, last-minute hitches kept them up late into the wee hours.

The $80 billion agreement they reached demonstrates that even in an era of corporate megamergers that require the efforts of battalions of investment bankers and lawyers, the most important deals still can come down to the leaders' outlook and character.

"To an unusual extent, the CEO's established this deal," said one participant. "Those two men deserve the credit."

Both chief executives, passionately analytical, ordered up mountains of studies and scenarios to make sure the merger would work whatever the price of oil. But both also agreed to keep their lawyers and investment bankers far away until they had an agreement virtually ready to be drafted. Most of the discussions were directly between two executives who regarded each other as among their few equals.

Those two leaders have had little to say themselves. And—with their companies' habitual secrecy reinforced by fears that any leaks might sink the merger as regulators begin to examine it—they have demanded that their board members, aides and outside advisers remain silent as well. Thus, the accounts of those individuals with some knowledge of the deal-making process and willing to speak are fragmentary and sometimes contradictory.

The origins of the deal rest on a series of obscure musings, dropped hints and preliminary approaches calling to mind the old joke about how porcupines make love—very carefully.

Exxon was once known as Standard Oil of New Jersey and Mobil as Standard Oil of New York, the two largest pieces of John D. Rockefeller's Standard Oil Trust, which was broken up in 1911. Initially, the two companies continued to share confidences as well as a headquarters at 26 Broadway in lower Manhattan.

Succeeding generations of ambitious executives took the two companies in very different directions, but they came to face similar challenges. Most recently, the falling oil prices of the 1990s—now lower after inflation than before the Arab oil embargo of 1973—has caused severe cutbacks that led to tens of thousands of layoffs at both companies.

With the price of oil taking another disorienting step down this year, the companies' chief executives finally concluded they had done all they could on their own. "The easy things are behind us," Noto put it earlier this week. "The easy oil, the easy cost savings—they're done."

Mobil—outflanked by Exxon, which is twice its size, and Royal Dutch/Shell Group, which is even larger—began hunting for partners. In Europe, Mobil combined its refinery and marketing operations with those of British Petroleum, even agreeing to let the British brand predominate. It knew that DuPont wanted to sell its Conoco oil company to the public or a sufficiently large buyer. Both B.P. and Amoco, the old Standard Oil of Indiana, were willing to discuss mergers of approximate equals.

Meanwhile, according to one Wall Street executive, Mobil was also suggesting that it might consider an outright sale. Investment bankers were encouraged just enough to present the idea to Exxon executives early this year, this deal-maker said, but it appeared to fall flat.

No wonder. Raymond was still saying Exxon had no need to resort to the mergers and partnerships that weaker companies were trying. If Mobil was rattled by an agreement between Shell and Texaco to team up in refining and sales in the United States, Exxon remained combative. Raymond even boasted last year that his lawyers were reviewing the Shell-Texaco agreement on antitrust grounds, adding that suing one's rivals was "the American way."

But then Raymond doesn't have to try hard to be intimidating. A Ph.D. in chemical engineering, with a heavy frame, rumbling voice and jowly visage, he seldom hesitates to let reporters, analysts or aides know when he thinks what they are asking or doing is just plain dumb.

Such attributes, combined with acknowledged technical brilliance, helped him drive his company to the limits of efficiency, while he remained cautious about costly new ventures abroad. But, according to associates, even Raymond was starting to bump against the limits of efficiency gains Exxon could achieve on its own.

If Exxon was to take any action, he felt, it had to have the scale and substance to truly improve his company. He first broached the subject of Mobil with his board this spring, receiving enough encouragement to take the next step.

By June, during an American Petroleum Institute meeting, Raymond and Noto were chatting about a Japanese refinery where they each have a stake, they told reporters after the deal was announced on Tuesday.

"Maybe we ought to have a conversation about the U.S.," Raymond suggested, perhaps with a view towards countering the Shell-Texaco partnership.

Noto responded in kind, saying, "Well, yeah, that and some other things."

About three weeks later they met in the Washington area, where Mobil has its Fairfax, Va., headquarters. Discussions moved slowly at first. But as the men pondered whether to begin more serious talks, they saw that the two companies were more complementary than it had appeared.

Their foreign ventures had surprisingly little overlap, with Mobil more devoted to developing natural gas. And Mobils' marketing ability—it popularized the self-service gas station—fit well with Exxon's huge and efficient crude oil volumes.

Noto also agreed early on that Raymond would be the boss. Though both are now 60, there would be no awkward attempt at having co-chief executives.

That Noto would accept a vice chairmanship at the combined company, to be called Exxon Mobil, surprised some who know him. "Lou Noto is a very—I don't want to say egomaniacal—he has a very big ego," said William Randol, an independent analyst.

Noto—compact and balding, with a brushy moustache—is much more the salesman and adventurer, a lover of sports cars and opera, comfortable chatting up reporters or literary luminaries. At the joint news conference on Tuesday, he repeatedly stepped in to rescue Raymond from awkward moments. Asked about their rapport, he said, "We do a bear act if you give us a moment."

But to associates, Noto had been making it clear that even a company as huge as Mobil might not be able to go it alone. That conviction was reinforced in August, when British Petroleum announced its $48 billion takeover of Amoco.

That news reverberated at Exxon as well, though some executives there almost made a point of not dwelling on it. "That would not have been the Exxon style," said one official.

As the talks turned earnest, the companies began exhaustive analyses. In a project code-named Highway, using far fewer people than normal to preserve secrecy, they tested the merger's benefits for years to come at a wide range of oil prices. Even if prices unexpectedly rebounded, they concluded, the deal would still pay.

Though they had agreed on the measures they would use to value their companies, agreement on a precise price came late. Discussions about antitrust issues also persisted.

Investment bankers and lawyers, however, were only brought in once Raymond, Noto and their boards were almost ready to have their agreement rendered on paper. By about mid-November, others at the companies began their first preparations to make the deal public.

Board members of both companies, who had been kept closely informed, were asked last week to convene in Manhattan Tuesday morning, the Mobil board at the company's midtown offices, the Exxon board at those of its bankers, J.P. Morgan.

Last-minute details, however, kept senior executives up until late Monday night, leaving some wondering whether the documents would be ready for the boards' votes by the time the markets opened.

With hardly an hour—if that—to spare, the Exxon board approved the deal unanimously. The Mobil, only six of whose 14 members would join the combined board, had one abstention or no. Minutes before the markets opened, the news was officially out.

Why diversify? Four decades of management thinking

Michael Goold
Kathleen Luchs

Executive Overview

This article explores both the thinking and practice of diversification during the last four decades, and our current understanding of diversification strategies that work and those that do not.

There have been relatively few influential ideas about what constitutes a successful strategy for a diversified company. In the 1960s, the spectacular performance of a few successful conglomerates seemed to prove that any degree of diversification was possible if corporate level managers had the requisite general management skills. In the 1970s, many diversified companies turned to portfolio planning, aiming to achieve an appropriate mix of growth and mature businesses. In the 1980s, many corporations restructured and rationalized, basing their strategies on "sticking to the knitting" and eschewing broad diversification.

Should chief executives in the 1990s aim to focus only on a few closely related businesses? Or should they aim to exploit synergies, or core skills, across a variety of businesses? Just how important are the managerial approaches of top executives in adding value to different businesses? These are the critical questions for corporate strategy today.

Large, diversified corporations have been under critical scrutiny for many years. In 1951 the prevailing view in America was summarized in an article in the *Harvard Business Review:*

> *The basic presumption is that a company turning from one type of activity to another is up to no good, especially if in the process it has become "big business."*[1]

Such companies were accused of being too powerful, and, in particular, of cross-subsidizing their different businesses to force competitors from the field. They were therefore seen as anti-competitive.

Today, diversified companies are also regarded by many commentators as being "up to no good," but for just the opposite reason; they are now charged with being uncompetitive. The problem is not that they are overmighty competitors, but that they add no value to their businesses. In 1987, Michael Porter wrote of the failure of many corporate strategies:

> *I studied the diversification records of thirty-three large, prestigious U.S. companies over the 1950–1986 period and found that most of them had divested many more acquisitions than they had kept. The corporate strategies of most companies have dissipated instead of created shareholder value. . . . By taking over companies and breaking them up, corporate raiders thrive on failed corporate strategies.*[2]

How has thinking about the rationale for diversified companies evolved during this period of time? Why has fear of the power of diversified companies been replaced with skepticism about their results? What have we learned, both about diversification strategies that work and those that don't work? There have been relatively few influential ideas about what constitutes a successful strategy for a diversified company. This article explores the development of these ideas, and examines current thinking about corporate level strategy.

Diversification and Corporate Strategy in the 1950s and 1960s

An important and enduring justification for the diversified company is the argument that the managers of these companies possess general management skills that contribute to the overall performance of a company. Kenneth Andrews argued that there had been a steady growth of executive talent in America, equal to the task of managing diversity. The establishment of business schools in the early twentieth century created the basis for the education of professional managers, and the divisionalized structure of large corporations provided the opportunities for younger managers to gain the requisite experience.[3]

General Management Skills

The idea that professional managers possessed skills that could be put to good use across different businesses rested on the assumption that different businesses nevertheless required similar managerial skills. This assumption received support from management theory. During the 1950s and 1960s much scholarly attention fo-

From *Academy of Management Executive,* Vol. 7, No. 3, 1993, pp. 7-25. Republished with permission of Academy of Management, P.O. Box 3020, Briar Cliff Manor, NY 10510-8020. Reproduced by permission of the publisher via Copyright Clearance Center, Inc.

cused on identifying basic principles of management, useful to all managers and applicable to all kinds of enterprises. Peter Drucker argued that "intuitive" management was no longer sufficient. He encouraged managers to study the principles of management and to acquire knowledge and analyze their performance systematically.[4]

The interest in investigating and analyzing underlying management principles continued into the 1960s. Harold Koontz wrote of the "deluge of research and writing from the academic halls." According to Koontz, it was the management process school, which aimed to identify universal principles of management, that held the greatest promise for advancing the practice of management.[5]

Theorists such as Koontz and Drucker naturally emphasized the issues and problems that were common across different types of businesses, since their aim was to help all managers improve their skills and the performance of their businesses. Though they did not explicitly claim that professional managers could manage any business, it was not a great leap to conclude that, if all managers face similar problems, professional managers might be able to use their skills in different businesses. Simple observation, as well as theory, supported this idea. Robert Katz noted that, "We are all familiar with those 'professional managers' who are becoming the prototypes of our modern executive world. These men shift with great ease, and with no apparent loss in effectiveness, from one industry to another. Their human and conceptual skills seem to make up for their unfamiliarity with the new job's technical aspects."[6] There was widespread respect for management skills, and business people were encouraged to apply their general management skills to improve the effectiveness of charities, universities, and government.[7]

In Europe, too, there was interest in general management skills. The founding of business schools in the U.K. and in France during the 1960s, and the growing interest in management training, was in part motivated by the perceived need to provide European managers with the same kind of general management skills as their U.S. competitors. Indeed, there was concern in Europe that the management skills of U.S. companies were so powerful that Americans would take over large chunks of European industry.[8]

Rise of Conglomerates

During the 1960s, the growth of conglomerates, with their numerous acquisitions of unrelated businesses across different industries, provided almost laboratory conditions in which to test out the idea that professional managers could apply their skills to many different businesses. Conglomerates such as Textron, ITT, and Litton not only grew rapidly, but also profitably, and top managers of these companies perceived themselves as breaking new ground. For example, David Judleson of Gulf & Western claimed, "Without the high degree of sophistication, skill, and effectiveness that management has developed only in the last two decades, the conglomerate could not exist. These management techniques provide the necessary unity and compatibility among a diversity of operations and acquisitions."[9] Harold Geneen used a system of detailed budgets, tight financial control, and face-to-face meetings among his general managers to build ITT into a highly diversified conglomerate.[10] In 1967, Royal Little, who masterminded Textron's broad diversification, explained that the company succeeded because, "we are adding that intangible called business judgement."[11] Textron had common financial controls, budgetary systems, and capital allocation procedures across its many businesses, but it provided few central services and had only a very small corporate office. The group vice presidents, who were responsible for a number of divisions, were appointed from outside the company. They acted as overseers and consultants to the divisions.

For more than twenty years, faith in general management skills seemed to justify a kind of virtuous circle of corporate growth and diversification.

These new American conglomerates were admired abroad. In the U.K., one writer wrote glowingly of Litton Industries and its spectacular growth across high-tech industries, claiming that the company was "... a technological achievement of its own, an operation in the technology of management as much as the management of technology."[12] Several British companies, such as Slater Walker, embarked upon a strategy of conglomerate diversification during the 1960s and 1970s. The emphasis in Britain, however, was more on identifying and buying companies whose assets were worth more than their stock market price and less on the application of sound, underlying general management principles by the top management group.[13]

Did the conglomerates add value to their numerous businesses across different industries? The practices of at least some conglomerates such as Textron held up well under academic scrutiny. Norman Berg argued that corporate executives in such companies were fulfilling new roles as "managers of managers." While he admitted that it was too early to draw firm conclusions about the long-term success of conglomerates, Berg suggested that corporate strategies based on improving the performance of a diverse collection of businesses would have important implications for the practice of management and also for public policy.[14]

For more than twenty years, faith in general management skills seemed to justify a kind of virtuous circle of corporate growth and diversification. Andrews summarized the basic premise, arguing that, "successful diversification—because it always means successful surmounting of formidable administrative problems—develops know-how that further diversification will capitalize and extend."[15] The conglomerate movement of the 1960s, involving extensive diversification across a wide variety of industries, seemed to demonstrate that the specialized skills and practices of corporate general managers enabled them to manage ever greater complexity and diversity.

Conglomerates and Performance Problems

There was little reason to question the belief that general management skills provided a sufficient rationale for diversified companies while such corporations were performing well and growing profitably. But by the late 1960s, conglomerates were encountering performance problems. In early 1969, the stock prices of conglomerates such as Litton, Gulf & Western, and Textron fell as much as fifty percent from their highs a year earlier, compared to a nine percent decline in the Dow Jones Industrial Average over the period, and one observer foresaw a round of conglomerate divestitures if such companies were to survive. Even ITT's consistent record of increased quarterly earnings over fifty-eight quarters during the 1960s and 1970s was broken in 1974.[16]

What became apparent was that sound principles of organization and financial control, coupled with a corporate objective of growth, were not, alone, sufficient to ensure satisfactory performance in highly diversified companies. Indeed, General Electric, a leader in the development of sophisticated techniques and principles for the management of a diverse portfolio of businesses, found by the early 1970s that its management approach had resulted in an extended period of what GE called "profitless growth." For example, the company's sales increased forty percent from 1965 to 1970, while its profits actually fell.[17]

By the late 1960s, there was an increasing awareness that a new approach to the management of diversity was needed.

Diversification and Corporate Strategy in the 1970s

As a response to the increasing recognition that large and diversified companies present particular management problems, increasing attention was devoted to the question of the issues on which general managers should focus their efforts.

The Concept of Strategy

One theme that emerged with increasing force during the 1960s and 1970s was the need for senior managers to focus their attention on the "strategies" of their companies. Strategy was more than long-range planning or objective setting; it was a way of deciding the basic direction of the company and preparing it to meet future challenges.[18]

C. Roland Christensen, one of the creators of the business policy course at Harvard during the 1960s, argued that the concept of strategy made it possible to simplify the complex tasks of top managers.[19] A focus on strategy prevented senior executives from meddling in operating details and day-to-day issues which should be left to more junior managers with direct responsibility for them. It allowed them to concentrate on the most important issues facing their companies—and it simplified management by providing a framework for decisions.

CEOs readily accepted that strategy should be their main and unique responsibility. During the late 1960s and 1970s many companies established formal planning systems, and the appropriate structure and uses of such systems received much attention from academics.[20] In the early 1970s, Louis Gerstner remarked on how quickly strategic planning had been adopted by companies, noting that, "Writer after writer has hailed this new discipline as the fountainhead of all corporate progress."[21]

The strategic frameworks, models, and tools being developed by academics and consultants focused mainly on strategic issues at the business unit level, and they were, therefore, less relevant in helping to define an overall strategy for companies with many different businesses. Andrews, however, defined the main task of corporate-level strategy as identifying the businesses in which the firm would compete, and this became the accepted understanding of corporate strategy.[22] This general concept of corporate strategy, though, did not provide much practical guidance to some of the problems managers of diversified companies confronted. In particular, it did not help them decide how resources should be allocated among businesses, especially when investment proposals were being put forward by a large number of disparate businesses, each with its own strategy. This problem was exacerbated when the aggregate demand for resources exceeded what was available.

Problems with Resource Allocation

Resource allocation decisions in diversified companies are a key part of corporate strategy, but they present particular difficulties. Corporate management must grasp the relative merits of investment proposals coming from a range of businesses in different sectors, with different time horizons, competitive positions, and risk profiles, not to mention management teams with differing credibilities. This can be complex. In the early 1970s, for example, a company such as ITT had to allocate resources among businesses that included telecommunications, insurance, rental cars, bakeries, and construction. With many divisions competing for funds, how could a company be sure it was investing in the best projects for future growth?[23]

Joseph Bower explored in detail how a large, diversified firm allocated resources. His research highlighted the gulf between financial theory, which saw the manager's task as choosing projects with the highest returns, and corporate reality, where all proposed projects showed at least the return required by the corporate hurdle rate for investment. In practice, divisional managers only proposed projects with acceptable forecast returns, and corporate-level managers had little basis on which to choose among projects.

Bower argued that investment decisions should not be made on a project-by-project basis, but had to be integrally related to a business's strategic product and market decisions.[24] During the 1970s, the new techniques of portfolio planning that were introduced by the Boston Consulting Group and others gained wide acceptance because they helped corporate executives to resolve practical problems of capital allocation in the context of an overall corporate strategy.[25]

Portfolio Planning

Portfolio planning provided corporate managers with a common framework to compare many different businesses. The industry attractiveness/business position matrix developed at GE, the Boston Consulting Group's growth/share matrix, and variations developed at other consultancies were used to classify businesses in terms of their strategic position and opportunities. These classifications helped managers both to set appropriate objectives and resource allocation strategies for different businesses, and to determine the overall cash requirements and cash generation of the corporate portfolio.[26]

The helicopter view provided by portfolio planning techniques was widely perceived as useful. For example, one CEO explained:

Portfolio planning became relevant to me as soon as I became CEO. I was finding it very difficult to manage and understand so many different products and markets. I just grabbed at portfolio planning, because it provided me with a way to organize my thinking about our businesses and the resource allocation issues facing the total company. I became and still am very enthusiastic. I guess you could say that I went for it hook, line, and sinker.[27]

During the 1970s, more and more corporations adopted portfolio planning, with the largest diversified companies being among the earliest adherents. One survey showed that by 1979, forty-five percent of the Fortune 500 companies were using some form of portfolio planning.[28]

In many companies, portfolio planning techniques became more than analytical tools to help chief executives direct corporate resources towards the most profitable opportunities: they became the basis of corporate strategy itself. The key concept here was the idea of a balanced portfolio: made up of businesses whose profitability, growth, and cash flow characteristics would complement each other, and add up to a satisfactory overall corporate performance. Imbalance could be caused, for example, either by excessive cash generation with too few growth opportunities or by insufficient cash generation to fund the growth requirements elsewhere in the portfolio.[29] Often, the first step towards balancing the corporate portfolio was to identify businesses that were a drain on corporate resources. Monsanto, for example, used portfolio planning to restructure its portfolio, divesting low-growth commodity chemicals businesses and acquiring businesses in higher growth industries such as biotechnology.[30]

Portfolio planning reinforced the virtuous circle of corporate growth and diversification that had been originally founded on general management skills. It helped corporate-level managers correct past diversification mistakes, leading to divestiture of weak businesses, and it encouraged them to invest in a mix of businesses, with different strategic (and cash) characteristics to balance their corporate portfolios and ensure future growth.

Problems with Portfolio Management

Even as an increasing number of corporations turned to portfolio planning, problems emerged in managing balanced portfolios.[31] Companies discovered that while certain businesses appeared to meet all the economic requirements of the corporate portfolio, they did not fit easily into the corporate family. It turned out to be extremely difficult, for example, for corporate managers with long experience of managing mature businesses in a particular industry sector to manage effectively their acquired growth businesses in new, dynamic, and unfamiliar sectors.

Research on how companies actually used portfolio planning confirmed the difficulties of managing businesses with different strategic characteristics, missions, or mandates. Philippe Haspeslagh investigated whether companies adjusted their systems of financial planning, capital investment appraisal, incentive compensation, or strategic planning to fit the requirements of their different businesses. The focus of his study was on the role played by general management, rather than on specific business-level strategies. He found that companies made few changes in their formal corporate-level systems, but corporate-level managers in successful companies did make informal attempts to adapt these systems to their businesses.[32] In another study on the effectiveness of portfolio planning techniques, the authors discovered that cash cows performed better in an organizational context of autonomy while fast-growing businesses benefited from more control. They concluded that the administrative context was an important variable in explaining business performance, and that many companies were taking the wrong approach to some of their businesses.[33]

In many companies, portfolio planning techniques became more than analytical tools to help chief executives direct corporate resources towards the most profitable opportunities: they became the basis of corporate strategy itself.

The recognition that different types of businesses had to be managed differently undermined the argument that general management skills, buttressed by the common frameworks of strategy and portfolio planning, provided the rationale for diversified companies. Many companies discovered that common systems and approaches, when applied to different kinds of businesses, could minimize value from those businesses. Portfolio planning helped corporate executives sort out the contribution of each of their businesses to the corporate portfolio, but it did not answer the other critical question confronting a diversified company: what contribution should the corporation make to each of its businesses?

Diversification and Corporate Strategy in the 1980s

During the 1980s, there was widespread skepticism about the ability of companies to manage and add value to diverse, conglomerate portfolios. Raiders such as Carl Icahn and T. Boone Pickens demonstrated that they could acquire even the largest companies, break them up, and realize huge profits. The takeover activity of the 1980s prompted a re-thinking of both the role of corporate management in large companies, and of the kinds of strategies that were appropriate for diversified companies.

Cost Cutting at Headquarters

What seemed most obvious about the corporate level in many companies was not its contribution, but its cost. Thus, attention shifted to cutting headquarters costs. Some companies turned central services into profit centers, charged with selling their services to the business units, while other companies disbanded some central functions altogether. The pruning of corporate staffs often meant devolving more authority to line managers in decentralized units.[34]

Cost cutting and the downsizing of corporate staffs, however, were not alone sufficient to demonstrate that corporate management could add value to their businesses, and the overall performance of large, diversified corporations also came under increasing scrutiny. Michael Porter published a study showing the high rate of divestiture of acquisitions among American corporations, arguing that the diversification strategies of many companies had failed to create value.[35] Also, the wave of takeovers caused executives to pay increasing attention to their company's stock price as analysts and raiders identified "value gaps," or the difference between the current stock market price of a company and its breakup value.[36]

Value-Based Planning

Faced with the threat from raiders and the criticism of academics such as Porter, chief executives devoted themselves increasingly to the task of creating shareholder value. Managers were encouraged to evaluate corporate performance in the same terms as the stock market (and raiders), using economic rather than accounting measures, and to take whatever actions were necessary to improve their company's stock price. Value-based planning, using the financial tools of discounted cash flow, ROE spreads, and hurdle rates, provided corporate managers with a fresh perspective on the link between stock prices and competitive strategy.[37]

A company's stock price, according to proponents of value-based planning, is determined by the value of the strategies of its businesses. However, it can be very difficult for managers to assess the strategies of dissimilar businesses: "... corporate level planners facing a portfolio of four, ten, dozens, or dozens and dozens of units do not know—probably cannot know—enough about each unit's competitive position, industry, rivals, and customers to make this determination."[38] One of the appeals of value-based planning is that, like portfolio planning, it offers corporate-level executives a means of evaluating many different businesses using a common framework. The corporate level can require business units to make strategic choices on the basis of economic returns, and doing this systematically across all units, it is argued, provides corporate management with the basis for making decisions on capital allocation.

Value-based planning techniques gained many adherents, especially among American corporations. In 1987 an article in *Fortune* described how "managements have caught the religion. At first reluctant, they pound at the door of consultants who can teach them the way to a higher stock price—a price so high it would thwart even the most determined raider."[39]

But value-based planning also has limitations as a guide to corporate strategy. It can help corporate managers to focus on the goal of increasing shareholder wealth and to understand the criteria that must be met to do so. It does not, however, provide much insight into the kind of corporate strategies that should be pursued to meet these criteria. A higher stock price is a reward for creating value. But the key question remains: How *can* corporations add value to diverse business portfolios? Perhaps the most influential view on this vital topic to have emerged during the 1980s is that they should "stick to the knitting."

Stick to the Knitting

The concept of corporate success based on core businesses, or stick to the knitting, gained popularity in 1982 with the publication of Peters' and Waterman's *In Search of Excellence.* Successful corporations, they observed, did not diversify widely. They tended to specialize in particular industries and focused intently on improving their knowledge and skills in the areas they knew best.[40]

Stick-to-the-knitting advice was also a reaction against the analytical techniques and impersonal approach of much of strategic and portfolio planning. Bob Hayes and Bill Abernathy voiced these concerns in their article "Managing Our Way to Economic Decline." In their view, too many American corporations were being run by "pseudo-professional" managers, skilled in finance and law, but lacking in technological expertise or in-depth experience in any particular industry. They warned that portfolios diversified across different industries and businesses were appropriate for stocks and bonds, but not for corporations.[41] The need for experience and deep knowledge of a business was also emphasized by Henry Mintzberg, who criticized the "thin and lifeless" strategies that result from treating businesses as mere positions on a portfolio matrix. He argued that instead of broad diversity, we need "focused organizations that understand their missions, 'know' the people they serve, and excite the ones they employ; we should be encouraging thick management, deep knowledge, healthy competition and authentic social responsibility."[42]

The need for experience and deep knowledge of a business was also emphasized by Henry Mintzberg, who criticized the "thin and lifeless" strategies that result from treating businesses as mere positions on a portfolio matrix.

The widespread conviction that companies should stick to the knitting increased skepticism about the ability of corporations to manage and add value to diverse portfolios. It reinforced the practical pressures created by the corporate raiders and contributed to a wave of retrenching. From the mid-1980s onwards, a goal for many corporations has been to rationalize their portfolios to overcome the perceived disadvantages of broad diversification.

Corporate Restructuring

Restructuring (whether voluntary or not) has frequently led to the disposal of corporate assets. In 1985, for example, General Mills announced its intention to focus on its core businesses of consumer foods and restaurants, and the company sold off its toy and fashion businesses.[43] More recently, General Signal embarked on a strategy of "back to the basics," retreating from its earlier major investments in high-tech businesses to focus on its traditional "boring" products such as industrial mixers.[44]

Restructuring has been widely regarded as a salutary correction to the excesses of broad diversification. Michael Jensen has argued that corporate break-ups, divisional sell-offs, and LBOs are critical developments that can prevent the wasteful use of capital by managers of large public corporations, and other recent academic studies support the view that restructuring does help improve the performance of corporations.[45] But restructuring implies a sense of which businesses a company should retain and which it should divest. How should the core businesses be selected?

One answer is that companies should restructure to limit their businesses to one, or a few, closely related industries. In this way, managers stick to what they know well, and are best able to exploit corporate expertise. This approach is consistent with stick-to-the-knitting advice, but it is not a complete answer. Successful companies such as GE, Hanson, and Cooper Industries nevertheless have businesses in many different industries. Furthermore, sticking to a single industry does not necessarily limit complexity or ensure that companies expand into areas they "know." During the 1980s, companies such as Prudential and Merrill Lynch sought to combine different types of financial services businesses. They discovered that businesses such as insurance, stockbroking, and banking, though all in the financial services industry, nonetheless required very different approaches, resources, and skills.[46]

Another reservation about a stick-to-the-knitting strategy based on limiting diversification to closely related businesses is that, despite extensive research, empirical evidence on the performance of companies pursuing more and less related diversification strategies is ambiguous and contradictory. Many studies have compared the performance of single-product firms, companies that diversify into related products, markets, or technologies, and unrelated conglomerates, but no firm relationship between different diversification strategies and performance has been discovered.[47]

Some concept of what constitutes a "core portfolio"—or the corporate "knitting"—is required, though, if restructuring is to result in long-term improvement in corporate performance.

Diversification and Corporate Strategy in the 1990s

The main issues for corporate strategy in the 1990s have therefore emerged as how to identify the businesses that should form a core portfolio for a corporation, and how to find ways of adding value to those businesses.

Three main alternative answers to these questions have received support in current management thinking:

1) diversification should be limited to those businesses with synergy;

2) the corporate focus should be on exploiting core competences across different businesses; and

3) successful diversification depends on building a portfolio of businesses that fit with the managerial "dominant logic" of top executives and their management style.

Synergy

Synergy occurs when the performance of a portfolio of businesses adds up to more than the sum of its parts. The concept of synergy is based in part on economies of scale; two or more businesses can lower their costs if they can combine manufacturing facilities, use a common salesforce, or advertise jointly, and in this way the combined businesses are worth more than they would be on a stand-alone basis.[48]

In much of the current management literature, synergy has become virtually synonymous with corporate-level strategy. Michael Porter views the management of interrelationships between businesses as the essence of corporate-level strategy, arguing that without synergy a diversified company is little more than a mutual fund.[49] Rosabeth Moss Kanter, too, argues that the achievement of synergy is the only justification for a multi-business company.[50] In a review of the literature on mergers, Friedrich Trautwein, a German academic, found that managers almost always justified diversification moves in terms of the synergies available, and that most of the advice in the management literature on diversification was based on the concept of realizing synergies.[51]

Those who view synergy as the essence of corporate-level strategy, including Porter and Kanter, acknowledge that companies find it difficult to gain synergy benefits and that the failure rate is high.

In practice, however, many companies have found it very difficult to gain benefits from a corporate strategy based on synergy.[52] Acquisitions aimed at realizing synergies can be especially risky; for example, two academic commentators have noted that anticipated synergy benefits "... show an almost unshakable resolve not to appear when it becomes time for their release."[53] Quantitative evidence appears to support the observation that synergies are hard to achieve; a recent study on takeovers concluded that most gains arise from asset disposals and restructuring rather than from synergy.[54]

Those who view synergy as the essence of corporate-level strategy, including Porter and Kanter, acknowledge that companies find it difficult to gain synergy benefits and that the failure rate is high. Much of the current literature, therefore, focuses on implementation—what companies have to do to gain benefits from sharing skills or activities across businesses. Porter, for instance, discusses the need for the evolution of a new organizational form, which he calls the "horizontal organization." These organizations facilitate interrelationships across different businesses by overlaying horizontal structures, systems, and managerial approaches onto the vertical relationships which currently characterize the ties between business units and corporate management.[55] Kanter describes the emergence of the "post-entrepreneurial corporation," which aims to create the relationships and management processes required for cross-business cooperation.[56] Christopher Bartlett and Sumantra Ghoshal argue a similar case for the complex problems facing multinationals attempting to make the most of their businesses in different countries. In their view, multinationals need to develop new organizational capabilities so that components, products, resources, people and information can flow freely among interdependent units. Bartlett and Ghoshal describe such an integrated network as a "transnational organization."[57]

Transnational or horizontal or post-entrepreneurial organizations, by definition, capture many synergy benefits because they have the organizational capabilities to manage complex interrelationships across businesses. There are, however, very few examples of companies that represent these new kinds of organizations, at least in full-fledged form. Consequently, much of the advice on synergy remains theoretical and prescriptive.

There is evidence, furthermore, that managing complex interrelationships to create synergies across businesses is not the only means of creating value. Michael Goold and Andrew Campbell, in their study of strategic management styles, found that companies such as Hanson and Courtaulds, which placed very little emphasis on synergy as a source of corporate value added, performed at least as well as companies that placed more emphasis on linkages across businesses.[58] These findings are reinforced by successful multi-business companies such as KKR, the leveraged buy-out specialists, and Berkshire Hathaway, managed by the renowned investor Warren Buffet, which are collections of independent businesses, and whose strategies are not based on exploiting synergies across their businesses. The assumption that synergy is the only rationale for a group of companies does not fit the available evidence, and this suggests that not all corporations need to focus their efforts on constructing and managing portfolios of interrelated businesses.

Synergy remains a powerful concept in our understanding of corporate strategy, but it is difficult to accept that it is the "one best way" to create value in a multi-business company. For some companies, the advantages of managing stand-alone businesses may outweigh the long-term investment required to create linkages among those businesses, and the potential for synergy may simply not exist in some corporate portfolios. We need to discover more about when synergy is an appropriate corporate strategy, and we need to learn more about how companies successful at managing interrelationships across businesses go about it.

Core Competences

Another approach to corporate strategy stresses building on the core competences of the corporation. This can be seen as a particular case of synergy, with corporate value creation dependent on exploiting unique skills and capabilities across a portfolio of businesses. Gary Hamel and C.K. Prahalad focus on technological competences. They argue that the corporate portfolio should not be perceived simply as a group of businesses, but also as a collection of such competences. In managing the corporate portfolio, managers must ensure that each part draws on and contributes to the core competences the corporation is seeking to build and exploit. Even a poorly performing business may be contributing to an important core competence, and if managers divest such businesses they may also be discarding some of their competences. If corporations are unable to transfer a core competence from one business to another, then they are wasting their resources. According to Prahalad and Hamel, many of the current management approaches of Western corporations, including SBUs, decentralization, and resource allocation practices, undermine the ability of corporations to build core competences, since autonomous businesses seldom have the resources or vision to build world class competences.[59]

Hiroyuki Itami, a Japanese academic, focuses on building the corporation's "invisible assets," such as expertise in a particular technology, brand names, reputation, or customer information. Such assets, he argues, can be employed throughout the firm without being used up, and they are the only sustainable source of competitive advantage.[60] Philippe Haspeslagh and David Jemison, authors of a recent study on acquisitions, support a capabilities-based view of corporate value creation, defining core capabilities as managerial and technological skills gained mainly through experience. Such capabilities can be applied across the corporation's businesses and make an important contribution to customer benefits.[61] It can be difficult to define a corporation's capabilities objectively, but understanding what they are can provide important insights into its sources of competitive advantage and the strategic options of the firm.[62]

The assumption that synergy is the only rationale for a group of companies does not fit the available evidence, and this suggests that not all corporations need to focus their efforts on constructing and managing portfolios of interrelated businesses.

The work on core skills, capabilities, or resources has generated much interest. Walter Kiechel, in *Fortune* magazine, describes how some executives are perceiving their role, and that of the corporate management, as guardians and promoters of the company's core skills, and sums up the current understanding of these concepts: "To the extent that such skills can be exploited by each of the company's businesses, they represent a reason for having all those businesses under one corporate umbrella—much better reason, the experts add, than the fabled synergies that multi-business companies of yore were supposed to realize but seldom did."[63]

But corporations that do base their strategy on core competences have to be careful that the overall competence-based strategy does not become an excuse for poor performance or poor judgment. IBM, for example, acquired Rolm to gain access to the smaller company's expertise in PBX systems. Five years later, however, following heavy losses, IBM sold a majority stake in Rolm to Siemens. Some commentators think that IBM was too optimistic about Rolm's competences and potential and not sufficiently knowledgeable about changes underway in the PBX market or within Rolm.[64] It can be difficult to judge when an investment in a business is justified in terms of building a core competence, particularly if it means suspending normal profitability criteria and if the investment is in an unfamiliar business area.

Another danger with the competence approach to corporate strategy is that businesses may require similar core competences, but demand different overall strategies and managerial approaches. Texas Instruments, for example, attempted to exploit the core competence it had developed in its semiconductors business in areas such as calculators, watches, and home computers. It failed in these new areas not because it lacked the core semi-conductor competence, but because its top management had no experience in managing such consumer-oriented businesses.[65] Similarly, Procter and Gamble applied its skills in product innovation and consumer promotion to a soft drinks business, Crush, but eventually divested the business because it ran into unfamiliar problems managing the local bottlers who largely control distribution of soft drinks.[66] Core competences may add value in specific areas in a variety of different businesses, but this is no guarantee that, overall, a company will be able to manage those different businesses successfully.

The work on core competences and capabilities broadens our understanding of a corporation's resources, and points out the important role of corporate management in building such resources and ensuring that they are used to best advantage. As with synergy, however, it is difficult to accept that this is the only way to add value to a corporate portfolio. Corporate executives are concerned not only with building skills and competences in their businesses, but also with allocating resources to them, approving their plans and strategies, and monitoring and controlling their results. These important "shareholder" functions can also be a source of added value, if done well. Some companies such as Berkshire Hathaway and Hanson lay far more stress on these shareholder functions than on competence building; and, in all companies, the shareholder functions occupy a vital place, even where the management of core competences is also a focus of attention.

Dominant Logic and Management Style

A third approach to corporate success focuses on how corporate management adds value to a portfolio of businesses, in particular in its shareholder role. C.K. Prahalad and Richard Bettis argue that the more diverse a firm, the more complex the problems in managing it. Diversity, however, cannot be defined simply in terms of the number of products or markets in which a firm competes; the strategic variety of the firm's businesses is a more significant measure of its diversity. With firms in strategically similar businesses, executives can use common methods and approaches, using a single managerial dominant logic: "A dominant general management logic is defined as the way in which managers conceptualize the business and make critical resource allocation decisions—be it in technologies, product development, distribution, advertising, or in human resource management."[67]

When managerial dominant logic does not match the needs of the business, tensions and problems arise. Corporate management is liable to appoint the wrong managers to the business, to sanction inappropriate plans and investments, to control against the wrong targets and to interfere unproductively in the managing of the business.

Goold and Campbell's work on strategic management styles shows how dominant logic works in specific companies. In their research on large, diversified companies they identified different types of strategic management styles, with the main styles being Financial Control, Strategic Control, and Strategic Planning. The different styles each added value, but in different ways and to businesses with different characteristics and requirements. Financial Control companies, for example, have distinctive administrative and control systems, emphasizing the setting and meeting of annual budget targets. Although they may invest in a wide variety of industries, the portfolios of businesses of successful Financial Control companies share common characteristics.[68] Hanson is a good example: "The company's strategy is to focus on mature, stable businesses: 'We avoid areas of very high technology. We do not want to be in businesses which are highly capital intensive, where decision making has to be centralized or which rely on huge and sometimes expensive research with a prospect of a return sometime or never.' "[69]

If corporations are unable to transfer a core competence from one business to another, then they are wasting their resources.

In this view, the dominant logic or management style of the corporate management group is central to the performance of a diversified firm, and a group of businesses is best managed when the dominant logic of top managers matches the strategic characteristics and requirements of the businesses. The importance of the "fit" between top managers and the businesses in the corporate portfolio has also been emphasized by executives. Orion Hoch of Litton, for example, has explained the reasons for Litton's extensive divestments and restructuring: "Our aim was to go back to businesses that we could be comfortable with .... We want to get back to doing what we were good at doing."[70] Gary Roubos, CEO of Dover Corporation, argues that the company is a successful conglomerate because it invests only in businesses in which it has considerable management "feel," even though these businesses are highly diverse: "Automatic lifts and toggle clamps are different—but they have much more in common than, say, investment banking and selling soap."[71]

Dominant logic may help explain why conglomerate diversification can succeed, and also why diversification based on synergy or core competences can fail. If conglomerate diversification, such as that of Hanson, is based on businesses with a similar strategic logic, then it is possible for corporate management to take a common approach and to add value to those businesses. On the other hand, businesses with opportunities for sharing activities or skills, or ones requiring the same core competence, may nonetheless have different strategic logics. This makes it difficult for corporate management to realize synergy or exploit a core competence across the businesses. Oil companies that diversified into other extractive, energy or natural resource businesses in pursuit of synergies or core competences tended to find that the benefits they sought were overwhelmed by the problems caused by dissimilarities in strategic logic between the new businesses and the core oil businesses.

The concepts of dominant logic and management style offer some promising insights into both successful and unsuccessful diversification efforts, but there are unanswered questions.[72] Should diversified corporations aim to build portfolios of strategically related businesses, to ensure that top management and corporate systems and approaches do add value? Or should corporations seek to differentiate their approaches—develop "multiple dominant logics"—to manage businesses with different strategic characteristics successfully?

Goold and Campbell discovered that companies tend to adopt a particular strategic management style, even though the style was usually implicit, and that it was difficult for managers to cope with a variety of approaches or styles. They argued that CEOs should aim to focus their portfolios on the kinds of businesses which would gain benefits from their strategic management style.[73] On the other hand, authorities on multinationals argue that the increasing complexities of globally spread businesses and international competition require corporations to develop new capabilities to manage businesses facing different strategic issues. C.K. Prahalad and Yves Doz maintain that the winners in the struggle for global competitive advantage will be those companies that can develop differentiated structures, management processes and systems, appropriate to the wide variety of their businesses.[74] Bartlett and Ghoshal describe how the "administrative heritage" of companies emphasizes a particular approach to issues such as coordination across businesses, but they argue that the idealized transnational company should be able to combine different approaches and develop "a full arsenal of coordinating processes, practices, and tools, and to use those mechanisms in the most effective and efficient manner."[75]

The question of whether it is possible to differentiate your management approaches to add value to many different kinds of businesses remains open. Bartlett and Ghoshal found evidence that some companies were seeking ways to encompass much more variety, but none had yet become a true transnational. We need more research to establish when it is appropriate to differentiate your management approaches to encompass the needs of diverse kinds of businesses, and when it is reasonable to adjust the corporate portfolio to a particular management style, or to a single managerial dominant logic. Work is also needed to clarify how to operationalize the concepts of dominant logic and strategic relatedness. We do not yet know how the limits of a dominant logic should be defined, how managers and corporations develop a new strategic management style, or if this is even possible.

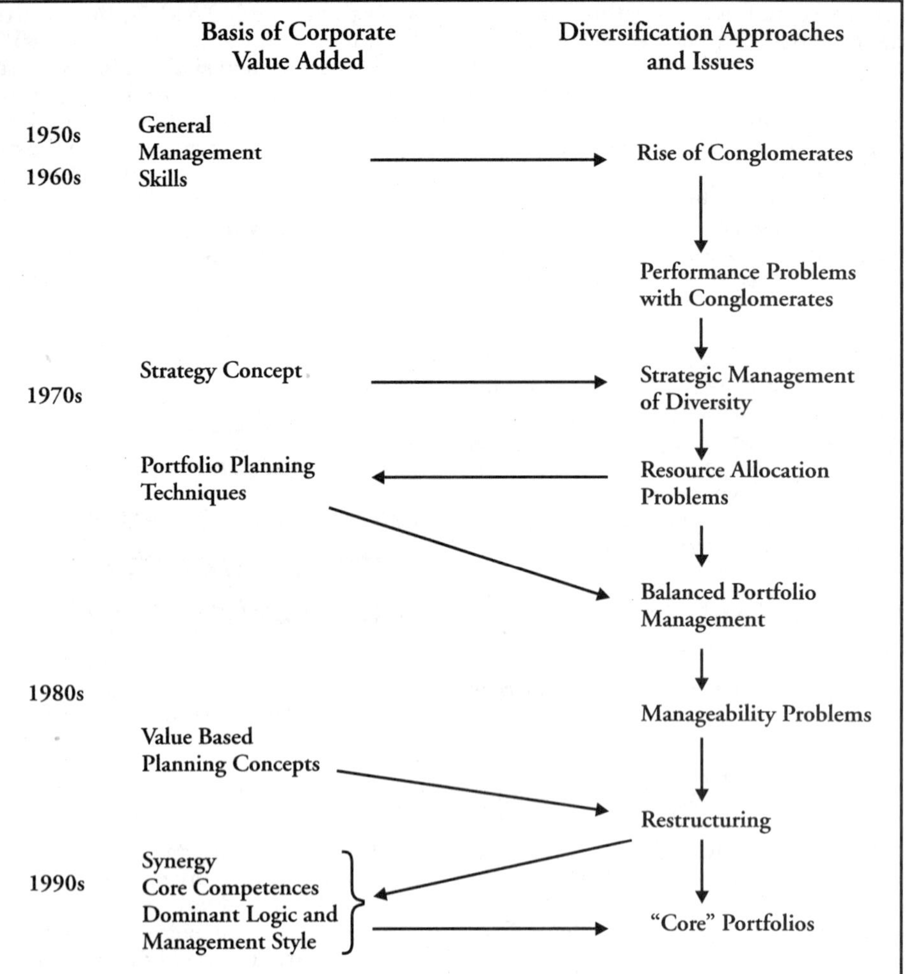

Exhibit 1. Evolution of Thinking on Corporate Strategy and Diversification

The Challenge of Diversification

During the last four decades, managers and academics have sought both to understand the basis of successful diversification and to address the problems created by it. Exhibit 1 summarizes the evolution of thinking and practice during this time.

From the 1950s onwards, the development of management principles and the professional education of managers led to the belief that general management skills provided the justification for diversification. Diversified companies and conglomerates were seen to add value through the skills of their professional top managers, who applied modern management techniques and generalized approaches to a wide variety of businesses across different industries. During the late 1960s, however, the performance of many conglomerates weakened, and a new approach to corporate management of diversity was sought. The concepts of strategy and strategic management provided a new focus for senior management's attention during the 1970s, but soon proved unable to resolve many of the choices and trade-offs involved in resource allocation in the multi-business firm. Portfolio planning techniques helped many companies improve capital allocation across businesses with different strategic positions, and led to the idea of balanced portfolio management. But such analytical approaches overlooked the problem of manageability. Many companies found it difficult to manage businesses facing different strategic issues, and during the 1980s poor corporate performance again became a critical issue. Raiders, executives, and academics realized that many diversified corporations were not creating shareholder value, and there was a wave of takeovers, corporate break-ups, and restructuring. The main themes of corporate strategy during the 1980s became restructuring back to core businesses and a resolve to stick to the knitting.

As we move into the 1990s, it has, however, become increasingly clear that there is no consensus on what sticking to the knitting in practice implies, or on how companies should be adding value to their remaining core businesses. Among the currently popular themes, the search for synergy and the building of core competences each have significant followings. But both views need to be complemented with some account of how the corporation can discharge its shareholder functions well. Here the concept of understanding the dominant strategic logic of a portfolio, and its compatibility with the approaches of top management, seems promising.

In our view, it is probable that a full account of corporate strategy and of diversification will need to draw on several of the strands of thought we have reviewed. Ultimately, diversity can only be worthwhile if corporate management adds value in some way and the test of a corporate strategy must be that the businesses in the portfolio are worth more under the management of the company in question than they would be under any other ownership.[76] To achieve this goal with a diverse group of businesses, it may be necessary to restructure portfolios to allow more uniformity in dominant logic and management style, more effective means of realizing synergies and more sharing of core competences.

Endnotes

1. Kenneth R. Andrews, "Product Diversification and the Public Interest," *Harvard Business Review,* July 1951, 94.
2. M.E. Porter, "From Competitive Advantage to Corporate Strategy," *Harvard Business Review,* May–June 1987, 43.
3. Kenneth R. Andrews, *op. cit.* 91–107; "Toward Professionalism in Business Management," *Harvard Business Review,* March–April 1969, 49–60.
4. Peter Drucker, *The Practice of Management* (New York, 1955; re-issued Pan Books, 1968), 21.
5. Harold Koontz. "The Management Theory Jungle," *Academy of Management Journal,* Vol. 4, No. 3, December 1961, 175.
6. Robert L. Katz, "Skills of an Effective Administrator," *Harvard Business Review,* January–February 1955, 37.
7. Arthur B. Langlie, "Top Management's Responsibility for Good Government," and Thomas Roy Jones, "Top Management's Responsibility to the Community," both in H.B. Maynard, ed., *Top Management Handbook* (New York, NY: McGraw-Hill, 1960); Andrews, *op. cit.*; Y.K. Shetty and Newman S. Perry, Jr., "Are Top Executives Transferable Across Companies?" *Business Horizons,* June 1976, 23–28.
8. Richard Whitley, Alan Thomas, and Jane Marceau, *Masters of Business? Business Schools and Business Graduates in Britain and France* (London: Tavistock Publications, 1981); J.-J. Servan-Schreiber, *The American Challenge,* translated by Ronald Steel (London: Hamish Hamilton, 1968).
9. David N. Judelson, "The Conglomerate—Corporate Form of the Future," *Michigan Business Review,* July 1969, 8–12; Reprinted in John W. Bonge and Bruce P. Coleman, *Concepts for Corporate Strategy* (New York, NY: Macmillan, 1972), 458.
10. Harold Geneen, with Alvin Moscow, *Managing* (New York, NY: Doubleday, 1984).
11. Norman Berg, "Textron, Inc.," HBS Case Study, 373–337, 1973, 16.
12. R. Heller, "The Legend of Litton," *Management Today,* October 1967; reprinted in Igor Ansoff, (Ed.), *Business Strategy* (Penguin Books, 1969), 378.
13. Jim Slater, *Return to Go: My Autobiography* (London: Weidenfield and Nicolson, 1977), 91.
14. Norman A. Berg, 'What's Different about Conglomerate Management?" *Harvard Business Review,* November–December 1969, 112–120.
15. Kenneth R. Andrews, "Product Diversification and the Public Interest," *Harvard Business Review,* July 1951, 98.
16. Robert S. Attiyeh, 'Where Next for Conglomerates?" *Business Horizons,* December 1969, 3944; Reprinted in John W. Bonge and Bruce P. Coleman, *Concepts for Corporate Strategy* (New York, NY: Macmillan, 1972); Geneen, *op. cit.*, 43.
17. Michael Goold and John Quinn, *Strategic Control* (Hutchinson and Economist Publications, 1990): Richard G. Hamermesh, *Making Strategy Work* (New York: John Wiley & Sons, 1986), 3; William K. Hall, "SBUs: Hot, New Topic in the Management of Diversification," *Business Horizons,* February 1978, 17.
18. Peter Drucker, "Long-Range Planning: Challenge to Management Science." *Management Science,* Vol. 5, No. 3, 1959, 238–49; Igor Ansoff, *Corporate Strategy,* (New York: McGraw-Hill, 1965); Alfred P. Sloan, *My Years with General Motors* (New York: Doubleday, 1963 (re-issued by Penguin Books, 1986); Alfred D. Chandler, Jr., *Strategy and Structure* (Cambridge: MIT, 1962) (re-issued 1982); Myles L. Mace, "The President and Corporate Planning." *Harvard Business Review,* January–February 1965, 49–62.
19. C. Roland Christensen, and others, *Business Policy: Text and Cases* (Richard D. Irwin, 1965).
20. R.F. Vancil and P. Lorange, "Strategic Planning in Diversified Companies," *Harvard Business Review,* January–February 1975, 81–90; Peter Lorange and Richard F. Vancil, *Strategic Planning Systems* (New Jersey: Prentice-Hall, 1977); K.A. Ringbakk, "Organized Planning in Major U.S. Companies," *Long Range Planning,* Vol. 2, No. 2, December 1969, 46–57; Norman A. Berg, "Strategic Planning in Conglomerate Companies," *Harvard Business Review,* May–June 1965, 79–92.
21. Louis V. Gerstner, "Can Strategic Management Pay Off?" *Business Horizons,* Vol. 15, No. 6, December 1972, 5.
22. Kenneth R. Andrews, *The Concept of Corporate Strategy,* 1971. Revised Edition (Homewood, IL: Richard D. Irwin, Inc., 1980), 35.
23. Berg, *op. cit.*
24. Joseph L. Bower, *Managing the Resource Allocation Process* (Harvard Business School Press, 1970). Harvard Business School Classics Edition, 1986.
25. Bower, *op. cit.*; Hamermesh, *op. cit.*
26. William K. Hall, "SBUs: Hot, New Topic in the Management of Diversification," *Business Horizons,* February 1978, 17–25; George S. Day, "Diagnosing the Product Portfolio," *Journal of Marketing,* April 1977, 29–38.
27. Hamermesh, *op. cit.*, 30.
28. Philippe Haspeslagh, "Portfolio Planning: Uses and Limits," *Harvard Business Review,* January–February 1982, 58–73.
29. Barry Hedley, "Strategy and the 'Business Portfolio,' " *Long Range Planning,* February 1977, 9–15; Charles W. Hofer and Dan Schendel, *Strategy Formulation: Analytical Concepts* (New York: West Publishing, 1978).
30. Hamermesh, *op. cit.*, 71.
31. Richard A. Bettis and William K. Hall, "The Business Portfolio Approach—Where It Falls Down in Practice," *Long Range Planning,* vol. 16 no. 2, April 1983, 95–104.
32. Haspeslagh, *op. cit.*
33. Richard G. Hamermesh and Roderick E. White, "Manage Beyond Portfolio Analysis," *Harvard Business Review,* January–February 1984, 103–109.
34. Rosabeth Moss Kanter, *When Giants Learn to Dance* (London: Simon & Schuster, 1989) 94; Thomas More, "Goodbye, Corporate Staff," *Fortune,* December 21, 1987.
35. Porter, *op. cit.*
36. David Young and Brigid Sutcliffe, "Value Gaps—The Raiders, The Market or the Managers?" Research Paper, Ashridge Strategic Management Centre, January 1990.
37. Alfred Rappaport, *Creating Shareholder Value: The New Standard for Business Performance* (New York, NY: Free Press, 1986); Bernard C. Reimann, *Managing for Value* (Oxford: Basil Blackwell, 1987).
38. William W. Alberts and James M. McTaggart, "Value Based Strategic Investment Planning," *Interfaces,* January–February 1984, 138–151; see also Enrique R. Arzac, "Do Your Business Units Create Shareholder Value?" *Harvard Business Review,* January–February 1986, 121–126.
39. John J. Curran, "Are Stocks Too High?" *Fortune,* September 28, 1987, 24.
40. Thomas J. Peters and Robert H. Waterman, *In Search of Excellence* (New York, NY: Free Press, 1982).
41. Bob Hayes and Bill Abernathy, "Managing Our Way to Economic Decline," *Harvard Business Review,* July–August 1980, 67–77.
42. Henry Mintzberg, *Mintzberg on Management* (New York, NY: Free Press, 1989), 373.
43. Michael E. Porter, "General Mills, Inc.: Corporate Strategy," HBS Case Study 9-388-123, 1988.
44. Seth Lubove. "Dog with Bone," *Fortune,* April 13, 1992, 106.
45. Michael Jensen, "The Eclipse of the Public Corporation." *Harvard Business Review,* September–October 1989, 61–74; S. Chatterjee, "Sources of Value in Takeovers: Synergy or Restructuring—Implications for Target and Bidder Firms," *Strategic Management Journal,* vol. 13. no. 4, May 1992, 267–286; S. Bhagat, A. Shleifer, R. Vishny, "Hostile Takeovers in the 1980s: The Return to Corporate Specialization," Brookings Papers on Economic Activity: Microeconomics 1990.
46. Robert M. Grant, "On 'Dominant Logic', Relatedness and the Link Between Diversity and Performance," *Strategic Management Journal,* vol. 9, no. 6, November–December 1988, 639–642; Robert M. Grant, "Diversification in the Financial Services Industry," in Andrew Campbell and Kathleen Luchs, *Strategic Synergy,* (London: Butterworth Heinemann, 1992).
47. There is an extensive literature on this topic. See Richard P. Rumelt, *Strategy, Structure and Economic Performance* (Boston, MA: Harvard Business School Press, 1974); Richard P. Rumelt, "Diversification Strategy and Profitability," *Strategic Management Journal,* vol. 3, 1982, 359–369; Richard A. Bettis, "Performance Differences in Related and Unrelated Diversified Firms," *Strategic Management Journal,* vol. 2, 1981, 379–393; Kurt H. Christensen and Cynthia A. Montgomery, "Corporate Economic Performance: Diversification Strategy Versus Market Structure," *Strategic Management Journal,* vol. 2, 1981, 327–343; Gerry Johnson, and Howard Thomas, "The Industry Context of Strategy, Structure and Performance: The U.K. Brewing Industry," *Strategic Management Journal,* vol. 8, 1987, 343–361; Anju Seth, "Value Creation in Acquisitions: A Re-Examination of Performance Issues," *Strategic Management Journal,* vol. 11, 1990, 99–115.
48. Igor Ansoff, *Corporate Strategy* (New York, NY: McGraw-Hill, 1965).
49. Michael E. Porter, *Competitive Advantage* (New York, NY: Free Press, 1985).
50. Kanter, *op. cit.*, 90.

51. Friedrich Trautwein, "Merger Motives and Merger Prescriptions," *Strategic Management Journal,* vol. 11, 1990, 283–295.
52. Vasudevan Ramanujam and P. Varadarajan, "Research on Corporate Diversification: A Synthesis," *Strategic Management Journal,* vol. 10, 1989, 523–551; Andrew Campbell and Kathleen Luchs, *Strategic Synergy* (London: Butterworth Heinemann, 1992).
53. Richard Reed and George A. Luffman, "Diversification: the Growing Confusion," *Strategic Management Journal,* vol. 7, 1986, 34.
54. S. Chatterjee, "Sources of Value in Takeovers: Synergy or Restructuring," *Strategic Management Journal,* vol. 13, no. 4. May 1992, 267–286.
55. Porter, *op. cit.*
56. Kanter, *op. cit.*
57. Christopher A. Bartlett and Sumantra Ghoshal, *Managing Across Borders: The Transnational Solution* (Harvard Business School Press, 1989).
58. Michael Goold and Andrew Campbell, *Strategies and Styles* (Oxford: Basil Blackwell Ltd., 1987).
59. C.K. Prahalad and Gary Hamel, "The Core Competence of the Corporation," *Harvard Business Review,* May–June 1990, 79–91; Gary Hamel and C.K. Prahalad, "Strategic Intent," *Harvard Business Review,* May–June 1989, 63–76.
60. Hiroyulki Itami, *Mobilizing Invisible Assets* (Harvard University Press, 1987).
61. Philippe Haspeslagh and David B. Jemison, *Managing Acquisitions* (New York, NY: Free Press, 1991), 23.
62. Robert M. Grant, "The Resource-Based Theory of Competitive Advantage: Implications for Strategy Formulation," *California Management Review,* Spring 1991, 114–135; Andrew Campbell, "Building Core Skills," in Andrew Campbell and Kathleen Luchs, *Strategic Synergy* (London: Butterworth Heinemann; 1992); George Stalk, Philip Evans, Laurence E. Shulman, "Competing on Capabilities," *Harvard Business Review,* March/April 1992, 57–69.
63. Walter Kiechel, "Corporate Strategy for the 1990s," *Fortune,* February 29, 1988, 20.
64. Robert D. Hof and John J. Keller, "Behind the Scenes at the Fall of Rolm," *Business Week,* July 10, 1989, 82–84.
65. C.K. Prahalad and R.A. Bettis, "The Dominant Logic: A New Linkage Between Diversity and Performance," *Strategic Management Journal,* vol. 7, 1986, 495.
66. Patricia Winters, "Crush Fails to Fit on P&G Shelf," *Advertising Age,* July 10, 1989.
67. Prahalad and Bettis, *op. cit.*, 490.
68. Goold and Campbell, *op. cit.*
69. Andrew Campbell, Marion Devine, and David Young, *A Sense of Mission* (London: Hutchinson, 1990), 242.
70. *Barron's,* May 20, 1991.
71. F.J. Aguilar, "Groen: A Dover Industries Company," HBS Case 9-388-055, 1988.
72. Michael Goold and Andrew Campbell, "Brief Case: From Corporate Strategy to Parenting Advantage," *Long Range Planning,* vol. 24, no. 1, February 1991, 115–117.
73. Goold and Campbell. *op. cit.*
74. C.K. Prahalad and Yves L. Doz, *The Multinational Mission* (London: Free Press, 1987), 261.
75. Christopher A. Bartlett and Sumantra Ghoshal, *Managing Across Borders: The Transnational Solution* (Harvard Business School Press, 1989), 166.
76. Michael Goold and Andrew Campbell, "Corporate Strategy and Parenting Skills," Research Report, Ashridge Strategic Management Centre, 1991.

About the Authors

Michael Goold is a founding director and fellow of the Ashridge Strategic Management Centre, London, England. His research interests cover the management of multi-business companies. Prior to establishing the Centre, he was a senior fellow in the Centre for Business Strategy at the London Business School where he undertook the research into the role of the corporate headquarters in managing diversified companies that led to the publication, with Andrew Campbell, of *Strategies and Styles* (Blackwells, 1987). He has extensive consulting experience with senior management. He was a vice president of The Boston Consulting Group and continues to consult with a variety of clients, in addition to his research and teaching responsibilities. He holds a B.A. with first class honors in PPE from Merton College, Oxford, and an M.B.A. from the Stanford Business School, California.

Kathleen Sommers Luchs is an associate at Ashridge Strategic Management Centre, London, England. She has a Ph.D. from Yale University and has been a lecturer in history at Yale and Harvard Universities. She received an M.B.A. from London Business School in 1987 and is co-author, with Andrew Campbell, of *Strategic Synergy* (1992), a book on synergy issues.

A Powerhouse of Technology Decides to Split into 2 Units

An Effort to Compete in a More Focused Way

By LAWRENCE M. FISHER

SAN FRANCISCO—Responding to the ever-shifting fortunes of high-technology industries, the Hewlett-Packard Company, the cornerstone of California's Silicon Valley, announced today that it would split into two independent companies, one focusing on computers, printers and scanners, the other on electronic test equipment and medical technology products.

Wall Street greeted the move enthusiastically, sending Hewlett-Packard shares up $2.75 to close at $68.625 on the New York Stock Exchange.

Analysts said the split would allow Hewlett-Packard's computer and imaging businesses to compete more effectively with more focused companies that have lower cost structures, like the Dell Computer Corporation, Sun Microsystems Inc. and Lexmark International Group.

Although Hewlett-Packard's reputation was built on the quality of its test and measurement equipment—not to mention its legendary founding in the iconic Palo Alto garage 60 years ago—that business has been marked by higher overhead and slower growth than the company had realized in computers, printers and scanners.

"The company has been in too many businesses," said Steven Milunovich, an analyst with Merrill Lynch. "H.P. has actually done surprisingly well through the years with a diversified business, but the time has come for this kind of step. I think it should be a shareholder-enriching event."

Hewlett-Packard has struggled to meet its own or analysts' estimates of revenue growth, although it beat earnings estimates in the most recent quarter through rigorous cost-cutting. Test and measurement, which also includes medical products like ultrasound, patient monitoring devices and heart defibrillators, had averaged better than 10 percent revenue growth over the last decade, but in the most recent fiscal year, growth dropped to 1 percent, because of the Asian economic crisis and a slowdown in the semiconductor business.

"We still have quite a collection of businesses under one roof, which have become increasingly divergent in terms of their business models, the way they go to market, and the customers they serve," Lewis E. Platt, Hewlett-Packard's chairman, president and chief executive officer, said in a telephone interview.

After the split, the computer and imaging company will continue to be known as the Hewlett-Packard Company, while a new name will be chosen for the measurement company. Hewlett-Packard plans a public offering of 15 percent of the measurement company's outstanding shares by year-end, which would be the largest initial public offering in Silicon Valley history. The measurement business, including chemical-analysis and medical businesses, represented $7.6 billion of Hewlett-Packard's total revenue of $47.1 billion in the 1998 fiscal year.

"The focus we get from being separate will help our outbound message," Mr. Platt said. "What can you say about a company like H.P.?"

In contrast, he said, Sun Microsystems, a major competitor in large network server computers, "is out there with just one message."

"The complexity and confusion of having all these businesses under one roof outweigh the synergy of having them all together," he said.

Platt, 58, said he would remain chief executive until Hewlett-Packard's separation was completed. That is expected to take 12 to 18 months. A search for a successor is under way.

Aside from the printer business, where Hewlett-Packard has a commanding market share, the company has struggled to own any particular market segment the way Sun is identified with the Internet, Dell with personal computers or I.B.M. with large enterprise systems.

Analysts say that while Hewlett-Packard has credible offerings in all of those markets, it has lacked a coherent strategy to address any one of them.

What is not clear is whether spinning off test and measurement will change that picture, they said.

"I actually think test and measurement is the crown jewel," said James Moore, chief executive of Geopartners Research in Cambridge, Mass. "Test and measurement is where the technology tends to be, where a lot of the talent tends to be. The problem is on the PC side. It was a great mistake for them to plunge so heavily into PC's. They and Compaq got into a price war, and what neither company understood was that Dell was hitting them in a blind spot."

Dell has grabbed market share from Compaq Computer and Hewlett-Packard with a combination of a direct sales model, which eliminates the overhead of dealers and distributors, and custom configuration, which allows it to sell machines at higher average prices.

Even so, Mr. Platt said the companies' business models were actually coming closer together. "Dell's out now very aggressively recruiting dealers and distributors to help them serve customers who prefer to be served that way," he said. "While we started out with very different multi-tier strategies, we are converging."

At $10.2 billion, revenues in Hewlett-Packard's computer business increased 3 percent over last year; in contrast Dell grew sales by 38 percent in the same period. At the same time, revenue from the measurement organization declined 11 percent, with test and measurement down 14 percent, chemical-analysis up 8 percent, and medical-products down 13 percent.

Platt said one quarter's results did not drive the decision to split the company, but he conceded that they might have been a factor. "If we'd had quite a wonderful year, maybe there would have been less urgency," he said.

Edward W. Barnholt, Hewlett-Packard's executive vice president and general manager of the measurement organization, has been named chief executive of the new company.

"We'll work very hard to be an $8 billion start-up that will compete very effectively with companies of all sizes," Mr. Barnholt said.

Whatever name is eventually chosen for the new company, he said, it will likely reflect the legacy of Hewlett-Packard. "We certainly want to build on the heritage of H.P.," he said. "We don't want to leave that equity behind."

DEALS

HOW GILLETTE WOWED WALL STREET

It structured the Duracell buy to juice up earnings immediately

Two thumbs up? Try four, or even six. Such was the overwhelmingly positive reaction to news that Gillette Co. would pay $7.1 billion in stock to buy battery maker Duracell International Inc. In the two days after the deal was announced on Sept. 12, Duracell's stock shot up 27%, while Gillette's rose 8%. Together, the two added a remarkable $4.1 billion in market capitalization—an unusually large gain relative to the deal's size, says Steven N. Kaplan, a University of Chicago professor of finance. "The market," adds Kaplan, "says this is a huge home run."

Why such rave reviews? For starters, the deal seems a logical fit, combining two companies with premier consumer brands and stellar track records. Duracell is the top player in a global battery market expanding at double-digit rates. But it's lagging outside the U.S. and Europe, and Gillette's international marketing prowess could quickly add muscle. Even rivals are impressed. "What would have taken Duracell years to achieve on its own, Gillette has the

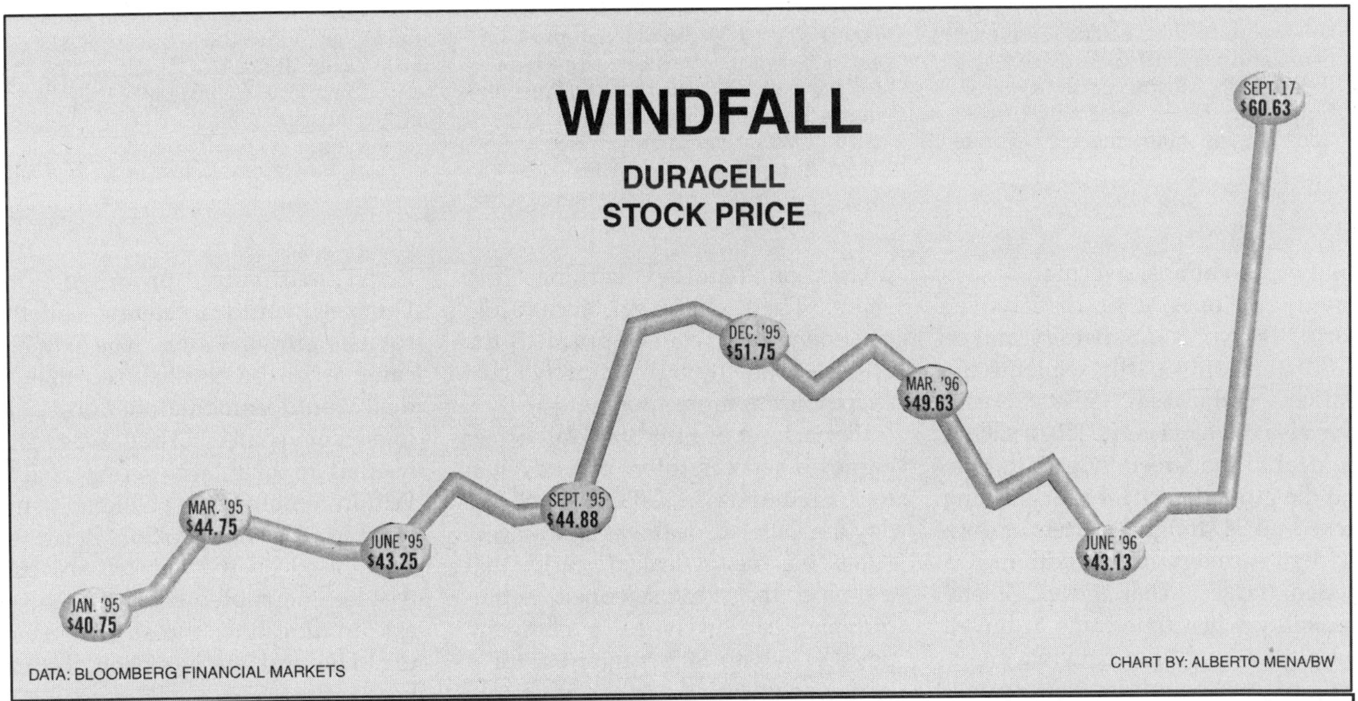

THE ART OF SELLING THE DEAL

With an all-stock deal, Gillette ignited Duracell's stock and kept analysts happy. But it may have shortchanged its own investors. Here's why:

CASH DEAL

At $58.50 a share, it would have cost $7.1 billion. But since Duracell's market/book ratio is high, Gillette would have had to take big annual deductions for goodwill and depreciation, depressing earnings.

STOCK SWAP

Gillette avoids huge deductions. But because it shares rose on the deal, the merger could cost several hundred million dollars more. Also, Gillette's ability to buy back stock will be restricted for two years.

AT DURACELL, AN EARLY CHRISTMAS

Chalk one up for the little guy. Sure, Duracell CEO Charles R. Perrin stands to earn some $26.5 million when Gillette acquires his company. And leveraged buyout firm Kohlberg Kravis Roberts & Co.'s original $350 million investment now is worth a total of $3.7 billion. Then there is the handful of unidentified market players who have sparked a Securities & Exchange Commission investigation by pocketing a nearly $1 million windfall from Duracell call options. But come December, when the deal is set to close, 8,231 Duracell workers in 39 countries will win, too.

That's because in November, 1992, every full- and part-time employee received options to purchase Duracell International Inc. stock for $33.94 a share. For most employees, that grant amounted to about 30% of annual pay. Rank and file production workers got approximately 400 options; engineers and managers took home many times more. Now, even the lowest-level employees have made a paper profit, on average, of more than $10,000—before taxes and exercise fees—based on the Sept. 17 closing price of $60.63. Employees can exercise all their options as soon as the merger becomes effective.

At Duracell's Bethel (Conn.) headquarters, the thrill of a huge one-time gain appears tempered by uncertainty about how the merger will play out. Employees have been told their jobs are secure. But they're faced with the unsettling choice of cashing out immediately or converting their holdings to comparable options on the stock of their new employer. "Do I want to let everything I have ride with Gillette when I'm not even sure what my future will be, or do I start exercising gradually now?" wonders Rob DaPra, assistant corporate controller. DaPra exercised 25% of his options last October and used the proceeds to help pay for a new home.

Merrill Lynch & Co., which administers Duracell's stock option plan, says it has seen a dramatic increase in the number of Duracell employees calling to find out the worth of their options. "Some people are very uneasy," says Sharon Roma, an assistant payroll manager who holds at least 600 options. Like 80% of Duracell's employees, Roma hasn't exercised any of her holdings—so far, "I have a 3-year-old daughter, and I figure maybe I can use them for her college education, so I'm going to let the options sit there." Experts say that's probably wise. At many companies, employees exercise their options prematurely, wasting much of the instruments' potential value, says Robert Salwen, president of consultants Executive Compensation Corp.

"VESTED INTEREST." Employees weren't the only winners at Duracell. Since the company doled out options, investors have seen their holdings appreciate nearly 100%, says Peter Chingos, a compensation consultant at KPMG Peat Marwick. And because the stock reserved under the option plan—7% of the company's outstanding shares—was modest, dilution of earnings per share has been minimal.

By setting aggressive target prices that determined when options would vest, Duracell helped ensure that its plan would do what it was supposed to do—produce higher value by effectively motivating workers. "Employees really do have a vested interest in how the company performs, and as we make those hurdles there's a real sense of accomplishment," says Gary Fox, general manager of headquarter services.

Says Salwen: "The company has succeeded in energizing their workforce," and now the workforce is a little richer. It's a storybook ending—and a textbook argument for employer stock options.

By Kerry Capell in New York

ability to do almost overnight," says David A. Jones, CEO of Rayovac Corp., the No. 3 U.S. battery maker.

But that only partly explains the market's enthusiasm. Gillette executives also did a masterful job of selling the deal to the Street. Indeed, they've laid the groundwork for years, having racked up 24 straight quarters of double-digit earnings growth with nary a missed target. That gave Gillette credibility when time came to unveil a deal that might normally have gotten a more skeptical look. Most analysts, for example, take it on faith that Gillette will be able to reverse a slowdown in Duracell's growth that began late last year.

What's more, Gillette executives deliberately structured the deal to cater to Wall Street's simplistic emphasis on reported earnings per share. They chose an accounting treatment that would appeal to the Street—even though it may cost shareholders more money.

For a taste of how the Wall Street game is successfully played, just look at trading in Gillette stock the day the Duracell deal was announced. After the news leaked early that morning, the stock swooned, a predictable reaction when a company pays a 25% to 30% premium for a large acquisition. Also, investors often assume that companies using stock in an acquisition are announcing that their stock is overvalued: Otherwise, why not pay cash?

But Gillette CEO Alfred M. Zeien quickly put on his salesman's garb. In a conference call with analysts, Zeien virtually promised that Duracell would accelerate Gillette's robust growth rate. The clincher came when he emphasized that the deal would immediately boost earnings per share. "That was all I needed to hear," says one analyst. Within moments, Gillette stock jumped $3 a share, to $67. Zeien was so focused on the market's reaction that he interrupted the conference to ask an aide how the stock was doing. He, and everyone on the call, heard it was up.

Making sure that the Duracell deal would immediately add to reported earnings was one of Zeien's key goals. But to do that, he had to ensure the deal was structured as a stock swap. If Gillette had paid cash for Duracell, which has a low book value but a high market value, the larger company would have absorbed at least $125 million in annual charges for goodwill and depreciation. To analysts focusing on the bottom line, that would have been a downer, and could have depressed Gillette's share price. A stock swap, by contrast, allows Gillette to employ a "pooling" accounting calculation, which merges the two companies' balance sheets and eliminates such pesky problems as extra goodwill.

Accounting experts say there is no economic difference between the two methods. "The market should be sophisticated enough to see through the accounting treatment," says William H. Coyle, a professor of accounting at Babson College. "But it often doesn't. So you have the accounting driving the behavior, which is not the way it should be." So important was the accounting strategy that one Gillette adviser says the company would have walked away had Duracell insisted on a cash deal.

PENALIZED. For Gillette shareholders, there are two downsides to a stock deal. First, it may already have cost them money. An all-cash deal at $58.50 per Duracell share (the price when the deal was announced) would have cost Gillette about $7.1 billion. But because Gillette's stock soared on the news, Duracell shareholders may get several hundred million dollars more. Another problem: The rules on pooling restrict Gillette's ability to buy back shares for two years, to the dismay of some institutional shareholders who see such buybacks as a way to soak up excess cash and boost the stock price. Gillette already has cut short a modest share buyback program.

Zeien admits that "a cash transaction might be the best thing to do for an individual who wants to hold the stock for five or 10 years," but says shorter-term holders would have been penalized by Wall Street's focus on earnings per share. "Anybody you ask will tell you that the stock price will go down" if a company takes on a huge slug of goodwill in an acquisition. Zeien also hints that the company might resume its share buyback program after the waiting period.

Gillette can hardly be blamed for playing Wall Street's game, and playing it well. After all, that's the currency by which companies are measured, and managers compensated. And to be sure, the enthusiasm for this deal among investors is genuine. Most observers believe Duracell will thrive under Gillette's vaunted management. But investors probably could have figured that out whatever accounting was used.

By Mark Maremont in Boston

The New INTEL

Craig Barrett is leading the chip giant into riskier terrain

BY ANDY REINHARDT

Intel Chief Executive Craig R. Barrett sounds nearly poetic when he describes why it has been so darn hard getting the giant chipmaker to charge into new businesses—and into the Internet Age, where the old rules of computerdom no longer hold. Not surprisingly, Barrett conjures up a Western metaphor. He does, after all, live in Arizona, commuting most weeks to Intel Corp.'s Silicon Valley headquarters. Barrett compares Intel's microprocessor business to the creosote bush, a tall desert plant that drips poisonous oil, killing off all vegetation that tries to grow anywhere near it. Microprocessors so dominated the company's strategy, he says, that other businesses could not sprout around it. Chips, he says, "are a dream business, with wonderful margins and a wonderful market position. How could anything else compete here for resources and profitability?"

How, indeed, unless you have a CEO who is kicking up a sandstorm to find a way. Nearly two years after Barrett took the reins at Intel, the chip giant is in the midst of a historic overhaul that is transforming its business and its culture—for a second time. The first, back in 1985, Intel fled the memory chip business and bet the farm on microprocessors, turning itself from a diversified maker of chips into one focused solely on producing the electronic brains of personal computers. It was a brilliant move that set up the company for a golden period of growth under legendary CEO Andrew S. Grove. But now, the days of Intel concentrating virtually all its energy and investment on PC chips are gone.

The Grove era is over. Instead, Barrett is reshaping Intel into a supplier of all sorts of semiconductors for networking gear, information appliances, and, of course, PCs. More startling, he's taking Intel into radically different

COMPUTER PROCESSORS

Still the heart of Intel's business, processors and companion chips for PCs and servers contributed 90% of revenues and 100% of profits in 1999. Analysts figure Intel's microprocessor business will account for less than 80% of total revenues in a couple of years.

THE BOSS Paul Otellini, 49, essentially No. 3 in the company, runs Intel's worldwide processor group. He's seen as a possible successor to Barrett.

PRODUCTS Pentium III and Celeron processors for desktop and mobile PCs; Xeon processors for servers and workstations. In the second half of this year, Intel will deliver its first 64-bit processor, called Itanium, which will help it grab more of the market for big corporate data systems. And it's about to introduce a gigabit chip, the fastest ever.

HOW INTEL STACKS UP Intel still has 84% market share in PC processors. But rival Advanced Micro Devices has hit big with its Athlon chip and Taiwan's Via also is coming on strong since buying the Cyrix processor from National Semiconductor.

ACQUISITION HELP Intel has made a few small acquisitions for its core business, such as graphics chipmaker Chips & Technologies and multiprocessing expert Corollary.

MARKET GROWTH The microprocessor sector just isn't the rocket ship it used to be.

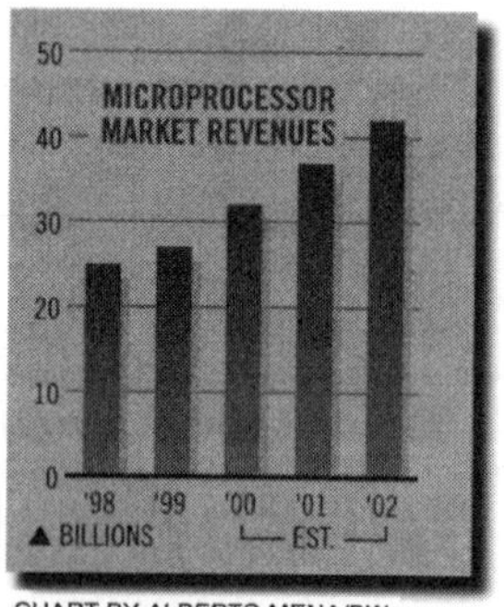

CHART BY ALBERTO MENA/BW

DATA: ROBERTSON STEPHENS, SEMICONDUCTOR INDUSTRY ASSN.

terrain, such as e-commerce, consumer electronics, Internet servers, and wireless phones. "We're putting a new image on top of the big powerful chip monster that eats the world," Barrett says.

And how. Last September, Intel unveiled a new family of chips for the networking and communications gear that zips data traffic through the arteries of the Internet. That's a $7 billion opportunity—and it's growing 30% faster than PC processors. In the same month, Barrett launched an even wilder scheme: Internet services, a $3 billion business worldwide that is nearly doubling each year. Intel opened the first of a dozen gigantic computer

INTEL'S PATH BEYOND THE PC

How the advent of the Internet and cheap PCs made Intel reboot

FEBRUARY 1997

Compaq unveils a $999 PC using a cheap Pentium clone chip. Intel execs downplay sub-$1,000 PCs as a fad, but the machines catch on, and Intel's share of the low end drops to 30%.

APRIL 1997

Barrett wants the troops to break their old habits and diversify. He compares Intel's microprocessor business to a creosote bush, a plant that kills off nearby vegetation.

JULY 1997

Barrett is named president in May and, fearing the impact of low-cost chips, kicks off the first of eight seminars for Intel's top brass. The classes are aimed at getting them to dream up new businesses.

OCTOBER 1997

Intel buys DEC's chip unit for $700 million. The deal contains a gem: Rights to the zippy StrongARM processor, which Intel adopts for some mobile and networking products.

DECEMBER 1997

Intel ends the year with record sales of $25 billion and a blowout $6.9 billion in profits. But analysts worry about the potential financial impact of cheap PCs.

JANUARY 1998

Intel surveys 2,000 Internet service providers and discovers they want simple servers that do jobs such as encryption. So Intel develops server appliances that debut two years later.

FEBRUARY 1998

To kick-start a networking business, Intel hosts a press event in San Francisco and unveils dozens of products, including routers and switches.

MARCH 1998

Barrett is named CEO. But lower chip prices in part prompt a warning of lower first-quarter results. To reclaim lost share, Intel launches the cheap Celeron chip. But it's poorly received.

JULY 1998

Barrett O.K.'s the launch of a new-business group to fund internal startups and asks manufacturing veteran Gerry Parker to head the new unit.

AUGUST 1998

The company forms a home-products group to develop Web appliances and Internet-enabled TVs and set-top boxes.

SEPTEMBER 1998

Five managers, led by Renee James, study the Web-hosting business—but it's a risky leap from making chips. The board gives it the O.K. six weeks later.

NOVEMBER 1998

Intel completes a crash, 12-month program to set up Web-based order taking for its customers. In 1999, online revenues soar quickly to $1 billion per month.

FEBRUARY 1999

Intel unveils plans to co-develop a digital signal processor with Analog Devices. This could help it gain ground in markets such as cell phones and consumer electronics.

MARCH 1999

Intel makes its largest acquisition, buying networking chipmaker Level One for $2.2 billion in stock. The company specializes in chips that connect network cards to wiring.

APRIL 1999

Intel announces a home networking kit, the first product it will sell directly to consumers over the Web. The product sends data over phone wiring in homes.

JUNE 1999

Straying far from its roots, Intel buys Dialogic, a maker of PC-based phone systems, for $780 million. Dialogic gives Intel technology for the convergence of voice and data networks.

SEPTEMBER 1999

Intel unveils 13 networking chips and opens its first Web-hosting center in Santa Clara. With a capacity for 10,000 servers, it could serve hundreds of e-commerce companies.

OCTOBER 1999

Intel acquires DSP Communications, a leader in wireless phone technology, and IPivot, a maker of gear for speeding up secure e-commerce transactions.

JANUARY 2000

Barrett spells out a plan to sell info appliances through phone companies and ISPs later this year. The devices use Linux software—not Windows CE from its long-time partner Microsoft.

FEBRUARY 2000

Intel launches a line of seven server appliances, called the NetStructure family, that speed up and manage Web traffic. This puts Intel in competition with Cisco Systems and others.

NETWORKING CHIPS

Intel is "deadly serious" about being a player in the fast-growing networking industry, says CEO Barrett. In the past, networking was a sideline to sell more PCs. Now, Barrett is pouring billions into acquisitions, hiring, and marketing.

THE BOSS Mark Christensen, 40, is a rising star at Intel. With the company 18 years, he helped drive networking sales from zero to about $1 billion in the 1990s. Now he leads a 2,500-person group and reports directly to Barrett.

PRODUCTS The Network Communications Group sells chips used in modems, network interface cards, switches, and routers. Customers include Lucent, Nortel, Ericsson, and Nokia. A new family of 13 chips rolled out last September features a so-called network processor, a programmable chip that speeds and simplifies the design of new networking gear.

HOW INTEL STACKS UP Lucent Technologies Microelectronics Group is No. 1. Stalwarts like Motorola and Texas Instruments also play major roles, while newcomers Broadcom and Conexant Systems are favorites with investors. Intel is barely a blip on the radar screen in the market as a whole, but it's strong in some segments such as chips for broadband.

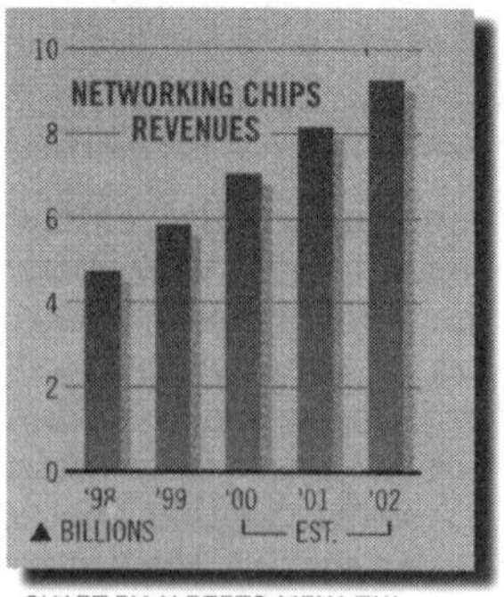

CHART BY ALBERTO MENA/BW

ACQUISITIONS Intel has spent big to get into this business. in 1999 it bought Level One Communications (for $2.2 billion), Softcom Microsystems (for $149 million), NetBoost (215 million), and the telecom chips group of Stanford Telecommunications (price not disclosed).

MARKET GROWTH Such chips are among the fastest-growing of all categories.

DATA: MERRILL LYNCH & CO., COMPANY REPORTS

centers that it's building around the world to run Web and e-commerce sites for other companies. Over the next two years, the chipmaker will spend $1 billion on this elaborate network of Internet data facilities.

WHAT THE NEW INTEL LOOKS LIKE

The old Intel was dedicated to a single product. But Barrett has divided the company into five groups, the better to pursue new products and acquisitions.

WEB WAR. Barrett's handiwork didn't stop there. In October, he paid $1.6 billion to buy DSP Communications Inc., a leading maker of digital wireless phone technology. Then, in January, Intel rolled out an ambitious plan to sell branded information appliances—screen phones, e-mail stations, TV set-top boxes— through phone companies and Internet service providers. And in February, the company barged into yet another new business, announcing a family of special-purpose network servers that manage Web traffic. The boxes will go head-to-head against gear from networking powerhouse Cisco Systems Inc. and a host of smaller rivals. "Craig stepped on the gas much more aggressively than I would have," concedes Grove, now Intel's chairman.

Each of these new schemes is ambitious in its own right. Taken together, they're a watershed. Within five years, Barrett intends all of Intel's new thrusts to be $1 billion-plus businesses and No. 1 or No. 2 in their markets. He's betting they will help Intel grow 15% to 20% a year, up from its paltry 8% compound growth over the past two years. So far, Wall Street is buying Barrett's vision, driving Intel shares up 40% since Jan. 1—easily the best growth among the 20 most widely held stocks in the U.S. By 2001, figures Merrill Lynch & Co. analyst Joseph A. Osha, products other than processors will make up a quarter of Intel's $38 billion in revenues and contribute nearly a third of its revenue growth. "Barrett is undertaking nothing less than a reinvention of Intel," says analyst Drew Peck of SG Cowen Securities Corp.

But no one is sure what he'll wind up with when he's done. Intel already is late to the Internet party. And the company is trying to break into new markets that already have scores of entrenched competitors. The result: Two years into Barrett's makeover, much of the payoff for Intel remains in the future. PC components are still the heart of its business, generating 90% of revenues and 100% of profits. "No organization its size can turn on a dime," says Peck. "This will be a slow, ponderous process, and meanwhile, expectations are very high."

Make that sky-high. Investors already are treating Barrett's plan as if success were a sure thing. That doesn't leave much margin for error. Barrett has to ensure that Intel's cash cow microprocessor business keeps throwing off beaucoup bucks to pay for the new gambits. In early March, for example, Intel will unveil the fastest PC chip ever sold, a Pentium III that runs at one gigahertz, or one billion cycles per second. But Intel's track record in its core business last year wasn't so good. The company had a rash of blunders in 1999—microprocessors and chipsets delivered months late, embarrassing design

COMMUNICATION PRODUCTS

Nine years after launching its first networking gear, Intel has only a single-digit share of a $20 billion market. Now it's aiming for fast-growth segments: Home networking, broadband modems, PC-based telephony, and server appliances.

THE BOSS John Miner, 45, used to run the company's servers and work-stations effort. Barrett tapped him last July to head a new 3,000-person Communications Products Group. Miner is gung ho: "Barrett says he'd rather come running after me and pull me back than have to push me out to the edge."

PRODUCTS Intel's lineup includes Ethernet hubs, small networking switches, and routers. It recently rolled out a line of specialized servers that manage Web traffic and speed up e-commerce. And it sells PC-based phone systems.

HOW INTEL STACKS UP Intel is up against 3Com, Nortel and Cisco in home and small-business networking. As it pushes into broadband modems, it crosses Alcatel, Motorola, and others. And in specialty markets such as Web appliances and PC phones, it bumps into Alteon, Natural Microsystems, and others.

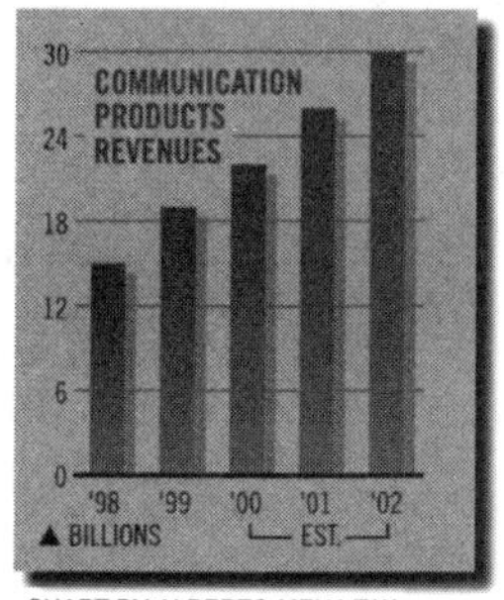

CHART BY ALBERTO MENA/BW

ACQUISITIONS Intel's most active area. In 1997, it bought Case Technology (for $72 million), a maker of low-end networking boxes. Since then, it has gobbled up the likes of IPivot ($500 million), which makes secure e-commerce servers; and Dialogic ($732 million), a leader in PC-based phone systems.

MARKET GROWTH Network gear is big business, but growth is slowing.

DATA; CAHNERS IN-STAT, COMPANY REPORTS

bugs, and supply shortages. Even loyal customers like Dell Computer Corp. (DELL) and Gateway Inc. have taken the highly unusual step of publicly blaming the chip giant's gaffes for their recent earnings problems. Gateway was so incensed over supply problems that it's giving some orders to archrival Advanced Micro Devices Inc., which has caught up to Intel in chip performance.

That's prompting analysts to wonder if top management is prepared to handle the swirl of new initiatives. For starters, Intel is heading into territory unfamiliar to its executives—all of them veterans deeply rooted in chips. Analysts worry that the company's pell-mell rush into new businesses lacks focus. "They're throwing spaghetti against the wall to see what sticks," complains analyst Jonathan J. Joseph of Salomon Smith Barney. And rivals snort that Intel lacks key expertise in networking and data services—though they admit that its rich profits give it the means to buy into new markets. Barrett himself concedes that in its new endeavors, Intel will have to "compete, scratch, and claw for market share"—a bracing change from Intel's near-monopoly in PC processors.

PC POTHOLE. Barrett had little choice. After 10 years of 30%-plus compound annual growth, Intel hit a mile-wide pothole in 1998. Earlier attempts to expand into new businesses such as modems and video conferencing had gone nowhere. Then falling PC prices, computer industry consolidation, and increased competition piled on top of one another, causing Intel's revenue growth to slow to 5%, while earnings declined for the first time in a decade. The bad news drove Intel's stock down 30% and kept it off its peak for most of 1998.

The biggest culprit in Intel's slowdown was a changing PC landscape. For the first time since the IBM Personal Computer exploded onto the market in 1981, PCs were losing some of their luster. Instead of clamoring for more power to run fatter software programs, many customers just wanted cheap PCs to get online. Low-cost PCs meant low-cost chips, something rivals realized faster. Peering into the future, says Frank Gill, Intel's former top networking exec who retired in 1998, "Intel could see that the next 10 years wouldn't be as lucrative in processors." Adds Barrett: "It used to be that the PC was the center of the action, but now it's clearly the Internet."

There's no question that Intel is now a believer. Just look at the company's semiannual developers' conference on Feb. 15. As 3,200 digit heads crammed into a ballroom at the Palm Springs (Calif.) convention center, giant video screens flashed to life and the unmistakable riff of Steppenwolf's *Born To Be Wild* blared into the hall—only it had new lyrics: "Get your modem running, head out on the I-way. Looking for e-ventures, and whatever comes our way. Born to be wired." It was the warmup for a speech by Grove, the legendary chip warrior who barely sounded as though he were still in the semiconductor business, as he went on about e-commerce, gigabit networks, and facilities filled with servers. "For the first time in 15 years, we have found it necessary to change our corporate mission statement," said Grove. Now, instead of being just the leading purveyor of PC technology, Grove says, Intel aims to make the building blocks for the entire Net Economy.

To do that means undoing much of what Grove put in place. Within weeks of taking over in May, 1998, Barrett began dismantling Grove's rigidly centralized management structure, eventually breaking Intel into five groups whose managers report directly to him. He loosened Intel's conservative financial management to let

NEW BUSINESS

Intel's New Business Group has pumped more than $50 million into 25 small projects. They vary from a secure medical ID system for doctors on the Net to terminals installed in the backs of seats at Madison Square Garden.

THE BOSS Gerry Parker, 56, is a widely respected 31-year Intel veteran who previously ran the company's manufacturing. Why an operations guy in business development? Because he makes things happen. "We're looking for as many ideas as possible," Parker says.

PRODUCTS Only a few projects have been revealed. One, an Oregon startup called Vivonic, will sell a $230 digital handheld health planner that links to a PC and a Web site. Another, called PassEdge, is developing technology for protecting digital content. And the first of a dozen Web-hosting centers is now open in Santa Clara, Calif.

HOW INTEL STACKS UP It's too early to say how Intel's startups will do. But Intel is not the first to spy the opportunity for Web hosting. The top players, including Exodus and IBM, have 30% of the market—with Intel nowhere in sight. Intel thinks it can break in by offering soup-to-nuts e-commerce services.

ACQUISITIONS In 1998, Intel bought Seattle-based iCat, a maker of easy-to-use e-commerce programs aimed at small to midsize businesses.

CHART BY ALBERTO MENA/BW

MARKET GROWTH Web hosting is one of the fastest-growing segments of the information technology business.

DATA: INTERNATIONAL DATA CORP., COMPANY REPORTS

more of its $12 billion cash hoard flow to acquisitions, equity investments, and internal startups. "We had to change the culture and the way we run our business," he says. Most of all, Barrett had to wean Intel from the defining strategy of the Grove era, when growth lay in stimulating demand for ever-more powerful PCS.

To flesh out his vision, Barrett has been on a spending spree. He's buying companies to beef up Intel's product line and help shed its notorious "not-invented-here" syndrome. In 1999 alone, the company spent $6 billion snapping up 12 companies—more, for the first time ever, than it spent on capital equipment, and nearly as much as the research-and-development and capital budgets combined. In a bid to mine fresh ideas within the company, the 60-year-old CEO has poured some $50 million into 25 homegrown startups that could someday become new product lines or be spun off as subsidiaries. And hundreds of other ideas are in the pipeline. Gerhard H. Parker, the Intel veteran who heads the company's New Business Group, says people are so excited about the opportunity that an employee recently chased him into the bathroom clutching a business plan. "It's wonderful to see that kind of enthusiasm," Parker says. "It wouldn't have happened a few years ago."

BATTING AVERAGE. Not without Barrett. While Grove is known for his fiery temper, Barrett is cool as ice. In his years before becoming CEO, he was known occasionally to bring a baseball bat to meetings to ensure—humorously—quick capitulation from intransigent colleagues. A native of the Bay Area, he studied metallurgy at Stanford University and went on to become an associate professor in the school's engineering department. After a sabbatical year working for Intel in 1973, he returned to Stanford for one day, then chucked it all and went back to Intel for good, rising through the ranks on the strength of his operational skills. He's credited with turning the company from an 80-pound weakling into an 800-pound gorilla in manufacturing, largely through inventing a technique called "Copy Exactly" in which every Intel plant is identical, down to the colors of paint. That made it easy for Intel to roll out new production techniques to all its factories—and dramatically boost quality and productivity.

So how did Mr. Manufacturing get Intel's troops jazzed about something besides their beloved microprocessor? He didn't need a baseball bat. When Compaq Computer Corp.'s $999 PC hit the market in February, 1997, carrying a chip from rival Cyrix Corp., Intel executives began to worry that cheap PCS could choke off its growth engine. Soon, inexpensive machines were flooding the market, and by mid-summer, Intel competitors AMD and Cyrix had grabbed 20% of the U.S. retail PC market, their highest share in half a decade.

That's when Barrett and then chief Grove decided to split Intel's Pentium line into distinct price and performance bands to target different markets. They devised the Celeron line for inexpensive PCS and the Xeon family for high-powered servers and workstations, while keeping the flagship Pentium III aimed at the middle tier of the market. Despite a cool reception at first, the Celeron has helped Intel climb back to 62% market share in sub-$1,000 PCS, up from 30% a year ago. And analysts now expect revenues from server-class chips to top $6.7 billion by 2001, up from $3.4 billion last year. The segmentation strategy has helped Intel maintain its juicy 60% gross margins by balancing high- and low-end sales.

But Barrett understood that segmentation alone wouldn't put Intel back on the growth curve investors had come to expect. Given Intel's size, growing at 20% per year required coming up with $5 billion or more in new reve-

INFORMATION APPLIANCES

A few years ago, Intel was convinced that PCs were the ultimate information appliance. But the possibility that something simpler or cheaper could attract millions of non-PC households became too attractive to ignore.

THE BOSS Claude Leglise, 44, who used to manage outside software developers, got a new mandate in August, 1998, "to move Intel into the home, somehow," he says. Just 18 months later, Intel rolled out services and prototype products that should appeal to consumers and Internet service providers.

PRODUCTS As yet undelivered, they'll use Celeron chips and Linux—not Microsoft Windows CE—software, and will be sold through phone companies and ISPs. Possible models include screen phones, e-mail terminals, and TV set-top boxes.

HOW INTEL STACKS UP There are zillions of rivals—from startups such as Network Appliance to giants like Motorola/General Instrument. Intel is behind since it hasn't shipped any products yet. Another promising avenue: Intel is moving aggressively into chips for wireless phones.

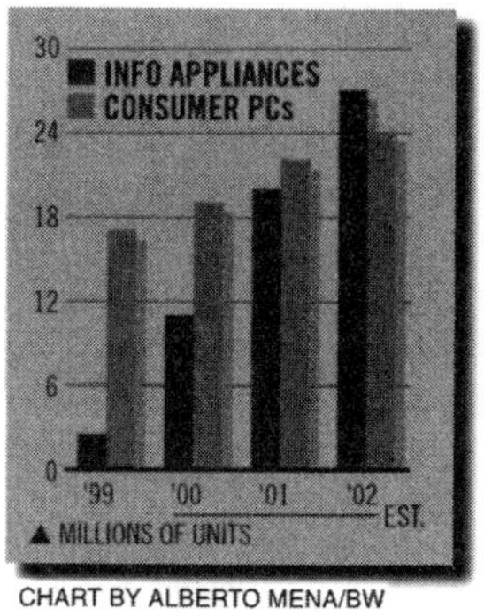

CHART BY ALBERTO MENA/BW

ACQUISITIONS DSP Communications ($1.6 billion).

MARKET GROWTH PC unit sales in the U.S. are expected to be eclipsed in 2002 by combined sales of e-mail terminals, Web pads, screen phones, Internet-enabled TVs, and other such high-tech gizmos.

DATA: INTERNATIONAL DATA CORP., COMPANY REPORTS

nues every year. And that meant Barrett had to think big. "He was looking to build Intel's next $25 billion business and knew he would have to significantly expand its charter," says David B. Yoffie, a professor at Harvard business school and a member of Intel's board.

THINKING GREEN. The CEO-to-be knew the first place to start was inside Intel. In July, 1997, he arranged for three corporate strategy gurus to conduct a seminar series for Intel's top 400 managers. In eight groups of 50, executives retreated for a week to hotels near Intel's offices in Santa Clara, Calif., Phoenix, and Portland, Ore. "We had to figure out how to grow new businesses in the shadow of the creosote bush," Barrett says.

The first day was led by Robert A. Burgelman, a Stanford Business School professor who has studied Intel for years and co-teaches a course at the school with Grove. Burgelman specializes in helping companies develop and nurture an entrepreneurial spirit. He urged seminar attendees to divide Intel's businesses into "blue" products, its old bread-and-butter chips businesses, and "green" products—everything new. The goal was to get managers to jump faster on green ideas and escape the gravitational pull of the blue status quo. Executives at Intel now routinely use the blue vs. green descriptions when discussing strategies. "There's been a freeing up of thinking," says Paul S. Otellini, the head of Intel's processor unit.

On the second day, managers learned about the threat posed by so-called disruptive technologies. Clayton M. Christensen, a Harvard B-school professor and author of *The Innovator's Dilemma,* explained how makers of cheap steel reinforcing bars, known as rebar, once dismissed as insignificant by industry giants, had nibbled their way into the market for higher-value steel. The PC had done the same thing to mainframe computers, he said.

"DIGITAL REBAR." The third day of the seminar focused on business ecosystems. Led by James F. Moore, president of consultancy GeoPartners Research Inc. and author of *The Death of Competition,* the session taught Intel execs that to move beyond the familiar PC world, they would have to construct new webs of relationships and help seed emerging business ecologies. In the first few months of the seminar series, when Intel still believed that cheap PCs would be a short-lived craze, "there was a lot of denial of the message," Moore says. Then, with AMD's market share soaring, the mood turned to despair.

The big breakthrough came in September, 1997. At a dinner with Grove and other top execs following a seminar, the famously paranoid Grove latched on to the rebar story as an analogy for cheap PCs. "If we lose the low end today, we could lose the high end tomorrow," he exclaimed. From then on, Grove referred to cheap PCs as "digital rebar," and Intel became more aggressive in promoting the Celeron, even at the risk of cannibalizing sales of pricier chips.

Intel's execs also began to accept the idea of widening the company's mission. Their vehicle of choice was an investment fund Intel launched in 1991 to dribble money into PC industry startups whose products or technologies gobbled up PC power and, in the words of Grove, created "waves of excitement" among potential PC buyers. Now

After seeing Intel squeeze PC makers, says one analyst, networking outfits "are suspicious of their intentions"

THE THRILL OF 'CLAWING FOR MARKET SHARE' IS BACK

Craig R. Barrett, CEO of Intel Corp. since May 1998, is as cool as his predecessor Andrew S. Grove was hot. But don't let Barrett's placid mien fool you: He's as tough as they come, with a biting wit. Trained as a metallurgist, Barrett quit his job as a Stanford University engineering professor to join Intel in 1974. He rose to the top on his operation's talent—Barrett is credited with turning Intel into a nonpareil manufacturer—but in the past two years, he has been moving into the role of visonary-in-chief. Barrett spoke with BUSINESS WEEK *correspondent Andy Reinhardt in the* CEO*'s unadorned conference room.*

Q: *How is Intel changing?*

A: We are still driving our core [microprocessor] business as hard as ever, and [it's] still doing pretty well. But we've supplemented it with new growth initiatives, which are very exciting and very different for us. We are acquiring companies, acquiring people, and putting a new image on top of the big, powerful chip monster that eats the world.

Whether it's networking or cellular communications, server appliances, or server farms, there's a lot more buzz and energy, which is causing the company to change the way it behaves. It's not just the big machine continuing to roll on. [We have] a bunch of smaller businesses starting up, which are forced to compete, scratch, and claw for market share.

Q: *You've started other businesses before. What's different this time?*

A: A lot of the initiatives we had in the past were not so much new business thrusts as something designed to augment and support the existing Job 1 business. But when you look at server farms [facilities with rows of computers] or cellular communications, these are pretty well removed from microprocessors. They're quite different, not just a pimple on our core business.

Q: *Why are you undertaking such a massive overhaul of your business?*

A: The PC was at the center of computing during the '90s, but if you look at the next decade, the Internet is clearly it. The PC is still very important in the Internet era. But if you want to be involved in this new era, you have to look for the new growth opportunities. That's exactly what we're trying to do.

Q: *Why are you doing so many acquisitions?*

A: We recognized one of the changes we had to make to continue to grow was to pump up the acquisitions. We really can't develop all this technology internally, so we had to go outside. This is generally accepted now as one of the ways people grow. . . . Let's stop being sqeamish; let's just go out and do it.

Q: *Your plan to host the Web operations of others baffles some people because it's so different from manufacturing chips. What expertise does Intel have to offer?*

A: If the argument were that we run big silicon factories so we can run big server farms, I would question it, too. But you have to look at it from the standpoint that we run Intel.com 24 hours a day, 365 days a year. We went from selling nothing online to more than $1 billion a month over our own infrastructure. We have expertise in this space. Forget about silicon factories.

Q: *What about your plan to sell information appliances? Couldn't they undermine sales of* PCs*?*

A: The Internet is too big, too powerful, too multifaceted not to have multiple points of entry. but the real question is, if you're going to send e-mail with photo attachments, how are you going to do that? I would argue that you're going to do that on a standard, fairly rich PC, not on a hand-held device. As long as it works that way, the PC is still at the center of the action.

renamed Intel Capital, the fund has vastly expanded its outlays, from about $300 million in 1997 to $1.2 billion last year, and has stakes in more than 350 software and Internet companies.

Intel Capital has scored some notable hits, including eToys, Red Hat, and Inktomi. Its holdings are now valued at more than $8.2 billion, and it kicked $327 million in pretax income into Intel's fourth-quarter results—half of the company's 6 cents upside earnings surprise. But Intel Capital wasn't conceived primarily as a moneymaker. The investment in eToys, for example, was seen simply as a way to boost the growth of e-tailing—and the purchase of PCs. "My goal is to expose the company to every facet of the Internet economy," says Leslie L. Vadasz, manager of the fund. "It has already lead to an opening of minds." The model worked so well that in 1999 Intel set up a separate $250 million fund to encourage software development for its new 64-bit Itanium processor and a similar $200 million fund to spur adoption of its new networking chips.

After the seminar series ended in 1998, the minds of Intel's managers were opened a bit more than the company could handle. At each session, attendees had broken into groups to dream up new business ideas. But "Barrett had gotten all these people excited with nowhere to go," says D. Craig Kinnie, director of Intel Architecture Labs, a research group in Oregon. The new CEO soon realized he needed more than just a cultural awakening: He had to change Intel's inflexible structure to allow new ideas to thrive.

WAD OF CASH. That July, Barrett came up with a solution. He and chief financial officer Andy D. Bryant threw out Intel's rulebook for funding new programs and established the New Business Group. Rather than setting tight budgets and subjecting internal startups to rigorous reviews, they were treated like venture-capital-financed companies and given a wad of cash to spend until it ran out. Under this scheme, Parker's unit has launched about 20 seed projects, each with three or four employees and a budget of several hundred thousand dollars. Seven larger projects have received $5 million to $10 million in funding. The ideas range from a scheme to equip doctors with secure IDs to encourage online medicine, to installing 3,000 information terminals on the backs of seats at Madison Square Garden for hockey fans to look up information on their favorite players. Two potential spin-offs: An Intel business called Vivonic, based in Oregon, will sell handheld computers that help users monitor their diet and fitness starting this spring. Another Portland-based venture, called PassEdge, is set to be launched this April with technology for protecting online content, such as digital music and movies, against illegal copying.

By far, Intel's biggest gamble is its nascent Web-hosting business. The idea of running Net data centers had been floated in 1996 but was shot down because top execs didn't grasp the coming rise of Web services. Two years later, in September, 1998, Barrett directed Renee James, Grove's chief technical aide, to explore the idea again. She pulled in a team of five people and spent six weeks cobbling together a plan. "We pored over reams of data, but in the end we took a flyer," James says. Intel's board quickly approved the plan in November, and by January, 1999, it was launched. Just nine months later, Intel opened its first data center in Santa Clara. With a capacity for 10,000 servers, the center is now barely occupied. So far, only about a dozen companies—including Citigroup, an Excite@Home shopping service, and several customers from Intel's Pandesic joint venture with SAP Corp.—are using the service.

Web services couldn't be further from the chip industry. But Intel execs argue that being in the business will give the company insight into e-commerce trends. Plus, it's an insurance policy in case computing moves to a pay-for-service model and PCs are eclipsed by devices connected to Web servers. Besides, Intel executives point out, the company already does $1 billion in online business every month. "We run Intel.com 24 hours a day, 365 days a year," Barrett says. "We went from selling nothing online to more than $1 billion a month over our own infrastructure. We have expertise in this space."

WIRELESS WAY. Still, analysts remain ambivalent about the likely success of the program. "I just don't get it," says Manoj Nadkarni, president of consultancy ChipInvestor.com, an investment research house based in Federal Way, Wash., that specializes in chip companies. Noting that the leading independentWeb-hosting outfits, Exodus Communications Inc. and Verio Inc. are still losing money, Nadkarni and other analysts wonder what kinds of margins Intel can get from the business. Barrett won't comment on profits. Competitors, naturally, can't resist. "This is a mistake," says William L. Shrader, CEO of Internet service provider PSInet Inc., pointing out that Intel is going into business against its customers. "Intel looks like a joke. They'll retreat in less than two years as gracefully as possible." Adds Ellen Hancock, CEO of Web-service rival Exodus Communications: "It's a stretch for them to say they have some expertise here. We've taken years to set up our operations."

Barrett rejects such notions but admits that Intel Online Services isn't the centerpiece of his strategy. By comparison, networking and communications are "an order of magnitude" more important, he says, because the communications industry is larger than computing, yet Intel "doesn't play nearly as significant a role there." Intel, however, does stand a good chance of becoming a major supplier of wireless chip technology. The purchase of DSP Communications, combined with a joint venture with Analog Devices to develop a new digital signal processor chip, could give Intel a bigger piece of the explosive mobile-phone business. It's already the No. 1 supplier of memory chips used in cell phones. By packaging DSPC's software with Intel's energy-efficient StrongARM processor, Barrett figures he can parlay that position into selling the more profitable brains of wireless Internet-ready phones. It's a huge opportunity: Researcher International Data Corp. figures such devices could surge to 536 million units in 2003, up from 85 million in 2000. "Wireless access is the second coming of the Internet," says IDC researcher Iain Gillott.

But rivals aren't rolling over. The $7 billion communications chip sector is on fire, with projected 20% growth this year. Established players are beefing up their portfolios. Motorola, Conexant, and Lucent Technologies, for instance, all recently bought network processor startups, and IBM has a chip of its own. Competitors pooh-pooh Intel's prospects, arguing it lacks expertise in custom chips and analog circuits—both crucial for networking. "Intel doesn't understand the communications market," snaps John T. Dickson, president of Lucent Microelectronics Group, the No. 1 supplier of communications chips. What's more, says Charles Boucher of Bear, Stearns & Co., after seeing how Intel sucked the profits out of the PC makers, networking companies "are suspicious of their intentions."

Adding talent through acquisitions could help, but Intel's track record in promoting outsiders is poor: Only three CEOs from the 20 companies Intel has bought in the last three years are now among its top 92 executives. Most others have stayed, but they toil deeper in the ranks. By contrast, Cisco's top tier is populated with former heads of acquired companies. Intel acknowledges, too, that while its overall turnover remains an enviable 4% per year, it has had trouble holding on to younger, midlevel managers who are defecting to dot-coms. Says one former Intel exec: "There aren't any whiz kids there."

Barrett is undaunted. He's driving Intel at a pace it has never known before, even during the heyday of "only-the-paranoid-survive" Grove. The new chief executive is bent on leaving a legacy every bit as large as Grove's, but he's managing a far more complex enterprise facing much greater challenges. If anything, the need to prove that Intel's success wasn't just a fluke has its managers fired up. "We felt like we had succeeded before the Net," says Sean Maloney, Intel's worldwide sales and marketing manager. "Now, we have to prove it all over again." And show the world that Intel is no creosote bush.

By Andy Reinhardt in Santa Clara, Calif., with bureau reports

LEVERAGED BUYOUTS

HOW FORMICA GOT BURNED OUT BY BUYOUTS

Wall Street doesn't talk about the dark side of debt-financed takeovers. Here's why

If Formica Corp. were a human being, it would be flat on the couch in intensive therapy. Formica, a world leader in laminated countertops, is what you might call a corporate orphan looking desperately for a home. Over the past 14 years, Formica has been the neglected, even abused, stepchild of two conglomerate parents. It has endured three leveraged buyouts. It has weathered a seemingly endless array of owners and board members, not to mention a plethora of corporate strategies and restructurings. Its latest LBO was just last year. On Feb. 17, Formica tapped the public markets for a second time, selling $215 million of junk debt.

LUSH RETURNS. Formica, one of the last survivors of the 1980s deal craze, is not alone. Other companies with a seemingly endless array of parents include Avis Rent A Car, Coldwell Banker, Consolidated Cigar, MGM Studios, and Simmons Co. (table, "Life on the Block"). They and their brethren illustrate an important but overlooked niche of the booming acquisition and buyout market. While dealmakers can make a mint, the constant shuffling of corporate orphans from buyer to buyer can sometimes inflict severe pain.

For instance, Wall Street loves to tout LBO successes. The typical story: Investors buy out the existing company, typically with substantial debt, perhaps 70%. Because of the leverage, the new owners, who own the bulk of the equity, have a strong incentive to aggressively streamline operations and get rid of all the deadwood. When the company is eventually sold, because so little equity was put in the deal, the returns are magnified. Current annual rates of return to the buyout artists are around 25%—below the 35% returns of the late 1980s, but still very lush.

In Formica's case, the private investors came out very well. If you had participated in LBO No. 1 in 1985 and sold out in LBO No. 2 in 1989, when Formica's cash flow was growing at about 14% a year, you would have made four to five times your investment. And if you had held on for 10 years, you would have made $10 for every dollar that you invested.

But Wall Street doesn't usually talk about the dark side of the process. "It's not healthy for the same companies to be bought and sold," says Howard H. Stevenson, a professor at the Harvard business school and author of *Do Lunch or Be Lunch: The Power of Predictability in Creating Your Future.* "Repeated LBOs are a disaster . . . you pay down debt, get new debt, new bosses, and [create] havoc within the organization."

In the case of Warren (N.J.)-based Formica, with $551 million in reve-

FORMICA
TALE OF AN ORPHAN

1956
American Cyanamid, a chemical conglomerate, buys Formica, the world's leader in decorative laminates.

1985
LBO #1:
Formica CEO Gordon D. Sterling and management, along with Shearson Lehman and Donaldson, Lufkin & Jenrette, take company private for $200 million with $153 million in debt. Sales in 1984 were $334 million with $15 million in profits.

1987
To try and help pay down debt, the company goes public, selling 5.3 million shares raising $64 million.

1989
LBO #2: After suitors take big stakes, company is taken private again by management, Dillon Read, and Masco. Highly leveraged, the company heads into a U.S. recession, followed by a downturn in Europe. Sales and earnings are lackluster.

1995
Beset by fierce price competition and an economic slump, Formica is purchased for more than $600 million by BTR Nylex, an Australian subsidiary of BTR, a British industrial conglomerate.

1996
Under BTR, Formica goes through several management shakeups. CEO Vince Langone, along with CFO David Schneider, are asked to leave. Formica distributors complain that product has become unavailable and service erodes.

1997
BTR's stock takes a 60% plunge from 1997 to 1998.

1998
LBO #3: Formica is acquired for $405 million by CVC European Equity Partners, a venture capital unit of Citicorp, and DLJ. CEO Langone and CFO Schneider are brought back by DLJ to head the company once again.

1999
In February, Formica sells $215 million of high-yield debt to the public and works on regaining market share lost under BTR. The major tasks are to cut costs, improve manufacturing, launch new products, and shore up customer service.

DATA: BUSINESS WEEK

nues, all three of its LBOs were done with the same man at the helm—Vincent P. Langone. But even with the guidance of a driven and highly praised CEO, the constant shuffling of owners has taken its toll. Over the years, Formica has struggled continually with oppressive debt, which deterred the company's growth. An acquisition by a division of British conglomerate BTR PLC in 1995 didn't help either. BTR made several costly strategic mistakes, battering Formica's net income and market share further.

HOT LBO MARKET. All of this has had a severe impact on Formica. In the past 15 years, the market share of decorative laminates of rival Wilsonart International Inc., a division of Premark International Inc., has risen from 25% to 50%, while Formica's share has slumped from 50% to 25%, mainly due to Formica's revolving-door ownership. Says Nicholas P. Heymann, an analyst with Prudential Securities Inc. in New York, "You have basically had a complete swap of leadership in the laminate market in the past 15 years." And while Formica has lost money in the last nine out of 10 years, Wilsonart's earnings have more than tripled, says Heymann.

"I think the company would probably be bigger today than it is" without all the changes, says Ilan Kaufthal, vice-chairman of Schroder & Co., an investment-banking firm in New York. Kaufthal sat on Formica's board of directors for 10 years beginning in 1985. "In my opinion," he adds, "[the company] would have been more profitable and perhaps would have gotten further in terms of its market share."

The slew of beaten-up orphans in the marketplace hasn't stopped the LBO business from getting hotter and hotter. Buyout funds raised $54.5 billion in 1998, up 58% from 1997 and 10 times higher than in 1992, according to *Buyouts* magazine. To be sure, over the past few years, LBO firms have reduced the average leverage of a deal from 90% to 70% and are funding additional capital for acquisitions and internal growth. Still, with the pace of LBO transactions accelerating, the number of recycled orphans can only grow.

Prior to its turbulent saga of serial ownership, Formica led a placid life. Formed in 1913, the company was originally designed to replace the mineral mica with a laminated material for industrial and electrical uses—hence the name "for mica." By the 1930s, its decorated laminated product became a national rage in American kitchens. When Formica went international in the late 1940s, its name became one of the best-recognized in the world.

"ARROGANT." But by 1985, Formica had lost its sheen. It had been owned by American Cyanamid Co., a pharmaceutical and diversified chemical company, for almost 30 years. As a small division—$334 million in sales—of a conglomerate with $3.5 billion in revenues, Formica was neglected. "Formica for years had pretty significant erosion of its market position," says Kaufthal. "Competitors were aggressively stealing market share," says Alvin Levy, a retired distributor for a Formica rival. "Formica's managers were very, very arrogant."

Anxious to shed non-core divisions, American Cyanamid put several up for sale, including Formica.

One ex-director wonders if Formica would exist today had it continued to languish under Cyanamid's control

The company was an ideal LBO candidate: Despite inroads by competitors, it still had a strong brand name and, most importantly, steady cash flows. Langone, then a 42-year-old Cyanamid vice-president, was assigned to offer Formica to buyers, one of whom suggested an LBO. "We really didn't know much about LBOs," remembers Langone about the deal. "We were corporate guys."

But Langone and his boss, Gordon D. Sterling, liked what they learned and decided to bid for the company. They recruited as partners Shearson Lehman Brothers Capital. The Sprout Group, the investment arm of Donaldson, Lufkin & Jenrette, also participated. The price: $200 million, financed with $153 million of junk debt.

Not surprisingly, life after the LBO at Formica changed drastically. As part of a conglomerate, says Langone, "You weren't looking hard at overhead." But after taking the company private, Langone and Sterling were consumed with reducing debt. "I did worry that Formica may have been too heavily leveraged," says Kaufthal.

BAD TIMING. Between 1985 and 1989, Formica managed to implement new strategies, such as expansions into Europe and Asia, says Langone. And in the late 1980s, the company added Surell—a product that competed with DuPont Co.'s Corian, a synthetic marble. Yet Langone admits that Corian still dominates the synthetic marble market. "My recollection was that very little was accomplished to diversify or leverage the Formica brand during that period," says T. J. Dermot Dunphy, CEO of Sealed Air Corp. in Saddle Brook, N.J., who sat on the Formica board from 1985 to 1989.

To help ease the debt burden, Formica in 1987 floated an IPO for 35% of the company, raising $64 million. With a chunk of debt retired, Langone planned to significantly expand the business over the next five years.

But the public company soon attracted suitors, such as Great American Realty, a subsidiary of Great American Management, and Investment Inc., a Chicago-based investment firm. With Formica clearly in play, Langone arranged a second LBO. "My motivation in life is not necessarily to buy and sell companies but to build them. But I still felt there were things I could do with the business," he says.

When Shearson and DLJ declined to participate, Langone turned to Dillon Read & Co. along with Masco Corp., a manufacturer and distributor of faucets, fixtures, and kitchen cabinets. The $400 million deal was financed with more than $300 million in debt. The timing, September, 1989, couldn't have been worse. "I didn't know soon after we closed the deal we would go straight into a recession in the U.S. for several years," says Langone.

The prolonged dreary economic conditions plus fierce price competition took their toll. Sales and earnings were lackluster. Yet Formica in 1995 was acquired by a division of BTR PLC, an ailing British-based industrial conglomerate, for $620 million.

For Formica, it was like being owned by Cyanamid all over again, only worse. The company was beset with management shakeups. Langone and Chief Financial Officer David T. Schneider were forced out. Distributors complained of poor customer service. Formica continued to lose money and its market

LIFE ON THE BLOCK

While the dealmeisters clean up, targets often are repeatedly bought and sold.

CONSOLIDATED CIGAR Bought twice by Ronald O. Perelman, plus a management LBO. Recently sold to French tobacco company Sieta.

COLDWELL BANKER In 1981, Sears acquires Coldwell. In 1993, it is sold to the Fremont Group, an investment arm of Bechtel. HFS buys the company in 1996 and spins off company-owned brokerage offices into company called National Realty Trust. HFS, Apollo Management Group, and Bear Stearns acquire assets of NRT.

MGM STUDIOS Kirk Kerkorian buys company a total of three times. In 1991, Crédit Lyonnais takes over the ailing studio after owner Giancarlo Parretti runs MGM into the ground. Kerkorian, who bought the company again in 1996, now owns 90% after taking it public in 1997.

SIMMONS CO. Bought and sold by four different LBOs owners since 1988, including Merrill Lynch Capital Partners, Wesray, Investcorp, and Fenway Partners.

AVIS In 1962, investment bank Lazard Frères buys Avis. It is later purchased by ITT, Norton Simon, Esmark, Beatrice, Wesray, Avis employees, and finally to HFS. In 1997, HFS takes the company public.

share kept slumping. BTR refused to comment.

Luckily, BTR's ownership was not to last. Two years later, the conglomerate divested Formica along with other non-core divisions. Wall Street no longer appreciated BTR's collection of disparate businesses.

Meanwhile, DLJ had put Langone and Schneider on retainer. They were looking for another LBO, specifically a building-products company with a strong brand name. "We examined 30 to 40 companies, but we didn't find anything we really loved," says Peter Grauer, managing director of DLJ Merchant Banking.

That is, until Formica came on the block again. DLJ and CVC European Equity Partners bought Formica last May for $405 million, $215 million less than what BTR paid for it in 1995. Langone and Schneider returned to reclaim their former posts. Already distributors have noticed the change. "The service is much better under Vince Langone," says Adele Beck, owner of KB Laminate Supply Inc., a Formica distributor in Providence, R.I. Now, the new owners are working to regain lost market share.

As for the cost that 14 years of revolving ownership has taken on the company? While former director Kaufthal says he thinks Formica would have been a lot better without the constant changes, he also wonders if it would even exist today had it continued to languish under Cyanamid's control.

But of course, to Langone this is all academic. Right now, he's just hoping the third LBO will work like a charm. For more than 50 years, Formica has been enhancing homes worldwide. Now, maybe it's finally found a permanent home. Knock on wood.

By Debra Sparks in New York

Prada Goes Shopping

By Lauren Goldstein

Patrizio Bertelli transformed Prada from a stuffy family company into a fashion powerhouse. And he's just warming up.

If you want to impress the CEO of a European fashion house, tell him (and they are mostly hims) that you're going to meet Patrizio Bertelli, the CEO of Prada. Eyebrows climb skyward, eyes widen, mouths gape and then shut. "He's a brilliant businessman," says Domenico De Sole, the CEO of rival Gucci. "You can quote me on that."

When Bertelli began working with Prada in 1978, the company was best known for luxury luggage. It had one store, in downtown Milan. Now Prada makes everything from lingerie to ski pants and owns 132 stores around the world. Bertelli can take much of the credit for that transformation, but success is just one of the reasons his peers are intrigued by him. Bertelli is also an enigma who fires employees on whim; a notorious control freak who insists that the desks, chairs, lamps, paper, trash cans, pencils, pens, and even staples in the U.S. office be imported from Italy; a feisty Tuscan who once smashed a mirror because it wasn't installed to his specifications. And lately Bertelli has exasperated industry colleagues by making inexplicable business decisions that somehow work out. Most annoying.

For instance, last summer Bertelli spent about $260 million, much of it borrowed, to buy 9.5% of Gucci—a company nearly twice Prada's size. Fashion gossips had a field day. Prada couldn't afford to take over Gucci, they noted. As for Bertelli's musings about exploring synergies, how naive could he be? The companies were competitors, for crying out loud! Gucci released a press notice saying "no discussions are contemplated" with Prada.

Bertelli had the last laugh, grossing $140 million when he sold the shares in January. To add salt to Gucci's wounds, he sold them to Bernard Arnault, chairman of LVMH Moet Hennessy Louis Vuitton, furthering that company's attempt to take over Gucci. The deal "changed their perception of me," Bertelli says of his peers. "They think that I can see the future."

Bertelli may not be able to see the future, but that deal put him in the role of the one to watch. Now he has his sights set on bigger game—forming his own luxury-brand conglomerate. In March, Bertelli struck a deal worth as much as $40 million with New York-based Austrian designer Helmut Lang for 51% of his trademark for the next three years. Bertelli also formed a joint venture (Prada owns 49%) with the De Rigo Group to make Prada sunglasses. And in August he announced the purchase of 8.5% of Church & Co., an English shoemaker. Recently Bertelli announced he was acquiring a controlling stake of German designer Jil Sander, making Prada Italy's first privately owned luxury-goods group. And not just any group—Lang and Sander occupy the same space on the fashion continuum as Prada. If the organizing principle of LVMH is luxury, Prada's is hip modernity.

What makes Bertelli rare among fashion moguls is that he is a hardheaded manager who is also integral to the creation and maintenance of the Prada look—a look that has influenced everyone from Giorgio Armani to the Gap. Prada is known for its cutting-edge design—and Prada wouldn't be Prada without Bertelli.

When Bertelli met his future wife, Miuccia Prada, at a trade show in 1978, it was, among other things, business at first sight. Bertelli was the owner of a leather factory in Arezzo; Prada was looking for someone to manufacture her bags. What she found at Bertelli's stall were knockoffs of her own creations. "You copied my stuff!" she yelled at him. Bertelli, the story goes, was indeed copying her designs—and doing it so well that Prada contracted with him to produce a new version of her bags. As they worked together, Bertelli began to guide her on ways to grow the business, which was little changed from the company her grandfather had founded in 1913 to make things like walrus-leather trunks. Eight years after the stormy meeting at the stall, they were married. In 1996 their respective businesses merged too, under a new holding company called Prapar B.V. Bertelli officially became the CEO of the Prada group. In fact, he had been effectively running the company almost from the moment he met Miuccia.

The Bertelli-Prada combination was a match made in business heaven. Miuccia Prada was determined to take the company's products into the modern age. And she did just that. The breakthrough was a simple black nylon bag she created in 1978. The women who tried it became addicted. It was light and indestructible, and matched everything. Perfect.

Bertelli recognized that the appeal of such products was wider than that of walrus leather and broadened the company. In 1983, Bertelli began to open more Prada stores. First came a second outlet in Milan, a sleek and minimal place that could not have been more different from the baroque design of the original store. In 1985 came a collection of shoes and another fashion breakthrough—a quilted black nylon tote bag with a gold-chain strap that was a takeoff of the famous Chanel bags. In 1989 Prada branched out into clothing.

By the end of the '80s Prada had stores in New York, Paris, Madrid, and Los Angeles. In the 1990s, Prada pulled out of several retail accounts as its own stores began sprouting up like luxury Gaps. This expansion had the advantage of allowing Bertelli to control the environment in which the products were displayed. (Control is a strategy he is fond of: Everything Prada sells is made by it or by a company it controls.) In terms of the product, too, Bertelli kept innovating. In 1993 the company introduced a less expensive line called Miu Miu, the nickname of Miuccia. In 1994 it was clothing for men and in 1997 a line of activewear called Prada Sport, which is on track to sell $200 million of goods this year. Cosmetics and home furnishings are planned. Not everything worked quite as intended. The 1996 burnt-orange and avocado-green prints, for example, were well represented at discounters the next season. But Prada's track record is so good that even its bad ideas are regularly filched—fashion's highest form of flattery.

To understand what makes Prada so influential, you have to understand what it is not. Prada is not beautiful like Dior, classic like Armani, sexy like Gucci, or tacky like Versace. But at various times it is each of those things. Prada, when it is on its game, is the perennial Next Big Thing. To the untrained eye, Prada products look a bit, well, strange. The skirts can seem dowdy, blouses baggy, shoes ungainly.

Orange-suede drawstring booties and black mink vests with nylon hoods are not for everyone. But to the fashion intelligentsia, Prada is fashion's future—and its objects are works of art. A Prada store even looks like a gallery. The walls are a soothing tea green, the shoes are displayed like sculpture, a pair of bikini pants and a bra are exhibited under glass. "They're far ahead of everyone," says Stacey Kaye, the merchandise manager at Henri Bendel.

Prada needs to be. Customers looking for the Next Big Thing are a lot harder to please than the customers of all-American style. Prada's core customers take fashion very seriously. To meet their demands, Prada must change constantly without veering off into the banal or the unsellable.

Bertelli is responsible for managing this balancing act. Miuccia Prada is the head designer, but Bertelli oversees everything the company's designers do. And when he and Miuccia disagree? The yelling begins. This type of management is unusual in a fashion CEO; typically, the business brains leave the creative to the creatives. Bertelli "is very much into the product," says Patrizio di Marco, a senior executive at Louis Vuitton and former president of Prada's U.S. operations. "He can redo completely a collection of bags in an afternoon." As unusual as a CEO-designer is, what really makes Bertelli stand out is that he knows how to push fashion to the edge—think Lucite shoes and rubber dresses—and also to sell it. Many fashion houses are so ahead of the times they can barely meet the payroll.

By comparison, Bertelli says Prada's revenues have grown on average 25% a year for the past five years, and he expects them to reach nearly $1 billion this year. (Prada is a private company, but Bertelli provided FORTUNE with audited annual reports.) In 1998, the figures show, Prada had a net profit of $77 million. That's not a great return, but Bertelli maintains that his costs are high because he's aggressively expanding the business. Overhead, for instance, had increased from 38% of sales in 1997 to 43% in 1998. Unlike other luxury-goods brands, Prada pretty much held its ground during the Asian downturn: Some 33% of its revenues came from the region last year, vs. 37% in 1996. Bertelli slashed prices in Asia to maintain market share during the slump, a decision that looks wise now that things are improving. And thanks to the new stores, revenues in the Americas were up 48% in 1998.

Bertelli loves products, but to keep the Prada demand at fever pitch, he is ruthless with them. To get the pick of Prada, you've got to get to the stores early because the must-have items of the season go quickly. And they won't necessarily be back. In 1994 Prada's bestselling bags were those black quilted nylon totes. Bertelli decided to phase them out. Why would anyone kill their most popular line? To move on to "next."

Next is usually the instinct of youth. Bertelli is 52. What kind of 52-year-old could be responsible for the Teflon-wool hiking skirt in stores this season? Well, he has gray hair, and when he met with FORTUNE he was wearing a white, short-sleeved, button-down shirt (he's said to love Brooks Brothers), with pencils in his breast pocket. Black-rimmed glasses rested in front of him on the table. This is the man whose name stirs up jaded fashion execs? This is the visionary behind one of the most influential fashion companies in the world? He looks like a professor.

To stay ahead of the fashion world, Bertelli sucks information, impressions, all he can, from everyone and everything around him. "He is an intelligent sponge," says di Marco. Bertelli puts it more floridly: "It is not fashion that changes lifestyles," he says. "It's lifestyles that change fashion. Many designers have not realized that yet." The results of Bertelli's constant search for inspiration can be seen in Prada's chic take on the fanny pack and its Technicolor L.L. Bean-ish boots. "Anytime an object communicates something, it can become fashionable," Bertelli believes.

Bertelli's roots belie his fascination with things arty and modern. He describes himself as "a normal guy" but admits he has workaholic tendencies. His father died when he was a boy, and his mother ran a shoe store in Arezzo. When Bertelli was still a teenager he started his own business—making and selling bags and belts. By 20 he had three people working for him. "I have always worked," Bertelli says. "And I have always had fun." Eventually Bertelli had fun making shoes and other leather goods under the names Sir Robert and Granello. Then he met Miuccia.

The couple and their two sons live in her family's 19th-century villa, which is filled with contemporary art by the likes of Dan Flavin and Brice Marden. Bertelli's friends say he is an excellent cook who invites favorite staff members home for dinner. He's an avid sailor who has spent some $50 million of the company's money—again to the consternation of his peers—to enter a Prada team in the America's Cup race next year.

But according to former employees, Bertelli is also a nightmare of a boss: a micromanager with a temper. He is known for frequently shouting at anyone who doesn't follow his instructions or at, well, anyone who is around at the wrong time. "The environment is very unprofessional, terror-stricken," said one recruiter who has worked with the company.

The big question for Prada's future is, Can a man with Bertelli's obsessive need for control manage a group of diverse brands from different countries, each endowed with a visionary of its own? Even Bertelli isn't sure. "The issue of managing another brand is a mystery to me," he admits. There's also the danger that if you take Bertelli's attention away from Prada, you take the spirit away from the company. And then, of course, there is the perennial question asked from the sidelines of the runways each season: Can Prada still deliver the Next Big Thing?

TELECOMMUNICATIONS

DOC EBBERS' MIRACLE DIET

The tight-fisted CEO is remaking MCI in WorldCom's image

WorldCom Inc. CEO Bernard J. Ebbers didn't waste any time in showing MCI Communications Corp.'s senior brass that the free-spending days of the second-largest long-distance company were over. When he summoned MCI's top 20 executives to a pow-wow in Destin, Fla., last July—two months before the two companies merged—he gave them several weeks' notice. Why? He wanted the execs, who were accustomed to plush corporate jets and first-class comfort, to scrounge up discount airfares. When they got there, more surprises awaited: Instead of finding the usual company limos that would whisk them to their hotels, they had to elbow their way to the rental-car-counter. No buffet was set up for their arrival. And they had to double up in hotel rooms.

Ebbers—known as "Bernie" through out the industry—was just as welcoming. First on the meeting's agenda: He warned that anyone who left the room during the presentation couldn't return until the break. Then he told them that under the WorldCom regime, they would have to submit monthly revenue statements—or "monrevs"—so he personally could police their spending. "It was a tough change," says one MCI exec.

Since WorldCom completed its $37 billion acquisition of MCI, Ebbers has brought a new slim-fast management approach to the long-distance company. To pay for the deal, he promised Wall Street that he would slash $2.5 billion in costs, rising to $5.6 billion by 2002. About half the savings in 1999 would come from putting their customer's phone and Internet traffic on each other's networks to avoid leasing links from other companies. What's more, Ebbers wants to ax MCI's overhead—one of the industry's cushiest at 30% of revenues—to about 23% this year. As part of that effort, MCI WorldCom Inc. has laid off 2,215 workers so far.

But there are some who fret that Ebbers will take his penny-pinching ways too far. MCI veterans say that if the cuts deepen, it could destroy the company's key strength—the marketing magic that helped break AT&T's monopoly. MCI is simply different from WorldCom, they argue. While WorldCom, based in Jackson, Miss., has focused on small to midsize businesses, Washington-based MCI excels at snagging consumers and high-end corporate customers—markets where you need to spend money to make money. "The world has changed for Bernie," says a former MCI exec. The company insists Ebbers won't cut core sales and marketing—he'll cut back office staff instead.

CRITICAL WEAKNESS. Just as important, Ebbers lacks several key strategic assets even after combining the two companies. One critical weakness: MCI WorldCom has no presence in the booming wireless industry. Ebbers has resisted buying a wireless company because the service hasn't been important to business customers. But analysts think the service is too popular to ignore any longer. Moreover, MCI WorldCom lacks a broad local-service offering for residential customers. Even in New York, where the company said it would offer local service, it has taken only minor steps. "Watch what they do, not what they say," says James G. Cullen, president of Bell Atlantic Corp.

Still, Ebbers' high-stakes gamble to take over MCI seems to be paying off. On Feb. 11, MCI WorldCom reported fourth-quarter revenues surged 14%, to $8 billion for the combined companies, while net income hit $428 million after a loss in the year-earlier period. Investors sent the stock soaring 5.5% that day, to $80.44. "We are continuing to gain confidence in our ability to execute," Ebbers told analysts at the time. Indeed, WorldCom out-performed every other major phone company last year, boosting its stock 137%, vs. 60% for Sprint Corp. and 24% for AT&T.

And Ebbers doesn't plan on slowing down. He has positioned MCI WorldCom to capitalize on the fastest-growing segments of the telecom industry—data and international services. With the globe's largest Internet backbone, MCI WorldCom's data business is on a pace to triple, to $23.2 billion, by 2002, estimates Sanford C. Bernstein & Co.'s analyst Tod A. Jacobs. By contrast, AT&T's data revenues will be $13.9 billion, according to Jacobs.

Foreign shores may be just as lucrative. By building its own communications networks overseas, MCI WorldCom is expected to boost international sales 40% annually, to about $5 billion, in 2002. "They're going to go through Europe and the rest of the world and take market share from the fat and

To pay for MCI, Ebbers promised $2.5 billion in cost cuts this year,

happy incumbents," says Jeffrey Heil, director of equity investments at the University of California, a large shareholder.

A key advantage in the U.S. and abroad is that MCI WorldCom is determined to build its own network—and not rely on competitors like the Baby Bells. "We don't want to negotiate with 48 other phone companies to do something," says John W. Sidgmore, MCI WorldCom's vice-chairman.

BUY N' SLASH. Ebbers' secret to success is tried and true. Since the former high school basketball coach got into the phone business in 1983 with the purchase of tiny long-distance reseller LDDS, he has bought 67 phone companies, changing their name to WorldCom in 1995. After buying companies, he slashes expenses and consolidates all traffic on a single network. Small wonder that his first yacht was named Aquasitions.

Ebbers is applying the same bottom-line philosophy at MCI WorldCom. On Sept. 27, the new company's top sales managers gathered at the America's Center in St. Louis. The folksy Ebbers told stories to help set the priorities for the new company. He said that one employee who is a single mother had been able to send her kids to college because of her WorldCom stock. Another woman had recently been able to buy a house in a better neighborhood thanks to her WorldCom shares. The point: Employees should focus on boosting shareholder returns. He then told them that everyone would receive stock options.

The new ethos of sacrificing expenses for profits is spreading throughout the organization. Ebbers sold three of MCI's five corporate jets and eliminated company cars for everyone but himself and Chairman Bert C. Roberts Jr., the former MCI chairman. And at the end of last year, the water coolers disappeared from MCI's headquarters in Washington. "It sent a signal that this is not the old MCI," says one former MCI exec. While some employees feel such trivial cost-cutting is silly, many with new stock options in hand are in favor of trimming the fat.

It helps that Ebbers' down-to-earth attitude has made him popular among workers. Often clad in jeans and cowboy boots, the CEO drops in unannounced to MCI employees' offices for an informal hello—something that MCI's Roberts didn't do. One secretary mistook Ebbers for the fax-machine repairman.

He doesn't live like a typical CEO, either. He likes to hang out with friends in Jackson at casual restaurants like Tico's Steakhouse. The 57-year-old divorcé is living temporarily in a modest double-wide trailer home on his soybean farm while he's building a house. He rides his tractor for fun. His prime indulgences are a new yacht, called Countach, and an enormous tract of land in British Columbia.

Ebbers' cowboy ways may change how MCI treats customers. In the past, MCI sought big-name accounts such as NASDAQ for the credibility and the brand-building these projects brought. But under WorldCom, these deals may be evaluated on whether they haul in enough dough. "Large deals are having to be justified purely on hard numbers," says an MCI exec who recently left.

The cultural changes are likely to lead to the departure of some key MCI staffers. Insiders question the future of Timothy F. Price, former MCI president and now CEO of MCI WorldCom's communications business. While Price has been a champion of expensive sales promotions, Ebbers may pull the plug on such goodies, including the MCI Classic PGA tournament. The contrast in styles has led to widespread rumors that Price is on his way out. The company insists nothing is amiss.

HOW BERNARD EBBERS IS TIGHTENING MCI'S BELT

DON'T GO NEAR THE WATER WorldCom removed all the water coolers from MCI's Washington headquarters. It's a symbol of the new penny-pinching attitude. Now staffers drink tap water or buy their own bottles.

ARE TOWELS EXTRA? MCI executives who visit WorldCom's Jackson (Miss.) headquarters tend to bunk at the $59-a-night Hampton Inn—owned by Ebbers. In the past, MCI executives stayed at places like the Ritz-Carlton, where rooms run $200 or so.

GOOBYE CORPORATE JETS. HELLO COACH Top execs are encouraged to fly with low-cost carriers like Southwest Airlines. To get even cheaper rates and direct flights to Mississippi, they're driving 30 miles to Baltimore-Washington International Airport. On Southwest, that can mean a round-trip fare to Jackson of $186, instead of $2,872 for a first-class seat on Delta. Meanwhile, WorldCom has sold off three of MCI's corporate jets.

HAIL, GOOD FELLOW Ebbers has eliminated the use of cushy corporate cars for everyone but Chairman Bert Roberts Jr. and himself. Now execs hail cabs or rent cars.

SORRY, I CAN'T AFFORD FRIES WITH THAT Execs are keeping receipts for any business lunches over $5. In the past, they didn't need any paperwork for their expense reports unless bills topped $25.

As MCI WorldCom hits the rocky post-honeymoon phase, telecom veterans think Ebbers should keep some of the old MCI. "I hope the culture that emerges will be a balance between the two," says former MCI exec Stephen Von Rump. So far though, MCI WorldCom is looking a lot more like WorldCom than like MCI.

By Catherine Yang in Washington, with Peter Elstrom in New York

Market Place: Midwest Express Profits by Pampering Passengers

By EDWIN McDOWELL

MILWAUKEE—Susan Dietman of Plano, Texas, has been flying Midwest Express between Dallas and Milwaukee almost every weekend for four years. Asked why she was so loyal, she ticked off some familiar reasons: adequate leg room, good food, nonstop flights and attentive service. Then she added a new one:

"When I pulled into the Dallas airport over Labor Day," said Ms. Dietman, an information systems manager at J.C. Penney, "it was threatening rain and the front window on the passenger side of my car disappeared inside the door, and I couldn't get it up." A Midwest ticket agent came to her rescue, spending 45 minutes fixing it.

"Then he took my tickets," Ms. Dietman said, "and while I drove to the parking lot he checked me in."

If that ticket agent's skills were surprising, his attitude was not—not to Midwest Express loyalists, anyway.

"A lot of airlines take the position, 'You have to fly. We're here, so get on board,' " said Don D. Johnson, a frequent flier and the owner of American Mail Service, a direct-mail company in Ralston, Neb. "Midwest Express people have the attitude that you represent money in their pocket, so how can they help?"

At a time when many carriers, judged by their economy-class service, could be called Spartan Air, Midwest consistently wins awards for pampering passengers on its all-coach planes. And while other carriers seem eager to lure ever more passengers with cut-rate fares, Midwest resists this temptation, content with its own modest, but profitable, niche.

Indeed, analysts also love Milwaukee-based Midwest Express, which traces its origins to 1948, when Kimberly-Clark Corp. began transporting its employees to remote mill locations in a prop plane.

In 1984, it started commercial service with two leased jets and daily flights from Milwaukee to Boston, Dallas and Appleton, Wis. Spun off by Kimberly-Clark in September 1995, it is on course toward its 11th consecutive profitable year—a span that includes five of the worst years in airline history. In the two years since that spinoff, the stock has doubled.

The shares closed Monday at $30.75, up 50 cents.

"From 1990 through 1994, only Midwest Express and Southwest were profitable every year," said Timothy Hoeksema, Midwest's 50-year-old chairman, president and chief executive, in a recent interview at the Milwaukee headquarters. To be sure, some of those profits were razor-thin. In the fallout from the Persian Gulf war, Midwest's earnings in 1991 nearly vanished: 2 cents a share, from 46 cents in 1990. But nearly all other airlines were in the red.

Hoeksema, who flew his first solo flight at 16 and later became Kimberly-Clark's chief pilot, is widely credited with imbuing Midwest Express with a culture unparalleled in commercial aviation.

"He's been able to transfer to the airline business the philosophy and business principles of the corporation, including the zeal for pleasing the customer," said Dennis Crabtree, vice president for operations.

From the beginning, Midwest Express' strategy has been relatively simple: focus primarily on business travelers in cities with strong business bases that have few if any nonstop flights—especially nonstops to and from Milwaukee or Omaha, where in 1994 the carrier established a mini-hub.

The one time Midwest Express departed from its game plan, entering the highly competitive Milwaukee-Detroit market in 1988, it suffered substantial losses before pulling out four years later.

When Midwest said recently that it would acquire eight MD-80s, for delivery through 1999, Hoeksema said it was part of a strategy "of profitable and controlled growth." Some existing routes, he added, are candidates for expansion, and some new routes may be coming.

For all the adulation, relatively few people have flown Midwest Express. Although it now ventures as far afield as New York, San Diego, San Francisco and Orlando, Fla., most of its 35,000 yearly flights—about the number flown by Delta, United or American in less than three weeks—are not much longer than 600 miles, compared with an industry average of just under 1,000.

Its 1.4 million passengers last year were a blip next to the 581.2 million passengers flown by the nation's big airlines, or even the 62 million commuter airline passengers.

How has Midwest, with so few passengers, earned such lofty praise? One big reason is that at a time when coach passengers are routinely shoehorned into narrow, knees-to-chin seats, Midwest's all-coach fleet—24 DC-9s and two (soon to be 10) MD-80s—features all-leather seats that are several inches wider and deeper than is typical in economy class. And there are no middle seats.

In this year's Consumer Reports Travel Letter rating of coach seats, Midwest's DC-9s received a "comfort score" of 100 and its MD-80s a 98, while most other carriers scored between 64 and 80.

"Their seats are the equivalent of first-class seats on most aircraft," said Ernest Hanchey, a project manager with HKS Inc., an architectural firm in Dallas, who flies Midwest Express to Milwaukee about every two weeks. "But I also like the fact that you get a real meal instead of a bistro bag."

Midwest Express pampering includes free newspapers at check-in, free champagne at breakfast and free wine at lunch and dinner—meals served on china with silverware and linen napkins. Dinners include lobster and steak, poached salmon, lobster thermidor, shrimp cocktail and fruit.

After lunch and dinner, the carrier serves its trademark chocolate chip cookies, hot from the on-board oven.

Despite shorter flights than those of most other airlines, Midwest spends more on food than any other carrier in the United States, an average of $9.59 for each passenger, according to Consumer Reports, about $2 more than American and United spend and more than twice the outlays of the other big airlines. At the bottom of the list were U.S. Airways, spending $2.50, and Southwest, which averages just 20 cents on its flights under three hours.

"Back in the early 1990s, when airlines were bleeding money," Hoeksema said, "we could have saved millions cutting back on our food, but we would have lost our reputation."

Indeed, Midwest is so uniformly popular with its customers that, unlike almost all the sizable airlines, it has not even been included in the Transportation Department's ranking of customer complaints in recent years because it has not received the minimum 10 complaints a year.

The revenues of Midwest Express Holdings—the parent company of Midwest and Skyway Airlines, Midwest's eight-year-old commuter line—have grown an average of 24 percent a year for 10 years. Its net income increased to almost $21.8 million last year, or $3.40 a share, compared with $19.1 million in 1995, or $2.77.

Moreover, the airline's revenue for each passenger flown, or "yield," rose 8.1 percent last year, to 19.3 cents a mile. While the eight-month suspension of the 10 percent excise tax on airline tickets helped, Midwest's yield still far exceeded the industry average of 12.9 cents.

Its secret? While Midwest generally keeps its fares in line with those of its rivals, it rarely matches their rock-bottom promotional fares and keeps a careful check on seat inventory.

"On our Monday morning flights to New York," Hoeksema said, "we may only have four seats open for lower fares."

Hoeksema disclaims any desire to become "a huge airline."

With no debt, cash flow last year of $29.4 million, a $55 million line of bank credit and a backup $20 million from Kimberly-Clark until 2000, "Capital is not our growth constraint," he said. "The constraint to our growth is how fast we can grow without losing our focus and control of our quality."

His goal, he said, is to expand capacity 12 percent to 18 percent a year, to continue to be a good place to work and to earn the best return for stockholders. Midwest became 100 percent publicly owned in May 1996, when Kimberly-Clark, which had moved its headquarters from Neenah, Wis., to Dallas, sold its remaining 20 percent stake. Officers, directors and employees own about 6.4 percent of the 6.4 million shares.

Salaries at Midwest Express, a nonunion airline, are well below those of the major carriers, but about average for a carrier its size: pilots earn about $75,000 a year, and flight attendants' pay ranges from $14,500 to $24,000. Employees also received a bonus of 8 percent of their base salary last year from a profit-sharing plan.

Brenda Skelton, senior vice president for marketing services, attributes the carrier's success to its discipline in everything from routes to fares to its fleet.

And Midwest buys used aircraft almost exclusively, paying about $8 million, half for the plane itself, the other $4 million to rebuild it and install "hush kits"—noise-reduction devices that most airlines are installing to comply with the Dec. 31, 1999, deadline for meeting federal noise reduction requirements.

"A new aircraft," Ms. Skelton said, "would cost north of $20 million." While Midwest is acquiring those eight MD-80s, for an undisclosed sum, it is considering turning the deal into a sale-leaseback.

The Midwest fleet is about 23 years old, one of the oldest in the industry, but is relatively youthful based on a more important gauge, landings and takeoffs, or "cycles." Noting that DC-9s are certified for a life of at least 100,000 cycles, Robinson-Humphrey, the Atlanta brokerage firm, noted in a research report earlier this year that the Midwest fleet averages fewer than 50,000 because it buys planes with fewer cycles.

The only blot on the Midwest Express safety record occurred in September 1985, when one of its DC-9s crashed on takeoff in Milwaukee, killing all 31 aboard. The National Transportation Safety Board ruled that the probable cause was pilot error.

Fittingly for an airline that evolved from a corporate culture, most Midway Express flights are designed so business travelers can get where they are going and return that night. And business travelers are in the majority even on its two daily nonstops to Orlando, arguably the family leisure capital of the world.

"When we thought about serving Orlando, we weren't interested in the $89 round trip; we said let's serve it as a business market," said Bob Bahlman, Midwest's chief financial officer. "If we wanted market share instead of profitability, we'd have five round trips a day, instead of two."

Similarly, the airline flies a daily nonstop between Milwaukee and San Francisco. But in the winter, it shifts that plane to Phoenix, which attracts many Midwestern "snowbirds." It also serves the Florida cities of Tampa, Fort Myers and Fort Lauderdale in winter, then shifts those planes to more profitable markets.

"In the beginning, we were afraid we might not get our regular passengers back, especially in San Francisco," Bahlman said. "But," he added, a satisfied gleam in his eye, "when we return, they're there waiting."

Specialized Hospitals Taking Over Health-Care Market

By ALLEN R. MYERSON

EDINBURG, Texas—As traditional hospitals with more offerings than Macy's decline, a new type is taking their place: the specialized hospital or clinic, designed to conquer a profitable niche.

Profit-making hospital chains are leading the way in opening category healers like heart hospitals, cancer centers and rehabilitation facilities. But many general hospitals, for profit or not, are also choosing to become more specialized. More alert than ever to where they are making and losing money, these hospitals are expanding and marketing their most profitable services.

In South Texas, Universal Health Services, the nation's third-largest hospital chain, bought Edinburg Hospital, an outdated general hospital, from the city three years ago. Universal Health built a new hospital, which opened on Aug. 1 with a traditional range of services but also a focus: delivering babies, in a women's pavilion with its own wing and a colonnaded entrance as prominent as the main one. The company is meanwhile guiding the older building through its own recovery, as a specialized hospital for rehabilitation and long-term care.

At its McAllen Medical Center, however, 20 minutes to the south, Universal Health is competing against someone else's specialty hospital. Just down the street there lies the new McAllen Heart Center, with a revolving red heart mounted on the roof. By agreeing to share profits with doctors, it lured five McAllen Medical Center cardiologists. McAllen Medical rushed to expand its own heart program before its rival opened last year, advertising itself on television as a "state of the heart hospital for cardiac care."

Often, the huge number of patients the category healers handle leads to improved quality and lower costs. Sanck Health Care's cancer centers at nine hospitals, soon to include St. Vincent's in New York, please health maintenance organizations with low costs and chemotherapy patients by staying open 24 hours a day, with valet parking always available. The Columbia-Presbyterian Medical Center, having opened a Center for Women's Health on Manhattan's East Side three years ago, offering one-stop shopping for specialists, is considering another at the hospital's Washington Heights campus. And the Healthsouth Corp.'s rehabilitation hospitals throughout the country boast of lowered costs and shortened stays.

"There's a transformation from a health care system organized primarily by the providers to a system organized by the needs of the patient," said Regina Herzlinger, a Harvard Business School expert on hospitals. "A hospital that does everything for everybody just won't be as efficient as a focused provider." In her new book, "Market-Driven Health Care" (Addison-Wesley), she cites McDonald's as an instructive example of "focused factories" that can deliver consistent products or services at lower cost.

But having hospitals behave more like purveyors of french fries can have untoward consequences. Traditional hospitals accuse their new competitors of draining away the most profitable services, leaving more complicated or money-losing treatments to them. While the McAllen

Heart Center's emergency room caters largely to cardiac cases, the McAllen Medical Center gets the car-crash and shooting victims.

Larger hospitals are finding it more difficult than ever to support costly services like emergency helicopters, neonatal intensive care and trauma centers for gunshot wounds. "If the services to generate positive income wind up getting taken out of institutions like this," said Michael Israel, chief executive of Duke University Hospital, "how do you find the funds to provide the services society needs?"

When overburdened public hospitals in Los Angeles and Chicago had to limit the number of trauma patients brought in by ambulance, private hospitals reduced their services so they would not receive a costly deluge. Federal laws prohibit patient dumping, but hospitals are not obligated to handle accident victims whom they cannot capably treat.

Many hospital administrators acknowledge that specialized competitors have forced them to become more cost-conscious and focused themselves. Hospitals are improving their efficiency enough to have raised their profits or surpluses to 5.7 percent of revenues in 1995, according to the most recent figures. The gain was the highest since 1986. Many hospitals are also receiving higher payments from Medicaid to compensate those with large shares of uninsured patients.

Competition, stingier government payments and the dictates of HMOs have closed more than 700 general hospitals in a decade, leaving 5,200 in 1995, according to the American Hospital Association. But in the same decade, the nation gained almost 100 rehabilitation hospitals, for a total of 171. A catch-all category of other specialty hospitals, including cancer and heart, rose to 110 in 1995, from 74 in 1989.

Many that remain general hospitals have still become more specialized. The chains try to buy clusters of hospitals in a region, then economize by parceling out specialties. Tenet Healthcare Inc., the nation's second-largest chain after Columbia/HCA Healthcare, has 12 hospitals in South Florida. It steers most heart surgery to just three, whose open-heart operations have risen one-third in four years. "We put services where they are needed," said Michael Focht, Tenet's president. "You do not need to have two open-heart programs within five miles."

Hospitals find surgery especially profitable. In heart and orthopedic surgery most of all, even routine procedures still pay well and require elaborate scans and tests. Delivering babies, unpopular until a few years ago because of the liability risks, has become a money-making activity because of high Medicaid reimbursement.

Medcath Inc., based in Charlotte, N.C., pronounces itself so pleased with its heart hospital in McAllen that it opened another one in Little Rock, Ark., last March, with others starting business in Tucson, Ariz., this month, Phoenix next spring, Austin late next summer and then Bakersfield, Calif., and Dayton, Ohio.

In Texas, where managed care has taken hold only recently, Denton Cooley's Texas Heart Institute at St. Luke's Hospital is one of the busiest surgery centers in the nation, with 2,400 operations a year—costing about 20 percent less than those offered by most competitors, with measurably better outcomes.

Among those newer to the game, the Heart Institute at Winthrop-University Hospital in Mineola, N.Y., more than tripled its open-heart surgery volume over five years. The Long Island hospital's publicity campaign includes mailing calendars to every household in its area, with more frequent bulletins to the elderly.

Healthsouth takes marketing much further in trying to endow its 135 rehabilitation hospitals and thousand or so clinics with a brand name as recognizable as Wal-Mart. Sports stars helping to publicize the brand include Michael Jordan, Tom Glavine and Emmitt Smith. Healthsouth has become especially profitable by figuring out how to offer rehabilitation for everything from sports injuries and birth defects to strokes and some surgery for much less than general hospitals can.

In trying to hang on to their more profitable departments, some hospitals are finding themselves defenseless against the new, specialized breed. From Houston's Methodist Hospital, the city's largest, a group of about 18 orthopedic surgeons left with dozens of nurses and aides two years ago for Columbia/HCA's new Texas Orthopedic Hospital nearby.

At Methodist, they had to compete for beds and operating rooms. At Texas Orthopedic, the 10 operating rooms, 46 hospital beds, 43 day-surgery recovery beds, physical therapy rooms and new doctors' offices are exclusively theirs.

" 'All the beds are mine?' the doctors said," according to Marsha Casey, a former Methodist executive. "'Wow. I'm there.' "

Several of the doctors became hospital co-owners, sharing in the profits. Texas Orthopedic, handling only a limited range of injuries, can offer its services more profitably than less specialized hospitals. If a patient has a heart attack, she will be whisked to another hospital, maybe Methodist.

This summer, Columbia/HCA also announced plans to turn a former general hospital in Houston into a children's hospital, and the company is considering new children's hospitals elsewhere. The ability of such Columbia/HCA hospitals to attract and keep their staffs is likely to suffer, however, because of plans by the company's new management to avoid having doctors as investors.

To attract medical stars, hospitals can wind up bidding against each other, sometimes into the millions, threatening the cost savings that set them apart. The Salick cancer centers build new operations and offer much higher pay.

The company might soon face a very familiar rival. Earlier this year, Zeneca PLC, a British drug maker, bought control of Salick Health Care, forcing out Bernard Salick, the founder. Salick pondered his next move for all of a day, then formed a new company to open AIDS centers. He soon hired David Ho, the researcher who developed the drug "cocktail" now preferred in AIDS treatment. Salick plans his first AIDS center in New York, opening in perhaps a few months, with others in Los Angeles, Miami and San Francisco. He also plans to return to cancer care.

Salick Health Care, meanwhile, is trying to specialize even further by opening breast centers for detecting and treating breast cancer and other ailments. The first breast center opened in Manhattan on East 61st Street between York and First avenues earlier this year. With construction set to begin on its first cancer center in New York, at St. Vincent's, by the end of the year, Salick Health Care hopes to have four or five more hospital sites around the area.

But not every specialty pays off, making some niche programs just as vulnerable as many mainstream operations.

On Manhattan's East Side, Lenox Hill Hospital closed its New York Pain Treatment Program in February. While the program never had a loss, said Norman J. Marcus, the program's director, it was not as profitable as areas like orthopedic and heart surgery, in which Lenox Hill is expanding.

The pain program will survive only as a much smaller, independent entity with five doctors instead of the former 30.

In a prepared statement, Terence M. O'Brien, Lenox Hill's chief operating officer, said the the hospital evaluates programs based first on its patients' needs. But, he added, "Our programs must also prove to be economically viable and consistent with our strategic plans and mission."

Marcus put it differently. "You want to do things," he said, "that bring in the greatest amount of money in the shortest period."

Predators and Prey: A New Ecology of Competition

by James F. Moore

For most companies today, the only truly sustainable advantage comes from out-innovating the competition.

Successful businesses are those that evolve rapidly and effectively. Yet innovative businesses can't evolve in a vacuum. They must attract resources of all sorts, drawing in capital, partners, suppliers, and customers to create cooperative networks.

Much has been written about such networks, under the rubric of strategic alliances, virtual organizations, and the like. But these frameworks provide little systematic assistance for managers who seek to understand the underlying strategic logic of change. Even fewer of these theories help executives anticipate the managerial challenges of nurturing the complex business communities that bring innovations to market.

How is it that a company can create an entirely new business community—like IBM in personal computers—and then lose control and profitability in that same business? Is there a stable structure of community leadership that matches fast-changing conditions? And how can companies develop leadership that successfully adapts to continual waves of innovation and change? These questions remain unanswered because most managers still frame the problem in the old way: companies go head-to-head in an industry, battling for market share. But events of the last decade, particularly in high-technology businesses, amply illustrate the limits of that understanding.

In essence, executives must develop new ideas and tools for strategizing, tools for making tough choices when it comes to innovations, business alliances, and leadership of customers and suppliers. Anthropologist Gregory Bateson's definition of *co-evolution* in both natural and social systems provides a useful starting place. In his book *Mind and Nature,* Bateson describes co-evolution as a process in which interdependent species evolve in an endless reciprocal cycle—in which "changes in species A set the state for the natural selection of changes in species B"—and vice versa. Consider predators and their prey, for instance, or flowering plants and their pollinators.

Another insight comes from biologist Stephen Jay Gould, who has observed that natural ecosystems sometimes collapse when environmental conditions change too radically. Dominant combinations of species may lose their leadership. New ecosystems then establish themselves, often with previously marginal plants and animals at the center. For current businesses dealing with the challenges of innovation, there are clear parallels and profound implications.

To extend a systematic approach to strategy, I suggest that a company be viewed not as a member of a single industry but as part of a *business ecosystem* that crosses a variety of industries. In a business ecosystem, companies co-evolve capabilities around a new innovation: they work cooperatively and competitively to support new products, satisfy customer needs, and eventually incorporate the next round of innovations.

For example, Apple Computer is the leader of an ecosystem that crosses at least four major industries: personal computers, consumer electronics, information, and communications. The Apple ecosystem encompasses an extended web of suppliers that includes Motorola and Sony and a large number of customers in various market segments.

Apple, IBM, Ford, Wal-Mart, and Merck have all been or still are the leaders of business ecosystems. While the center may shift over time, the role of the leader is valued by the rest of the community. Such leadership enables all ecosystem members to invest toward a shared future in which they anticipate profiting together.

Yet in any larger business environment, several ecosystems may vie for survival and dominance: the IBM and Apple ecosystems in personal computers, for example, or Wal-Mart and Kmart in discount retailing. In fact, it's competition among business ecosystems, not individual companies, that's largely fueling today's industrial transformation. Managers can't afford to ignore the birth of new ecosystems or the competition among those that already exist.

Whether that means investing in the right new technology, signing on suppliers to expand a growing business, developing

James F. Moore is president of GeoPartners Research Inc., a management consulting firm in Cambridge, Massachusetts, that specializes in issues of business strategy and implementation.

crucial elements of value to maintain leadership, or incorporating new innovations to fend off obsolescence, executives must understand the stages that all business ecosystems pass through—and, more important, how to direct the changes.

A business ecosystem, like its biological counterpart, gradually moves from a random collection of elements to a more structured community. Think of a prairie grassland that is succeeded by stands of conifers, which in turn evolve into a more complex forest dominated by hardwoods. Business ecosystems condense out of the original swirl of capital, customer interest, and talent generated by a new innovation, just as successful species spring from the natural resources of sunlight, water, and soil nutrients.

Every business ecosystem develops in four distinct stages: birth, expansion, leadership, and self-renewal—or, if not self-renewal, death. In reality, of course, the evolutionary stages blur, and the managerial challenges of one stage often crop up in another. Yet I've observed the four stages in many companies over time, across businesses as diverse as retailing, entertainment, and pharmaceuticals. What remains the same from business to business is the process of co-evolution: the complex interplay between competitive and cooperative business strategies (see the table, "The Evolutionary Stages of a Business Ecosystem").

The Birth of Business Ecosystems

Bet on a seed innovation that can lead to revolutionary products.

Discover the right customer value proposition.

Design a business that can serve the potential market.

During Stage 1 of a business ecosystem, entrepreneurs focus on defining what customers want, that is, the value of a proposed new product or service and the best form for delivering it. Victory at the birth stage, in the short term, often goes to those who best define and implement this customer value proposition. Moreover, during Stage 1 of a business ecosystem, it often pays to cooperate. From the leader's standpoint, in particular, business partners help fill out the full package of value for customers. And by attracting important "follower" companies, leaders may stop them from helping other emerging ecosystems.

The rise of the personal computer is a revealing example of ecological business development. In the early 1970s, a new technology—the microprocessor—emerged with the potential to spawn vast new applications and dramatically reduce the cost of computing. Yet this innovation sat dormant for several years. By 1975, hobbyist machines like the Altair and IMSAI had penetrated a narrow market. But these computers were not products that could be used by the average person.

Starting in the late 1970s, Tandy Corporation, Apple, and others introduced early versions of what would eventually become the personal computer. The seed innovation they all chose was the microprocessor, but these first designers also recognized that other products and services had to be created to bring the whole package together. These ranged from hardware components to software to services like distribution and customer support.

Apple and Tandy each had a different strategy for creating a full, rich ecosystem. Apple worked with business partners and talked about "evangelizing" to encourage co-evolution. While the company tightly controlled its basic computer design and operating system software, it encouraged independent software developers to write programs for its machine. Apple also cooperated with independent magazines, computer stores, and training institutions—and even seeded a number of school districts with Apple IIs.

Tandy, on the other hand, took a more vertically integrated approach. It attempted to buy and then own its software, ranging from the operating system to programming languages and applications like word processors. The company controlled sales, service, support and training, and market development by selling exclusively through its Radio Shack stores. At the same time, it discouraged independent magazines devoted to its TRS-80 machines. Therefore, Tandy's simpler and more tightly controlled ecosystem did not build the excitement, opportunities, and inner rivalries of Apple's, nor did it harness as much capital and talent through the participation of other companies.

Tandy's approach got the company out front fast; in 1979, it had sales of $95 million compared with Apple's $47.9 million. However, Tandy's tight control of its ecosystem ultimately led to slower growth at a time when establishing market share and a large user base was essential to success. By 1982, Apple's $583.1 million in sales had decisively passed Tandy's $466.4 million.

Meanwhile, a third business ecosystem emerged in the early days of personal computing. It never rivaled Apple's orTandy's in size, but it did help IBM enter the fray. This third ecosystem centered around two software companies: Digital Research and Micropro. In 1977, Digital Research made its software operating system CP/M available independent of hardware. That separation allowed almost any small manufacturer to assemble components and put out a usable personal computer. Overnight, a variety of small companies entered the business, building on the same Zilog microprocessor used in the early Tandy machines.

In 1979, Micropro brought out a word processor that ran on CP/M-based machines. Wordstar was the first truly powerful word processor, and it took an important group of potential PC customers—writers and editors—by storm. Demand for CP/M machines soared, fueling the growth if not the fortunes of small companies like Morrow and Kaypro.

But during the first stage of any business ecosystem, co-evolving companies must do more than satisfy customers; a leader must also emerge to initiate a process of rapid, ongoing improvement that draws the entire community toward a grander future. In the Apple and Tandy ecosystems, the hardware companies provided such leadership by studying the market, defining new generations of functionality, and orchestrating suppliers and partners to bring improvements to market. In the CP/M ecosystem, however, the hardware companies were bedeviled by rivalry among themselves. Infighting kept down prices and profit margins, and none of the CP/M companies could afford heavy advertising programs.

In Stage 1, established companies like IBM are often better off waiting and watching carefully as a new market sorts itself out. The iterative process of trying out innovative ideas and discovering which solutions are attractive to customers is hard to accomplish in a traditional corporate culture. And the diverse experimentation that thrives in an entrepreneurial scene provides more "genetic diversity" from which the market can ultimately select the fittest offering.

Established companies can subsequently replicate successful ideas and broadcast them across a wider market. In other words, they can enter the market at Stage 2 by appropriating the developmental work of others. Meanwhile, original ecosystems that succeed, like Apple's, do so by consciously nurturing a full community of partners and suppliers right from the start.

Expansion: Capturing Territory

Compete against other ecosystems to control strategic markets.

Stimulate demand for your product or service offerings.

Meet demand with adequate supply.

In Stage 2, business ecosystems expand to conquer broad new territories. Just as grasses and weeds rapidly cover the bare, scorched ground left after a forest fire, some business expansions meet little resistance. But in other cases, rival ecosystems may be closely matched and choose to attack the same territory. Direct battles for market share break out. Fighting can get ugly as each ecosystem tries to exert pressure on suppliers and customers to join up.

In the end, one business ecosystem may triumph, or rival ecosystems may reach semistable accommodations. Think of a hardwood forest that borders a grassland. The zone of conflict at the boundary may shift from year to year, but it never completely wipes out either ecosystem.

In general, two conditions are necessary for Stage 2 expansion: (1) a business concept that a large number of customers will value; and (2) the potential to scale up the concept to reach this broad market. During the expansion stage, established companies can exercise enormous power in marketing and sales, as well as in the management of large-scale produc-

The Evolutionary Stages of a Business Ecosystem

	Cooperative Challenges	Competitive Challenges
Birth	Work with customers and suppliers to define the new value proposition around a seed innovation.	Protect your ideas from others who might be working toward defining similar offers. Tie up critical lead customers, key suppliers, and important channels.
Expansion	Bring the new offer to a large market by working with suppliers and partners to scale up supply and to achieve maximum market coverage.	Defeat alternative implementations of similar ideas. Ensure that your approach is the market standard in its class through dominating key market segments.
Leadership	Provide a compelling vision for the future that encourages suppliers and customers to work together to continue improving the complete offer.	Maintain strong bargaining power in relation to other players in the ecosystem, including key customers and valued suppliers.
Self-Renewal	Work with innovators to bring new ideas to the existing ecosystem.	Maintain high barriers to entry to prevent innovators from building alternative ecosystems. Maintain high customer switching costs in order to buy time to incorporate new ideas into your own products and services.

tion and distribution, literally crushing smaller ecosystems in the process.

IBM, for example, entered the personal computer business in 1981. In contrast to its own history and culture of vertical integration, IBM followed and extended the Apple model of building a community of supporters. IBM took on partners and opened its computer architecture to outside suppliers. Moreover, it adopted a microprocessor from Intel that incorporated all of the instructions available in the Zilog microprocessor in Tandy and CP/M machines. And IBM licensed MS-DOS, a software operating system from then tiny Microsoft, which was almost a near clone of CP/M. As a result, Wordstar and other popular application programs could easily be ported over to the IBM PC.

One of the most important managerial challenges in Stage 2 is to stimulate market demand without greatly exceeding your ability to meet it. IBM certainly stimulated demand for its new machine through a combination of heavy brand advertising, distribution through Sears and other channels, and building its own network of specialty stores. By anyone's measure, IBM's approach to expanding its PC ecosystem was a major success. Its personal computing business grew from $500 million in 1982 to $5.65 billion by 1986, and IBM's ecosystem rapidly dominated the market.

Automobiles: An Old-Fashioned Timeline

An ecological approach can be used to analyze the evolution of any major business. However, a look at how the old-line automobile companies evolved reveals a different time scale than that of almost any new business today. Historically, the evolutionary stages of an established ecosystem like Ford's or GM's often took decades to play out; but now businesses can be born and die in a matter of years. Managers used to focus on directing the action within a particular stage rather than on how to move from one stage to another. Yet transition between stages has currently become a managerial fact of life.

The major U.S. automobile ecosystems took about three-quarters of a century to evolve, a phenomenal length of time compared with the rise and fall of high-tech businesses like personal computers. However, early automobile executives were well aware of the need to forge a community of suppliers and customers.

Birth of the Horseless Carriage. The late 1800s were a time of experimentation, as the first automobile pioneers struggled to grasp the potential of individualized, motorized transportation. Ransom E. Olds and a handful of others established viable automobile business ecosystems by the turn of the century. Their machines worked reasonably well, were accepted by a small but dedicated number of customers, and could be profitably produced.

Expansion Battles. The next 20 years carried the automobile business deep into the second stage of ecological competition. In 1904, William C. Durant began building what would become General Motors. Henry Ford founded the Ford Motor Company, and, in 1908, he introduced his mass-produced, mass-marketed Model T. Near-legendary battles between Ford and GM ensued—struggles as much for soul and future definition of the business as for simple market share.

Ford's approach was based on vertical integration, carefully engineered production, and product simplicity. Ford's ecosystem had what we now would call "scalability"; by 1914, his company produced over 267,000 cars and held 48% of the market.

Durant's strategy for GM, however, was, based on acquisitions of early companies, marketing might, sales coverage, and product variety. Durant's ecosystem captured market share by pooling and integrating the markets and the production facilities of a variety of smaller companies. However, by 1920, General Motors had nearly collapsed because of the inability of Durant's management systems to control such a complex collection of business entities.

From about 1910 to 1930, industry leaders directed the large expansion of the automobile market, reconfiguring the major ecosystems in the process. Alfred P. Sloan's design for General Motors, initiated in 1920, is most notable and involved the simultaneous ouster of Durant. Sloan's design specifically allowed for the management of a complex business ecosystem by breaking up the diverse company into product lines, which, in turn, could be focused like Ford's mass-produced lines. Sloan also centralized financial oversight of decentralized product lines, and GM became the prototype of the modern multidivisional company.

Community Leadership. By the 1930s, battles for community leadership and bargaining power revolved around the principal supplier to the auto industry: labor. In the late 1920s, around 500,000 people worked in the Detroit area car factories. Working conditions were dangerous; one auto body plant was known as "the slaughterhouse." But by the mid-1930s, the United Auto Workers Union had formed. In 1937, the UAW achieved a landmark victory when GM recognized the union as an official representative of its employees.

Over time, organized labor brought workers crucial bargaining power, which the union used to force the companies to share the spoils of victory. The tug-of-war between workers and companies continued for decades, mediated with varying effectiveness by the U.S. government. While it protected workers, this form of ecosystem struggle also carried with it high costs: work-rule rigidity and the polarization of workers and management. These costs would come back to haunt the U.S. automobile business in the next stage of ecosystem development.

The Threat of Obsolescence. Labor-management struggles continued into the 1970s, until both sides were driven together by a much deeper crisis: the obsolescence of the management approaches, business practices, and systems of production that had been only incrementally improved since the 1920s. The near collapse of the U.S. automobile business came, of course, at the hands of the Japanese. The Toyota ecosystem, for one, was capable of unheard-of levels of product variety, quality, and efficiency at the time. This powerful new business ecosystem was based on a combination of customer-focused design, concurrent engineering, flexible manufacturing, dedicated workers, and networks of suppliers, all tied together through statistically refined management practices.

Therefore, the automobile industry, as traditionally defined, found itself in a full-fledged ecological war, defending against a new wave of business ecosystems. Self-renewal proved difficult, and companies like Ford and Chrysler had nearly collapsed by the late 1970s. The superiority of Japanese approaches ultimately forced the transformation of the world automobile business into what we know today.

However, IBM also generated much more demand than it could meet. The company maintained high prices, which encouraged others to enter the market by setting a high price umbrella under which they could thrive. Compaq, for example, became the fastest company to join the *Fortune* "500" based on supplying machines to meet demand in the IBM ecosystem.

IBM did its best to keep up with demand. In the early 1980s, it invested directly in several key suppliers to help it grow fast enough to meet the market. Intel, for example, received $250 million from IBM in 1983. Concerned about its image as an insensitive behemoth, as well as possible antitrust objections, IBM managers carefully assured these suppliers that the help came without any strings attached.

IBM's relationships with suppliers were basically nonexclusive. Obviously, suppliers like Intel, Microsoft, and Lotus were happy to help the success of Compaq and others because it allowed them to diversify the risk of overdependence on IBM. For its part, IBM was flush with more demand and success than it knew what to do with. Top managers didn't focus on slowing the development of clone makers and nonexclusive suppliers—or keeping crucial elements of value like the microprocessor in-house. At first, IBM didn't attack new competitors within its ecosystem through the courts, through special promotions, or by lowering its own prices.

However clear the threat from the rest of the pack appears to us now, at the time, IBM and its business partners were pleased. By 1986, the combined revenues of companies in the IBM ecosystem were approximately $12 billion, dwarfing the Apple ecosystem's revenues of approximately $2 billion. IBM's leadership also forced Tandy and essentially every other non-Apple maker of personal computers to dump their proprietary designs and offer IBM PC compatibles.

In contrast with IBM, the story of Wal-Mart's retailing ecosystem shows how top management can take the right precautions when a business is expanding (see the insert, "The Evolution of Wal-Mart: Savvy Expansion and Leadership"). In general, Stage 2 rewards fast expansion that squeezes competing ecosystems to the margin. But managers must also prepare for future leadership and leverage in the next stage. To do so, companies need to maintain careful control of customer relationships and core centers of value and innovation. Moreover, they must develop relationships with their suppliers that constrain these followers from becoming leaders in Stage 3.

Leadership: The Fight for Control in an Ecosystem

Guide the ecosystem's investment directions and technical standards.

Make sure the ecosystem has a robust community of suppliers.

Maintain bargaining power by controlling key elements of value.

While the lion and antelope are both part of a healthy savanna ecosystem, they also struggle with each other to determine to what extent each species expands within it. Similarly, in business ecosystems, two conditions contribute to the onset of the leadership struggles that are the hallmark of Stage 3. First, the ecosystem must have strong enough growth and profitability to be considered worth fighting over. Second, the structure of the value-adding components and processes that are central to the business ecosystem must become reasonably stable.

This stability allows suppliers to target particular elements of value and to compete in contributing them. It encourages members of the ecosystem to consider expanding by taking over activities from those closest to them in the value chain. Most of all, it diminishes the dependence of the whole ecosystem on the original leader. It's in Stage 3 that companies become preoccupied with standards, interfaces, "the modular organization," and customer-supplier relations.

For example, by the mid-1980s, the IBM PC technical architecture defined the de facto business structure for the personal computer business as a whole. Virtually any company could figure out how to make components and services that would dovetail effectively with other elements of the PC ecosystem. Of course, this was a mixed blessing for IBM. The openness of its computer architecture encouraged third parties to support it, dramatically accelerating the ecosystem's growth. Yet this same openness decreased the dependence of suppliers on IBM's leadership, laying the foundations for Stage 3 "clone wars."

Lotus, Intel, Microsoft, and other suppliers started working together to determine common standards for hardware and software, with and without IBM's involvement. Other ecosystem members welcomed this new leadership since it seemed fairer to suppliers and more innovative than IBM's.

Belatedly, IBM sought to enforce its patents against clone makers, seeking licenses from major players—one of the many strategies that failed. A grim milestone of sorts was achieved in 1989 when clone shipments and product shipments from other smaller companies bypassed those of major personal computer manufacturers. Thus IBM was relegated to competing head-on with myriad "box makers." IBM still retained a large share of the market but only through offering extensive discounts to large volume purchasers.

Which brings us to the new structure of today's "Microsoft-Intel" ecosystem: Microsoft, with gross margins estimated at 80%; Intel, with gross margins of 40% and 50% on its new chips; and IBM's PC business with margins of about 30%, a far cry from the 70% to 90% margins in its mainframe business.

In Stage 3, bargaining power comes from having something the ecosystem needs and being the only practical source. Sometimes this sole-source status can be established contractually or through patent protection. But fundamentally, it depends on constant innovation—on creating value that is critical to the whole ecosystem's continued price/performance improvement. During expansion, IBM didn't find a way to keep innovating or even to achieve economies of scale. Power shifted to chips and software, areas in which IBM did not excel.

Now both Intel and Microsoft have bargaining power through control of a critical component. Each is a strong leader and plays the role of *central ecological contributor.* Central contributors maintain the much-coveted chokehold within a business ecosystem. In short, other members can't live without them. This central position enables them to bargain for a higher share of the total value produced by the ecosystem. For example, Intel and Microsoft have gross margins that are almost double the average for their whole ecosystem.

Central contributor status is maintained in part by the investments others have made in being followers. Hardware and software vendors have made heavy investments in Microsoft operating systems and in applications that work with Intel chips. Switching to other vendors would be risky and expensive; if possible, other co-evolving companies don't want the burden of learning how to work with a new leader.

In addition, central companies reinforce their roles by making important innovative contributions to the performance of the ecosystem as a whole. Intel, for instance, has enormous scale advantages in the fabrication of microprocessors. Its chip volumes allow it to work out fabrication-process advances sooner than other chip vendors. Ironically, IBM held a license to manufacture Intel-designed microprocessors. With its large volumes during the expansion stage, IBM could have been the one taking the fabrication and price/performance lead in chips—and it could have denied Intel the scale to keep up.

Finally, followers value a central contributor because of its grip on customers. End users are drawn to Microsoft operating systems and Intel chips because so many software applications are available for them. In turn, developers keep turning out such applications because they know Microsoft and Intel are customer gateways.

To some extent, these two companies achieved their current central position by being in the right place at the right time—that is, by serving IBM. Intel and Microsoft clearly appreciate what they have now and are working effectively to maintain their central contributions. Still, some companies like Wal-Mart have systematically gone about building a strong ecosystem, one that guarantees a leading role for themselves.

In any case, for dominant companies, the expansion and leadership stages of an ecosystem can make or break them. In Stage 3, lead producers must extend control by continuing to shape future directions and the investments of key customers and suppliers. And for healthy profits, any company in the ecosystem—leader or follower—must maintain bargaining power over other members.

Self-Renewal—or Death

Track new trends that may upend the ecosystem.

Build a management team that can, if necessary, start a new ecosystem.

Balance stability and change by incorporating new innovations.

Stage 4 of a business ecosystem occurs when mature business communities are threatened by rising new ecosystems and innovations. Alternatively, a community might undergo the equivalent of an earthquake: sudden new environmental conditions that include changes in government regulations, customer buying patterns, or macroeconomic conditions. Moreover, these two factors reinforce each other. An altered environment is often more hospitable to new or formerly marginal business ecosystems.

In fact, how a dominant company deals with the threat of obsolescence is the ultimate challenge. Just because Microsoft and Intel are leaders now doesn't mean their current ecosystem is immortal. Nor does it mean that Microsoft NT ("New Technology" operating software) will form the basis for its successor. After all, Novell and UNIX Systems Laboratories have merged and will put forth a new generation of software, looking to strengthen a new ecosystem. Both Hewlett-Packard and Sun Microsystems remain strongly entrenched. And Motorola is now manufacturing a new generation microprocessor to be sold by both IBM and Apple, along with a jointly developed new software operating system.

Leading successive generations of innovation is clearly crucial to an ecosystem's long-term success and its ability to renew itself. Today's pharmaceutical companies provide some interesting insights into three general approaches to self-renewal, which can be used alone or in combination: (1) dominant companies can seek to slow the growth of a new ecosystem; (2) they can try to incorporate new innovations into their own ecosystems; or (3) they can fundamentally restructure themselves to try coping with a new reality.

During the past few decades, pharmaceutical companies have operated under a relatively consistent, if largely implicit, social compact with government regulators. In exchange for investing heavily in product and process innovation, drug companies have been allowed comparatively high margins and protection from competition through patent laws and lengthy approval processes. Traditional pharmaceutical ecosystems, therefore, have evolved around three major functions: R&D, testing and approval management, and marketing and sales. Each of these functions is expensive, hard to perfect, and thus presents a barrier to new competitors. In the past, these functions were carried out within large, vertically integrated companies that did not, until recently, consider themselves networked organizations.

In the 1980s, generic drug manufacturers that specialized in producing off-patent drugs posed a threat to the established pharmaceutical houses. The dominant companies responded by blocking these rival ecosystems in order to minimize their expansion. This included lobbying to slow generic drug enabling legislation and to reinforce the natural conservatism of the U.S. Food and Drug Administration. Well-funded marketing and sales efforts convinced thousands of individual physicians to continue prescribing mostly branded drugs. While the generic drug manufacturers were able to establish alternative ecosystems, their penetration of the market has been held to about 30%, with little price cutting by the dominant companies.

Meanwhile, a variety of small biotechnology start-ups posed an even greater threat to the traditional pharmaceutical powerhouses. In general, biotech researchers concentrate on isolating complex substances that already exist in the human body and finding ways to manufacture them—for example, human insulin and human growth hormone. As many as one biotech try in ten may prove successful, which keeps the R&D cost down to between $100 million and $150 million per marketable product. Compare this with the traditional pharmaceutical average of 10,000 chemical tries to identify one marketable drug—and R&D costs of $250 million to $350 million per product.

Many of the founders of and investors in biotechnology start-ups believed that low R&D costs would provide the basis for creating whole new business ecosystems that could compete with the established drug companies. For example, Genentech, one of the pioneering biotech companies, clearly intended to establish itself as a full competitor. By the mid-1980s, Genentech had five products in the market and was marketing three itself. It licensed its first two products: alpha-interferon to Hoffmann-La Roche and insulin to Eli Lilly. Using the cash from these licenses, Genentech sought to manufacture and market human growth hormone and tissue plasminogen activator on its own. Yet in 1990, 60% of Genentech was sold to Hoffmann-La Roche for $2.1 billion. A similar fate has befallen almost all of the original biotech companies.

In essence, these companies misjudged the difficulties of mastering the testing and approval process. The first biotech managers bet on the assumption that testing and approval would, like R&D, be less expensive and problematic than it was for their traditional competitors. Since biotech products were existing molecules already resident in the human body, these products would presumably require much less testing than synthetic chemical compounds. However, the FDA approval process in the United States, which grants access to the most important market worldwide, has not borne this out. From 1981 to 1991, only 12 biotech products were approved for general marketing.

Strapped for cash and unable to raise much more from their original investors, most biotech companies ended the 1980s in no position to lead their own business ecosystems. Biotech managers and investors were attracted to alliances with traditional companies and thus merged new business ecosystems with powerful existing ones. In turn, dominant companies like Merck, Eli Lilly, and Bristol-Myers began to think like business ecosystem builders. In order to snap up licenses, patents, and talent to strengthen their own R&D, these companies affiliated themselves with the biotech companies rather than simply blocking their new rivals.

Of course, the leaders of a mature business ecosystem sometimes have no choice but to undertake profound structural and cultural changes. Pharmaceutical ecosystems now face new threats and a profoundly altered environment. The social compact to protect drug company profits in exchange for product and process innovation is breaking down. The public, government, and corporations all want health care costs reduced. Drug company leaders see lean times ahead as they confront the possibility of price and profit caps, as well as consolidated purchasing of drugs by HMOs and government agencies.

Responding to this environmental shift will force changes across all major functions. Companies will probably have to limit R&D spending and focus it carefully. Managers are likely to design a testing and approval process that highlights not only efficacy but also cost/benefit performance of new treatments. Finally, companies will probably market and sell less directly to individual physicians, focusing instead on negotiations with experts who represent third-party payers and government.

> From an ecological perspective, it matters not which particular ecosystems stay alive; it's only essential that competition among them is fierce and fair.

But despite the difficulties of such a complex business environment, managers can design longevity into an ecosystem. During the expansion and leadership stages, for instance, companies can work hard to micro-segment their markets, creating close, supportive ties with customers. These customers will then remain committed to a particular ecosystem long enough for its members to incorporate the benefits of new approaches.

And visionary executives like Merck's Roy Vagelos can sometimes lead an ecosystem so that it rapidly and effectively embraces anticipated developments—be they new technologies, regulatory openings, or consumer trends. Ultimately, there is no substitute for eternal vigilance. As Intel's Andy Grove noted recently, "Only the paranoid survive."

Clearly, pharmaceutical companies—and any other venture threatened by continual innovations—can no longer allow their particular ecosystems to evolve without direction. Using an ecological approach, executives can start making strategic changes by systematically questioning their company's current situation: Is the company linked with the very best suppliers and partners? Is the company betting its future on the most promising new ideas? Are suppliers leading the way in commercializing innovation? Over the long run, how will the company maintain sufficient bargaining power and autonomy to guarantee good financial returns?

Examining a company's key competitors from a business ecological point of view is also important: What hidden web of customer and supplier relationships have competitors worked to develop? Who do they depend on for ideas and supplier support? What are the nature and benefits of those relationships? How do these compare with what the company has?

The Evolution of Wal-Mart: Savvy Expansion and Leadership

An ecological analysis of Wal-Mart reveals how a relatively small company, starting in a rural area of the United States, could turn its original isolation to advantage by creating a complete business ecosystem. Wal-Mart developed and continues to refine an offer that customers find nearly irresistible: low prices on a variety of brands as diverse as Gitano jeans and Yardman lawn mowers. Moreover, CEO Sam Walton managed the company's expansion superbly and increased bargaining power during the leadership stage.

The Birth of Discounting. In the early 1960s, Kmart, Wal-Mart, and other discounters recognized that the Main Street five-and-dime was giving way to the variety store. And variety stores, in turn, were threatened by the large discount store. In order to buy a wide range of goods at low prices in one location, customers were increasingly willing to get into cars and drive to malls or other non-Main Street locations.

Kmart and Wal-Mart appeared on the discount scene at about the same time. The Kmart stores were actually owned by old-style S.S. Kresge, which reinvented itself as a suburb-oriented discount retailer, with big stores located near existing malls and towns of more than 50,000 people. Kmart stores carried items aimed at the lower end of suburban tastes.

By the late 1960s, Wal-Mart had worked out the basic structure of its own business ecosystem: Wal-Mart stores, which supplied a variety of well-known brands, were located in relatively sparsely populated areas. The company went into towns of 5,000 people, particularly where several of these towns might be served by one store. Wal-Mart products were up to 15% cheaper than those available in "mom-and-pop" stores.

While the original Wal-Mart locations could support one store, the customer population wasn't large enough to maintain two rival discounters. Thus once Wal-Mart established a store in a particular area and had beaten back weak local retailers, it was seldom threatened with future local competition from other discounters, including Kmart.

Expansion: Planning for a Chokehold. Once its business strategy was up and running in a number of discount stores in the American South and Mid-West, Wal-Mart's top executives concentrated on developing organizational capabilities that would let it scale up successfully. They were obsessed with three things:

☐ Building a set of incentives that would ensure employee commitment to local stores, which led to a complex system of training, oversight, bonuses, and stock-purchase plans for workers.

☐ Managing communication and control of a network of remotely located stores, which required close monitoring of a carefully drawn set of measures that were transmitted daily to Wal-Mart headquarters in Bentonville, Arkansas.

☐ Setting up an efficient distribution system that allowed for joint purchasing, shared facilities, systematic ordering, and store-level distribution of a large number of different goods. This third obsession ultimately became Wal-Mart's trademark hub-and-spoke

Wal-Mart Takes Off

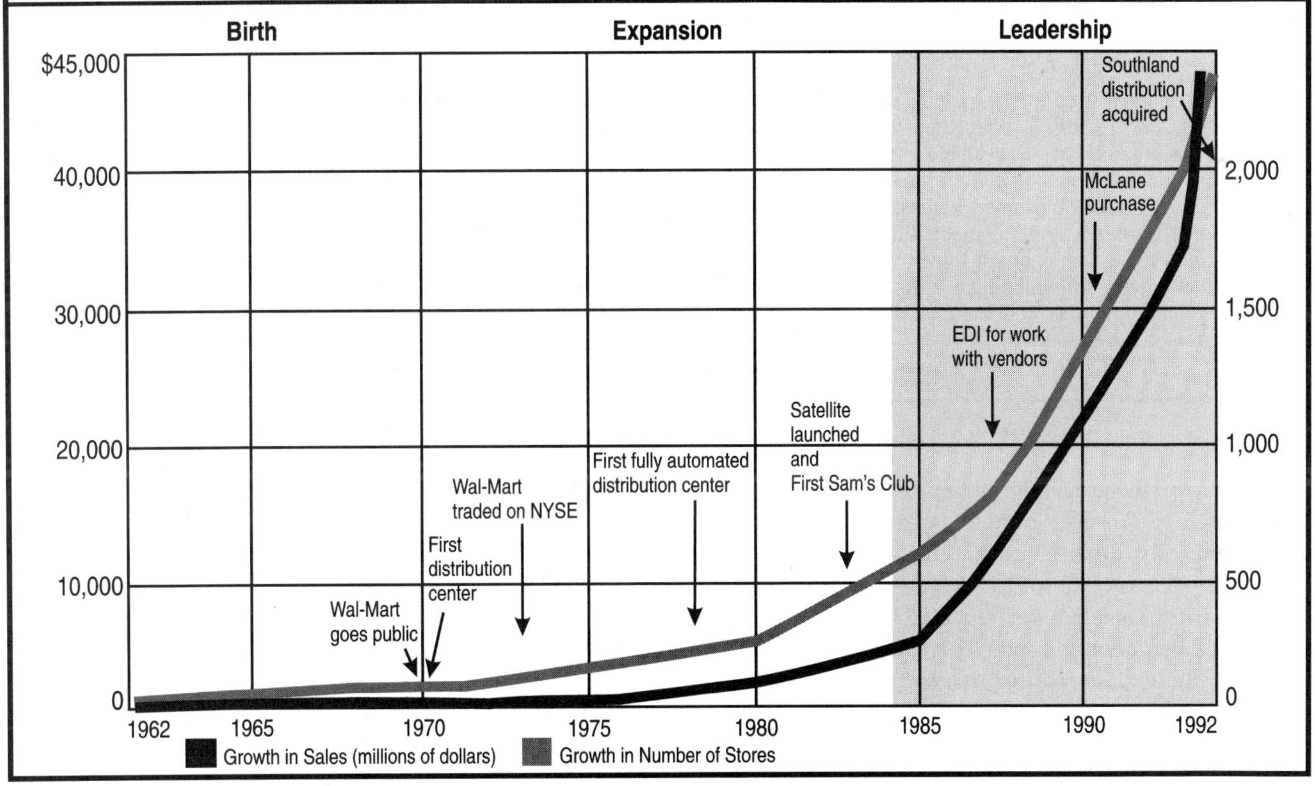

distribution system: warehouses served constellations of stores located no more than a day's drive from the center.

In 1970, Wal-Mart went public to raise funds for its expansion. That same year, the company built its first hub-and-spoke distribution center—embarking on a strategy of targeting a large geographic area, setting up a distribution center, and then populating the area with as many stores as the territory would support. Wal-Mart not only filled the needs of customers in small towns but also saturated entire regions, making it uneconomical for competitors to enter as either distributors or local store owners.

The number of Wal-Mart stores grew rapidly, from 32 in 1970 to 195 in 1978—when the first fully automated distribution center opened—to 551 in 1983—when Wal-Mart launched its own satellite, creating a communication network to keep in daily touch with its now far-flung empire.

Leadership: Building Bargaining Power. By 1984, Wal-Mart's managerial agenda changed. What was in the birth and expansion stages a race to develop systems and conquer territory now became a concerted effort to build bargaining power. As the leaders of a highly successful and visible business ecosystem, Wal-Mart managers worked on continuing to assert the company's vision over other community members, including suppliers like Procter & Gamble, Rubbermaid, and Helene Curtis Industries.

First, Wal-Mart resisted the temptation to charge higher prices in the markets and regions it dominated. Instead, top managers still viewed each market as "contestable"—as a potential opening for rivals if WalMart ceased to give the maximum possible value to customers. Continued customer leadership, in turn, enhanced the Wal-Mart brand and further cemented the company's place in the minds and buying habits of consumers. Wal-Mart's system of "everyday low prices," in which there's no need for weekly sales or special promotions, has now become a standard in discount retailing.

Second, Wal-Mart—now a very large and powerful channel to customers—started putting heavy pressure on suppliers to keep their prices down. Moreover, WalMart compelled its suppliers to set up cross-company distribution systems to attain maximum manufacturing efficiency. For example, in 1987, Wal-Mart and Procter & Gamble reached an unprecedented accord to work together through extensive electronic ordering and information sharing between the companies. In return, Wal-Mart gives better payment terms than the rest of the retailing industry: on average, Wal-Mart pays its suppliers within 29 days compared with 45 days at Kmart.

Third, Wal-Mart continued to invest in and enhance its own fundamental economies of scale and scope in distribution. By the leadership stage, distribution had become the crucial ecological component of the Wal-Mart ecosystem. In fact, Wal-Mart's distribution chokehold has allowed the ecosystem as a whole to triumph over others like Kmart's. While suppliers, big and small, may chafe under Wal-Mart's heavy hand, it's also clear that most of them need this particular leader to survive. The graph "Wal-Mart Takes Off" is a testament to the company's dominance and bargaining power in the leadership stage.

Finally, Wal-Mart has extended its reach into adjacent territories and ecosystems. In 1983, Wal-Mart entered the membership discount market with its Sam's Club, which by 1992 included 208 clubs that contributed over $9.4 billion in revenues. In 1990, Wal-Mart incorporated another ecosystem by acquiring McLane Company, the nation's largest distributor to the convenience store industry. McLane, under Wal-Mart's control, now serves about 30,000 retail stores, including 18,000 convenience stores. And in 1992, Wal-Mart also acquired the distribution and food processing divisions of Southland Corporation. Southland operates a large chain of 7-Eleven convenience stores, and this acquisition added as many as 5,000 more 7-Eleven stores to the McLane/Wal-Mart customer base.

And to prepare the ground for organizational breakthroughs, managers need to consider how the work of their company might be radically different: What seed innovations might make current businesses obsolete? What would it take to catalyze a cluster of ideas into a new and vital business ecosystem? What type of community would be required to bring these new ideas to the widest possible market?

Asking these questions, let alone acting on the answers, has become a difficult necessity for all companies. Superficially, competition among business ecosystems is a fight for market share. But below the surface, these new competitive struggles are fights over who will direct the future.

Yet it's precisely in the role of conscious direction that a strictly biological metaphor is no longer useful. Business communities, unlike biological communities of co-evolving organisms, are social systems. And social systems are made up of real people who make decisions; the larger patterns are maintained by a complex network of choices, which depend, at least in part, on what participants are aware of. As Gregory Bateson noted, if you change the ideas in a social system, you change the system itself.

I anticipate that as an ecological approach to management becomes more common—as an increasing number of executives become conscious of co-evolution and its consequences—the pace of business change itself will accelerate. Executives whose horizons are bounded by traditional industry perspectives will find themselves missing the real challenges and opportunities that face their companies. Shareholders and directors, sensing the new reality, will eventually remove them. Or, in light of the latest management shifts, they may have already done so.

Unfortunately for employees and investors, this often occurs only after the companies involved have been deeply damaged. Companies that once dominated their industries, as traditionally defined, have been blindsided by new competition. Whether such companies can find the appropriate leadership to renew the ecosystems on which their future depends remains an open question. If they cannot, they'll be supplanted by other companies, in other business ecosystems, that will expand and lead over the next few years.

For the individuals caught up in these ecosystem struggles, the stakes are high. As a society, we must find ways of helping members of dying ecosystems get into more vital ones while avoiding the temptation of propping up the failed ecosystems themselves. From an ecological perspective, it matters not which particular ecosystems stay alive; rather, it's only essential that competition among them is fierce and fair—and that the fittest survive.

The Changing Art of Becoming Unbeatable

The rise of infotech is the largest trend in business, but when seeking your company's lasting competitive edge, there's someplace else you should look.

Geoffrey Colvin

What do you want most in the world? I don't mean in your personal life, I mean in your role as a business titan out there every day battling the forces of evil in your industry. My guess is that if you close your eyes and think big, what you'd really like—more than a smaller cell phone or a bigger monitor, more even than reliable copiers—is a sustainable competitive advantage.

Those are the three little words business people seem to be longing to hear more and more, and it isn't surprising. These days you almost suspect that no advantage is sustainable. AT&T thought it had a sustainable competitive advantage: mammoth size and a great brand. IBM thought it had one: a humongous installed base. So did Apple: the coolest technology. All of them were wrong, and now everybody's worried. Banks wonder whether we'll conduct our finances with non-bank companies of some kind, possibly online. Kodak must dominate digital photography or risk becoming insignificant. Everywhere you look, you see companies—big, powerful ones—getting their foundations knocked out from under them by forces that just hadn't been important before.

Welcome to life in the age of infotech. The common thread in all these cases is that information technology, either directly or through its effects, obliterates competitive advantages that had seemed almost invulnerable. Market dominance, like Digital Equipment's in minicomputers? Wiped out when the world shifted to PCs. A respected name, like Sears? Overcome by Wal-Mart, with superior logistical systems and a ferociously competitive culture.

The dawning realization is that in the age of infotech, infotech is rarely a source of sustainable competitive advantage. How could it be otherwise? Part of this technology's marvel is that it's so cheap and widely available. What I've got, you've got, or can get. Yes, some companies have built businesses on infotech superiority, but that's a mean and relentless game. Federal Express, for example, maintains an infotech system that analysts say is as much as 12 months ahead of competitors'. Staying there costs the company a billion dollars a year.

The fact is that for most of us, most of the time, infotech will not catapult us ahead of the competition in any reliable way. You must keep your infotech current with that of competitors—otherwise you're dead—but for sustainable competitive advantage you'll have to look elsewhere.

Where? The answer I'm hearing from executives around the world and in all sorts of industries is: in the most distinctively human elements of business—culture, leadership, character. This is potentially soggy turf, where it's easy to platitudinize and avoid confronting anything meaningful. But many in business are realizing that they have no choice. Recalls Vincent DiBianca, a senior vice president at CSC Index: "Fifteen years ago I couldn't use the word 'culture.' It was too soft. Now everyone wants to know how to change it."

This profound shift in attitude is happening now for at least three sound reasons.

- **The rise of infotech is making customers enormously more powerful.** It's arming them with truckloads of information, for starters. In business-to-business selling this is part of the thunderous advance of E-commerce, which is enabling buyers to check prices and specifications offered by suppliers around the globe instantly and continually. You hear occasional brave talk from companies about how they'll configure their Websites so that buyers will have a hard time making direct price comparisons with competitors, but we all know how that goes: Companies that enable price comparisons to be made most easily gain an advantage, forcing everyone to do it, like it or not.

Consumers are getting similar power through infotech, using intelligence they acquire via the Internet to choose—and often buy—cars, insurance, computers, books, airline seats, brokerage services, and much else. As a result, sellers of every one of those things are being forced to compete on price, and they hate it.

Buyers gain further advantage in an information economy because new competitors enter businesses so easily. This is most apparent in the software, information, and service industries, where you may need only a big idea and a little cash to get yourself launched. No matter what business you're in, it probably has too much capacity anyway. In industries around the world, from cars to chemicals to computers, overcapacity threatens to commoditize just about everything.

How do you compete in a world like this? Not on price if you can help it, but rather through innovation and service, both of them nearly magical results of human interactions that will never be easy to engineer or even understand.

• **Knowledge has become the scarce resource constraining most businesses.** Former Shell executive Arie de Geus argues persuasively that this is a millennial shift. A thousand years ago in Europe, he notes, land and natural resources were the critical factors in creating wealth; if you had them, you were rich, and otherwise you were poor. Then, some 500 years ago, production finally began to exceed the needs of current consumption; that's called savings, which led to bigger ships, new machines, and an economy that was exploding, with financial capital the resource no one could get enough of. Today, he says, capital is more abundant than ever in history, and while a struggling entrepreneur might not see it that way, the point is valid. "Our predecessors had to court banks," he says. "Now banks court us."

Conclusion: "The critical resource is now people and the knowledge they carry," says de Geus. "Just look at the success of capital-poor and brain-rich companies." He's right. Everyone's favorite example is Microsoft, which over its life has created more wealth (as of the end of last year, measured by market value added) using $5.7 billion of capital than Exxon has using $88.4 billion. While Microsoft's products are pure intellect, the point can be made just as forcefully in manufacturing. Cisco Systems, maker of computer hardware, has created more wealth using $2.8 billion of capital than Du Pont has using $35.6 billion. Dell Computer has created more wealth with just $418 million of capital than Burlington Northern has with $20.4 billion.

So managing a company's ideas has become at least as important as managing its money. Jack Welch, CEO of General Electric, for years said his job had only two main parts: allocating capital and choosing people. A few years ago he added a third: transferring ideas. (Just for the record, he has created more wealth than any CEO in history.) And if the contents of quirky human brains are now the world's critical production factor, management changes profoundly. As de Geus says, "You can no longer manage in the old style. You must now optimize people." How do you do that? To begin with, he says, "without very high trust you will never get maximization of brain potential." So trust is key—and we're off into the deep woods of human interaction, culture, and character.

• **Infotech contributes to extremely fast and discontinuous change, making speedy response vital to success.** As strategy guru Gary Hamel notes, "We live in a discontinuous world—one where digitalization, deregulation, and globalization are profoundly reshaping the industrial landscape." Yet most companies have built their success on incremental changes, such as line extensions, steady productivity improvements, and ever faster cycle times. Valuable as those things are, they aren't good enough when radical change strikes. Then success demands equally radical rethinking of strategy.

Hamel has thought a lot about how companies can achieve that, and while he doesn't talk much about culture, that's a large element in what he prescribes. Getting new voices—especially young voices—into strategizing is crucial, he says. So is creating new conversations, deep exchanges between people in the company who don't usually have them. He stresses the importance of "the emotional commitment of individuals at the bottom of the organization who are being asked to devote their lives to carrying out a new strategy" and discusses how to increase it.

I don't suppose you have to call this culture, but that's what it's all about. If culture is what people do when no one is telling them what to do (as good a definition as I've ever heard), then Hamel's prescription for strategy innovation—"the next fundamental competitive advantage for companies around the world"—amounts to a culture that calls forth certain behaviors continually. Yet again, the key to competitive advantage seems to rest on factors that are about as human as you can get. As Hamel says, "To all you strategists and corporate leaders eager to create value—get a soul!"

Bottom line: The more that infotech revolutionizes business, the more economically valuable are the exclusively human qualities of the people who work in a company. Researchers are even beginning to focus on this relationship. A new study from Wharton examines the effects of money invested in infotech capital (hardware and software) vs. money invested in IT workers in the banking industry. The study found that the capital investments "may be a strategic necessity to stay even with the competition," but the investments in the workers yielded far greater returns. Says Patrick Harker, one of the study's authors: "Machines can't give you a competitive advantage. It's all about the people."

No one expresses the particular power of a cultural advantage better than Herb Kelleher, founder and CEO of Southwest Airlines, famed for its strong culture of humor and individual responsibility. Once—mostly to provoke him, I admit—I tried telling Herb that his culture wasn't all that important. "I can explain Southwest's success," I said. "You fly one type of aircraft, serve no meals, transfer no luggage, give no assigned seats, fly mostly short hauls, and always charge the lowest fares on your routes. There's the formula. What's culture got to do with it?" Perhaps steam did not actually shoot out of his ears, but it looked as if it would. He slammed the table and said, "Culture has everything to do with it—because everything you said our competitors could copy tomorrow. But they can't copy the culture, and they know it." Actually, some of his competitors, notably United on certain California routes, later tried to copy almost everything I mentioned. But Herb was right: They couldn't copy the culture and got beat.

There's no avoiding it. The eternal search for sustainable competitive advantage is leading us straight into the squishy softness of culture and character. Many business people won't like it. They won't be comfortable talking with colleagues about trust, honesty, purpose, values, and other topics out of the self-help section of the bookstore. They will have to face the fact that they will likely be eaten alive by competitors who confront these issues with relish.

You may say that this was always true.

It was.

What is so crucially important is that in the age of infotech, it is truer than ever, and getting truer every day.

FedEx CEO Smith Bets His Deal with Cisco Will Recast The Future of Shipping

By Douglas A. Blackmon

What does Federal Express do now, in a world that may not absolutely, positively need it overnight?

Frederick W. Smith foresaw today's fast-cycle economy a quarter-century ago when he created Federal Express, a company obsessed with speed and reliability. He leapfrogged the rest of the transportation industry, and FedEx's parent, FDX Corp., became a $17 billion-a-year landmark of the new economy.

Now, the need for a fast but pricey delivery service, something that was a brilliant bet not that long ago, isn't so clear. Indeed, the rate of growth in FedEx 's delivery volume within the U.S., which accounts for about two-thirds of the company's revenue, has slowed significantly this year.

Some of the reasons are clear: E-mail delivers documents instantly. Low-cost truck lines, discount air carriers and even ocean vessels now provide tracking of shipments via the Internet. Big FDX rivals such as United Parcel Service of America Inc. and Airborne Freight Corp. offer reliable ground and air services, along with versions of the elaborate information systems that once distinguished FDX from the pack.

But something bigger is also threatening FedEx: Companies are a lot smarter than they used to be.

A big part of FedEx's business has traditionally come from firms that would suddenly realize they were short of key parts needed for their production, or that they were low on goods demanded by their customers. Because those companies couldn't plan their needs particularly well, they relied on FedEx to make up in speed what they lacked in precision.

Now, many businesses are deploying complex new "supply chain management" systems. Those systems are designed to eliminate much of the unpredictability in their operations—and also much of the need for the kind of expensive, rapid-fire delivery FedEx excels at providing.

So Mr. Smith, the 55-year-old chairman and CEO of FDX, is making two more big bets. First, he is gambling that his company can remake itself by slowing some things down. The company is improving its delivery services that compete more directly with UPS and the U.S. Postal Service. It has invested $500 million in the past two years to double capacity at its RPS unit, a business-to-business delivery network acquired in 1997. RPS transports packages more slowly, more cheaply and with much higher profit margins. FDX is also planning to build at RPS a residential ground-delivery network, though it won't be available nationwide for several years.

Second, and more ambitiously, FDX is trying to recast itself as a major provider of the very management systems that threaten the company. Mr. Smith wants to design a network that can supplant a company's inefficient stream of faxes and phone calls with digital exchanges of information about demand, factory schedules and the availability of materials.

Working at their best, such systems would select the most logical, most economical type of transport—air, land or sea—for delivering packages on time. They would also coordinate customs clearances around the world and minimize the amount of time any item sits in a warehouse along the way. If this idea pans out, assembly lines won't need to be shuttered unexpectedly due to a sudden drop in consumer demand, and factories won't have to pay huge premiums in overtime to handle busy times.

"That is absolutely the way the world is going to work," says Mr. Smith. "If we aren't successful in this area, we aren't going to be successful at all."

And indeed, if this strategy really jells, it could enable some companies to dispense with warehouses altogether. That is exactly what FDX is hoping to do, and it isn't starting small: Its first client is Internet hardware behemoth Cisco Systems Inc.

That said, Mr. Smith's bets are loaded with risk. For starters, the company says it has spent "tens of millions of dollars" and devoted hundreds of employees to devising the new software and systems. Also, such programs have been notoriously difficult to implement at many companies.

And the business is swarming with rivals. Andersen Consulting, at times teaming up with truck and leasing company Ryder System Inc., supplies supply-chain systems to dozens of companies. International Business Machines Corp. and i2 Technologies Inc. are big software players too—minus the trucks and planes. The reason for the competition is simple: These systems are at the heart of business-to-business electronic commerce, a category expected to hit $1.3 trillion of transactions by 2003. That would dwarf expectations of consumer spending on the Web by 10 to 1, according to Forrester Research.

Deep in the fray, of course, is UPS, the giant nemesis of FDX. The company's chairman, James P. Kelly, describes UPS as "a global conveyor belt" arranging just-in-time delivery of materials and data from anywhere in the world.

UPS has already had powerful success in e-commerce by leveraging its ground delivery system, which reaches nearly all addresses in the U.S. Because of its massive volume, UPS's costs per package on residential deliveries are tiny. So UPS can charge rates much lower than air freight and still make money. That, coupled with electronic tracking and guaranteed delivery dates, has made UPS the preferred method of delivering consumer goods purchased over the Internet. A survey found that 55% of all online purchases last Christmas were shipped via UPS. FDX carried only about 10%.

Mr. Smith dismisses UPS's lead in residential e-commerce and its inroads on overnight packages. He says e-commerce transactions between businesses will be vastly more profitable, and adds that FDX is heavily focused on leveraging the international delivery network it has spent billions to build, particularly in Asia. Still, in shipping goods between businesses, FDX concedes that it rarely wins more than about 25% of the packages shipped by its 300 biggest and best customers.

And with expected 1999 revenue of $26 billion, UPS has far greater financial resources than FDX. It is expected to become an even more potent player this month, when the company plans to hold a $4.1 billion initial public offering, the largest American IPO ever.

UPS scoffs at Mr. Smith's new vision as overkill at best, recycled software at worst. "We don't believe we are software developers," says its e-commerce chief, Mark Rhoney. Companies making that gamble "are trying to go a bridge too far."

UPS says it can achieve the same efficiencies by using existing, less expensive software and its own highly advanced warehousing and logistics unit. "Maybe you don't need an inventory completely in motion at all times," says UPS spokesman Steve Holmes. "There's debate over that theory."

But working to FedEx's advantage is this fact: The company has an impressive history of technology breakthroughs.

In the 1980s, Mr. Smith began to give away more than 100,000 desktop computers packed with FedEx software, designed to link and lock in thousands of customers to its ordering and tracking systems. FedEx was the first to equip its drivers with hand-held scanners capable of alerting customers when packages had been picked up or delivered.

And, in 1994, FedEx was the first big transport firm to launch a Web site with tracking and tracing capabilities. "It was very clear to me that this was going to change the whole way that people interacted with each other," Mr. Smith says. "What I didn't understand was how rapidly it would be adopted."

Other companies did figure that out, though, and began pushing software programs to wring efficiencies out of transport and delivery services. Mr. Smith urged his executives to come up with a smart response, but he had a hard time persuading them to invest in technology that didn't have a clear payoff for the transportation side of the business. "It was enormously frustrating," he says. "It took a long time for me to get across to people . . . how profound I thought this was going to be and what a different set of disciplines it was going to require to be successful. We couldn't continue to conduct business as usual.

"The benefits were not necessarily predictable, but the risks were potentially just so injurious that we just had to go out and do them," Mr. Smith says. "It became obvious that it wasn't a big deal, but the deal."

In the meantime, FDX made other moves that put the company at a disadvantage in the consumer e-commerce boom. It dismissed much of the residential delivery business in the U.S., as well as the movement of low-value goods between businesses. FDX dumped most of its catalog mail-order customers in the mid-1990s, and in 1997 changed its pricing structure to drive away other low-profit customers.

That strategy boosted earnings during a grueling price war, but it also gave UPS the opportunity to distinguish its residential delivery services. FDX is largely blocked out of the competition for consumer e-commerce deliveries. That has hurt the company on Wall Street. Shares of FDX, flying high a few months ago on reports that the company would make a huge Internet play, have fallen more than 30% since May to just over $40 a share.

So now, FDX is preparing to embark on its new strategy. And its first guinea pig, beginning this month, is Cisco Systems, the Silicon Valley Internet hardware maker that transacts 80% of its sales over the Web. FDX is scheduled to begin coordinating all of Cisco's shipping over the next two years—and in the following three years, gradually eliminate virtually all of the company's warehousing.

Here is how that ambitious plan would work: The company relies on factories in the U.S., Mexico, Scotland, Taiwan and Malaysia to make the dozens of finished parts its customers want. Now, Cisco often holds on to each part at a warehouse near the factory so the whole order can be shipped to the customer at once.

But Cisco's business is booming—its revenue has grown 40% annually over the past three years—and the company doesn't want to continue building warehouses, paying for reshipping, and owning tens of millions of dollars of inventory while it awaits transit. Beyond that, the company needs more flexibility to be able to drop or add manufacturers at a moment's notice. So Cisco wants a far more advanced system for moving products.

The idea: Merge the orders in transit. As many as a hundred different boxes destined for a single customer would be shipped independently as soon as they are manufactured—and they would all arrive at a customer's door within hours of each other. The parts could be assembled right there, never spending a moment in a central warehouse.

FDX and Cisco began talking about this idea back in the spring of 1997. The following January, Mr. Smith met with Cisco's senior officers at their San Jose, Calif., headquarters and then spoke privately with the CEO, John Chambers. The two executives struck a chord about how manufacturing and transportation companies should evolve in a networked economy.

Meanwhile, Cisco discussed the plans with its other transportation suppliers. Several, including UPS, said they could handle the job using their current logistics programs.

But in the end, Cisco picked FDX because the company said it was willing to overhaul its entire operation. FDX is creating a unique system that will automatically select routes for an endless number of Cisco shipments: routers made in Mexico, hubs from Scotland, switches from the U.S. Breaking with a past practice that often rankled customers—pushing customers exclusively into FedEx services—the new software is supposed to pick whatever type of transportation is most effective and economical. So, it's quite possible that FDX's system will route deliveries on ships, airplanes or trucks owned by other companies, even UPS.

In addition to planning every shipment, FDX must coordinate customs controls as a package moves from country to country. As the system is fully phased in, management of all shipping shifts to an FDX "command and control center." Gradually, Cisco's need for warehouses is supposed to disappear as more orders are merged in transit. Just as critical, the real-time status of this massive synchronization is to be constantly available on the Internet.

"FedEx said, 'We will change our networks, our capabilities, our structures to allow you to do that,' " said Lincoln Holland, the Cisco vice president for logistics overseeing the project. "They said that's our vision of the world. . . . Now we are just hoping they can create a product that will work for us."

Creating competitive (dis)advantage: Learning from Food Lion's freefall

Gregory G. Dess and Joseph C. Picken

Executive Overview

Many lessons can be learned from the avalanche of bad press and the strategic errors that overwhelmed Food Lion in the early 1990s. Although the focus of the press reports was on worker exploitation and unsanitary practices in food preparation, Food Lion's core problems go much deeper. This company provides a springboard example to illustrate the dysfunctional outcomes of a myopic vision of strategy. Food Lion's fundamental strategic error was not uncommon: It based its strategy on an organizational strength that did not create a sustainable competitive advantage. We address the benefits gained from expanding the boundaries of a firm's value chain to incorporate both suppliers and customers, adding value in multiple activities and in multiple ways, and achieving close integration of value-creating activities.

> Success doesn't beget success. Success begets failure because the more that you know a thing works, the less likely you are to think that it won't work. When you've had a long string of victories, it's harder to foresee your own vulnerabilities.
>
> Leslie Wexner, CEO. The Limited, Inc. [1]

In the early 1990s, few firms were ridiculed as much as the retail grocery chain Food Lion. Starting with an exposé on ABC's *PrimeTime Live* charging employee exploitation, false package dating, and unsanitary meat handling practices, Food Lion faced an avalanche of bad press. The result was not only a blow to its reputation, but also sharp declines in sales and earnings. What makes the Food Lion story so fascinating is the company's astonishing change in fortune. Few corporations have rewarded their initial investors as richly. Food Lion's original 100-odd investors have been treated royally: A single share of stock bought for $10 in 1957 split into more than 12,000 shares by 1991—with a value of over $200,000![2] Food Lion's employees have not fared nearly so well, however, and their discontent is a major source—but certainly not the only cause—of Food Lion's problems.

Food Lion was formed in 1957 in Salisbury, North Carolina, by three former Winn-Dixie employees—Wilson Smith, and brothers Ralph and Brown Ketner. Stock was peddled at $10 per share to any takers in Salisbury. Tom Smith, one of the store's first employees, is presently chairman and CEO. Food Lion was hardly an overnight success, and struggled during its first 10 years of operation. Nothing seemed to work. Trading stamps, contests, and drawings all failed to draw customers. However, 1967 marked the turning point.

That year, Ralph Ketner pored over six months of receipts and determined that if Food Lion lowered its prices on all 3,000 items and sales increased 50 percent, the company would survive. The strategy paid off, the company was reborn as a resolute cost cutter, and the slogan LFPINC (Lowest Food Prices in North Carolina) soon appeared on bumper stickers. By 1983, annual sales topped $1 billion. Over the next nine years, sales and net income grew at more than a 22 percent annual clip—to $7.2 billion and $178 million, respectively. Buoyed by its market success in the Southeast, Food Lion boldly opened 100 stores in Texas, Louisiana, and Oklahoma in the early 1990s. Then disaster struck, and the downside of Food Lion's fervent quest for cost control became strikingly evident.

The first blow against Food Lion came on November 5, 1992 when ABC's *PrimeTime Live* news program uncov-

From *Academy of Management Executive,* Vol. 13, No. 3, 1999, pp. 97-111. Republished with permission of Academy of Management, P.O. Box 3020, Briar Cliff Manor, NY 10510-8020. Reproduced by permission of the publisher via Copyright Clearance Center, Inc.

ered charges of unsanitary meat handling practices and false package dating. Jean Bull, a meat wrapper who had worked in 12 different Food Lion stores over a 13-year period, charged:

> I have seen my supervisor take chicken back out of the bone can, make us wash it and put it back out, and it was rotten. It's just unreal what they'll do to save a dime. They take that pork that's already starting to get a slime to it, it gets what they call a halo to it, a kind of green tinge to it, and they take and put that into a grinder with sausage mixture, and they put it back out for anywhere from 7–10 days, as fresh, home-made sausage. And it's rotten.[3]

Throughout its history. Food Lion's nonunion status and labor practices have not endeared the firm to its employees or the United Food and Commercial Workers (UFCW) Union. In its efforts to organize Food Lion's employees, the UFCW has applied pressure by bringing violations to the attention of the Department of Labor, reportedly mailing more than a million brochures to consumers to remind them of the *PrimeTime Live* exposé. Shortly after the *PrimeTime Live* broadcast, the Labor Department began investigating violations of child safety laws and pressures by management for employees to work off the clock, that is, work after quitting time without pay. In August, 1993, the firm agreed to pay $16.2 million to settle charges of more than 1,000 violations in the largest settlement ever by a private employer over wage and work-hour violations.

Unfortunately, timing is everything. These problems surfaced shortly after Food Lion had begun its major expansion into the Southwest, where it faced strong, entrenched competition. In Dallas-Fort Worth, where the company planned to open 54 new stores, Kroger, Albertson's, and Winn-Dixie were well-established national players with excellent locations. Strong regional competitors included Tom Thumb, Minyard's, IGA, Simon David's, and Danal's. These competitors had fine-tuned their market analysis to the point where they offered a product mix tailored to the economics and demographics of local neighborhoods. Into this foray, Food Lion's stringent cost-control strategy dictated smaller stores (33,000 square feet versus the 45,000–70,000 square-foot stores of competitors), limited product selection, and fewer employees. Store managers, operating within the confines of stringent cost controls, lacked the resources and flexibility to respond to the highly competitive and focused competitive environment. Whatever competitive position Food Lion had hoped to build quickly eroded with the *PrimeTime Live* report and surrounding controversy.

Whatever competitive position Food Lion had hoped to build quickly eroded with the* PrimeTime Live *report and surrounding controversy.

What went wrong at Food Lion? Was it worker exploitation? A management team out of touch with operations? A failure to adapt to new markets? Too much focus on the bottom line—or, for that matter, on the top line?

What Went Wrong at Food Lion? The Fundamental Strategic Error

Food Lion was extremely successful for many years. Its performance soared after it adopted an across-the-board cost-cutter strategy in 1967. By 1983, annual sales had reached $1 billion; by 1992, they surpassed $7 billion. With such extraordinary performance, management continued to pursue and reinforce its proven success formula of stringent cost controls in every new store. Food Lion's everyday-low-price strategy required that store workers perform multiple tasks to exacting time standards. Company rules and procedures dictated the time to be used for unloading delivery trucks, trimming produce for display, and a variety of other operational tasks. Labor was budgeted based on a store's sales volume. If sales were down, a manager was forced to accomplish the same tasks and provide the same service level with fewer employees—contributing to pressures for employees to work off the clock. As Food Lion expanded into the Southwest, however, it entered a different competitive environment—a more sophisticated market where cost control alone was insufficient to ensure success. Figure 1 illustrates a typical retail grocery distribution model and compares it with the primary activities of the grocery distribution value chain to describe Food Lion's competitive problem.

As illustrated in Figure 1 the value chain includes three upstream and two downstream activities. Upstream activities, such as inbound logistics, warehouse and consolidation operations, and outbound logistics, are concerned with purchasing, inventory management, and trucking operations, and in most companies are highly centralized and tightly controlled. Downstream activities, like sales and marketing and customer service, are focused on the local market—with the possible exception of certain regional advertising and promotional functions—and are primarily the responsibility of local store managers. The upstream activities of most grocery chains look pretty much the same. Chains differ considerably, however, in the way they manage their downstream operations and in the amount of autonomy and discretion granted to local store managers.

Food Lion effectively reduced costs in its upstream activities. The powerful chain was able to establish strong bargaining positions with suppliers of products (e.g., grocery items, produce, meat) and services (e.g., transportation). Its strong cost culture and rigid control

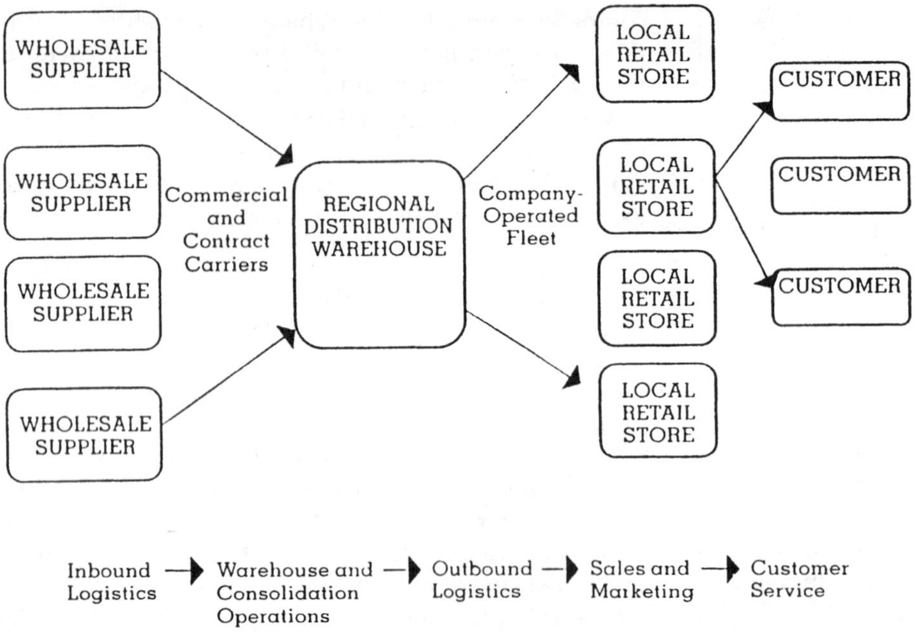

FIGURE 1
Retail Grocery Distribution Model and Value Chain

systems had traditionally served it well in creating a competitive advantage. This same approach was equally effective in squeezing out costs when applied to the downstream activities. Store operations is where the giant chains interact with individual customers. In the Dallas-Fort Worth market, Food Lion's competitors also focused on cost control upstream, but worked hard to differentiate their stores by focusing on product selection and customer service downstream. In these markets, the public had come to expect a wider variety of product offerings, excellent customer service, and a pleasant ambiance.

The root cause of Food Lion's failure was myopia about what the organization was trying to accomplish.

In this case. Food Lion's ruthless cost cutting backfired. Its small stores, limited selection, and rigid cost and manpower control procedures contributed to a rather spartan atmosphere—long on efficiency but short on customer service amenities, an approach that fell flat in its new markets. Food Lion's single-minded focus on stringent cost control throughout the value chain, reinforced by an untimely run of bad publicity, led to a competitive failure. Forced to retreat, Food Lion by the end of 1994 had closed as unprofitable more than half the new stores it had opened in the Southwest in 1991.

Food Lion's fundamental strategic error was that it based its strategy on an organizational strength that did not create a sustainable competitive advantage. The company's principal strength lay in its ability to drive down costs—the foundation of its success as it came to dominate Southeastern markets. As the company expanded into the Southwest, its narrowly focused generic strategy of cost leadership fell apart. Differences in the competitive environment dictated a different approach. By continuing to blindly pursue its traditional cost-cutter approach, Food Lion apparently missed the message: the essence of competition in the Dallas-Fort Worth market called for greater product variety and a higher level of customer service in their store operations. Even in Food Lion's traditional markets, its high-pressure management tactics and hard-nosed employee practices came home to roost when *PrimeTime Live* offered employees a chance to vent their frustrations by blowing the whistle.

The Food Lion debacle is not unique. Many organizations base their strategies on organizational strengths that do not create competitive advantages, or rely so heavily on a single source of competitive advantage that they fail to recognize the need for a different approach when environmental conditions change.[4]

The root cause of Food Lion's failure was myopia about what the organization was trying to accomplish. That nearsightedness carried the strategy of cost cutting to a dysfunctional extreme. Danny Miller describes such behavior in his book *Icarus Paradox*, showing how an organization's success often sows the seeds of its ultimate failure. He takes his title from the Greek legend of Icarus, who flew so high and so close to the sun on his artificial wax wings, that they melted and he plunged to his death. "The paradox, of course, is that his greatest asset led to his demise. And that same paradox applies to many outstanding companies today: their victories and their strengths often seduce them into the excesses that cause their downfall."[5]

Miller provides numerous examples of companies—including Gulf & Western, A&P, Wang, and ITT, that made similar strategic errors. What did they miss? Where did they go wrong? Part of the answer may lie in the way their top strategists understood, interpreted, and applied the traditional tools and guidelines for strategy formulation.

Limitations of Traditional Approaches

The traditional approaches to the analysis and formulation of strategy—SWOT analysis, industry analysis,

Porter's five forces model, and the related notion of generic strategies—all require an initial analysis and assessment of the organization and its competitive environment.[6] The so-called SWOT analysis, an examination of the firm's internal strengths and weaknesses and an assessment of the opportunities and threats posed by the competitive environment, is probably the best known and most widely used. Industry analysis adopts a similar perspective.[7] Each examines the organization and its relationships and interactions with the other entities in its competitive environment. There's nothing wrong with these approaches, which have much to contribute. But by themselves, they rarely point the way to developing sustainable competitive advantage. Let's look at some of the limitations:

Strengths May Not Lead to Advantage

A firm's strengths and capabilities, no matter how unique or impressive, may not enable the organization to achieve a competitive advantage in the marketplace. It would be a little like having a concert pianist in a street gang who has a skill that is unique in that environment, but that hardly helps to attain the gang's goals. Similarly, the skills of a highly creative product designer offer little competitive advantage in a firm that produces low-cost commodity products where little differentiation is encouraged or is essential to be competitive. Basing a strategy solely on the foundation of an organizational strength or capability that cannot by itself create or sustain a competitive advantage is a wasted effort. Food Lion's expansion into the Southwest failed, in large part, because it blindly replicated the formula that had worked so successfully in its traditional Southeastern markets. Food Lion's management apparently failed to recognize that its traditional strengths in cost control were not enough to create sustainable advantage in the very different competitive market conditions it encountered in the Southwest.

Too Narrow a Focus

Strategists who rely on traditional definitions of their industry and competitive environment frequently focus their sights too narrowly on current customers, technologies, and competitors. By so doing, they fail to notice important changes on the periphery that may trigger the need to redefine industry boundaries and identify a whole new set of competitive relationships. In Food Lion's traditional markets, it set the standard: A successful supermarket was a food store, period.

Store layouts and product mix varied little from store to store. In the Dallas-Fort Worth marketplace, however, consumers had come to expect much more. The one-stop shopping experience typically involved, along with groceries, amenities such as pharmacies, optical shops, branch banking, floral shops, bakeries and specialty delicatessens, on-site photofinishing, hardware, small appliances. toys, tapes and CDs, and video rentals. Many competitors offered a cup of coffee at the door and trays of free samples in the meat, deli, and produce sections. Clearly the competitive ground rules were very different, and in retrospect it is apparent that many of Food Lion's traditional management practices, formulas, and routines did not work well in the more sophisticated competitive environment of Dallas-Fort Worth.

A One-Shot View of a Moving Target

A major weakness of both the SWOT and industry analysis techniques is that they are static analyses that focus much of their attention on a snapshot in time. Static analysis is a little like studying a single frame of a motion picture. You may be able to identify the principal actors and learn something about the characters and the setting, but it's really tough to get much insight into the plot. Competition among organizations is played out over time—circumstances, capabilities, and strategies change—and a static analysis falls short of understanding the dynamics of the competitive environment. Perhaps Food Lion's planners and strategists, intrigued by the growth prospects and attractive market demographics, missed the more subtle differences in the competitive environment. Or perhaps they noticed the differences, but blinded by their long history of success as a cost cutter, chose to ignore them and assumed that consumers would welcome their new approach. The implications of these differences in competitive conditions must have become apparent to local store managers soon after Food Lion began its Southwest expansion, but their hands were tied. The new stores were so small and the management practices so well-entrenched, that local managers could not change the formula enough to adapt and survive.

Overemphasizing a Single Dimension of Strategy

The misunderstanding of generic strategies may also contribute to an inappropriate emphasis on a single dimension of competitive advantage. In 1980, Michael Porter introduced the notion of three potentially successful generic strategies—cost leadership, differentiation, and focus—that could, if consistently implemented, enable firms to outperform their rivals.[8] Quick response has been offered as a fourth option.[9] Generic strategies were originally presented as mutually exclusive alternatives—an organization that attempted to hedge its bets by pursuing more than one generic strategy at a time would invariably end up stuck in the middle, worse off than it was before. For many, the concept of a generic strategy—"Low cost becomes the theme running through the entire strategy"—was so simple and so appealing that managers tended to forget Porter's admonition that "quality, service, and other areas cannot be ignored." In Food

Lion's case, "cost control" was the theme—and apparently the only theme—that the company recognized. Although quality, service, and other areas were not entirely ignored by top management, the strong and consistent emphasis on cost control clearly had an influence that may have caused employees and local managers to cut corners on quality and deemphasize customer service to an extent that was clearly detrimental. It is important to understand, as we will discuss later, that Porter's notion of generic strategies can sometimes be taken too literally. The notions of cost leadership, differentiation, and focus are useful in conceptualizing and developing strategy but, as the case of Food Lion clearly shows, excessive reliance on a single dimension of strategy frequently leads to difficulties.

The examples clearly show that a one-dimensional focus on an organization's greatest strengths may lead to disaster. The limitations of the traditional approaches to analysis are also apparent—and the connection between misreading the competitive environment and problems in strategy formulation is obvious. It's far from clear, however, where this all leads. Just how does an organization go about creating competitive advantage?

Creating Competitive Advantage by Focusing on the Value Chain

The Food Lion example demonstrates that the single-minded pursuit of a narrowly-defined source of competitive advantage is often insufficient to guarantee success. Organizations that have created sustainable competitive advantages typically do not rely on a single strength, but strive to identify and pursue multiple strategies and approaches. Porter's three generic strategies of cost leadership, differentiation, and focus, as well as quick response, can, if used appropriately, contribute to competitive advantage. The key is to identify where and how to apply these strategic techniques.

Since traditional approaches to strategic analysis have limitations that may lead to strategic errors, how do strategists avoid decisions that lead to disadvantage? What approach should be pursued? In our experience, there is no simple solution, but there are some useful guidelines. Most organizations that have created significant competitive advantages and sustained them over time tend to:

Understand the Business as a Process

The concept of the value chain—looking at the organization as a sequential process of value-creating activities—is a powerful conceptual tool for understanding the building blocks of competitive advantage. Porter argued that five primary activities—inbound logistics, operations, outbound logistics, marketing, and sales and service—contribute to the physical creation of a product or service, its sale and transfer to the buyer. and customer service after the sale. Support activities—including purchasing, human resource management, information systems, research and development, and organizational infrastructure—either add value by themselves or indirectly support the primary activities. Although these generic value chain activities are useful for illustrating the basic concepts, we have found them awkward in practical application. The categories are applicable to manufacturing organizations but difficult to apply to other kinds of businesses. In addition, a focus on the generic value chain de-emphasizes the important interdependencies between the firm and other organizations and the ways in which these linkages can be used to add value for the ultimate end-user.

Organizations that have created sustainable competitive advantages typically do not rely on a single strength, but strive to identify and pursue multiple strategies and approaches.

We strongly advocate the development of a process-oriented view of the firm as an essential first step in understanding the organization and its position in the competitive environment. In our experience, developing a unique and specific value chain tailored to represent the strategic situation, and including all key service and support activities, is preferable to an attempt to force-fit the generic value chain of predetermined primary and support activities to all situations.[10] It is important to conceptualize the value chain in its broadest context, without regard to organizational boundaries, and to explicitly place the organization into the context of the broader value chain that involves suppliers and intermediate customers, as well as the ultimate end-user. We prefer to describe the value chain more generally as a sequential arrangement of processes or activities that operate on inputs, add value, and collectively produce a product or service created for and delivered to an end-user.

This definition helps to conceptualize an organization's role as an integral part of a larger value chain that may include upstream suppliers and intermediate customers in the firm's downstream channels of distribution. In addition to a thorough understanding of the activities that create and add value within the organization, managers must also understand how value is created for the end-user through interactions with other organizations in the larger value chain. Strategists who use the value chain to conceptualize their organizations as part of a larger process frequently gain valuable insights that are hidden from those who tend to view the organization as a self-contained entity with clearly defined boundaries that isolate it from its environment.

Strategists who use the value chain to conceptualize their organizations as part of a larger process frequently gain valuable insights that are hidden from those who tend to view the organization as a self-contained entity with clearly defined boundaries that isolate it from its environment.

Expand the Boundaries to Include Suppliers and Customers

Strengthening the competitive position of a business in an industry often requires managers to look beyond their organizational boundaries. They must ask themselves: How can we enhance the value chains of our suppliers and customers? They must view their firm's value chain as part of a system of value chains. The hotly contested automobile industry provides an example of the way manufacturers, by working closely with their suppliers, can improve quality, and reduce costs and cycle time with the benefits shared by both parties.

Honda has developed a mini-reengineering program aimed at strengthening its suppliers.[11] Early in its partnership with Donnelly Corporation, a mirror producer located in Holland, Michigan, Honda sent engineers to study two of the suppliers' plants. "Time goal," according to Jim Wehrman, a Honda purchasing manager. "is to give almost a consultant's outside view of the operation." Overall, Honda hopes Donnelly will reduce costs about 2 percent a year, with both companies sharing the savings. Donnelly has built an entirely new plant to make Honda's mirrors. Not only does Honda get low-cost, high-quality components, but Donnelly's payoff is impressive: from $5 million in sales in the first year, the partnership is expected to grow to $60 million in a little over a decade. In this case, Honda has integrated its value chain with that of a supplier, to the mutual benefit of both organizations.

Robin Transports, a trucking firm, provides another example of how tight linkages between the value chains of a firm and its customers can create competitive advantage.[12] Robin Transports has designed its trailers and operational procedures to support General Motors's inbound logistics strategies. The trailers have been designed with fabric walls to enable them to be unloaded from both sides as well as from the rear, enabling parts to be delivered closer to GM's assembly lines, in places where standard trailers cannot be used. Robin also loads the trailers to permit them to be unloaded in sequence for ease of handling and delivery at the specified times when the parts are needed. GM has reduced inventories by utilizing just-in-time (JIT) deliveries and realized productivity improvements through more efficient materials handling. In exchange, it has designated Robin Transports as a preferred supplier with a premium rate. The lesson: Robin Transport's competitive position was strengthened by directing its efforts at one of its customer's critical value chain activities—inbound logistics.

Identify Strengths and Weaknesses at Each Link in the Chain

Once one begins to view the business as a process, or series of parallel processes. it becomes only natural to assess the organization's strengths and weaknesses in the value chain, and to identify sources of competitive advantage and areas of relative weakness at this level of analysis. In developing competitive strategies, managers must identify, sequence, and prioritize activities that add value for the customer or end-user. Effective managers strive to strengthen value chain activities amid relationships that add value, and eliminate those that don't contribute.

The processes and techniques of SWOT analysis are appropriate and useful at this level. Industry analysis also becomes more meaningful when addressed in the context of the value chain. The ways in which individual value activities combine to create unique organizational capabilities become apparent from an understanding of their interrelationships and interdependencies. Benchmarking is often used to compare an organization's performance at the level of individual primary or support value activities with best-in-class performers, regardless of industry. Benchmarking is also useful in identifying ways that organizational performance can be enhanced.

Add Value in Multiple Activities and in Multiple Ways

Managers should strive to determine what activities add customer value, what relationships among value-creating activities are most important, and what forms of competitive advantage can be successfully exploited at each stage in the value chain. Successful firms with enduring sources of competitive advantage not only identify activities that add value, but also recognize the important interrelationships among value activities.

These organizations seek to add value at multiple points along the value chain and in a variety of different ways, each of which complements and reinforces other value-creating activities. Businesses pursuing a competitive advantage of differentiation succeed by creating unique bundles of products and/or services that are highly valued by customers. Attributes that businesses use to differentiate their products and services include: desirable product features, favorable image and reputation, convenient and quality after-sales service, manufacturing consistency and reliability, technological innovation, and status symbols.

Lexus, for example, has established itself as a premier nameplate by selling cars of exceptional quality with superior customer service.[13] Without question. Lexus must establish and maintain close ties with its dealers, providing resources such as advertising materials, parts supplies and, of course, automobile inventories. One could easily imagine the futility of Lexus's superb marketing, sales and service efforts if it could not maintain tight tolerances to product specifications in the manufacturing operations, or if procurement was unable to acquire high-quality components. Clearly, superb marketing and service—by itself—would be inadequate to support Lexus's differentiation strategy.

Successful firms with enduring sources of competitive advantage not only identify activities that add value, but also recognize the important interrelationships among value activities.

An example of how one key element of strategy can enhance three forms of competitive advantage—cost leadership, differentiation, and quick response—is Southwest Airlines' well known 15-minute turnaround time between flights.[14] By halving the standard 30-minute turnaround, Southwest saves approximately $175 million in capital expenditures alone through more efficient utilization of its aircraft. Greater aircraft utilization enables the airline to offer more flights—a source of differentiation because it provides customers with a greater selection and availability of arrival and departure times between destinations. Ensuring such tight turnarounds requires superb coordination among several value chain activities, including ticketing, catering, baggage handling, fueling, maintenance, weight and balance calculations, and flight plans and local clearances.

Achieve Close Integration of Value-Creating Activities

A firm that successfully exploits all three forms of competitive advantage is Atlas Door, which achieves its position through the close integration of all its value-creating activities.[15] A manufacturer of industrial doors in a wide variety of sizes, materials, and constructions, Atlas entered the industry determined to beat the four-month period that competitors typically required to complete an order. To do this. Atlas invested in information systems and related processes to set up a just-in-time factory that vastly exceeded industry norms for delivery logistics. It also developed computer-aided design (CAD) capabilities so that a customer could describe a door to an Atlas engineer over the phone. During the conversation, the engineer would then draw up the order while the customer answered questions. Figure 2 highlights some of the important relationships among value chain activities at Atlas Door.

CAD enables Atlas to provide better customer service and improve sales and marketing efforts through tighter customer interfaces and quicker response time to orders and changes. In addition, the CAD system permits Atlas to develop more accurate raw material requirements. The added precision improves product quality and lowers defect rates and scrappage. The CAD system also reduces design time, thus lowering labor costs. The information systems amid related processes and procedures that support the JT inventory system also provide many sources of competitive advantage. Customer orders are handled more efficiently, elevating customer service, lowering costs, and enabling more efficient throughput from procurement through outbound logistics. Orders are filled more quickly and less warehousing space, lighting, and staffing are required. And, since only cheese and wine improve with age, losses due to damage and theft are reduced.

Focus on the Dynamics of the Competitive Environment

The competitive environment is in continual flux, as customers, suppliers, and competitors enter and depart, as technologies evolve, and competitive initiatives are launched and countered in the arena. The pitfalls of static analysis must be avoided, and firms must focus on the ongoing dynamics of the competitive marketplace. This extraordinarily difficult task becomes considerably more manageable when viewed in the context of any organization's key value activities. By narrowing the focus to only those market factors and trends that affect the organization's key value activities, the bewildering complexity is reduced considerably, and interpretation becomes easier and more direct. Had Food Lion focused separately on the upstream and downstream activities in its value chain, the differences between its approach and those of its competitors might have been interpreted differently. The competitive moves its rivals used to counter Food Lion's low price strategy might also have been more easily understood.

Innovate by Adding Value in New and Unique Ways

During the 1980s, much attention was focused on the competitive advantages of cost leadership and differentiation, in particular, through high standards of quality.[16] Many firms became so adept at combining these two forms of competitive advantage that the Japanese began referring to the situation as *atarimae hinshitsu,* one in which "value is taken for granted." When a particular form of competitive advantage becomes so common and widespread that it is accepted as the minimum standard for industry participation, firms must find new forms of competitive advantage in order to sustain above-normal levels of profitability. During the early 1990s, many firms have discovered that they could regain competitive advantage by shifting their focus to speed or response time. Many academics, consultants, and executives have extolled the virtues of speed and quick response. "Ultimately, speed is the only weapon we have," says Intel Corporation's Andrew S. Grove.[17] Kathleen M. Eisenhardt of Stanford University says: "The best strategies are irrelevant if they take too long to formulate."[18] "Speed kills the competition," says Richard D. Stewart, CEO of the Computer Corporation of America.[19] And George Stalk, Jr., of the Boston Consulting Group,[20] says: "As a strategic weapon, time is the equivalent of money, productivity, quality, even innovation."

Speed can be a particularly strong source of competitive advantage when a supplier provides a critical element of its customer's product or production process. If downtime is extremely costly, reliability and quick response become paramount concerns. Caterpillar's capabilities in rapidly supplying parts for its large and costly earth-moving equipment have one objective minimizing costly downtime for its customers.[21] The company's new state-of-the-art Service Information System gives both dealers and key customers instant access to parts and service information and helps forge a three-way partnership among Caterpillar, the dealer, and the customer. This partnership is critical, for example, in keeping the all-Caterpillar fleet of machines up and running at Pegasus Gold's three Montana mines. The dealers keep product support specialists on-site and train mine personnel in the use of Caterpillar software and maintenance programs. Quarterly meetings among Pegasus, the dealers, and Caterpillar have also helped to keep machine availability above 95 percent, reducing Pegasus's equipment costs by 25 percent.

When a particular form of competitive advantage becomes so common and widespread that it is accepted as the minimum standard for industry participation, firms must find new forms of competitive advantage in order to sustain above-normal levels of profitability.

Some analysts view quick response as just another form of differentiation. The example of Caterpillar, however, illustrates that responsive logistics support can itself be a powerful source of competitive advantage. When customers are dependent on suppliers for quick response to minimize downtime, rapid availability of replacement products, parts, or services takes on paramount importance.

Focus on Strengths by Outsourcing Non-Critical Functions

Competitive advantage can be enhanced by focusing organizational attention primarily on those activities that are critical to the development of that advantage, and outsourcing noncritical functions that can be performed more effectively or more efficiently by other.[22] Strategic outsourcing is not just about reducing costs; in many cases the resulting reconfiguration of the value chain can redefine the terms of engagement in the competitive arena. One example is Pepsico's cost leadership strategy at its Taco Bell unit. CEO John Martin introduced the K-minus concept (the K stands for Kitchen) in 1989 to drive down costs and improve the focus on service.[23] Under this plan, many food production activities such as crushing beans, dicing cheese. and preparing beef were removed from the restaurants and centralized in contractor-run commissaries. The cost savings allowed Taco Bell to slash prices. Equally important, the company was able to reduce the average size of its restaurant kitchens by 40 percent, freeing up more space and employees to serve customers.

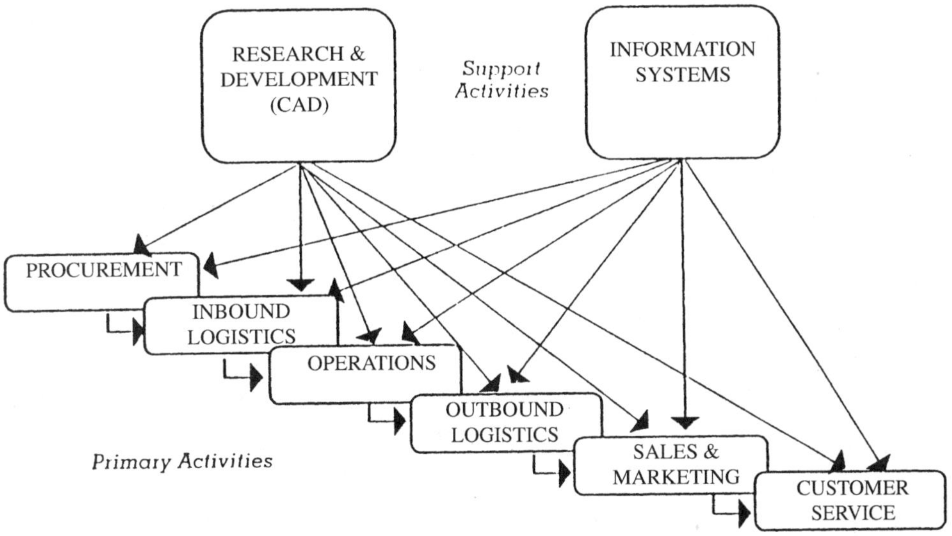

FIGURE 2
Support Activities Provide Close Integration of Value Chain Activities

Leveraging the Value Chain: The Example of Wal-Mart

One of the most successful retailers of all time, Wal-Mart has seen sales and profits increase over the last five years by 89 percent and 53 percent, respectively—both measures better than twice the retailing industry average.[24] The company's stock roughly tripled between June 1995 and June 1999. Wal-Mart has broadened its product offering to include groceries, fast food, and other items, and exports its data systems, drive, and efficiency to international markets. Already the dominant discounter in Canada and Mexico, Wal-Mart is expanding to such other huge markets as China, Indonesia, the U.K.. and Brazil. Although the international division accounted for 5 percent of corporate sales in 1997, its revenues are projected to reach $27 billion, or 17 percent of total sales, by 2000.[25]

Much of Wal-Mart's success can be attributed to its strategic focus and emphasis on key elements of the value chain. The value chains of mass-market retailers like K-Mart, Target, and Wal-Mart have historically looked very much like the retail grocery distribution model illustrated in Figure 1. The critical success factors in the industry have traditionally included purchasing power, distribution efficiency, retail location, and merchandising. The successful competitors have all emphasized cost control and efficiency in purchasing and distribution operations, and operated low-overhead facilities. Competitive rivalry has focused primarily on location, pricing and differentiation in merchandise mix, and promotion.

Over the past decade, Wal-Mart has left its competitors in the dust, and is now moving in on the traditional turf of a number of other retail distribution industries. For years, Wal-Mart offered pharmacies in addition to its traditional merchandise mix. Many Wal-Mart outlets now also feature such consumer services as optical shops and photo finishing. The chain's new superstores include a full line of groceries, meats, and produce, as well as in-house fast food outlets. As Wal-Mart increasingly moves into product areas that were formerly the domain of grocery chains, the revenues and profits of traditional food retailers like Food Lion are likely to be adversely affected.

What is the secret of Wal-Mart's success? Let's take a look at one example of how Wal-Mart has redefined the industry's value chain—and how it competes successfully on all three forms of competitive advantage.

Wal-Mart is ostensibly in the business of selling moderately priced goods to the public.[26] A number of years ago, however, Wal-Mart took a closer look at the industry's value chain and decided to reframe the competitive challenge. Although its competitors were focused primarily on retailing—merchandising and promotion—Wal-Mart concluded that they were not so much in the retailing business as in transportation logistics and communications. And that was the battleground on which it chose to compete. By redefining the rules of competitive engagement in a way that played to its strengths, Wal-Mart achieved a competitive advantage that dominates its industry.

A central element of Wal-Mart's strategy is the logistics technique known as cross-docking. Goods are continuously delivered to Wal-Mart's warehouses, where they are selected, repacked, and then dispatched to stores—often without sitting in inventory. Instead of spending valuable time in the warehouse, merchandise crosses from one loading dock to another in 48 hours or less. This enables Wal-Mart to achieve the economies associated with full-truckload purchasing, while avoiding the usual inventory and handling costs, reducing Wal-Mart's cost of sales by two to three percent relative to its competitors.

By redefining the rules of competitive engagement in a way that played to its strengths. Wal-Mart achieved a competitive advantage that dominates its industry.

The benefits to Wal-Mart and its customers multiply. Lower costs help make possible Wal-Mart's everyday low prices, which help the company save even more by eliminating frequent promotions. Stable prices also lead to more predictable sales, thus reducing stockouts and excess inventory. Fewer stockouts boost customer satisfaction and loyalty. Lower inventories translate into increased flexibility, permitting Wal-Mart to adjust the merchandise mix in response to changing consumer preferences. Finally, everyday low prices bring in more customer traffic, which translates into higher sales per retail square foot.

These economies make it easier for Wal-Mart to afford to staff its stores with greeters and additional check-out clerks, and to reward employee performance and loyalty with stock ownership and profit-sharing. Loyal and dedicated employees and better customer service are an element of differentiation that, in the long run, translates into more loyal customers.

Although cross-docking seems a valuable concept, the practice isn't easily imitated and diffused throughout the industry. If such imitation were easy, Wal-Mart's competitive advantage would only be temporary. However, cross-docking is extremely difficult to manage. To make it work, Wal-Mart had to make strategic investments in a variety of interlocking support systems, which would be extremely difficult to copy, thus strengthening Wal-Mart's competitive advantage. The systems involve:

- Continuous contact among Wal-Mart's distribution centers, suppliers, and every point of sale in every store to ensure that orders can be executed within a matter of hours.
- Fast and responsive transportation, including 19 distribution centers serviced by nearly 2,000 company-owned trucks.
- Fundamental changes in managerial control that allow the stores to pull products when and where

they need them, instead of having suppliers push products into the system. Such an approach places a premium on frequent, informed cooperation among stores, distribution centers, and suppliers—with far less centralized control.

- Information systems that provide store managers with detailed data about customer behavior, along with a fleet of airplanes that regularly ferry store managers to the Bentonville, Arkansas, headquarters for meetings on market trends and merchandising.
- A video link connecting each store to corporate headquarters and every other store.
- Programs like stock ownership and profit sharing geared to making personnel responsive to customers.

Clearly, the logistics strategy of cross-docking and sophisticated information systems reduce costs in a number of ways and, by reducing inventories and shortening procurement cycle times, increase Wal-Mart's flexibility and responsiveness to changing consumer preferences. As the company broadens its product offering and expands into new markets, it is likely that the benefits associated with its finely tuned logistics and information management systems will yield sustainable advantages in these new markets as well.

In creating its position of sustainable competitive advantage, Wal-Mart has understood the business as a process and expanded the boundaries to include its suppliers and customers. It has identified its strengths, added value in multiple activities and in new and innovative ways, and leveraged its capabilities to enhance the flexibility of its operations through the close integration and coordination of interdependent activities.

We have found, however, that taking a strategic inventory often helps managers identify and focus on the sources of competitive advantage within their own firms.

Can Wal-Mart's success be duplicated in any industry? Perhaps. Easier said than done? No question. We have found, however, that taking a strategic inventory often helps managers identify and focus on the sources of competitive advantage within their own firms.

Taking a Strategic Inventory

Figure 3 presents a set of questions and guidelines designed to help managers relate the concepts described in this article to their own organizational context. We illustrate the use of the strategic inventory by analyzing how Wal-Mart has created competitive advantage through the use of new logistics techniques. Then, revisiting the Food Lion example, we point out how the strategic inventory might have revealed some of the flaws in its Southwestern expansion strategy. Finally, we take a look at Food Lion's recent performance, including some of the efforts it has made to reverse its fortunes.

Wal-Mart: Creating Competitive Advantage

Using the strategic inventory to analyze Wal-Mart's strategy provides insight into how the firm has created competitive advantage by leveraging its strengths across the value chain.

1. *Where is value created for the ultimate customer?* Wal-Mart creates value for its customers throughout the value chain. Its purchasing power and efficiencies in inbound and outbound logistics are reflected in lower consumer prices. Its information systems, low inventory levels, and responsive distribution systems enable store managers to anticipate and quickly respond to changing customer needs. Its staffing practices and employee incentives emphasize a level of customer service that translates into satisfied customers.
2. *What important relationships exist among the value chain activities?* From the perspective of internal customers and suppliers, many important relationships exist. Clearly, inbound and outbound logistics are closely linked through the cross-docking strategy. Information systems are vital in adjusting the merchandise mix to reflect consumer preferences, placing orders with suppliers, and coordinating the movement of merchandise along the value chain. Wal-Mart's product coding and marking strategies link suppliers, company operations, and customers to shorten checkout lines, reduce errors, and continuously monitor sales and stocking levels. These practices ensure efficient flow of goods from producer to store shelf, and ultimately to the consumer.
3. *What forms of competitive advantage are emphasized?* Multiple forms of competitive advantage are emphasized throughout Wal-Mart's value chain. Low cost is Wal-Mart's primary source of competitive advantage. Quick response is also important, not only ensuring that the shelves remain fully stocked, but also lowering handling and inventory carrying costs. Wal-Mart also emphasizes differentiation by the breadth of its product line and its consumer-friendly strategies of everyday low prices, consistent quality, fully-stocked shelves, and loyal, well-trained, and customer-oriented employees.
4. *What forms of competitive advantage are emphasized by competitors?* Wal-Mart's competitors emphasize product differentiation and low cost as their primary sources of competitive advantage. Given the breadth of Wal-Mart's offering, it is difficult for com-

Figure 3
Strategic Inventory

1. **Where in the organization's value chain do we create value for the ultimate customer?** (Value chain activities may vary for each organization.)

Value chain activity	Is value added? (Yes/No)	How is value created for the customer?
Inbound logistics		
Operations		
Outbound logistics		
Sales and marketing		
Service		
Procurement		
Research and development		
Information systems		
Management and administration		

2. **What are the important relationships among the activities of the value chain? What kinds of interdependencies exist?** For each activity, identify both internal customer/supplier relationships and interdependencies and the important linkages and interfaces with external suppliers and customers.

	Inbound logistics	Operations	Outbound logistics	Sales and marketing	Service	Procurement	R&D	Information systems	Management and administration
External suppliers	X					X	X	X	X
Inbound logistics		X						X	X
Operations	X		X					X	X
Outbound logistics		X		X	X			X	X
Sales and marketing			X		X			X	X
Service				X				X	X
External customers				X	X		X	X	X

3. **For each of the value-creating activities identified above, what form of competitive advantage is emphasized?** What activities and/or relationships among activities need to be strengthened to improve the organization's competitive advantage?

- ✦ Do we add value in multiple activities and in multiple ways?
- ✦ Will our competitive advantage survive in a changing environment?
- ✦ Can we innovate by adding value in new and unique ways?
- ✦ Can we add value by expanding the boundaries to include our suppliers?
- ✦ Can we add value by expanding the boundaries to include our customers?
- ✦ Can we add value by focusing on a few key activities and outsourcing the rest?

4. **What forms of competitive advantage are emphasized by our competitors?** What opportunities and risks does this suggest?

---

petitors to achieve more than parity in product differentiation. The inability to match Wal-Mart's advantage in distribution logistics places competitors at a disadvantage in competing on cost or responsiveness. This makes it more difficult to establish a differentiation advantage based on long-term customer satisfaction and loyalty. By relying on multiple sources of competitive advantage, Wal-Mart is less vulnerable to a competitor that emphasizes only a single competitive strength.

Food Lion's Narrow Focus

Food Lion's narrow focus provides a stark contrast to Wal-Mart's complex and highly integrated approach to competitive advantage. Food Lion's traditional strategy was based on price leadership. which required establishing a superior cost position across the entire value chain. Food Lion's weapon of choice was control. Management's obsession with cost control alienated its employees and organized labor, and apparently caused it to ignore many of the important relationships and interdependencies between upstream and downstream activities. As Food Lion expanded into the Dallas-Fort Worth market, it became clear that it did not fully understand the role of differentiation-based competition in these markets.

How has Food Lion fared since 1992? In 1993, the year after the *PrimeTime Live* exposé, Food Lion earned only \$4 million—less than 0.1 percent on sales—compared with \$205.2 million in 1991.[27] In 1994, Food Lion began to retrench—closing 87 unprofitable stores, including 50 of the 103 stores it opened in the Southwest during 1991. Its growth and expansion is now focused primarily in its core markets, and includes the acquisition of competitors in Florida and North Carolina.

Food Lion's credibility and reputation suffered greatly. Its stock fell from a split-adjusted \$18 per share in 1992 to about \$6 in 1993. From 1993 to 1998, annual revenue growth slowed to less than 6 percent. By 1998, earnings had recovered to the level achieved in 1991, but net income as a percentage of revenues was only 2.3 percent, compared with 3.2 percent in 1991. Between 1993 and mid-1999, the stock slowly crept up from \$6 to about \$11 but earnings per share have increased rather impressively from \$.44 in 1996 to \$.48 in 1997 and \$.57 in 1998. The bottom line: Food Lion was badly wounded by its ill-conceived expansion out of its familiar territory and by the ABC report—both partly consequences of its obsession with cost control.

While still primarily a low-cost competitor Food Lion has clearly increased its emphasis on differentiation, focusing more attention on the downstream activities of sales, marketing, and customer service.

What has Food Lion learned, and how has it changed its strategy to more accurately respond to the requirements of a changing marketplace? While still primarily a low-cost competitor, Food Lion has clearly increased its emphasis on differentiation, focusing more attention on the downstream activities of sales, marketing, and customer service.

The company is currently updating and enlarging its existing stores, and experimenting with new formats, such as larger store-within-a-store nonfood departments, to compete with the super centers. Food Lion is also emphasizing customer service and convenience by building more stores in its core markets and expanding operating hours, many to 24 hours per day.

Several new initiatives are designed to foster closer relationships with customers and suppliers. The company has successfully introduced the MVP Customer Card that offers graduated discounts to the company's best shoppers. This program has become popular both with customers and with the vendors who support the program. In late 1996, Food Lion announced a partnership with the Mom & Pops Bakery Division of WSMP, Inc. The program, called Homestyle Meals to Go!, features hot or cold entrees and side dishes that can be prepared in minutes at home. These initiatives appear to represent a tentative response to the forms of differentiation-focused advantage emphasized by some of Food Lion's competitors. It appears that Food Lion's management learned a number of lessons from its aborted efforts to expand into Southwestern markets and began to take the necessary steps to achieve relative parity on the important dimensions of competitive differentiation.

Lessons and Suggestions

Many lessons can be learned from Food Lion's reversal of fortune during the 1990s. It should be clear that an organization's strengths, no matter how great, don't necessarily translate into sustainable competitive advantages. A narrowly focused competitive strategy that succeeds under one set of market conditions may not fare so well in a different competitive environment.

We have demonstrated by example that a well-grounded understanding of the sources of advantage in, and the interrelationships among, the elements of an organization's value chain are essential to the development of sustainable competitive advantage. Wal-Mart illustrates how a firm can outperform its competitors by redefining the industry's value chain and expanding the firm's boundaries to include both suppliers and customers. We have provided a set of guidelines for using the value chain as a powerful tool to identify and understand the sources of sustainable competitive advantage. Finally, we have included the strategic inventory as a practical resource to help managers understand the sources of competitive advantage in their own organizations.

Our final suggestion to managers: use the strategic inventory as a self-test of your own understanding of the sources of competitive advantage available to your firm. Then ask other managers, from at least three different levels in your organization, to do the same. Compare the answers. The results may surprise you. Perceptions about the most important value chain activities, their interrelationships, and the forms of competitive advantage for which a firm is striving can vary dramatically both within levels and across levels in an organization. Such inconsistent perceptions waste resources and time and can result in forfeiture of promising opportunities.

Acknowledgment

This article is based on our 1997 book, *Mission critical: The seven strategic traps that derail even the smartest companies.* Burr Ridge, IL: Irwin Professional Publishing. Observation of both successful and failed strategies across a broad range of companies and industries has led us to identify common patterns of strategic failure, which we have labeled as the seven strategic traps. While the same strategic errors seem to be repeated, over and over again, by managers apparently unable to learn from the mistakes of those who have gone before, the authors believe that most strategic failures are avoidable. Strategies need not be brilliant, just as long as they are sound. well-conceived, and avoid the most common strategic errors. It doesn't take the world's greatest leader to succeed in implementation, just one who doesn't make any really dumb mistakes. And the most important lesson of all is that it's not that hard to avoid the most common strategic traps—if you know what to look for. By understanding the mistakes others have made, and avoiding the most common strategic traps, prudent managers can navigate around the rocks and shoals and plot a safe course to reach their organization's strategic objectives.

Endnotes

1. *Fortune.* 1994. Can The Limited fix itself? October 17:161–172.
2. Sources for the Food Lion example include: *The Washington Post.* 1993. Labor's food fight: Food Lion tests strength of supermarket union. March l:C1; *The Washington Post.* 1993. Food Lion to settle claims it violated U.S. labor laws. August 4:A1; *The Washington Post.* 1994. Food Lion accused of selling outdated infant formula. February 4:B2; Value Line: Food Lion Inc. 'V.' November 18:1500; *Forbes.* 1994. Lionized no more. January 17:16; *Wall Street Journal.* 1993. Food Lion to pay big settlement in labor case. August 3:A3–A4.
3. Wolfe, J. Food Lion comes toTulsa . . . "Hello, I'm Diane Sawyer;" in Hitt, M. A., Ireland, R. D. & Hoskisson. 5. E. 1995. *Strategic management: Competitiveness and globalization: 584.* Minneapolis/St. Paul: West Publishing Company.
4. "An example of firms that have overemphasized differentiation strategies are the Japanese automobile manufacturers (e.g.. Toyota, Honda, and Nissan). These firms have, in effect, overemphasized their strengths in high quality manufacturing, excellent R&D, and technological innovation. This has led to many examples of gold plating, such as excessively narrow seams and costly soundproofing technology on inexpensive models. See, for example, *Wall Street Journal.* 1994. Why Toyota will endure in the U.S. car market. October 17:A1; Apple Computer illustrates the downside of the excessive use of quick response strategy with its failed introduction of the Newton personal digital assistant. See, for example, *Byte.* 1994. Apple's high-tech gamble. December:50–70.
5. Miller, D. 1990. *The Icarus paradox.* New York: Harper Collins.
6. See, for example, Ansoff. I. 1965. *Corporate strategy.* New York, McGraw-Hill; Porter, M. E. 1980. *Competitive strategy.* New York: Free Press; Porter. M. E. 1985. *Competitive advantage.* New York: Free Press; and Andrews. K. 1987. *The concept of corporate strategy* (3rd ed.) Homewood. IL: Irwin, for representative examples.
7. See Porter, M. E. 1980 op. cit., for a definitive treatment of the approach and methodologies used in industry analysis.
8. Ibid., 34–46.
9. Stalk. G., Jr. 1989. Time: The next source of competitive advantage. *Harvard Business Review* 66(4):41–51.
10. J. B. Quinn in *Intelligent enterprise.* New York: Free Press. (1992:37) recommends that "all nonproduction elements in the value chain, and at corporate staff levels need to be redefined as 'services' which can either be produced internally or potentially outsourced to external firms."
11. *Fortune.* 1994. The new golden rules of business. February 21:60–64.
12. Boxersox, D. J. 1990. The strategic benefits of logistic alliances. *Harvard Business Review,* 68(4):35–45.
13. *Fortune.* 1994. Service is everybody's business. June 27:52; *Fortune.* 1993. Companies that serve you best. May 31:74–78.
14. *Southwest Airlines News.* 1993. The Southwest Story. December 13:10.
15. Miller. A. & Dess, G. G. 1996. *Strategic management.* Second edition. New York: McGraw-Hill: 162.
16. Ibid., 158.
17. Vinton, D. E. 1992. A new look at time, speed, and the manager. *The Academy of Management Executive,* 6(4):7.
18. Eisenhardt, K. M. 1990. Speed and strategic choice: How managers accelerate decision making. *California Management Review,* 32(Fall):1–16.
19. Stewart, H. D. 1989. Speed kills the competition. *Chief Executive.* November–December: 46–49.
20. Stalk, G. Jr., op cit.
21. 1993 *Caterpillar Annual Report:* 16.
22. See Chapters 2 and 3 of Quinn, op. cit.. for a comprehensive discussion of the approach and rationale for strategic outsourcing.
23. *Fortune.* 1994. Service is everybody's business. June 27: 48–60.
24. *ValueLine.* 1997. Wal-Mart Stores. May 23: 1664 and *ValueLine.* 1997. Retail Store Industry. May 23: 1641.
25. *Business Week.* Wal-Mart Spoken Here. 1997. June 23:138–144.
26. The Wal-Mart example draws on Stalk, G., Evans, P., and Shulman, L. E. 1992. Competing on capabilities: The new rules of corporate strategy. *Harvard Business Review* 70(2): 140–147: and Kierinan. M. J. 1993. The new strategic architecture: Learning to compete in the twenty-first century. *The Executive.* 4(1):7–21.
27. The update on Food Lion draws on: ValueLine. 1997. Food Lion, Inc. "B." May 16:1507; *Food Lion News.* 1996. Announces a 41-store test launch of a Home Meal Replacement Program as part of its Food Lion Fast Initiative. November 13:1; *Food Lion News.* 1996. Food Lion Earnings up 22%. Same Store Sales up 6.7%. September 19:1; *Food Lion News.* 1996. Food Lion Posts Strong First Quarter—Same Store Sales Up 5.2%. April 4:1: and *Financial World.* 1997. Food Lion: King of the Jungle?: January 21:24, and 1996, 1997, and 1998 Food Lion *Annual Reports.*

Gregory G. Dess holds the Carol Martin Gatton Endowed Chair in Leadership and Strategic Management at the University of Kentucky. His research on strategic decision making, competitive advantage, and organization-environment relations has been published in many leading academic and practitioner journals. *Contact: gdess@pop.uky.edu.*

Joseph C. Picken is a member of the adjunct faculty at the Cox School of Business at Southern Methodist University and president of Joseph C. Picken & Associates, which provides strategy, operations, and turnaround management services to emerging growth firms. Dr. Picken holds AB and MBA degrees from Dartmouth College and a Ph.D. in business administration from the University of Texas at Arlington. *Contact: jpicken@aol.com.*

Six Sigma Enlightenment; Managers Seek Corporate Nirvana Through Quality Control

By CLAUDIA H. DEUTSCH

Heard the latest management mantra? Six Sigma.

In consultant-speak, it denotes the path to a corporate nirvana where everything—from product design to manufacturing to billing—proceeds without a hitch. In engineer-speak, it means no more than 3.4 defects per million widgets or procedures.

In practice, Six Sigma is a statistical quality-control method that combines the art of the efficiency expert with the science of the computer geek. And a growing group of big no-nonsense companies like Allied Signal, Motorola and General Electric swear by it.

"Six Sigma has galvanized our company with an intensity the likes of which I have never seen in my 40 years at G.E.," said John F. Welch, the chairman of General Electric.

So fervent a proselytizer is Mr. Welch that G.E. has spent three years and more than $1 billion to convert all of its divisions to the Six Sigma faith. The GE Medical Systems unit recently introduced a $1.25 million diagnostic scanner, the first product that G.E. designed from start to finish using Six Sigma principles. Six Sigma teamwork enabled GE Plastics to produce 1.1 billion pounds more plastics without building one new plant. Over all, Mr. Welch credits Six Sigma with raising the company's operation profit margins to 16.6 percent from 14.4 percent.

So what exactly is this philosophy of flawlessness? First, the name. Sigma is the Greek letter that statisticians use to define a standard deviation from a bell curve. The higher the sigma, the fewer the deviations from the norm—or, in industry parlance, the fewer the defects. At One Sigma, two-thirds of whatever is being measured falls within the curve. Two Sigma encompasses about 95 percent. At Six Sigma you are about as close to flaw free as mere mortals can get.

No company can really achieve that kind of perfection, of course. But as with any religion, Six Sigma presents an ideal state toward which adherents continually strive.

"Six Sigma gets people away from thinking that 96 percent is good, to thinking that 40,000 failures per million is bad," said James E. Morehouse, a vice president of the consulting firm of A. T. Kearney Inc.

Six Sigma was developed more than a decade ago at Motorola. But since then, it has been embraced by numerous corporations and is even included in courses on quality at the Harvard Business School.

As applied in industry, Six Sigma is a rigorous statistical method of breaking a customer's requirements into tasks or steps, and setting the optimum specification for each part of the process, based on how the parts interact.

"Six Sigma translates fuzzy customer requirements into technically measurable responses," said Maurice L. Berryman, a Six Sigma consultant in Dallas.

Here is an example: Say a customer wants to be billed on the same day each month. With Six Sigma, making that happen means analyzing the interaction of everything involved in processing that customer's order.

When and how does the sales department send through paperwork, and at what point does a difference in days, hours, even minutes, have an impact on when the bill goes out? Does it make a difference when shipping coordinates with billing? How long does mail sit in the mail room, and at what point does it matter?

Once everything is quantified, the what-if scenarios begin: Would a stricter paperwork processing schedule in sales make mail room bottlenecks irrelevant? Would adding a person in accounting give the mail room an extra hour's leeway?

In principle, Six Sigma is little different from the type of analysis that Frederick W. Taylor, the industrial efficiency pioneer, might have performed with stopwatch and notebook a century ago. But in Six Sigma analyses, there are thousands of permutations and combinations—probably too many for the human mind to fathom, although easy enough for even a moderately speedy computer. Thus, modern information technology has made Six Sigma a practical way to identify the optimum configuration of most products or processes.

"Six Sigma gets people from all over the organization to work together on improving the end product, not just their individual piece of it," said Frank Jones, a Six Sigma specialist at the management consulting firm Booz-Allen & Hamilton.

Scanner Analyses Cost $50 Million

In the case of the new GE Medical Systems products—a superfast diagnostic scanner called the Lightspeed—200 people spent nearly three years and almost $50 million to run 250 separate Six Sigma analyses. While one team was checking out the reliability of measurement devices, another was figuring out which factors affect the scanner's life, while yet another was dissecting image quality into factors that could be massaged to filter out picture-blurring electronic noise.

The Lightspeed, like many diagnostic scanners, employs computed tomography, or CT. CT scanners work by sending electromagnetic waves through the body and recording the amount of energy that comes out. Since various tissues and organs absorb energy differently—bones absorb more than flesh, for example—the emerging waves, in the form of light, yield a good picture of the internal landscape they have passed through. The scanners let doctors study wafer-thin cross sections of parts or all of a patient's body without making any incision.

GE Medical Systems, which already controls 39 percent of the $1.6 billion global market for scanners, has high hopes for the Lightspeed. The new scanner captures multiple images simultaneously, requiring only 20 seconds to do full-body scans that once took three minutes—important because patients must remain perfectly still during the scan. And unlike previous CT scanners, the Lightspeed does not need to cool down for as long as three minutes between uses.

"The speed is breathtaking, and it ran without downtime from the start," said Dr. Carl Ravin, the chairman of the department of radiology at Duke Medical Center.

The Lightspeed is not perfect, of course. But Six Sigma enabled GE Medical to anticipate which compromises doctors would accept. For example, the Lightspeed takes slightly thicker scan slices than doctors normally specify, but no one complained because the thicker slices were virtually free of electronic noise.

"Six Sigma let us predict the amount of variability that customers will tolerate before they perceive it as a defect," said Marc Onetto, who oversees Six Sigma projects at Gems, as GE Medical Systems is commonly known.

The Problem of Human Error

Of course Six Sigma itself is not perfect, either, since it cannot compensate for human error. Take what happened when Gems tinkered with the computer that translates the data the scanner collects into images an operator can read.

CT scanners generate a lot of heat, and the heat often caused the printed circuit boards to overload. A Six Sigma team figured out that by perforating the metal box that holds the boards, they could dissipate the heat. They were right—except that they forgot to check what other impact that change might have.

Gems started sending out scanners with perforated computer boxes. The holes compromised the structural integrity of the metal, the metal warped outward and the circuit boards loosened—causing as many failures as the heat had.

Gems technicians spotted the problem during field tests, and the company corrected it by reinforcing the metal before any scanner was running at a hospital or a clinic. But the mistake taught Gems an important lesson about Six Sigma.

"You must take it step by step," said Charles H. Young, a Gems spokesman who has been steeped in the process. "You get into trouble if you compromise the rigor of the process. You can't skip steps and jump to premature conclusions."

Customer Demand Drives Project

The Lightspeed project started, as so many new products do, with customers clamoring for more, better, faster.

By late 1995, Gems knew that Siemens, Toshiba and other competitors were working on faster scanners. The company also knew it could probably get its own faster version ready, approved by the Food and Drug Administration and on the market before the 1998 Radiology Society of North America show, the annual December trade exposition at which the medical equipment industry displays its latest wares. But readying a scanner as radically different as the Lightspeed was an iffier proposition.

"Going for that quantum leap in technology in that time frame was one of the toughest decisions of my career," said Vivek Paul, the general manager of the CT business at Gems. "We shifted development resources from existing products, and that left us very vulnerable if Lightspeed couldn't be built in time."

In January 1996, the race against the clock began.

The most important parts of the scanner are the tubes, which focus the waves, and the detector, which translates them into pictures. So they received the heaviest attention.

The old tubes, which cost $59,000 each to replace, had long been a thorn in GE's side. Hospitals and clinics wanted them to operate for at least 12 hours a day, for 6 months; typically, they lasted only half that long. Moreover, Gems was scrapping some $20 million in tubes each year because they failed preshipping performance tests. Even so, a disturbing number of faulty tubes were slipping past inspection, only to be pronounced dead-on-arrival—Gems really does call them D.O.A.'s—at the customer's door.

So the Gems Six Sigma teams deconstructed the tubes. They knew that one problem involved the petroleum-based oil in the tube, which prevents short circuits by isolating the anode, which has a positive charge, from the negatively charged cathode. The oil often deteriorated after a few months, but they did not know why. By using statistical what-if scenarios on all parts of the tube, however, the researchers learned that the lead-based paint on the inside of the tube was adulterating the oil. By November 1996 they had developed a paint that would preserve the oil and protect the tube.

Solving Leaks In Vacuum Tubes

CT scanners generate X-rays by bombarding metals with high-speed electrons. Even a few air molecules can slow the electrons down, so the tube needs a total vacuum. But too many tubes were reaching the end of the production line with "beads" —tiny openings, usually where glass and metal are sealed, that let air leak in.

So Gems engineers made a list of things that could cause a vacuum leak. Through Six Sigma analysis, they ruled out type and length of glass. But they did learn that the metal pin through which current flows into the tube tended to tarnish, which would loosen the seal. They also found other significant factors: the type of gas used in processing the tube, and the speed with which the glass cooled down after going through a heat-treating furnace.

Thus informed, the engineers used computer modeling to test numerous combinations of different temperatures, gases and such. They wound up "pre-oxidizing" the metal pin, roughening its surface and helping it adhere to the glass. They replaced the hydrogen gas with nitrogen. And they changed the heating process from one in which tubes move continuously through the furnace to one in which they are processed in fixed batches, making the heating and cooling periods easier to control.

"Six Sigma gave us a methodical way to test how changes in one factor would interact with changes in others," said Beth Hulse, the engineer who led the project.

Trying to eliminate all leaks would have put Gems way behind deadline and way over budget. And it was now early 1997. So Gems settled for a process that cut the preshipment scrap rate by 40 percent and that has eliminated D.O.A.'s so far. And while the new tubes are priced at $85,000, or 40 percent more, they carry a one-year warranty.

Helping Reduce False Readings

Converting an electron beam to X-ray images is not an efficient process. Only about 1 percent of the energy that hits human tissue emerges as light, with the rest dissipated as heat. And that heat can affect the quality of the image.

Statistical analysis showed that adding a $100,000 resistor would control the temperature. But the same tests also revealed that changing a few inexpensive capacitors elsewhere in the tube, and redesigning how the wires are padded, would yield a similar result.

Another way to cut down on fuzzy images and false readings—detection of tumors that are not really there, for example—would have been to tighten the specifications for the focal point, the accuracy with which the electron beam hits the target issue. But that would have involved a costly tube redesign.

By April 1997, a Six Sigma team had learned that widening the tungsten wires that cover many of the wave-receptor cells in the detector plate would create a bigger target, thereby compensating for any tiny inaccuracies in the beam's trajectory.

Although this change requires giving the patient a higher dose of X-rays during the scan, the dose is still within the medically accepted margin of safety. "By making the data collection process less efficient, we made the scanner as a whole more efficient," said Gary Strong, a Lightspeed designer.

But the image quality still needed improvement. The detector surface in each scanner has thousands of "pre-amp chips," semiconductor components that amplify the light signals so that a computer can read them. But each chip emits some energy itself, which in turn gets picked up by other chips, causing extraneous rings or shadows in the image.

Redesigning the chips, Gems concluded, would take at least eight months, which could mean missing the target date for field tests: April 1998. But Six Sigma analyses showed that Gems could get the same result by relaxing specifications for the relationship between the amount of energy that comes into and out of the pre-amps, and by writing simple software that would allow the computer to control the variation. The project was completed last March—just before the deadline for the field tests.

The Lightspeed, which went on the market in September, costs 25 percent more than older scanners but seems to be a hit. Gems has installed 12 Lightspeeds, and has orders for 50 more.

But the Six Sigma work at Gems is far from over. The Gems chief executive, Jeffrey R. Immelt, is working on projects to find a better way to position flexible tabs—the items that keep electrons in alignment as they travel across the detection panels. And he will soon join a team that will apply Six Sigma methods to reduce variances in customer service.

"Six Sigma lets you approach problems with the assumption that there's a data-oriented, tangible fix at the end," Mr. Immelt said. "And that is a radical culture change."

DIAMONDS AND TIRES AND BRAS, OH, MY!

Inside the Cult of Costco

BY SHELLY BRANCH

"HAVE YOU HEARD THE SALMON STORY?" JIM SInegal, the unassuming CEO of Costco warehouse clubs, has a favorite tale he likes to tell, and yes, it involves a fish. But to do the story justice, he needs visual aids—color slides and a projector—that are presently jammed in the belly of a big metal cabinet. "Where is that . . . thing?" he wails, anxious to get the low-tech show under way. "Here we go! Here we go!" Sinegal, who could pass for a high school science teacher in his plaid shirt and aviator glasses, stands back to admire the salmon he's beamed up on the wall. "We took this product that we'd been selling for $5.99 a pound [click, advance] and improved it—deboning it, trimming it. And every step along the way, as we picked up volume? We lowered the price."

Not many CEOs boast about nudging prices south, nor are they apt to brag about slicing margins. But Costco's low-price logic isn't quite the same as other retailers': it applies to everything from salmon to emerald-cut diamonds. Unlike predictable discounters, which can numb shoppers with sales and sensible bargains, Costco has figured out that a low price, artfully affixed to high-quality, high-end merchandise, can transcend the pedestrian notion of "discount." Played out in Costco's cement-floor aisles, the high/low shopping experience becomes a powerful middle-class elixir.

"PEOPLE COME IN HERE AND THEIR ATTITUDE IS, **WHAT'S THE CATCH?"** COSTCO CEO JAMES SINEGAL SAYS.

Other "clubs," such as BJ's Wholesale and Sam's, attempt as much but are no match for Costco. Formally called Costco Wholesale and based in Issaquah, Wash., the company has 289 stores and $24 billion in annual revenue. That's nearly 200 fewer than Sam's—which is owned by Wal-Mart—and an estimated $1 billion more in revenue. Not only is Costco the largest and most profitable chain of its kind; it is also noticeably more bourgeois, attracting some of the most overeducated, overemployed hoarders (just ask the millionaires at Microsoft, who can pick up Costco membership applications on the company campus). "[Costco] has this shock thing about low prices, but that's not the whole story," says Daniel Barry, an analyst with Merrill Lynch. "Costco is relentless in its mission to have a treasure-hunt feel, to create a place that's exciting to shop. By the way, nobody you ever talk to dislikes Costco. The worst thing they say is, 'I walked out of there spending $250.' "

Costco, for the uninitiated, is the place where individual and business customers, paying $35 to $100 per year for "membership," buy 24 rolls of toilet paper or none at all. This is where laundry detergent and Italian olive oil come in drums big enough to dunk a toddler, and where a 1,000-piece lot of Ralph Lauren golf jackets, selling 75% below retail at $19.99 each, will vanish in an afternoon. In its three-acre stores, Costco somehow promotes both gluttony and thrift: Where else in America can you shop for a $20,000 engagement ring—at Costco, there's often a waiting list for them—then proceed to the health and beauty aisle for a lifetime supply of panty shields?

The vast array of product, actually, is one of retailing's better illusions. A Wal-Mart Supercenter carries as many as 125,000 items; a grocery store stocks roughly 40,000. Not so at cavernous Costco, where you'll find just 4,000 carefully chosen products. This makes it easier for the company to manage inventory and to obsessively monitor prices. Three-quarters of the stuff is "basic," like tuna fish and paper towels; the other items are discretionary, often with high-end names such as Godiva and Waterford. The store's periphery offers a variety of services: film developing, a pharmacy, and a tire shop. Crazy product juxtapositions—face creams next to crackers—are all part of a selling formula that homes in on the middle-class tastes for cross-shopping and impulse purchases. "This is the great psychological display of what we're all about," proclaims Sinegal, pointing to shopping carts that look as if they contain the bounty of Bloomingdale's, Home Depot, and

A&P. This is a CEO who makes you wonder if he wouldn't slip a few caskets in among the Cheerios, as long as the price was right.

Fully one in four American households harbors a card-carrying Costco member. And FORTUNE is on hand in Newport News, Va., as the club's universe gets a little bit bigger. By 10 A.M. on this weekday grand opening for the chain's 275th store, the 600-slot parking lot is full (does anybody work in this town?). At the door, a "symphonic" baby grand piano, tagged at $12,229.99, churns out Bette Midler's "the Rose" all by itself. Strolling in slow motion with pork loin samples and mini-tacos in hand, gawking shoppers twist their heads to survey the pristine piles—of Starbucks coffee, of Nike golf shoes, of 200-thread-count sheets—that reach toward the warehouse ceiling. "People come in here, and their attitude is, 'what's the catch?' " laughs Sinegal. "They say, 'these guys are charging you to shop with them. They've got all of this merchandise, the prices are great, so there's got to be a damn catch.' "

"I LAUGHED WHEN I REALIZED IT WAS A COPY," SAYS MARGO CLAYMAN OF THE COACH BAG KNOCKOFF SHE BOUGHT FOR $46.99.

Costco executives insist that their no-frills business is simple. Straightforward. It's a motto that they do seem to live by, starting with the white-plastic name badges that are mandatory chest gear for every employee, every day. But as I tour the new warehouse with Joseph Portera, Costco's belly-laughing executive vice president for operations, it becomes clear that the psychology behind Costco is actually pretty opaque. "The goal here is not to go in deep with selections but to go in broad," says Portera. "We want to surprise people at every turn. Even if you don't buy the Waterford crystal, it makes an impact on you." He pantomimes like one of the *Price is Right* girls. "Maybe you'll get a little irritated, knowing you could've [picked it up] last time but didn't, and now it's gone. So this time you'll stay awhile, and walk the entire building, to make sure you don't miss a thing."

Portera's words, when you think about it, sound a little bit like a thief's. And in a weird way, the Costco shopping experience does have the undertone of a heist. The lack of signage generates anxiety. (Where did you find those gorgeous Bormioli Rocco glasses?) And it is quite by design that the goods—whose astonishing variety reminds one of a certain proverbial truck—are stacked on pallets. Whether holding golf clubs or toilet paper (the club's No. 1-selling item), the pallets support giant cubic blocks of consumer goods, a little like freestanding sculptures. Dazzling in its understatement, the package, in effect, becomes the display.

The fact that Costco doesn't advertise extends the secretive, clubby aspect of the place. And here, significantly, is where Costco's practical and psychological aspects intersect. Not only would ads taint the thrill of the hunt for members, but they would also force the company to raise prices, which would in turn cause Costco's computers to go haywire: they are rigged to alert management when a price on an item exceeds its cost by 14% or more. High volume, after all, is the point here, not high margins. It works: Costco pulls in an average of about $91 million per store per year.

Costco shoppers appreciate the tightfistedness: they don't miss the ads or the lack of cushy customer service. Instead, Costco impresses and garners trust with its return-anything-at-any-time guarantee. The store backs everything it sells. No questions asked if you bring back a hose set or a set of pantyhose—ever. Costco is so confident about the quality of its goods that it even touts a "diamond guarantee," promising to pay a member $100 if a stone is appraised for less than double the Costco price. Such policies make Costco stand out in a time when other retailers have all but given up on customer loyalty. As Jim Hebert, a retail consultant in Bellevue, Wash., notes, the chain's 86% membership renewal rate is the highest in the industry and recalls the loyalty heyday of Nordstrom.

Some of the devout, I learn, are reluctant to send their spouses to Costco alone, for fear that they'll forget about the two gallons of milk and come home with a $1,000 stainless-steel grill. When marriage sours, Costco cards have been known to turn up in divorce settlements. Like alcoholics who lie about their Jack Daniel's consumption, some Costco shoppers fudge the frequency of their trips. "I'd say I come once a week," says one shopper, pushing a cart between pallets in the downtown Seattle store. Her friend rolls her eye. "Once a week? Pulleeeze!"

Since 1984, Costco has enlarged its red-plastic shopping carts four times. Thanks to serious foodies like Tim Rose, the senior vice president whose job it is to raise Costco's epicurean profile (the rotisserie chicken, at 2.75 pounds and $4.99, is a big seller), customer visitation is up from once every three weeks in 1995 to once every ten days. All the while, average checks have held steady at about $95, suggesting that people are buying in the same amounts, just a lot more often. "People feel happy at Costco, they really do" observes Kurt Barnard, publisher of *Barnard's Retail Trend Report*. "There's a sense of pleasure. They are content in having chosen a store where they feel they got their money's worth, and then some. Alas, in retail that's increasingly rare."

Some people, like Jon Carlin, a sales manager for Fujifilm, confuse their roles as Costco vendor, observer, and shopper. Last fall, when a ladies' $39.99 cashmere sweater hit the floor at Costco, Carlin found himself grabbing for fleece along with hordes of women who were—gasp—stripping to try on the goods. He emerged with ten pullovers. "I don't even have that many girlfriends," he laments. On Wall Street, where Costco is a retail-sector favorite, an analyst's bullishness on the stock seems directly proportionate to the high derived from his Costco sprees. DLJ's Gary Balther, who has a "buy" on the stock, recently picked up a leather Nautica jacket for $199; George Strachan of Goldman Sachs, who has Costco as a "top retail pick," includes a lengthy ode in his recent report. (. . . "I fantasize over—but do not buy—a $479 Dewalt ten-inch table saw. . . .") Michael Poyner, an analyst with London-based Credo Group, recalls his first Costco-induced trance: "There were these $20 wheelbarrows piled up to the ceiling," he says.

"They were bright blue, with rubber wheels. I mean, they were *pretty.* And I stood there, seriously thinking, 'I wonder if I could convince British Airways to pack one of these up for me?' "

Costco, of course, didn't come to mess with so many heads by accident. "Discount merchandising is not for the timid," says Sinegal, who co-founded the company in 1983 with chairman Jeffrey Brotman. Sinegal, it should be said, was mentored by the best of the best—Sol Price, the founder of Fed Mart and Price Club (the latter merged with Costco in 1993). In the industry, Sinegal is known as a tough but fair skinflint—someone who can slice fat from a crisp dollar bill. To furnish Costco's headquarters, Sinegal managed to scare up a bunch of castoffs—used desks and chairs from nearby Boeing. And when he's on the road, which is as much as 50% of the time, Sinegal takes the company's 11-seat Challenger jet only if he's got enough bodies to fill it. Most important: "We'd like it to be known that we are the toughest negotiators in the business. And that we're gonna come after [vendors] for every nickel we can, and we won't let up until we think we've got the price right on the merchandise." When asked, vendors are expected to change their factory runs to produce specially "built" packages that are ever bigger, ever cheaper. Costco's new Crystal Geyser 32-pack, for instance, brings the mineral water's per-bottle price down to 19 cents.

TOILET PAPER IS ITS BEST SELLER, BUT **COSTCO ALSO CARRIES HIGH-GRADE DIAMONDS**—AND THERE'S OFTEN A WAITING LIST.

Often, the "right price" is determined by how much cheaper Costco can make a product itself. "We sell a six-pack of Kodak 200-speed film for $21.99," says the CEO, who seems to have a price scanner embedded in his brain. "Then we have our own [private-label brand] for $6.99. How can you not provide that value for your customers? That doesn't mean we want to get rid of Kodak. But at some point, a vendor's going to realize that option is open. And it does create leverage for us."

Indeed, the company's private label, called Kirkland, has managed to bully down price points in several categories, such as over-the-counter drugs. Realizing the escalating power of the Kirkland brand, so to speak, some major manufacturers, such as Hanes and Whirlpool, have gone so far as to co-brand with the company. New on the floor, for instance, is an assortment of "Kirkland Signature by Whirlpool" appliances, including refrigerators and dishwashers. Today roughly 12% of Costco's products bear some sort of Kirkland mark.

Costco would always prefer to have a name brand on its floors. But because many high-end makers like Cartier and Cannondale recoil at the idea of seeing their goods in a warehouse setting, this isn't always possible. "I expect our buyers to do whatever they have to do, legally, to get [those items]," says Doug Schutt, the senior vice president in charge of "diverting" some $200 million worth of merchandise from unamenable vendors each year. To get hot products, Costco relies on third-party distributors. But so-called gray market channels are a bit unpredictable. Some suppliers, hoping to protect their higher-end retail customers, have been known to spurn Costco's offers "officially," then call up later to cut a direct, if quiet, deal.

If nothing else, the wheeling and dealing has taught Costco to play a kind of hardball that rivals the CEO's wicked racquetball game (he never misses a day on the court). This is especially true when it applies to another key merchandising strategy: knockoffs, to use the term of art. In recent months the company has tapped factories from Brazil to Mauritius to produce dead ringers for things like Tumi luggage, Cole Haan loafers, and Coach handbags. Schutt, whose fluency in labels would shame any serial shopper, is currently smitten with an Egyptian-cotton men's dress shirt that will soon be a Costco staple. At $36.99, it has mother-of-pearl buttons and is patterned after a Nordstrom design. If past efforts are any measure, the knockoff will be pretty damn good. On the Internet, Costco members chat heatedly about the fabrication of Kirkland pots ("I liked the Kirkland handles far better than the All-Clad," says one). Up in Boston, Margo Clayman is so proud of her $46.99 Coach-inspired bag that she refuses to remove the purse's hanging tag—a Coach detail that Costco didn't overlook. "It says 'Kirkland,' but no one comes close enough to tell the difference," she laughs.

If the Costco way, with its slavish devotion to discounts and knockoffs, seems distinctly American, guess again. Six years ago, when Costco was worrying, unnecessarily, about U.S. market saturation, the chain began exporting its buy-in-bulk mentality. It now has 20 warehouse stores in Britain, Taiwan, South Korea, and Japan. One of the first stops was Watford, England—a London suburb—where Costco operates one of its most successful stores. "At first people said, 'Huh? You don't buy rubber boats where you buy baked beans,' " recalls Jim Murphy, who manages Costco's seven U.K. locations. How things change. We are chatting in his office at the Watford branch. From our perch, three stories above the warehouse floor, we can see shoppers scurrying for liquor, Michelin tires, and Queen Green giant olives. "Bless her!" cries Murphy when he sees a woman wheel not one but two office chairs to the checkout lane.

For Costco, which has seen store sales grow by an average of 6% a year since 1995 and profits more than double in that time, to an estimated $542 million for 1999, an iffier frontier is the Internet. Costco.com was launched last September with no fanfare, no ads. Unlike the analog store, it is an all-high-end proposition, allowing even nonmembers to click their way through discounted Hungarian goose-down comforters and $17,000 Frank Mueller watches (chairman Jeff Brotman wears one). Traditionalist Sinegal was reluctant to go online at first, and the company is proceeding slowly with the site's expansion beyond 1,000 items. Perhaps that's just as well. As its shares have bested the S&P 500 by 24% in the past 12 months, Wall Street doesn't seem to be lobbying too hard for this particular chain to do too much tinkering beyond its bricks-and-mortar format. Apparently they know the deal: It's awfully hard to put Willy Wonka's factory inside a desktop box.

Unit 4

Unit Selections

34. **Publishers of Paperbacks Are Facing Sliding Sales,** Doreen Carvajal
35. **How Levi's Trashed a Great American Brand,** Nina Munk
36. **How NordicTrack Lost Its Footing,** *Business Week*
37. **A Makeover for the TV Dinner; Swanson Is Being Upgraded to Restore Market Share,** Constance L. Hays
38. **Reengineering Work: Don't Automate, Obliterate,** Michael Hammer
39. **Owens Corning: Back from the Dead,** Thomas A. Stewart
40. **A Close-Up Look at President Rick Wagoner and His Strategy for Reviving GM,** *Business Week*

Key Points to Consider

- It is important to differentiate systematic decline from organizational decline. Systematic decline affects all members of the industry and demands a reaction. Organizational decline indicates an internal managerial problem.
- Reengineering demands a radical change of procedure and policies, not an application of new technology to old systems.
- The process of turnaround is complicated, time consuming, expensive, and often impossible to accomplish.

DUSHKIN ONLINE Links | www.dushkin.com/online/

24. **Business Forecasting**
    http://forecasting.cwru.edu
25. **Marketing Energy Services to the Healthcare Segment**
    http://www.fuld.com/HealthCareReport/index.html
26. **Center for Organizational Theory (COT)**
    http://socrates.berkeley.edu/~iir/cot/cot.html
27. **Six Sigma for Manufacturing and Non-Manufacturing Processes**
    http://www.airacad.com/transact.htm
28. **Voice of the Shuttle**
    http://vos.ucsb.edu/shuttle/commerce.html

These sites are annotated on pages 4 and 5.

Organizational Change

Few will disagree with the idea of the knowledge-based organization as the dominant model for the modern enterprise. Accordingly, the primary assets of such organizations are people, along with the knowledge and expertise that those people bring to their firm. A most logical conclusion, then, is that as people are living, learning organisms, so also, in a collective sense, are their organizations. As their individual members grow and acquire skills and knowledge, organizations capture those capabilities from their workforce and leverage them into superior performance.

The U.S. business community enjoyed a long period during which they were basically unchallenged domestically and internationally. The period after World War II was particularly lacking in effective competition. Among the industrialized nations, the manufacturing facilities of Germany and Japan had been mostly demolished. Great Britain, France, and Italy had suffered extensive economic and physical damage. The politics of the Soviet Union eliminated any business activity in Eastern Europe by U.S. firms. Turbulence in China removed that country as a threat. Central and South American countries were only beginning to emerge.

In that context, to paraphrase management guru Tom Peters, it was impossible to mismanage an American firm! The prevailing strategic actions were incremental. Planning was not a very important part of the process.

But in the 1970s, a set of circumstances evolved that changed matters abruptly. To counter world political threats, the United States had taken an active role in rebuilding its defeated enemies. Germany and Japan benefited in many ways and were able to assume the roles of strong competitors quickly. The first of the oil crises hit with devastating results. Nagging social problems beset the country. The necessity for effective strategic directions of firms would change in a most dramatic manner.

The nature of the strategic response depends on the source of the new conditions. These sources might involve systematic changes, those that are felt industry-wide. All industry members are faced with the same factors causing the change. Changes in industry composition are often the result.

Organizational change, however, is confined to the individual firm. While the forces that precipitate change may be environmental, they are more likely to be related to the company's management, stakeholders, current strategy, structure, or rivals. Conceit, complacency, and conservatism, separately or in combination, may lead to a firm seeing its seemingly secure position deteriorate rapidly. Realignment of stakeholder interest may result in a strategy shift. Often these innovations come from leaders who are outside of the industry, although their targets inevitably are the industry leaders.

But change is difficult to accomplish. It involves an entirely new set of skills. Firms need to recognize the need for change and then they must make it happen. It is vital that a firm understands that the change process is difficult, time consuming, and one that requires a high degree of commitment from all levels.

Many companies have undertaken a significant strategic redirection in order to adapt to the changing environments. Probably the most recognized of these is to reengineer the company. Reengineering does not mean that a company replaces manual operations with technologically based activities. Rather, it suggests that entire processes are changed. Reengineering involves making drastic changes in the way the product or service is delivered and the way it is received by the customer. The banking industry, with automated tellers, electronic funds transfers, and online banking is a vivid case in point. Highly labor-intensive activities in the value chain in the past are now performed in real time on a totally automated basis. Some may argue that the resultant downsizing in personnel represents a drastic social price to pay for a new system. Few, however, would be willing to consider the customer charges that would be in place today if the old system had continued.

As we enter the twenty-first century, every organization in the world has been subjected to profound changes in its environments. Many now refer to this combination of events as the third industrial revolution. It has been characterized by enormous increases in productivity due to the use of sophisticated electronics and computers, new chemicals and materials, and new methods of distribution.

Arguments for and against the concept that changes are occurring faster than ever abound. Consider one measure of change. It took 40 years for the United States to have 10 million telephones in use. It took 20 years to have 10 million fax machines installed. It took less than 1 year to have the first 10 million users on the Internet.

Consumers embrace concepts such as Internet shopping and online banking. Business to business activities are automated and many are performed between and among computers. Design and manufacturing processes are more effectively and more efficiently done with computer programs.

A critical element of a firm's survival has always been speed. Speed in transactions, speed in operations, and speed in reacting and adapting to new methods remain the defining factors in an organization's success. In his book, *The Living Company,* Arie de Geus, a former executive with Royal Dutch Shell, pointed out how successful Shell has been in large part due to their view of Shell as an extended group of workers dedicated to learning. Describing decision making as a learning activity, he writes, "In this sense, strategy is simply the ability to learn. The organization's ability to learn faster (and possibly better) than the competition becomes its most sustainable competitive advantage."[1]

1. de Geus, Arie, *The Living Company,* Harvard Business School Press, Boston, MA: 1997, p. 157.

Publishers of Paperbacks Are Facing Sliding Sales

By DOREEN CARVAJAL

There was a time when the lowly and cheap paperback tucked on a drugstore rack was lavished with high praise, ranked in the revolutionary stratosphere with the advent of the Pill, or at the very least, air-conditioning or color television.

Publishers gleefully described the 1939 introduction of paperbacks as a revolution. And students of the late 1950s and early 1960s were labeled "the paperback generation"—a baby boom of masses raised on Dr. Spock's "The Pocket Book of Baby and Child Care" and inspired by copies of "Catcher in the Rye" that seemed engineered to fit in blue-jeans pockets.

But today there is less room in those pockets or, perhaps, some top publishers speculate, the aging eyes of that generation are growing a little dim for the printed type of the purse-sized, mass-market paperbacks, which were once promoted as "good reading for the millions."

Since 1995, the number of mass-market paperbacks sold in the United States has declined by almost 9 percent, falling to 484 million copies last year, about three times the percentage loss in consumer books overall. And the immediate future offers little comfort; the book industry's research arm, the Book Industry Study Group, is projecting continued slight annual declines for the paperback market over the next several years.

With the average price of a paperback climbing toward $7, the $1.5 billion market for the books remains profitable, but it has been losing an increasing share of market to discounted hardcovers, which chains and independent bookstores generally prefer to stock along with quality trade paperbacks, which are larger and more expensive than ordinary mass-market paperbacks.

The paperback has also been buffeted by other forces—the consolidation of the wholesale jobbers who stocked mass-market paperbacks in the United States' supermarkets and drugstores; sagging public interest in such genres as westerns; the general aging of the industry's biggest group of customers, and the declining popularity of mall stores that attracted more impulse buyers than superstores.

And then there are enough speculative, unproved theories in the publishing industry to pack a paperback chapter. Are people devoting less time to casual recreational reading and more to books offering professional enrichment? Are people simply reading less? Or are they getting their reading fix from audio-book tapes or the Internet?

"You've got a business that hit a wall; it's still a business, but no one can figure out how to make it grow," said Jack Romanos, the president of Simon & Schuster, which owns Pocket Books, the paperback publishing house that started the business in 1939 with the experimental publication of "The Good Earth" and "Wuthering Heights." "Culturally," he said, "we should care, because I believe that the paperback is the logical entry into the reading place."

Since 1993, the ubiquitous 4 1/4-by-7-inch mass-market paperback has slipped from 39 percent of book purchases in the United States to 36 percent in 1997, according to the most recent report from the Consumer Research Study on Book Purchasing.

Meanwhile, hardcover sales, while generally sluggish, rose to 31 percent of the market, from 28 percent. The same survey noted declines in paperback sales in outlets from supermarkets and drugstores to warehouse clubs and discount stores.

Confronted with that climate, paperback publishers have taken a variety of approaches, starting with the occupants of the top executive suites.

Within the last two months, Gina Centrello, the president of Pocket Books, departed after 16 years with the company and reappeared as the new head of a rival paperback publishing house, Ballantine. Soon after, Pocket Books announced the hiring of its new president and publisher, Judith Curr, who will be taking over a unit where mass-market paperback revenues were down last year by more than 4 percent.

Some paperback publishers have responded to reduced demand by trimming the number of titles that they offer and shipping copies more cautiously than in the halcyon days of paperback publishing, when shipments of a book like Jacqueline Susann's "Valley of the Dolls" could reach 15 million copies.

With the lone exception of the best-selling author John Grisham, marquee authors today are generally more likely to sell in the range of 1 million to 3 million.

And that makes some publishers wistful for the volume that was. "I do think these changes have had an effect," said Esther Margolis, the publisher of Newmarket Press and Ms. Susann's former publicity representative, who believes that people were clearly reading more then.

"Paperbacks were available, instantly available. If the covers were enticing, people who had never read books before read them. They weren't intimidating. They were little books that had pretty little covers and they were inexpensive and you could throw them away. It demystified the book for a lot of people."

Avon Books, a paperback publisher owned by the Hearst Corporation, is shipping 25 percent fewer copies of paperbacks than it did five years ago, while at the same time it has reduced the number of titles it publishes by 10 percent to about 300 a year, Avon's publisher, Lou Aronica, said.

Other paperback publishers like Pocket Books and Warner Books have also cut back on the titles they offer. Some have tinkered with price reductions without making much difference in sales. And generally they can't reduce prices dramatically, because of fixed costs for paper, shipping, author advances and the expense of unsold books returned by booksellers.

"Twenty-five years ago, we used to sell 8 to 10 mass-market paperbacks for every hardcover that we sold," said Laurence Kirshbaum, the chairman of Time Warner Inc.'s trade publishing group, which includes Warner Books. "Now the ratio is a 2-to-1 relationship. So there's been a tremendous transformation.

"The paperback market has settled in at a certain core, and it doesn't seem to be growing," he continued. "And what we've done at Warner is refine our distribution and cut. Something has been lost here in the sense that what used to be much more of a truly mass-market phenomenon has become more specialized and to some extent more elitist."

The contemporary history of the mass-market paperback in the United States dates to 1939, when Robert de Graff, an ambitious publisher, introduced a line of plastic-laminated books that sold for 25 cents each. Despite some debate over credit for the idea, legend has it that de Graff settled on this price after concluding as he tossed two bits into the toll booth at Jones Beach State Park on Long Island, N.Y., that nobody ever misses a quarter.

Within a few years, de Graff's company, Pocket Books, and its kangaroo mascot, Gertrude, ushered in the paperback revolution, creating an alternative mass distribution network.

It moved beyond the elite carriage trade of existing bookstores and turned to a sprawling network of magazine distributors who took books to where Americans walked—thousands of newsstands, candy stores, cigar shops and food stores. But with consolidation in the 1990s, these distributors have dwindled from a high of about 700 companies to a handful and the result is that they are stocking fewer books.

"It was a terrific bargain that was available in 500,000 outlets instead of 5,000," said Thomas Bonn, the author of "Undercover: An Illustrated History of American Mass Market." "You couple that with the return of World War II servicemen who were reading armed-service paperback editions and the postwar expansion of education, and you have the creation of a generation of readers. The paperback successfully defended reading because it was a format that could compete with television."

Many of the top executives in major publishing companies count themselves in the 1960s paperback generation that developed an appetite for reading with paperback versions of "Siddhartha," "To Kill a Mocking Bird" or "Slaughterhouse Five."

And so, they say, they speak with personal experience when they wonder whether readers from the baby-boom generation are shifting to more expensive hardcover formats simply because the larger type is more comfortable for their eyes.

So if readers are buying fewer paperbacks, where has their attention been diverted? A prevalent theory is that they are spending more time on competing diversions such as exploring the Internet.

Albert Greco, an associate professor of business at Fordham University who follows the publishing industry, said there were indications that some readers might be finding more entertainment on videotapes.

For the first time, in 1997, consumers spent more on home videos than on books, a narrow gap projected to increase through 2001, according to figures from the Statistical Abstract of the United States. The same figures show that consumers have increased spending for online access to the Internet, but those expenses are still less than spending on home videos and books.

"This is how people are voting with their dollars," Greco said. "In 1998, the average American spent $88.79 buying or renting videos and spent $88.09 on books. That's less time and fewer dollars being spent on reading. You can't rely on videos of Air Force One to create an enlightened electorate."

But readers still spend enough on paperbacks to convince publishers that it remains a viable business. "Like Broadway, it's that fabulous invalid, and every day there are rumors of its demise, but people keep showing up," said Irwyn Applebaum, the publisher and president of Bantam Books, which has been publishing paperbacks for more than 50 years.

"There's no question that the mass-market paperback business has declined and will probably continue to decline, whether you look at units or dollars or the number of titles that are produced. But the mass market is still a thriving, multifacted business. The bright spot is that on any given day people are still buying books."

At least one publisher has returned to the very roots of the revolution to keep his sales growing. Walter Zacharius, the founder and chairman of Kensington Books, the second-largest publisher of romance novels, keeps searching for new sales outlets—the critical element that powered the growth of Pocket Books and the paperback revolution.

On Valentine's Day last year, his company tried pitching romance-club memberships to a QVC cable television audience, an effort that did not succeed despite the heart-tugging efforts of one of his authors.

At age 75, Zacharius has struck a deal to distribute a line of black romance books through distributors of cosmetics aimed at black women. He is also negotiating to stock his new line of Latino romance novels in bodegas through Spanish-language newspaper distributors in California.

"I've read this all the time that it's tough to compete," Zacharius said. "They're crazy! We're competing. We're growing. We're more successful than last year. The truth is that this is garbage. I really think that people in the mass-market field cannot forget two words."

He pauses, savoring the words like a businessman's mantra in a scene from "The Graduate": "Mass market."

How Levi's Trashed a Great American Brand

While Bob Haas pioneered benevolent management, his company came apart at the seams.

BY NINA MUNK

When Robert Haas led the most recent LBO of Levi Strauss & Co. in 1996, he took one of the world's most successful brands and placed its entire future in the hands of four people: himself, an uncle, and two cousins. Other family shareholders had two choices: Cede all power to this group for 15 years, or cash out. Most stayed in.

It seemed a good bet at the time. Haas was the guy who had saved the troubled family company back in 1984. He shut dozens of plants, jettisoned unpromising subsidiaries, expanded overseas, and refocused on Levi's core product. In 1985 he took Levi Strauss semiprivate in a limited LBO. Levi's stock climbed more than 100-fold, from $2.53 a share (adjusted for splits) to $265 a share. Haas was a hero.

A Harvard MBA who worked for the Peace Corps and McKinsey before joining Levi Strauss, Haas had been lionized in management circles and business journals (such as the very one you're reading) for applying his enlightened management practices to an old-line clothing manufacturer. Haas chafed at the idea of merely dressing the world in riveted denim; he was intent on showing that a company driven by social values could outperform a company hostage to profits alone.

While shareholder-driven companies like Coke and Gillette rushed into China, Haas pulled out—to protest human rights abuses. He sent sewing machine workers to off-sites to reprogram them from a mentality of piecework to one of teamwork. And shortly before the latest LBO, he began a massive reengineering project that was supposed to make Levi Strauss the most responsive apparel company in the industry, reducing the time it took to get jeans to stores from three weeks to 72 hours.

If the family shareholders had been paying careful attention to what was really going on at Levi's well before the '96 LBO, they might have bet differently. Sometime around 1990, a great brand began coming apart at the seams. Levi's market share among males ages 14 to 19 has since dropped in half, it hasn't had a successful new product in years, its advertising campaigns have been failures, its in-store presentations are embarrassing, and its manufacturing costs are bloated. The reengineering—with an $850 million budget—was a disaster. J.C. Penney, Levi's biggest customer, reports that last fall Levi's delivered its all-important back-to-school line—get ready—45 days late. Says Levi's Thomas Kasten, who led the reengineering: "I don't think we fully accomplished anything, to be honest."

Since 1997 the company has announced plans to shut 29 factories in North America and Europe and to eliminate 16,310 jobs. A month ago it said 1998 sales had dropped 13%, to just under $6 billion. FORTUNE estimates that since the '96 LBO—since Bob Haas became unaccountable to anyone but his three relatives—Levi Strauss' market value has shrunk from $14 billion to about $8 billion. By comparison, crosstown San

Francisco rival Gap has grown from $7 billion to over $40 billion during the same period. "Bob is very smart," says a former Levi's executive. "But then the question is, 'What's he smart at? Is he smart at running an apparel company?' I think that's an open question."

Levi Strauss is a failed utopian management experiment. It's a story of what can happen when well-intentioned but misguided managers run a private company answering to no one. Above all, it's an epic tale of opportunity lost, of what might have been. Retailing people often compare Levi Strauss with Gap—not favorably. "Levi's has always had a lot of very technically oriented people who know how to make good, consistent product," says Howard Gross, CEO of Millers Outpost, a chain of 220 stores that sell Levi's. "But typically in apparel you have merchants, men like [Gap CEO] Mickey Drexler. I'm not sure Bob Haas has ever been trained to be a merchant. I'm not sure he's even been in a store, waiting on customers, talking to them so that he could hear them say, 'Why are the legs on those jeans so tight?' "

The criticism does not appear to bother Haas. "By personality and instinct, I am not the rock star CEO," says Haas, in an obvious reference to Drexler. "It's a fantasy to think that somebody in a corner office on the seventh floor in San Francisco can be all-seeing and all-knowing. It's crazy."

We're not writing an obituary for this 150-year-old company. Levi's is still one of the world's great brands, better known than Marlboro, Nike, or Microsoft. No one—not Tommy Hilfiger, not Lee, not Gap—comes close to it in jeans sales. And 75% of American men own a pair of Levi's Dockers khakis. Above all, Levi Strauss is a cash machine. As a privately held company, it does not divulge profits. But FORTUNE managed to get a look at its financials: Last year, on revenues of just under $6 billion, Levi Strauss produced $1.1 billion in cash flow. That's more than Tommy, Polo Ralph Lauren, Nautica, and Liz Claiborne—combined. More than Nike. More, by a pinch, than Gap.

It takes a long time to sink a great brand. "A big brand like Levi's is an aircraft carrier," remarks Steve Goldstein, who left the company last summer after a 20-year tenure, most recently as head of marketing for Levi's. "You can turn the engines off and the actual speed of the carrier will not slow perceptibly for a long time. With the Levi's brand we gradually dialed down our propeller speed and the carrier kept moving. People up on the deck said, 'We're still moving fast!' But those down in the engine room said, 'Whoa! We're going to be dead in the water!' "

For all his empathy toward the engine room, Haas is a man born to the bridge. Although he dressed casually for FORTUNE's photo shoot, Haas is not a casual man. Even his language is carefully in place. He speaks in paragraphs of elevated diction; an off-hand conversation can sound like a lecture. He's known for extraordinary (some say obsessive) attention to detail. Poring over press releases and in-house memos, he corrects split infinitives and misplaced modifiers. His handwriting is tiny and meticulous. He goes to bed at 9:30 P.M.

Haas envisions Levi Strauss as a company where a factory worker's voice is as likely to be heard as the CEO's. "He's not the sort of manager who says, 'Here's what you did wrong,' " explains Levi's former CFO George James. "Instead, he sits down, looks you in the eye, and asks, 'What do you think you did wrong?' " Because of his obvious sincerity, Levi's employees are fiercely loyal to him, although they don't always approve of his management style. "I love Bob to death, but he has a tendency to want to involve everybody in decision-making. He's compassionate to a fault," says Peter Thigpen, former president of Levi Strauss USA.

No matter how well-intentioned, group decision-making usually degenerates into endless meetings, task forces, memos, and e-mails. That's what happened at Levi Strauss. "Everything had to go into a corporate process, so nothing ever got resolved," says Robert

REPOSITIONING ITSELF

Levi's has figured out that kids don't wear the same jeans their parents do and that trendy retailers don't stock the same lines as J.C. Penney. So it's creating a portfolio of dozens of brands and sub-brands, from cheap basics to high-priced fashion.

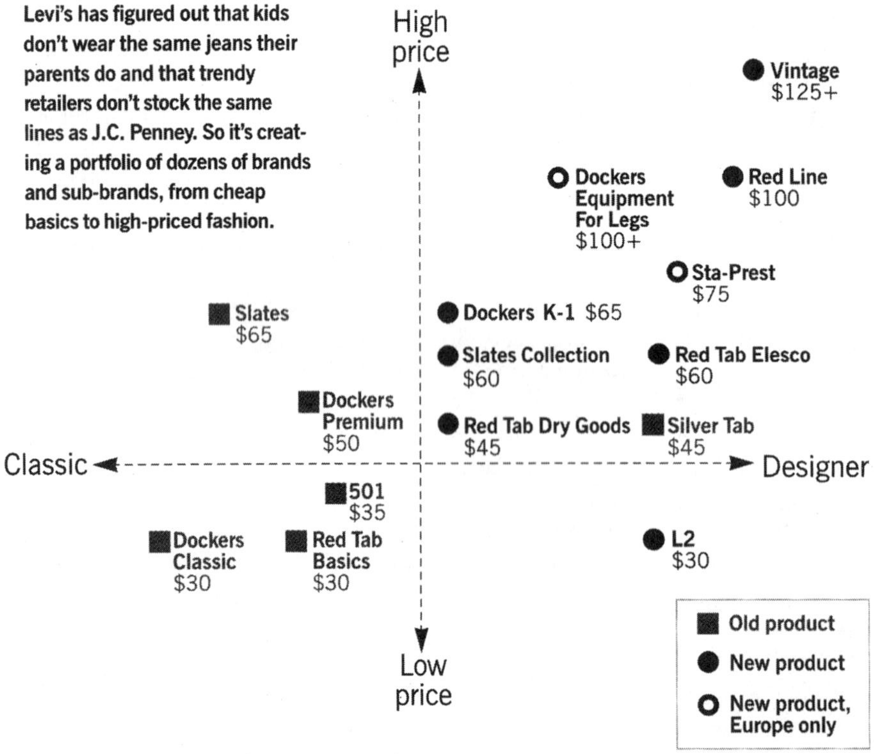

Siegel, who left the company after 29 years to become CEO of Stride Rite in 1993. "Almost half my time was spent in meetings that were absolutely senseless." Clearly frustrated even now, Siegel adds, "If you asked [Levi's executives] for the time, they would build you a clock, and still not be able to tell you the time." In the olden days—when Levi's was synonymous with jeans—none of that really mattered. But now Levi's doesn't just compete with Lee and Gap and Calvin Klein. Now it has hundreds of competitors with names like JNCO, Mudd, Arizona, Fubu, LEI, Kikwear, Badge, Union Bay, Canyon River Blues, Bongo, Stussy, Menace, Faded Glory—names that Levi's executives may or may not have heard of.

It's worth noting that Bob Haas has excelled at everything he's ever done. He was president of his primary school student body, editor of his high-school yearbook, and valedictorian of his 1964 class at UC Berkeley, where he was elected to Phi Beta Kappa. The business world never much interested Haas: He majored in English and considered becoming a Chaucer scholar. Then he joined the Peace Corps, where he spent two years in the Ivory Coast. Still, after returning from Africa, Haas dutifully attended Harvard Business School, like his father before him. When he graduated in 1968, he became a management consultant at McKinsey & Co. Some San Franciscans joke that to understand what's gone wrong at Levi Strauss, all you need to know is that Bob Haas was in the Peace Corps and worked at McKinsey.

Haas joined Levi's in 1973 as an inventory management analyst. In 1984, at 42, he became the fifth-generation family member to run the company (his father, Walter A. Haas Jr., was CEO from 1958 to 1976). Bob Haas had big plans. He wanted to create a company with a social mission, a purpose larger than sewing together pieces of 14½-ounce denim. "When I became CEO there was a cry: 'What are our values? What do we stand for as a company?' " he explains. "I said, let's fix the business issues first, but as soon as we have our business back on track we have to attend to our culture, because that's the glue that unites us, the beacon that guides our actions."

Levi Strauss has always believed in corporate philanthropy and social responsibility. When the firm went public in 1971, its offering prospectus made corporate history by warning that profits might be affected by a commitment to social programs. But Bob Haas wanted to go further—much further. In 1987 he developed the Levi Strauss Mission and Aspirations Statement, which promoted teamwork, trust, diversity, empowerment, etc., etc. Printed on recycled blue denim, the aspirations statement was hung on office walls, posted in factories, en-

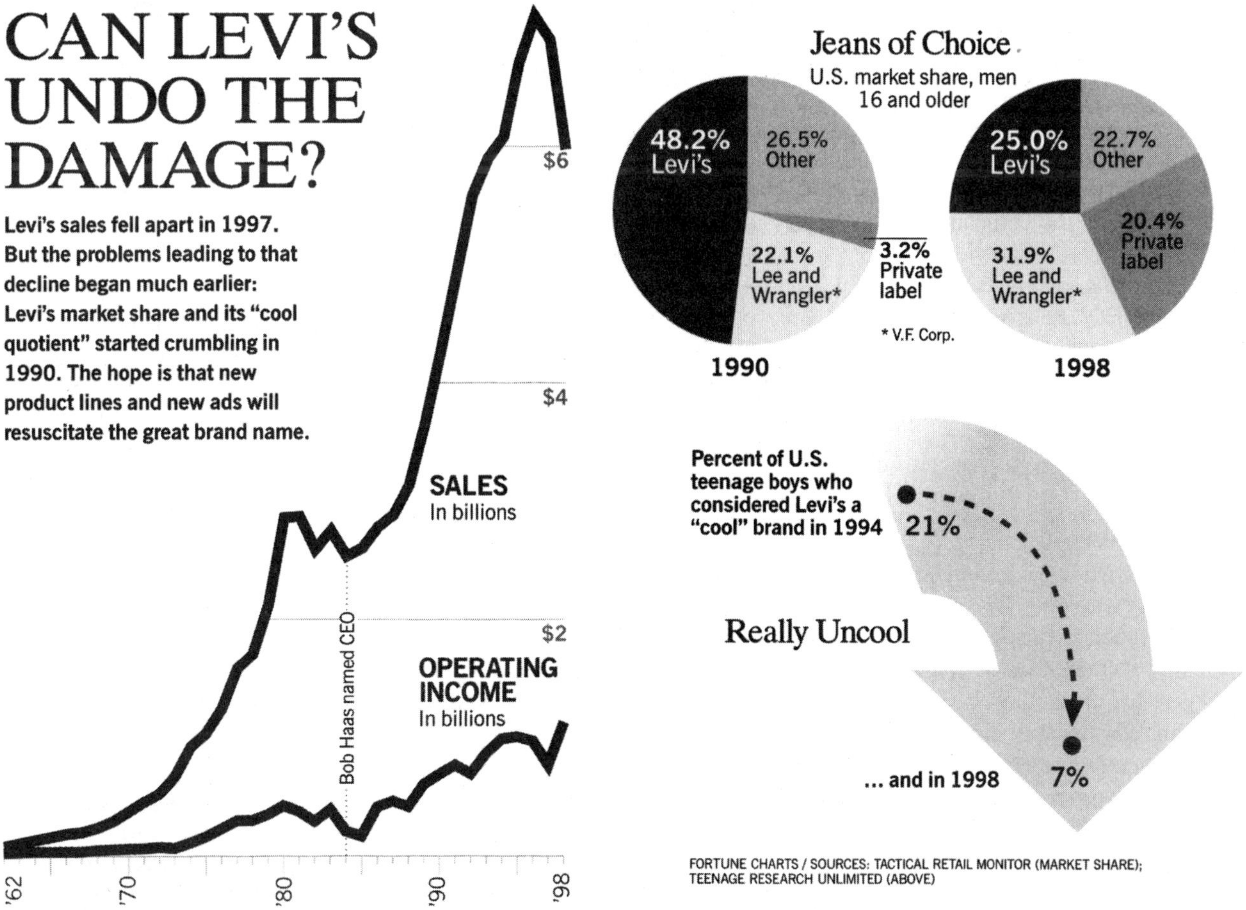

FORTUNE CHARTS / SOURCES: TACTICAL RETAIL MONITOR (MARKET SHARE); TEENAGE RESEARCH UNLIMITED (ABOVE)

closed in Lucite paperweights, and laminated on wooden plaques. For most CEOs, that would have done it: State your mission, act accordingly, and expect your employees to do the same. Haas, however, had something to prove: that a company driven by social values could outperform one driven by profits.

He changed Levi's compensation plans so that one-third of executives' bonuses reflected their ability to manage "aspirationally." He assigned 80 task forces to make the company more "aspirational." The work-and-family task force sent a 25-page questionnaire to 17,000 employees. The global-sourcing task force spent nine months creating guidelines that would hold Levi's overseas contractors to the highest possible standards of labor practices. A diversity focus group organized off-site sessions that paired white, male managers with women and minorities to discuss racial and gender stereotypes.

By the early 1990s, Levi's employees were attending the company's "core curriculum," a three-part, ten-day course that covered leadership, diversity, and ethical decision-making. Joined by at least one senior manager, groups of 20 employees discussed their vulnerabilities, shared their deepest fears, even composed their obituaries. "It was all about personal disclosure and human connections," says Barry Posner, dean of Santa Clara University's business school, who helped implement the core curriculum. "It was about asking, 'How do I find meaning in the workplace?' It was about seeing that work is noble, that we're doing more than getting pants out the door."

Bob Haas had discovered his vocation. At one time he distributed AIDS leaflets outside the company cafeteria. He gave a long interview to the *Harvard Business Review* called "Values Make the Company." He delivered a keynote speech on business and ethics to the Conference Board. Levi's wasn't just a garment company committed to social responsibility. It was a politically correct organization that happened to be in the garment business. "The problem is some people thought the values were an end in themselves," says Levi's President Peter Jacobi, who recently announced his retirement. "You have some people who say, 'Our objective is to be the most enlightened work environment in the world.' And then you have others who say, 'Our objective is to make a lot of money.' The value-based people look at the commercial folks as heathens; the commercial people look at the values people as wusses getting in the way."

In hindsight, the wusses did get in the way. For even as Bob Haas pioneered utopian management, the business began to look threadbare. Despite its enlightened benevolence, Levi's clung to old ways of doing things. It stopped innovating. It ignored, or was oblivious to, the marketplace. The "principled reasoning approach" to decision-making taught in the core curriculum didn't help. "Unless you could convince everyone to agree with your idea, you didn't have the authority to make a decision," says former CFO George James. "That made it very difficult to be responsive."

Case in point: Dockers, launched by Levi's in 1986. Dockers khakis were an immediate success, hitting the market just as American men began replacing suits with more casual attire. But in 1993, Dockers missed one of the biggest trends in the khaki market: wrinkle-resistant pants. As other manufacturers began selling them, Dockers stayed put. Sales collapsed. That same year, Levi's reported its first decline in profits since 1988.

The denim market was changing too. Levi's 501s used to be the hot jeans. "But in '93, kids started telling us the legs were too narrow," says Gross of Millers Outpost. In response, Millers Outpost created its own line of jeans with legs as wide as 23 inches. Then J.C. Penney and Sears got into the act, making jeans with flared legs and boot cuts. Tommy Jeans splashed the Hilfiger logo all over its baggy pants. JNCO introduced jeans with 40-inch-wide legs and 17-inch-deep pockets. Through it all, Levi Strauss kept on pushing its basic jeans, with 16-inch-wide legs and 6-inch pockets. At the same time, kids were spending more and more money at specialty stores like Hot Topic and Pacific Sunwear and Gap, whereas Levi's sold almost exclusively to now-out-of-favor department stores. It wasn't that Levi's management didn't see the changes. "We told Levi's about extreme fits," says Gross. "We showed them our numbers. We told them what kids were asking for. They even attended some of our focus groups. But they didn't want to believe."

"BOB HAAS IS SMART. *The questions is, 'What's he smart at? Is he smart at running an apparel company?' That's an open question."*

Or else they were distracted. In 1993, Levi Strauss embarked on something called the Customer Service Supply Chain initiative. Once again, what began as a well-intentioned project morphed into a monster. The stated goal of the initiative was to make Levi's more responsive to retailers. The company wanted to get new products to market in three months, down from 15 months, and to reduce the time needed to restock a pair of jeans from three weeks to 72 hours. Amazingly, no one seriously considered the possibility that getting a pair of jeans to stores in 72 hours might double or triple Levi's costs. "There was no cost boundary," says Tom Kasten, who headed the effort. "I mean, we talked a little about how it shouldn't cost more, but it really was an afterthought."

In June 1993, 200 of Levi's best people began designing a new supply chain. Many were vice presidents of important divisions, divisions that would now be without leaders. Others left work behind, forcing colleagues to do double duty. Joined by at least 100 Andersen consultants, the group took over the third floor of headquarters, soon covering the walls with vast organizational charts and maps. The place resembled a war room. The members of the Third Floor Brigade weren't just on a mission, they were, in their words, "creating a revolution." To convince skeptics at Levi's that this was serious stuff, they collected magazine cover stories on companies like IBM, GM, and Digital that were in turmoil because they had ignored their changing markets. Proselytizing, the Brigade blew up the covers, pasted them to poster boards, and carried them around the organization. "It created huge battle lines," says Jacobi, Levi's president. "There were Moonies and there were nonbelievers, and they avoided each other and said bad things about each other. But there was no way to get out of it. It was like quicksand."

The Customer Service Supply Chain initiative was no longer just about improving service to retail customers. It was about improving everything. Whole new categories of jobs were created. The Third Floor Brigade rewrote more than 600 job descriptions; all over the company people had to reapply for their positions. To help employees evaluate their aptitudes and handle the imminent changes, the Brigade put together a 145-page handbook called *Individual Readiness for a Changing Environment*. "Let yourself feel the loss, then let go and move on," it advised. "New ways should be viewed as neither right nor wrong, neither better nor worse, than the previous ones."

Levi's employees freaked out. Some who didn't get the jobs they had applied for, or re-applied for, broke down. Others simply quit. "It pushed me over the edge," says a former employee. The retailers—the people actually meant to benefit from all this—shook their heads in disbelief. "The reengineering changes had us confused as hell," says a buyer at one major Levi's account. "One minute there was no customer service, the next minute they'd overdo it." By the time Levi's board of directors put an end to the nonsense in late 1995, the reengineering team's budget had swollen by 70%, to $850 million. As for restocking basic product, J.C. Penney's standard is 20 days; Levi's average last year was 27 days.

How did this go on for so long? Simple. Haas has the power, and most family members seem content with the arrangement—despite the sagging value of their shares (which have declined by about 40% in three years), despite the fact that they get no dividends. "I've always looked on it as a long-term investment," says Robert Friedman, cousin to Bob Haas and a member of the Levi's board. Rumor has it some family members want out, or at the very least would like a new CEO. They won't get one. Other than the four men who control the votes, no one has any say in the company until 2011, when the shareholder agreement expires.

> "TO BE HONEST, *I don't think we fully accomplished anything," said the man who led Levi Strauss' reengineering effort.*

One family member who spoke to FORTUNE on the record is Richard Goldman, husband of Bob Haas' late aunt Rhoda Haas Goldman. In 1946, 4-year-old Bob Haas was the ring bearer at the Goldmans' wedding. Half a century later the Goldmans and Bob Haas were no longer speaking. Rhoda Goldman was the only member of the 12-person board who opposed the 1996 LBO. She and her husband didn't want to hand the company over to four people for the next 15 years. "It didn't make any sense to her or to me," Richard Goldman says. "As shareholders, we were surprised anyone would go along with it."

The disagreement wasn't just about control; like most squabbles, it was also about money. Levi's bankers at Morgan Stanley, valuing the shares at $189 each, said the firm was worth $10 billion. Bob Haas offered shareholders $250, a one-third premium. But the Goldmans' bankers at Robertson Stephens valued the stock at between $315 and $387. In response, Haas increased his offer to $265 a share, valuing the company at $14 billion. After a lengthy battle, the Goldman family decided to accept that offer, cashing out their 12.5% interest for $1.7 billion. They were lucky; if they had held on, their shares would now be worth about $950 million.

"One could argue that we overpaid, in light of subsequent events," says Bob Haas. "But I would much rather be restructuring and reinvigorating ourselves as a private company than trying to talk, not just to you, but to every security analyst and financial reporter in the world who wants to do yet another tedious story about our problems and offer gratuitous advice as to what went wrong and how to fix it. Those kinds of distractions get in the way of operating effectiveness."

Last year, Levi's redefined its utopian mission. The old one, which appeared in the preamble to the mission and aspirations statement, was: "To sustain responsible commercial success." The new one is simply, and ambiguously: "To be the casual apparel authority." So, once again, the company is in the midst of major organizational changes. It recently shifted to a brand-management structure long popular with consumer companies like Procter & Gamble and Sara Lee. So, once again, people are moving into new jobs, being given new titles. Because management now recognizes that one of Levi's problems was inbreeding, an urgent mandate is to fill one-third of all openings with outsiders. Headhunters have been directed to find a new president/COO from the outside. Already, Levi's has brought in as its new CFO William Chiasson, from Kraft Foods. Its new creative director for the U.S. youth market is Devon Burt, formerly of Nike.

Levi's finally understands what people in the fashion business have always known: Kids don't wear the same jeans as their parents. It recognizes that cool retailers won't be caught dead or alive stocking the same product as J.C. Penney. "The mistake we made was to make one brand for everyone—it ended up being nothing to anyone," says Robert Holloway, who heads Levi's U.S. youth market division. The company is now creating a portfolio of brands and sub-brands, each targeted at a different "tribe," in Levi's language. Some will be created in-house, others will be acquired from the outside.

Levi's big customers say they are cautiously optimistic about the new lines. But Levi's multibrand strategy is nothing more than what its competitors have done for years. Think of Gap, for example, with its high-end Banana Republic, its middle-of-the-road Gap, and its low-priced Old Navy. To reach the next level, to be a real player, Levi's has to become cool again. It must figure out how to appeal to a small, but hugely influential group of city dwellers who set fashion trends, a tribe Levi's calls "cultural creatives."

Late last year, in a bid to be culturally creative, Levi's furtively launched Red Line jeans, distributing them to just 25 cutting-edge shops, where they sell for $99. To position Red Line as far away from Levi's as possible, the unit's headquarters is in Venice, Calif. Nothing on Red Line jeans indicates that they have any relation to Levi's. The brand isn't mentioned on Levi's Website. So determined is Red Line to remain underground (i.e., cool) that its manager, Julia Hansen, refused to talk to FORTUNE, nor would she provide any product publicity shots.

Retailers report that Red Line is selling well. To Levi's, however, that's not really the point. It doesn't expect Red Line to have much impact on its bottom line; the idea is for the jeans to have a "halo effect," for the hipness associated with Red Line to somehow seep into Levi's other lines. The Dockers division is pursuing a similar strategy: To make its pants known as something other than the "uncool khaki" or the "fat man's khaki," it recently launched a hip line called K-1 Khakis. In Europe, there's a new Dockers line called Equipment for Legs, made of high-tech fabrics like Gore-Tex and targeted at the yuppie urban warrior.

It will be years before anyone knows if the new initiatives have worked. In the meantime, it seems reasonable to ask two basic questions: Would Levi Strauss be scrambling so desperately if it were a public company? And would Bob Haas still be CEO? Says Haas: "I wouldn't be CEO, because I wouldn't want to work in the company. It's that simple. My passion for this place is about doing the right thing for the enterprise, its people, the communities in which they operate, and making this a winning organization. My passion would be considerably diminished if I had to deal with the kinds of frivolous and nonproductive distractions that many of my peers at public companies have to deal with."

On Wednesday, June 12, 1996, a crowd of Levi Strauss employees gathered in San Francisco to hear a major announcement. Standing proudly before them, Bob Haas revealed a new incentive plan. With the company now fully in family hands, Haas could not offer employees stock options. Instead, he promised that if Levi's reached $7.6 billion in cumulative cash flow by 2001 (after three years, it's just $2.8 billion), every employee in the world, all 37,000 of them—from sewing machine operators in El Paso to salesmen in Barcelona—would receive a bonus worth one year's salary. Giddy employees cheered. Here was the latest confirmation that they were working for the world's most enlightened employer. Sincere notes of gratitude poured in to headquarters: "Bob, thanks for this great opportunity. Only 1,895 days to go! Many thanks, Estelle." And: "Bob, many thanks for your generous & exciting idea. What a great challenge to rise to, Paul T." And: "Bob, see you in 2001 for the big party! Kel."

One more thing: The party will be in utopia.

REPORTER ASSOCIATE *Jane Hodges*

HOW NORDICTRACK LOST ITS FOOTING

An infomercial pioneer's fast ride from mega-sales to Chapter 11

Not so long ago, an insomniac could barely get through a late-night channel surf without running into an ad for NordicTrack. And the saturation-ad strategy worked. By 1993, sales of its cross-country-ski machines were heading toward $500 million a year. By last October, NordicTrack was in Chapter 11. In this day of bulging bellies and short attention spans, fitness machines come and go like so many post-holiday diets. But how did this pioneer of infomercials fall so far so fast?

For starters, NordicTrack was a victim of its machine's durability. Lots of golfers and tennis players, for example, never stop looking for a longer-driving club or a racquet with a sweeter spot. But once you have a NordicTrack, you never need another one. In an industry in which impulse buyers seek get-thin-quick solutions, NordicTrack got hammered by a barrage of contraptions to flatten stomachs and harden thighs.

NordicTrack's somewhat complicated machine cost an average of $599, hundreds of dollars more than many of its rivals. Requiring coordinated movement of the arms and legs, it pushed users harder than the less daunting treadmill, whose sales have recently been revived by aging baby boomers. Besides all that, management fumbled an expansion into retail. "We weren't as nimble as we should have been," says NordicTrack Inc. President William E. Shepard with some understatement. Shepard, who was sent in by CML three months ago, is dismantling its nearly empty Chaska (Minn.) headquarters, which once housed 400 workers. It's now down to 25.

> "We need what Volkswagen did," says the president. "We need our own new Beetle"
>
> **NORDICTRACK'S WILLIAM SHEPARD**

PALTRY BID. From a peak of $477 million in 1993, NordicTrack sales slid to $267 million in 1997, a 44% decline. Over the past three years, NordicTrack posted nearly $217 million in operating losses for its parent, CML Group Inc. in Acton, Mass. CML also owns the Smith & Hawken gardening-products catalog and retail stores, which turned a small profit this year. One measure of NordicTrack's descent came on Nov. 30, when ICON Health & Fitness Inc., the Utah-based owner of brands like Weider weight-training products and the HealthRider aerobic machine, offered a paltry $6.6 million to the bankruptcy court, mostly to use NordicTrack's well-known brand name.

Still, compared with most exercise gizmos, NordicTrack was a marathoner in the $4 billion-a-year market for fitness machines. Started in a basement by Minnesota inventor Ed Pauls in 1976, the company rode the first wave of the fitness boom and quickly made a mark with innovative direct marketing, print ads, and an 800 number. By 1986, aided by a spike in cross-country skiing, Pauls sold out to CML for $22 million. Growth was meteoric.

By the time NordicTrack peaked in 1993, the home-fitness biz was diversifying and newcomers, such as abdominal tighteners and aerobic riders, were stealing NordicTrack's advertorial tricks. As the competition intensified and the costs of making commercials rose, NordicTrack strayed from direct marketing. It moved into traditional retail, setting up 125 permanent stores in high-rent shopping malls across the country and 100 mall-based kiosks during the November-to-February eat-too-much holiday season. The stores, small and carrying only NordicTrack machines, offered little room for customers to try out the equipment. And those who wanted to carry home their new toy had to wait for it to be shipped.

HOME RUNNERS. That clumsy expansion was "an invitation for disaster," says Gregg Hartley, executive director of the Fitness Products Council, the industry's trade association. But Shepard believes that NordicTrack can resuscitate itself at the mid-to-upper end of the home-fitness market by changing its retail approach. ICON, for example, sells its products at places like Sears, Roebuck & Co. and Sam's Club. "We need what Volkswagen did," Shepard says. "We need our own new Beetle."

Maybe, but the only fitness machine with any staying power seems to be the treadmill, with about $2 billion worth sold at retail outlets last year. "The people who are turning 45 now are the ones who started the running phenomenon 20 years ago," says Tom Doyle, research vice-president for the National Sporting Goods Assn. So these days, says Doyle, they're jogging in their rec rooms between taking the kids to soccer, sweating it out on the stationary bicycle, or huffing through weight training on a home gym. Sales of both bikes and gyms were up 15% last year. That's another reason why NordicTrack looks like roadkill on the baby boomers' fickle highway.

By Jay Weiner in Minneapolis

A Makeover for the TV Dinner; Swanson Is Being Upgraded to Restore Market Share

By CONSTANCE L. HAYS

Maybe it was the shifting cultural and demographic tides. Maybe it was corporate guilt over a badly neglected brand. Or maybe it was the phone call from the man who had spent his career in the poultry industry and was still confounded by a piece of fried chicken in his TV dinner that he could not trace to any particular part of the bird.

"Consumers like to be able to recognize what they're eating," observed Murray Kessler, president of the Swanson frozen foods division of Vlasic Foods International, which is based in this Philadelphia suburb.

Whatever finally forced the decision, this much is clear: after decades of inertia, the Swanson TV dinner, the archetypal frozen meal born during the Eisenhower Administration, is getting an overhaul.

That's what Swanson calls it, anyway. The company, after all, still features a menu that seems lost in a time warp, with main courses like fried chicken, Salisbury steak and roast turkey served with potatoes, corn and maybe some green beans. Some dinners still tuck a brownie into its own individual compartment, and the turkey still has a gooey cranberry concoction at its side. Swanson even acknowledges the stodginess of its product with a certain perverse pride.

"They have missed every single trend since the Korean War," said Jeffrey G. Kanter, an analyst with Prudential Securities. "It's one thing to miss the Thai food craze, but it's another to miss Italian."

But for an American icon like the TV dinner—named and packaged that way when the first ones came out in 1954 to suggest the meals represented all that was modern and sophisticated at the time—even modest tinkering can, perhaps credibly, be labeled an overhaul.

What Swanson is changing is that the fried chicken, its biggest seller even though it is now produced from fowl hacked into 19 illogical pieces, will be made from more appealing and at least recognizable cuts of meat.

There is also, in the Swanson saga, a note of corporate drama worthy of, say, "Dynasty" or "Dallas."

Robert F. Bernstock, now Vlasic's chief executive, lost a bid for the top job at the Campbell Soup Company last summer. And now that Vlasic has been spun off by Campbell, Mr. Bernstock wants badly to show his stuff. "The whole goal," he said of the latest changes, "was to do something significant and symbolic of how we could operate as a company."

It was high time Swanson did something. TV dinners—the label has stuck, even though the industry years ago dropped that couch-potato term from its packaging—are a $300 million business for the company. But competitors have proliferated, market share is plunging, and consumer complaints ("Need a microscope to find the chicken," one said) are at an all-time high.

Not surprisingly, the division was also losing money. The numbers are depressing: Vlasic has just 9 percent of the $4.5 billion frozen prepared-foods category, running fourth to Nestle, owner of the Stouffer's and Lean Cuisine brands, which has 26.4 percent, and Conagra, maker of Healthy Choice, Marie Callender's and other brands, which has 19.8 percent, and H. J. Heinz, with 9.3 percent, according to Information Resources Inc., which tracks sales in supermarkets and other large stores.

Vlasic is betting on the revamping of the TV dinner to become a benchmark success that could make the company seem a good bet for Wall Street, and set it on a path toward profitability and growth denied by its former handlers.

The company was created a year ago from what can best be described as leftovers. It was spun off as a hodgepodge of food businesses, including pickles, mushrooms and Argentine beef, that Campbell Soup decided it could get along better without. Mr. Bernstock is a kind of Campbell leftover, too, having lost his bid for the chief executive's job to Dale F. Morrison, an executive best known for producing impressive growth with Pepperidge Farm cookies and snacks.

While at Campbell, Mr. Bernstock headed the condensed-soup business, and he readily recalls what low priorities the businesses that now constitute Vlasic were. "It's a Statue of Liberty kind of analogy," he said. "Give us your tired, your poor."

Yet that set of circumstances begets a certain aggressiveness, a will to prove something, that some analysts predict could turn into healthy profits. "There's a lot of opportunity at Vlasic, because very one of these businesses was a forgotten child under the Campbell umbrella," said Mr. Kanter, the analyst. It might even outperform Campbell, he said, which is laboring mightily to increase profits and sales from soup.

Still, for Vlasic, that will take time, not to mention money. "After years of being neglected, you can't turn these businesses around overnight," said Erika Gritman Long, an analyst with J. P. Morgan. "It's going to take some significant, up-front investment that will hurt your earnings before you can turn them around." She projects Vlasic earnings for the current fiscal year, which closes at the end of the month, will total just 49 cents, down from an initial forecast of $1.29 made when the company was spun off.

The TV dinner emerged from the technological and societal changes of World War II, said Michael Stern, a columnist for Gourmet magazine and culinary historian. "During the war, there was a lot of promise that the techniques developed to feed the troops would spill over into civilian life and do what everyone seemed to want in the late 40's and 50's—provide more leisure time," he said. "The TV dinner was a great step in the convenience revolution. It goes hand in hand with the move out to suburbia."

And by helping to do away with daylong cooking of elaborate family meals, he said, it contributed to "the unraveling of the nuclear family."

"The idea was not that people would eat them in front of the TV," he added, "but that they were as modern as television." They also had an element of sophistication, as upwardly mobile families served them to underscore the point that they did not have a lot of time to spend in the kitchen.

As Mr. Stern pointed out, of course, it is the upwardly mobile people today who enjoy showing off their bread-baking and other old-fashioned skills.

The way the TV dinner was revised shows where Mr. Bernstock's business priorities lie. He chose Vlasic's best-known line and largest category, and rather than add one new product, he decided to work on everything at once. In the interest of saving money, some products, like an all-dark-meat dinner, were eliminated in favor of a mix of white and dark. A boneless white-meat dinner was added. New, slightly smaller chickens were tested and approved, because there would be less waste from discarded parts, and the company's plant in Fayetteville, Ark., was reconfigured to handle the changes.

Mr. Kessler, the Swanson president, recalled visiting factories around the country shortly after starting his new job in February. "When I got to the fried-chicken line, one of the people said to me, 'I'm not proud of our fried chicken right now,' " he said. "They weren't proud mostly because of the way we were cutting up the chicken."

Practices like "parts management," an effort to economically control how chicken was used, had failed, he added, and the elimination of ribs from breast meat, for example, made it difficult for people to tell what part they were getting. Complaints soared to 250 for each million unit sales, "and in this company, a red alert is about 10," he said. As profits fell the last five years, advertising was yanked away, and the stage was set for Swanson's big decline.

Once the chicken was reorganized, Mr. Bernstock ordered a new advertising campaign, one whose slogan will be "Make New Memories With Swanson," aimed directly at families. While one commercial from the 50's showed a mother swishing out the door in a fur stole, two commercials the company is now considering show parents enjoying TV dinners alongside their children. Ad spending, including the first TV commercials in a decade, will increase this year to $10 million from $5 million. In the 1980's, though, some $80 million was spent annually on advertising for Swanson and Vlasic's pickle brands. Executives are in the process of meeting with retailers around the country, to push orders of the dinners, and longtime distribution issues are being ironed out, Mr. Bernstock said.

"We all ate these things as kids, but we want to generate interest for a whole new generation of kids," he said, adding that his own four children, ages 14 to 21, eat their share of TV dinners. The typical frozen-dinner consumer is increasingly older, well beyond 21, though considered responsive to changes in packaging and product content.

"Heinz has seen benefits from revamping its Weight Watchers products," Ms. Long said. "Before they changed the products themselves, they changed the packaging and their volumes went up. You've got core users who need to feel there's some variety and some change there."

As for what else may be coming down the pike, Vlasic officials offer plenty of hints, but no details, about a new pickle product that is supposed to be unveiled in October. Analysts are puzzled about just what that may be, though Vlasic saw huge sales of its horizontally sliced pickles after it introduced them in 1995. "I don't know what they could do with a pickle," Mr. Kanter said. "I mean, Mother Nature grows cucumbers a certain way."

Reengineering Work: Don't Automate, Obliterate

Michael Hammer

Despite a decade or more of restructuring and downsizing, many U.S. companies are still unprepared to operate in the 1990s. In a time of rapidly changing technologies and ever-shorter product life cycles, product development often proceeds at a glacial pace. In an age of the customer, order fulfillment has high error rates and customer inquiries go unanswered for weeks. In a period when asset utilization is critical, inventory levels exceed many months of demand.

The usual methods for boosting performance—process rationalization and automation—haven't yielded the dramatic improvements companies need. In particular, heavy investments in information technology have delivered disappointing results—largely because companies tend to use technology to mechanize old ways of doing business. They leave the existing processes intact and use computers simply to speed them up.

But speeding up those processes cannot address their fundamental performance deficiencies. Many of our job designs, work flows, control mechanisms, and organizational structures came of age in a different competitive environment and before the advent of the computer. They are geared toward efficiency and control. Yet the watchwords of the new decade are innovation and speed, service and quality.

It is time to stop paving the cow paths. Instead of embedding outdated processes in silicon and software, we should obliterate them and start over. We should "reengineer" our businesses: use the power of modern information technology to radically redesign our business processes in order to achieve dramatic improvements in their performance.

Every company operates according to a great many unarticulated rules. "Credit decisions are made by the credit department." "Local inventory is needed for good customer service." "Forms must be filled in completely and in order." Reengineering strives to break away from the old rules about how we organize and conduct business. It involves recognizing and rejecting some of them and then finding imaginative new ways to accomplish work. From our redesigned processes, new rules will emerge that fit the times. Only then can we hope to achieve quantum leaps in performance.

Reengineering cannot be planned meticulously and accomplished in small and cautious steps. It's an all-or-nothing proposition with an uncertain result. Still, most companies have no choice but to muster the courage to do it. For many, reengineering is the only hope for breaking away from the antiquated processes that threaten to drag them down. Fortunately, managers are not without help. Enough businesses have successfully reengineered their processes to provide some rules of thumb for others.

Michael Hammer is president of Hammer and Company, an information technology consulting firm in Cambridge, Massachusetts. This article is based in part on work performed in association with the Index Group also a Cambridge-based consultancy.

WHAT FORD AND MBL DID

Japanese competitors and young entrepreneurial ventures prove every day that drastically better levels of process performance are possible. They develop products twice as fast, utilize assets eight times more productively, respond to customers ten times faster. Some large, established companies also show what can be done. Businesses like Ford Motor Company and Mutual Benefit Life Insurance have reengineered their processes and achieved competitive leadership as a result. Ford has reengineered its accounts payable processes, and Mutual Benefit Life, its processing of applications for insurance.

In the early 1980s, when the American automotive industry was in a depression, Ford's top management put accounts payable—along with many other departments—under the microscope in search of ways to cut costs. Accounts payable in North America alone employed more than 500 people. Management thought that by rationalizing processes and installing new computer systems, it could reduce the head count by some 20%.

Ford was enthusiastic about its plan to tighten accounts payable—until it looked at Mazda. While Ford was aspiring to a 400-person department, Mazda's accounts payable organization consisted of a total of 5 people. The difference in absolute numbers was astounding, and even after adjusting for Mazda's smaller size, Ford figured that its accounts payable organization was five times the size it should be. The Ford team knew better than to attribute the discrepancy to calisthenics, company songs, or low interest rates.

Ford managers ratcheted up their goal: accounts payable would perform with not just a hundred but many hundreds fewer clerks. It then set out to achieve it. First, managers analyzed the existing system. When Ford's purchasing department wrote a purchase order, it sent a copy to accounts payable. Later, when material control received the goods, it sent a copy of the receiving document to accounts payable. Meanwhile, the vendor sent an invoice to accounts payable. It was up to accounts payable, then, to match the purchase order against the receiving document and the invoice. If they matched, the department issued payment.

The department spent most of its time on mismatches, instances where the purchase order, receiving document, and invoice disagreed. In these cases, an accounts payable clerk would investigate the discrepancy, hold up payment, generate documents, and all in all gum up the works.

One way to improve things might have been to help the accounts payable clerk investigate more efficiently, but a better choice was to prevent the mismatches in the first place. To this end, Ford instituted "invoiceless processing." Now when the purchasing department initiates an order, it enters the information into an on-line database. It doesn't send a copy of the purchase order to anyone. When the goods arrive at the receiving dock, the receiving clerk checks the database to see if they correspond to an outstanding purchase order. If so, he or she accepts them and enters the transaction into the computer system. (If receiving can't find a database entry for the received goods, it simply returns the order.).

Under the old procedures, the accounting department had to match 14 data items between the receipt record, the purchase order, and the invoice before it could issue payment to the vendor. The new approach requires matching only three items—part number, unit of measure, and supplier code—between the purchase order and the receipt record. The matching is done automatically, and the computer prepares the check, which accounts payable sends to the vendor. There are no invoices to worry about since Ford has asked its vendors not to send them.

Ford didn't settle for the modest increases it first envisioned. It opted for radical change—and achieved dramatic improvement. Where it has instituted this new process, Ford has achieved a 75% reduction in head count, not the 20% it would have gotten with a conventional program. And since there are no discrepancies between the financial record and the physical record, material control is simpler and financial information is more accurate.

Mutual Benefit Life, the country's eighteenth largest life carrier, has reengineered its processing of insurance applications. Prior to this, MBL handled customers' applications much as its competitors did. The long, multistep process involved credit checking, quoting, rating, underwriting, and so on. An application would have to go through as many as 30 discrete steps, spanning 5 departments and involving 19 people. At the very best, MBL could process an application in 24 hours, but more typical turnarounds ranged from 5 to 25 days—most of the time spent passing information from one department to the next. (Another insurer estimated that while an application spent 22 days in process, it was actually worked on for just 17 minutes.).

MBL's rigid, sequential process led to many complications. For instance, when a customer wanted to cash in an existing policy and purchase a new one, the old business department first had to authorize the treasury department to issue a check made payable to MBL. The check would then accompany the paperwork to the new business department.

The president of MBL, intent on improving customer service, decided that this nonsense had to stop and demanded a 60% improvement in productivity. It was clear that such an ambitious goal would require more than tinkering with the existing process. Strong measures were in order, and the management team assigned to the task looked to technology as a means of achieving them. The team realized that shared databases and computer networks could make many different kinds of information available to a single person, while expert systems could help people with limited experience make sound decisions. Applying these insights led to a new approach to the application-handling process, one with wide organizational implications and little resemblance to the old way of doing business.

MBL swept away existing job definitions and departmental boundaries and created a new position called a case manager. Case managers have total responsibility for an application from the time it is received to the time a policy is issued. Unlike clerks, who performed a fixed task repeatedly under the watchful gaze of a supervisor, case managers work autonomously. No more handoffs of files and responsibility, no more shuffling of customer inquiries.

Case managers are able to perform all the tasks associated with an insurance application because they are supported by powerful PC-based workstations that run an expert system and connect to a range of automated systems on a mainframe. In particularly tough cases, the case manager calls for assistance from a senior underwriter or physician, but these specialists work only as consultants and advisers to the case manager, who never relinquishes control.

Empowering individuals to process entire applications has had a tremendous impact on operations. MBL can now complete an application in as little as four hours, and average turnaround takes only two to five days. The company has eliminated 100 field office positions, and case managers can handle more than twice the volume of new applications the company previously could process.

THE ESSENCE OF REENGINEERING

At the heart of reengineering is the notion of discontinuous thinking—of recognizing and breaking away from the outdated rules and fundamental assumptions that underlie operations. Unless we change these rules, we are merely rearranging the deck chairs on the Titanic. We cannot achieve breakthroughs in performance by cutting fat or automating existing processes. Rather, we must challenge old assumptions and shed the old rules that made the business underperform in the first place.

Every business is replete with implicit rules left over from earlier decades. "Customers don't repair their own equipment." "Local warehouses are necessary for good service." "Merchandising decisions are made at headquarters." These rules of work design are based on assumptions about technology, people, and organizational goals that no longer hold. The contemporary repertoire of available information technologies is vast and quickly expanding. Quality, innovation, and service are now more important than cost, growth, and control. A large portion of the population is educated and capable of assuming responsibility, and workers cherish their autonomy and expect to have a say in how the business is run.

It should come as no surprise that our business processes and structures are outmoded and obsolete: our work structures and processes have not kept pace with the changes in technology, demographics, and business objectives. For the most part, we have organized work as a sequence of separate tasks and employed complex mechanisms to track its progress. This arrangement can be traced to the Industrial Revolution, when specialization of labor and economies of scale promised to overcome the inefficiencies of cottage industries. Businesses disaggregated work into narrowly defined tasks, reaggregated the people performing those tasks into departments, and installed managers to administer them.

Our elaborate systems for imposing control and discipline on those who actually do the work stem from the postwar period. In that halcyon period of expansion, the main concern was growing fast without going broke, so businesses focused on cost, growth, and control. And since literate, entry-level people were abundant but well-educated professionals hard to come by, the control systems funneled information up the hierarchy to the few who presumably knew what to do with it.

These patterns of organizing work have become so ingrained that, despite their serious drawbacks, it's hard to conceive of work being accomplished any other way. Conventional process structures are fragmented and piecemeal, and they lack the integration necessary to maintain quality and service. They are breeding grounds for tunnel vision, as people tend to substitute the narrow goals of their particular department for the larger goals of the process as a whole. When work is handed off from person to person and unit to unit, delays and errors are inevitable. Accountability blurs, and critical issues fall between the cracks. Moreover, no one sees enough of the big picture to be able to respond quickly to new situations. Managers desperately try, like all the king's horses and all the king's men, to piece together the fragmented pieces of business processes.

Managers have tried to adapt their processes to new circumstances, but usually in ways that just create more problems. If, say, customer service is poor, they create a mechanism to deliver service but overlay it on the existing organization. Bureaucracy thickens, costs rise, and enterprising competitors gain market share.

In reengineering, managers break loose from outmoded business processes and the design principles underlying them and create new ones. Ford had operated under the old rule that "We pay when we receive the invoice." While no one had ever articulated or recorded it, that rule determined how the accounts payable process was organized. Ford's reengineering effort challenged and ultimately replaced the rule with a new one: "We pay when we receive the *goods.*"

Reengineering requires looking at the fundamental processes of the business from a cross-functional perspective. Ford discovered that reengineering only the accounts payable department was futile. The appropriate focus of the effort was what might be called the goods acquisition process, which included purchasing and receiving as well as accounts payable.

One way to ensure that reengineering has a cross-functional perspective is to assemble a team that represents the functional units involved in the process being reengineered and all the units that depend on it. The team must analyze and scrutinize the existing process until it really understands what the process is trying to accomplish. The point is not to learn what happens to form 73B in its peregrinations through the company but to understand the purpose of having form 73B in the first place. Rather than looking for opportunities to improve the current process, the team should determine which of its steps really add value and search for new ways to achieve the result.

The reengineering team must keep asking Why? and What if? Why do we need to get a manager's signature on a requisition? Is it a control mechanism or a decision point? What if the manager reviews only requisitions above $500? What if he or she doesn't see them at all? Raising and resolving heretical questions can separate what is fundamental to the process from what is superficial. The regional offices of an East Coast insurance company had long produced a series of reports that they regularly sent to the home office. No one in the field realized that these reports were simply filed and never used. The process outlasted the circumstances that had created the need for it. The reengineering study team should push to discover situations like this.

In short, a reengineering effort strives for dramatic levels of improvement. It must break away from conventional wisdom and the constraints of organizational boundaries and should be broad and cross-functional in scope. It should use information technology not to automate an existing process but to enable a new one.

PRINCIPLES OF REENGINEERING

Creating new rules tailored to the modern environment ultimately requires a new conceptualization of the business process—which comes down to someone having a great idea. But reengineering need not be haphazard. In fact, some of the principles that companies have already discovered while reengineering their business processes can help jump start the effort for others.

Organize around outcomes, not tasks. This principle says to have one person perform all the steps in a process. Design that person's job around an objective or outcome instead of a single task. The redesign at Mutual Benefit Life, where individual case managers perform the entire application approval process, is the quintessential example of this.

The redesign of an electronics company is another example. It had separate organizations performing each of the five steps between selling and installing the equipment. One group determined customer requirements, another translated those requirements into internal product codes, a third conveyed that information to various plants and warehouses, a fourth received and assembled the components, and a fifth delivered and installed the equipment. The process was based on the centuries-old notion of specialized labor and on the limitations inherent in paper files. The departments each possessed a specific set of skills, and only one department at a time could do its work.

The customer order moved systematically from step to step. But this sequential processing caused problems. The people getting the information from the customer in step one had to get all the data anyone would need throughout the process, even if it wasn't needed until step five. In addition, the many handoffs were responsible for numerous errors and misunderstandings. Finally, any questions about customer requirements that arose late in the process had to be referred back to the people doing step one, resulting in delay and rework.

When the company reengineered, it eliminated the assembly-line approach. It compressed responsibility for the various steps and assigned it to one person, the "customer service representative." That person now oversees the whole process—taking the order, translating it into product codes, getting the components assembled, and seeing the product delivered and installed. The customer service rep expedites and coordinates the process, much like a general contractor. And the customer has just one contact, who always knows the status of the order.

Have those who use the output of the process perform the process. In an effort to capitalize on the benefits of specialization and scale, many organizations established specialized departments to handle specialized processes. Each department does only one type of work and is a "customer" of other groups' processes. Accounting does only accounting. If it needs new pencils, it goes to the purchasing department, the group specially equipped with the information and expertise to perform that role. Purchasing finds vendors, negotiates price, places the order, inspects the goods, and pays the invoice—and eventually the accountants get their pencils. The process works (after a fashion), but it's slow and bureaucratic.

Now that computer-based data and expertise are more readily available, departments, units, and individuals can do more for themselves. Opportunities exist to reengineer processes so that the individuals who need the result of a process can do it themselves. For example, by using expert systems and databases, departments can make their own purchases without sacrificing the benefits of specialized purchasers. One manufacturer has reengineered its purchasing process along just these lines. The company's old system, whereby the operating departments submitted requisitions and let purchasing do the rest, worked well for controlling expensive and important items like raw materials and capital equipment. But for inexpensive and nonstrategic purchases, which constituted some 35% of total orders, the system was slow and cumbersome; it was not uncommon for the cost of the purchasing process to exceed the cost of the goods being purchased.

The new process compresses the purchase of sundry items and pushes it on to the customers of the process. Using a database of approved vendors, an operating unit can directly place an order with a vendor and charge it

Why Did We Design Inefficient Processes?

In a way, we didn't. Many of our procedures were not designed at all; they just happened. The company founder one day recognized that he didn't have time to handle a chore, so he delegated it to Smith. Smith improvised. Time passed, the business grew, and Smith hired his entire clan to help him cope with the work volume. They all improvised. Each day brought new challenges and special cases, and the staff adjusted its work accordingly. The hodgepodge of special cases and quick fixes was passed from one generation of workers to the next.

We have institutionalized the ad hoc and enshrined the temporary. Why do we send foreign accounts to the corner desk? Because 20 years ago, Mary spoke French and Mary had the corner desk. Today Mary is long gone, and we no longer do business in France, but we still send foreign accounts to the corner desk. Why does an electronics company spend $10 million a year to manage a field inventory worth $20 million? Once upon a time, the inventory was worth $200 million, and managing it cost $5 million. Since then, warehousing costs have escalated, components have become less expensive, and better forecasting techniques have minimized units in inventory. But the inventory procedures, alas, are the same as always.

Of the business processes that *were* designed, most took their present forms in the 1950s. The goal then was to check overambitious growth—much as the typewriter keyboard was designed to slow typists who would otherwise jam the keys. It is no accident that organizations stifle innovation and creativity. That's what they were *designed* to do.

Nearly all of our processes originated before the advent of modern computer and communications technology. They are replete with mechanisms designed to compensate for "information poverty." Although we are not information affluent, we still use those mechanisms, which are now deeply embedded in automated systems.

---

on a bank credit card. At the end of the month, the bank gives the manufacturer a tape of all credit card transactions, which the company runs against its internal accounting system.

When an electronics equipment manufacturer reengineered its field service process, it pushed some of the steps of the process on to its customers. The manufacturer's field service had been plagued by the usual problems: technicians were often unable to do a particular repair because the right part wasn't on the van, response to customer calls was slow, and spare-parts inventory was excessive.

Now customers make simple repairs themselves. Spare parts are stored at each customer's site and managed through a computerized inventory-management system. When a problem arises, the customer calls the manufacturer's field-service hot line and describes the symptoms to a diagnostician, who accesses a diagnosis support system. If the problem appears to be something the customer can fix, the diagnostician tells the customer what part to replace and how to install it. The old part is picked up and a new part left in its place at a later time. Only for complex problems is a service technician dispatched to the site, this time without having to make a stop at the warehouse to pick up parts.

When the people closest to the process perform it, there is little need for the overhead associated with managing it. Interfaces and liaisons can be eliminated, as can the mechanisms used to coordinate those who perform the process with those who use it. Moreover, the problem of capacity planning for the process performers is greatly reduced.

Subsume information-processing work into the real work that produces the information. The previous two principles say to compress linear processes. This principle suggests moving work from one person or department to another. Why doesn't an organization that produces information also process it? In the past, people didn't have the time or weren't trusted to do both. Most companies established units to do nothing but collect and process information that other departments created. This arrangement reflects the old rule about specialized labor and the belief that people at lower organizational levels are incapable of acting on information they generate. An accounts payable department collects information from purchasing and receiving and reconciles it with data that the vendor provides. Quality assurance gathers and analyzes information it gets from production.

Ford's redesigned accounts payable process embodies the new rule. With the new system, receiving, which produces the information about the goods received, processes this information instead of sending it to accounts payable. The new computer system can easily compare the delivery with the order and trigger the appropriate action.

Treat geographically dispersed resources as though they were centralized. The conflict between centralization and decentralization is a classic one. Decentralizing a resource (whether people, equipment, or inventory) gives better service to those who use it, but at the cost of redundancy, bureaucracy, and missed economies of scale. Companies no longer have to make such trade-offs. They can use databases, telecommunications networks, and standardized processing systems to get the benefits of scale and coordination while maintaining the benefits of flexibility and service.

At Hewlett-Packard, for instance, each of the more than 50 manufacturing units had its own separate purchasing department. While this arrangement provided excellent responsiveness and service to the plants, it prevented H-P from realizing the benefits of its scale, particularly with regard to quantity discounts. H-P's solution is to maintain the divisional purchasing organizations and to introduce a corporate unit to coordinate them. Each purchasing unit has access to a shared database on vendors and their performance and issues its own purchase orders. Corporate purchasing maintains this database and uses it to negotiate contracts for the corporation and to monitor the units. The payoffs have come in a 150% improvement in on-time deliveries, 50% reduction in lead times, 75% reduction in failure rates, and a significantly lower cost of goods purchased.

Link parallel activities instead of integrating their results. H-P's decentralized purchasing operations represent one kind of parallel processing in which separate units perform the same function. Another common kind of parallel processing is when separate units perform different activities that must eventually come together. Product development typically operates this way. In the development of a photocopier, for example, independent units develop the various subsystems of the copier. One group works on the optics, another on the power supply, and so on. Having people do development work simultaneously saves time, but at the dreaded integration and testing phase, the pieces often fail to work together. Then the costly redesign begins.

Or consider a bank that sells different kinds of credit—loans, letters of credit, asset-based financing—through separate units. These groups may have no way of knowing whether another group has already extended credit to a particular customer. Each unit could extend the full $10 million credit limit.

The new principle says to forge links between parallel functions and to coordinate them while their activities are in process rather than after they are completed. Communications networks, shared databases, and teleconferencing can bring the independent groups together so that coordination is ongoing. One large electronics company has cut its product development cycle by more than 50% by implementing this principle.

Put the decision point where the work is performed, and build control into the process. In most organizations, those who do the work are distinguished from those who monitor the work and make decisions about it. The tacit assumption is that the people actually doing the work have neither the time nor the inclination to monitor and control it and that they lack the knowledge and scope to make decisions about it. The entire hierarchical management structure is built on this assumption. Accountants, auditors, and supervisors check, record, and monitor work. Managers handle any exceptions.

The new principle suggests that the people who do the work should make the decisions and that the process itself can have built-in controls. Pyramidal management layers can therefore be compressed and the organization flattened.

Information technology can capture and process data, and expert systems can to some extent supply knowledge, enabling people to make their own decisions. As the doers become self-managing and self-controlling, hierarchy—and the slowness and bureaucracy associated with it—disappears.

When Mutual Benefit Life reengineered the insurance application process, it not only compressed the linear sequence but also eliminated the need for layers of managers. These two kinds of compression—vertical and horizontal—often go together; the very fact that a worker sees only one piece of the process calls for a manager with a broader vision. The case managers at MBL provide end-to-end management of the process, reducing the need for traditional managers. The managerial role is changing from one of controller and supervisor to one of supporter and facilitator.

Capture information once and at the source. This last rule is simple. When information was difficult to transmit, it made sense to collect information repeatedly. Each person, department, or unit had its own requirements and forms. Companies simply had to live with the associated delays, entry errors, and costly overhead. But why do we have to live with those problems now? Today when we collect a piece of information, we can store it in an on-line database, and electronic data interchange (EDI) make it easy to collect, store, and transmit information. One insurance company found that its application review process required that certain items be entered into "stovepipe" computer systems supporting different functions as many as five times. By integrating and connecting these systems, the company was able to eliminate this redundant data entry along with the attendant checking functions and inevitable errors.

THINK BIG

Reengineering triggers changes of many kinds, not just of the business process itself. Job designs, organizational structures, management systems—anything associated with the process—must be refashioned in an integrated way. In other words, reengineering is a tremendous effort that mandates change in many areas of the organization.

When Ford reengineered its payables, receiving clerks on the dock had to learn to use computer terminals to check shipments, and they had to make decisions about whether to accept the goods. Purchasing agents also had to assume new responsibilities—like making sure the purchase orders they entered into the database had the correct information about where to send the check. Attitudes toward vendors also had to change: vendors could no longer be seen as adversaries; they had to become partners in a shared business process. Vendors too had to adjust. In many cases, invoices formed the basis of their accounting systems. At least one Ford supplier adapted by continuing to print invoices, but instead of sending them to Ford threw them away, reconciling cash received against invoices never sent.

The changes at Mutual Benefit Life were also widespread. The company's job-rating scheme could not accommodate the case manager position, which had a lot of responsibility but no direct reports. MBL had to devise new job-rating schemes and compensation policies. It also had to develop a culture in which people doing work are perceived as more important than those supervising work. Career paths, recruitment and training programs, promotion policies—these and many other management systems are being revised to support the new process design.

The extent of these changes suggests one factor that is necessary for reengineering to succeed: executive leadership with real vision. No one in an organization wants reengineering. It is confusing and disruptive and affects everything people have grown accustomed to. Only if top-level managers back the effort and outlast the company cynics will people take reengineering seriously. As one wag at an electronics equipment manufacturer has commented, "Every few months, our senior managers find a new religion. One time it was quality, another it was customer service, another it was flattening the organization. We just hold our breath until they get over it and things get back to normal." Commitment, consistency—maybe even a touch of fanaticism—are needed to enlist those who would prefer the status quo.

Considering the inertia of old processes and structures, the strain of implementing a reengineering plan can hardly be overestimated. But by the same token, it is hard to overstimulate the opportunities, especially for established companies. Big, traditional organizations aren't necessarily dinosaurs doomed to extinction, but they are burdened with layers of unproductive overhead and armies of unproductive workers. Shedding them a layer at a time will not be good enough to stand up against sleek startups or streamlined Japanese companies. U.S. companies need fast change and dramatic improvements.

We have the tools to do what we need to do. Information technology offers many options for reorganizing work. But our imaginations must guide our decisions about technology—not the other way around. We must have the boldness to imagine taking 78 days out of an 80-day turnaround time, cutting 75% of overhead, and eliminating 80% of errors. These are not unrealistic goals. If managers have the vision, reengineering will provide a way.

OWENS CORNING: BACK FROM THE DEAD

The Company Was Mired in Debt, Besieged by Asbestos Litigation, and Headed Nowhere When Glen Hiner Left GE to Run It Five Years Ago. Here's How He Turned It Around.

Thomas A. Stewart

The trees have leafed out in Toledo, but the infant arbors spotted around a glittering new riverfront building aren't much to look at, and won't be for years. There's plenty to see inside, however. The building is Owens Corning's spanking-new headquarters and an apt symbol of the striking renewal of the 59-year-old maker of fiberglass insulation, glass composites, and roofing materials.

What CEO Glen H. Hiner and his team are doing at Owens Corning could be an object lesson in how to revitalize a company—"my way," says Hiner, "as opposed to Al Dunlap's way." It's also a story about the competitive logic of the New Economy: In the past year a series of moves in sales and marketing, information systems, and manufacturing and distribution have come together in a coherent strategy that is transforming this Midwestern maker of humdrum materials into a global competitor whose real business is knowledge.

If "Chainsaw" Al Dunlap's way is execution (as in beheading), Hiner's is execution (as in follow-through). The stock market loved Dunlap's quick cuts to the quick. And Hiner's approach has worked too: Owens Corning has racked up impressive numbers—including 21 consecutive quarters of year-over-year improved profits from ongoing operations. But Wall Street, so far, remains standoffish. There are reasons for that. Investment-based growth takes time. Owens Corning has a big housing-supply business in Europe, where economies are still flat. And though Owens Corning is convinced that it has burned off a cloud from ancient asbestos liabilities, their shadow still spooks the market.

Too, the company's balance sheet bears scars from a fierce takeover battle a decade ago. In that 1986 struggle, a hostile raid by Sanford Sigoloff's Wickes Cos. drove Owens Corning into a desperate recapitalization that left it with $1.65 billion in long-term debt, shareholders' equity of negative $1 billion, and a scrimp-and-save outlook so single-minded that virtually all investment stopped and over the next five years sales shrank by $74 million, about 3%, to $2.8 billion. The bad news got worse late in 1991, when Max Weber, CEO for just over a year, was taken ill and retired, dying of cancer 16 months later at 63.

Hiner, then 57, accepted the challenge of lifting the stones under which Owens Corning was pinned. Hiner was running Jack Welch's old shop, General Electric's plastics business, leading it from annual sales of $750 million to $5 billion in 13 years. Now he was going to a business half as large, but it would be his own show. Says Hiner: "There was an element of vanity in my deciding to go, and I admit to that. No matter what I did, plastics would always be the house Jack built."

Hiner brought with him a passionate belief that it's better to punch your way out of a corner than to play rope-a-dope. In 1993 he came out swinging: Enough with the debt—then about $900 million—he told the company; it's time to grow. By 2000, when Hiner will turn 65 and retire, he wanted Owens Corning to be a $5 billion company that would supply just about everything it takes to build a house, from insulation to siding to windows. And he vowed that the company would get 40% of its sales outside the U.S., up from 21% at the time; and productivity would grow 6% a year and profits twice as fast as sales. It was an ambitious agenda, but last summer progress was dramatic enough that Hiner made his goal tougher, proclaiming that Owens Corning would achieve it a year early, by 1999.

This CEO's egalitarian style has helped. Hiner used to be hidden in a 28th-floor aerie, but in the new headquarters, an open-plan three-story building, he is second-floor center—"in the middle of the middle"—with glass walls around his office. As he walks from his car—there is no reserved parking—he invariably falls in with whoever else is on the path to the building. He always eats in the cafeteria—bringing visitors like his old colleague Welch or, often, Corning alone and inviting himself to join a table. ("Sometimes when we see him heading our way, we duck and pretend to be deep in conversation," marketing director Karen Strauss admits.) So when the boss is in town, it's almost inevitable that everyone in the building sees him during the day—which gives him the chance to pop up, like the Lilac Fairy in The Sleeping Beauty, just when you need him.

"Symbols are easy," Hiner says, "but you've got to make the symbols work." It's worth noting what he could not do to make growth happen. A CEO can make acquisitions, which will account for about $1 billion of Owens Corning's sales growth. He can move capital to fund what's growing fastest and lend his presence and prestige to projects. He can hire, fire, and reassign. But CEOs can't create internal growth; they can only help the people who concoct and execute plays, ploys, and projects. Indeed, the revolutionary CEO has to be conservative too. Says Hiner: "The old culture had a very clear vision—raise cash to reduce debt. We've got to get out of that bunker, but I've got to honor the past. They were doing a good job at what they were told to do. If you come in and say, 'You were dumb,' you lose all your credibility." These guys could execute; the question was, execute what?

Hiner told them to see Owens Corning as customers did, from the outside. He hoped that would let the company break free from a set of long-held givens. Among them:

—Seasonality and cyclicality: Housing starts and remodeling projects ride the economy's hills and dales; in good times or bad, winter's dead.

—Big stockpiles: Every fiberglass line can make any grade of insulation, but the process—melting glass in glowing furnaces, spinning it in strands that can be 150 miles long, at a speed Rumpelstiltskin would envy, then sending it on to be cooled, sprayed with a fixative, and rolled—works best uninterrupted. Add that to seasonality, and you're condemned to build inventory.

—Costly shipping: Insulation is bulky and inexpensive; roofing materials are heavy and inexpensive. Ergo, distribution is a burden, not a source of advantage.

All true, but all beside the point to customers. Owens Corning was fighting for share in a $5 billion domestic roofing and insulation business. But the market that customers saw was a $320 billion worldwide home-remodeling business. Says Dave Brown, president of building-materials sales and distribution: "We were focused on the materials, but customers are asking for more than products."

In the hot home-improvement market—which has grown about 50% in the 1990s, thanks to retailers like Home Depot, Lowes Cos., and Builders Square (part of Kmart)—consumers think about projects, not products: adding a room, fixing the roof, turning the basement into an entertainment center. Stuff is secondary; their big concerns are unreliable contractors, scarce information, and unexpected problems. Builders and contractors, frustrated when materials don't arrive on time, also think in project terms; customers for Owens Corning's composites—automakers, e.g.—increasingly want component systems rather than just parts.

That insight was the seed of a big idea. By leveraging the Pink Panther brand—one of the strongest in any industry and certainly stronger than the brands of competitors like France's Saint-Gobain (Certainteed in the U.S.) and Schuller, the rechristened remains of the asbestos-tainted Manville name—Owens Corning could blow away the old givens. Instead of peddling pallets it could offer customers one-stop shopping and solutions to the problems projects pose—and by the way move a lot of product.

It was good thinking but for one thing: Owens Corning lacked the ability to carry it out. It had big gaps in its product line. Also, sales and distribution—organized by product—couldn't offer big retail customers a simple way to buy a multiplicity of things. Says Brian DeGeorge, a sales rep in North Carolina: "You could have a four-car wreck in a customer's parking lot, all of them driven by an Owens Corning salesperson." After the sale, retailers dealt with four different service centers, four different sets of terms, and four different invoices, and wrote four different checks. Third—least apparent and most difficult—the company couldn't execute its strategy for selling materials unless it totally reconceived how information flowed through it and to and from its customers.

First came filling the product line, so the company could sell everything needed for the "envelope" of a house: shingles, waterproofing, and venting for the roof; vinyl siding and windows; foam and fiber insulation and a pink plastic house wrap that acts as a final insulating barrier. In 1994, Owens Corning bought UC Industries, an 18-year-old New Jersey maker of rigid insulating foam—it looks like dense Styrofoam and is better for some applications than glass wool—and with it the services of co-founder Jerry Weinstein. Says Weinstein, who has an entrepreneur's zeal for making every possible sale: "Ten years ago Owens Corning would have sneered at a $50 million business like us—we would have been a rounding error."

UC Industries was the first of a series of buys; still highly leveraged, Owens Corning bought small, and only what would be profitable within a year. The biggest deal, also in 1994, was the insulation business of Pilkington, a British company, which in a stroke more than doubled Owens Corning's European capacity. Five more buys came in 1995—including two other small foam makers and a manufacturer of vinyl windows—and seven last year and this.

In the labs, Hiner's call for new ideas was rain after a drought. Research—run from a campus of buildings near Granville, Ohio, on what once was the farm of J.C. Penney's brother Herbert—had been cut by more than half when the company hunkered down to reduce debt. An acoustics lab, which had mostly worked on commercial buildings, closed entirely. It reopened last year with a new focus on sound insulation for appliances, cars, and homes. The last was a dream of a line extension: With a little science and a lot of marketing, Owens Corning showed that what keeps Jack Frost from chilling a bedroom will keep Pearl Jam from rattling a home office—and sales of Quiet-Zone products should rise 28% this year.

The reenergized R&D center also had a new wool fiberglass called Miraflex for do-it-yourselfers; it's cheaper to make than ordinary glass insulation and cheaper to ship because it can be compressed, and it gets a premium price because it's noticeably less itchy than the usual stuff. There were new composites and roofing materials: An up-market new shingle and a fake shake, called MiraVista, that looks like the real wooden thing but is fire-resistant.

By the end of 1995, sales were up from $2.8 billion to $3.6 billion, long-term debt down from $900 million to about $800 million. Operating income was rising smartly, mostly thanks to blocking-and-tackling improvements. The product line was richer—the company estimates its potential "take per home" for a 1,800-square-foot house was up from about $1,000 in 1993 to $4,000. To make that tangible, though, Owens Corning had to build something intangible: a new information culture and system.

In the old economy, information was a byproduct—a bill of lading, an invoice, a brochure: It was necessary gaudery, but value lay in the goods. Information systems, consequently, grew up around goods—which is why Owens Corning, like many companies, entered the mid-1990s with 200 incompatible systems, each dedicated to one or two tasks, such as counting shingles or invoicing insulation.

The new economy won't tolerate that, because information is becoming more valuable than goods. That realization came to Owens Corning independently and simultaneously in three different places. In the field, sales reps found that major accounts—fast-growing "big box" retailers like Home Depot and Lowes—needed information more than sales pitches. First, they wanted sophisticated logistics. A typical Lowes outlet, says Greg Wessling, general-merchandise manager for the North Carolina-based chain of 408 stores, deals with 5,000 to 7,000 vendors, carries 40,000 items, and has virtually no storage space. "Can you imagine the traffic jam at their back door?" asks Art Bender, who leads the Owens Corning team that calls on Lowes. "They'd like to have a truck come by at 2:35 and another at 4:30, each carrying a pallet or two of several different products. Our systems could only handle full trucks of one product."

Logistics is just a part of the demand for knowledge from stores like Lowes. "Their No. 1 request is training," says Bender, who manages a rep, Tisa Pacella, whose job is to provide it. Shoppers for insulation and shingles need trained salespeople on the floor, and companies like Lowes (which added 47 stores in 1996) and Home Depot (88 new stores) hire gobs of people, many of whom start knowing little more than the shoppers. Bender and Pacella often send Owens Corning training videos to Lowes headquarters to be beamed by satellite to store personnel.

To provide this knowledge-based selling, reps were pulled away from peddling single product lines—insulation, roofing, asphalt—and told to sell the company's whole line. Then customer service and fulfillment were folded in with sales to form a horizontal order-ship-service process under Alan Booth, former head of the insulation business, who now sports the title "process executive." Merely encouraging cross-functional cooperation—here's coffee and Danish, now make nice—isn't enough, Booth says: "When you're trying to get a common invoice for ten or 11 distinct businesses, you need someone to cut through and say, 'We'll do it this way.' " It's worked. For example, sales of insulating foam, which could have fallen through the cracks of the old organization, have grown 56%, to $40 million, in two years.

Back in Toledo, chief information officer Michael Radcliff, hired by Hiner from Honeywell in 1994, faced a similar basket of challenges: Maintaining the hodgepodge of legacy computer systems cost $35 million a year, and the damned things couldn't, even at their best, support the new strategy. Radcliff took a huge gamble: He bet his job—and almost the company—on his group's ability to install SAP, the immensely powerful and notoriously complex enterprisewide information-management software, across most of Owens Corning in just 18 months—about the time it usually takes to hook up just one business unit. He called the project Advantage 2000. SAP connects all the information that flows through a company in a single system, so that, for example, when a salesman enters an order, it automatically puts dibs on raw materials, schedules production and delivery, and prepares a bill—all with no more data entry. Says Hiner: "Electronic commerce will seal the deal with customers. They ought to be online with us, ought to know our inventory, ought to know when something is shipped, ought to be able to pay electronically, so we can give them multiple products in a way that looks like one product." It will vastly improve Owens Corning's ability to forecast sales and, says Richard Glosser, plant leader in Vise, Belgium, "allow us to substitute information for inventory."

But SAP is also the furthest thing from plug-and-play software: If you install it without completely mapping and reengineering business processes and ensuring the accuracy of all data—for example, clearing out all the fudge factors companies cook up over the years—you're doomed to chaos, possibly for years.

Today the job's on target, on budget, and ready for completion this fall. What made it work? First, Radcliff defined success in business terms—inventory reduction of 50%, a $100 million reduction in working capital, $5 million less for plant maintenance, an overall 1% increase in pretax earnings, etc.—and insisted that half the project staff came from the businesses, not from information systems. As a result, he says, no matter how messy things got, "the debate was 'How do I achieve the outcome?' and nothing else." Second, by starting with corporate finance, Owens Corning ensured that its first victims were numerate and computer-savvy, the best possible teachers. Then, rather than wimp ahead with small pilots, the company picked a major business thousands of miles from headquarters, whose legacy systems were the clunkiest in the company, where the work had to be done in several languages, and where people were thrilled to break the trail for the company. So thrilled, says Ann Senn, a Deloitte & Touche consultant who worked with Radcliff, that "I have never seen a business side pulling the tech side harder. We kept saying, 'Hey, wait a minute, slow down!' " After paying $110 million to install SAP and train people, Owens Corning will reap $15 million in savings in 1997, $50 million next year—and $80 million in 2000.

If the reinvention of Owens Corning shows anything, it's that there's no stopping halfway to beCorning a knowledge company: You either are or you aren't. Building-materials marketing director Karen Strauss knew nothing about plans for Advantage 2000 when she began to realize that knowledge was the most valuable thing she had to sell: If consumers knew how shingles and vents and soffits worked together to make a better roof, if they knew how to pick reliable contractors, if contractors knew how to help customers get financing or how to flog the Pink Panther brand, Owens Corning could sell pink houses, not just pink fiberglass.

Out of these thoughts Strauss and Dave Brown conceived System Thinking, a marketing vision that is the capstone of the company's strategy, joining all that Hiner & Co. has done with acquisitions, new products, sales and service, and Advantage 2000. With Owens Corning's potential take per home now over $6,000, System Thinking pushes the notion that roofing, exteriors, insulation, and sound are all systems—products that work together—and that by selling systems Owens Corning can significantly increase demand. Out of System Thinking are pouring ad campaigns and merchandising support, plus innovative programs like certification for contractors who meet Owens Corning's standards. There's also an ambitious program to sign up homebuilders to agree to use Owens Corning products wherever possible in exchange for marketing support and the right to brag about the brand. As of April, more than 100 U.S. builders had signed on to build a projected 7,500 new System Thinking Homes in 1997. Estimated incremental sales: $10 million.

In all these programs, knowledge pulls the product, not vice versa. Says Brown: "We'd never looked at information as a product before." The logic of Information Age competition is so seamless and compelling, Strauss says, that something like Advantage 2000 was "a happy inevitability"—for the logic drives sales, marketing, and systems all to the same place. For Owens Corning, they came together at the same time, though each began for its own good reason: pressure from customers, the pending breakdown of the old information systems, the hot pink-house idea.

Hiner, more modest than he should be for having the foresight to found a solid, long-term strategy, does take credit for helping to orchestrate its execution: "We didn't have the luxury of saying, 'Work on one thing and get it done, then another, then another.' But I'm a pretty good cheerleader, good at touching people and giving them a few kisses." He's needed that skill. In addition to a total revamping of sales and service, marketing, and information systems, the company has successfully completed 14 acquisitions, built or acquired facilities on every continent save Australia and Antarctica, taken aggressive financial and legal steps against its old asbestos liabilities, radically restructured human resources and compensation, and designed, built, and moved into the new building—all the while steadily increasing the efficiency of its core businesses.

Whether Hiner's kisses have turned Owens Corning into a prince of a company isn't yet proved. Overseas sales growth has been slow. There's that recently sidewinding stock price. The CEO wants to make "a really big acquisition" before he retires in 2000. But if the kisses take, Hiner's way will look pretty good.

A close-up look at President Rick Wagoner and his strategy for

REVIVING GM

As flashbulbs popped and music blared, General Motors President G. Richard Wagoner Jr. was beaming. Unveiling a crop of snazzy new concept cars at the Detroit auto show earlier this month, Wagoner's pride was palpable. "I pushed pretty hard for these," he said, momentarily shedding his customary awshucks modesty as he showed off three sleek hybrids that combine elements of cars, minivans, and sport-utility vehicles (SUVs). After years of churning out mostly unremarkable cars, GM finally had something to wow the audience. Wagoner couldn't have been happier.

That's not the only reason the athletic, 6-foot, 4-inch Wagoner is pleased. After a roller-coaster year in which GM was pummeled by a 54-day strike and a continuation of its seemingly endless market-share slide, the past few months have brought good news for Detroit's biggest carmaker. Six years of cutting costs and reshaping the way the lumbering giant designs and builds cars—much of it spearheaded by Wagoner, first as GM's chief financial officer and since 1994, as head of its core North American Operations (NAO)—seem to be paying off. GM has high hopes for its new Chevrolet Silverado and GMC Sierra full-size pickup trucks introduced last fall. And it's once-sluggish manufacturing operations have succeeded in revving up production to take advantage of the hot market for high-margin light trucks. Flat-out production has sent GM's fourth-quarter earnings from operations up a stunning 55%, to $2.19 billion, as profits in its North American auto operations more than doubled, to $1.7 billion. And next year should be even better. Analysts now expect GM's operating profits to increase 62%, to $6 billion.

GIDDY. Behind the scenes, too, GM watchers see cause for optimism. After years of preparation, the company is pushing ahead with plans this spring to spin off its auto-components group, Delphi Automotive Systems. And even GM'S most intractable problem, labor relations, shows signs of mending.

The combination has suddenly turned GM investors giddy. After driving the company's shares down from 76 to 47 over the course of last summer's strike, Wall Street has sent the stock up a stunning 89%, to a record high of 89, since October. In January alone, shares have risen almost 25%. "The market is telling us that this company is turning the corner," says Morgan Stanley Dean Witter auto analyst Stephen J. Girsky. And GM is likely to create more investor buzz on January 29 when analysts get a sneak peak at future models. Says Seth M. Glickenhaus of Glickenhaus & Co., a GM stockholder: "Finally, these people are coming out of their Rip Van Winkle sleep."

Investors are now counting on the 45-year-old Wagoner to keep up the momentum. Promoted last fall to president of GM's $130 billion global auto operations—which account for three-quarters of total revenues—Wagoner has played a pivotal role in getting GM back into fighting trim. His slow-but-steady overhaul of the North American unit won him the post—and has made him the leading candidate to succeed John F. Smith Jr., GM's 60-year old chairman and CEO. Smith, who has leaned heavily on Wagoner for years, credits him with doing a "superb" job. "We had to change virtually everything," Smith says. "Some things hadn't been touched since the beginning of time." The results are plain. After an $86 million loss in 1997, GM's North America auto business posted a $1.6 billion profit in 1998 and could soar to $3 billion in 1999. The improving outlook has won Wagoner kudos from the board as well. Says director John G. Smale: "GM under Wagoner has made more money in North America than it had in decades before him."

"NO PLAN B." Still, the year ahead will be Wagoner's acid test. The core of Wagoner's strategy for transforming GM has been a thorough renovation of its sagging product lineup. In the past two years, Wagoner has overseen the launch of 20 models—27% of GM's total 75 offerings—the Silverado and Sierra

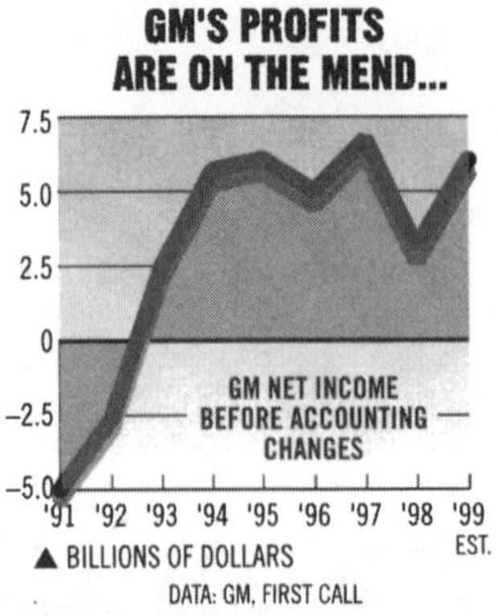

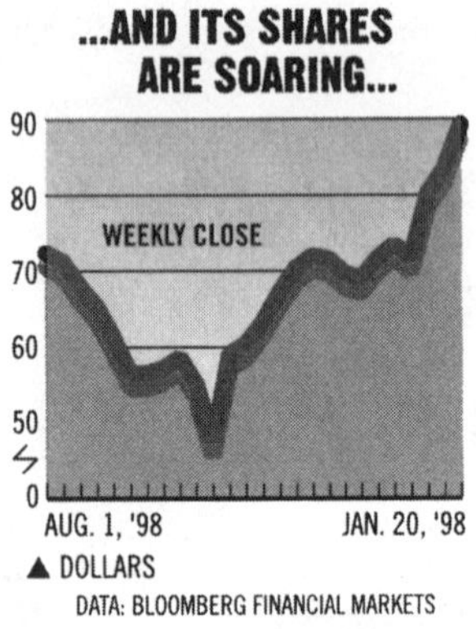

CHARTS BY ERIC HOFFMANN/BW

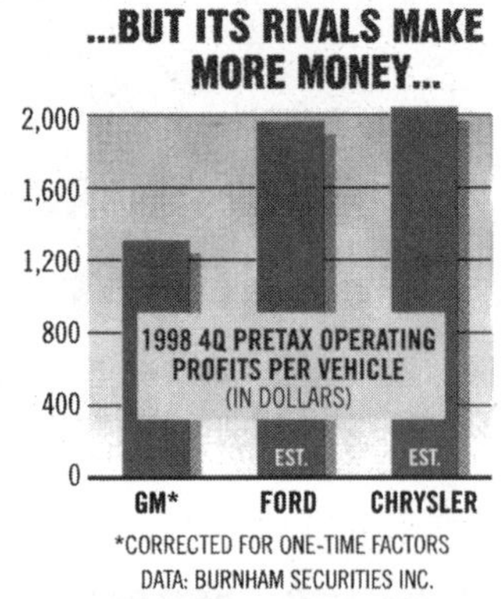

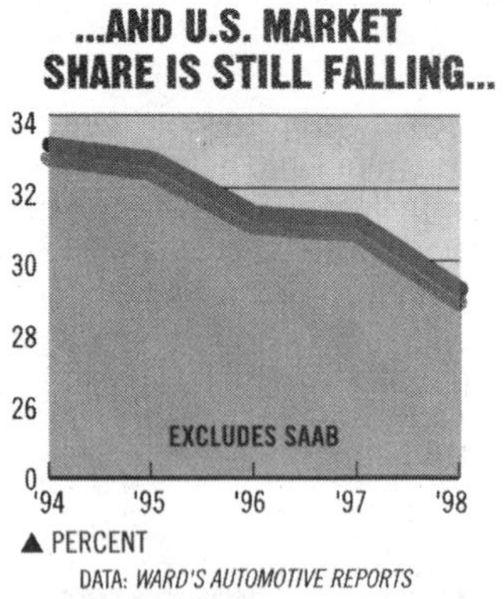

pickups, as well as a host of minivans and midsize cars. And later this year, GM will introduce four new SUVs, which could give another big jolt to profits. Wagoner and Smith had expected the new models to recharge GM's results throughout last year, but the strike cost it much momentum. In 1999, there are no excuses. "This is where the rubber hits the road," says Roy S. Roberts, GM's North American marketing chief. "There is no Plan B."

So how are they doing? Early indications seem promising: Sales of GM's redesigned minivans, such as the Chevy Venture and the Pontiac Montana, have more than doubled since 1995, the last year before redesigned models arrived. Sales for the seven new midsize models are up a more modest 5% since 1997, but even in this hugely competitive arena, GM has its stars: The Buick Century family sedan gained 38% for the year, while the Chevy Malibu rose 36%.

That's good—but is it good enough? For all his success, Wagoner still faces huge challenges. Overseas, Brazilian and Asian units are wracked by economic woes, even as GM's European operation—long one of the company's most profitable units—struggles to regain its footing. His biggest job, though, will be halting GM's decades-long market-share slide in the U.S. In the four years Wagoner headed the NAO's $94 billion business, GM's share of the U.S. market slipped down a further four percentage points, to 29.2%. The precipitous fall reflects myriad problems that can be boiled down to this: Many people today are turned off by GM cars. "At the end of the day, what really counts is the hardware," says Joseph S. Phillippi, an analyst at Lehman Brothers Inc. "GM is still, in most respects, one generation behind all its competitors."

Despite recent efforts to rejuvenate GM's brands and the progress with a smattering of new models, names like Oldsmobile and Buick seem tired. Even worse, GM remains years behind rivals in shifting production to the popular pickup and SUV models. And as car buyers defected in droves, GM has been left with a huge infrastructure of poorly located, aging dealerships and underutilized, outdated factories. Certainly, GM has made huge strides. But unless it generates excitement over new

WAGONER IS DRVING GM FORWARD . . . BUT HE STILL FACES MAJOR CHALLENGES

Restored domestic auto profits from a $982 million loss in 1993 to a $1.6 billion gain in '98 and an estimated $3 billion in '99.

➤ Whittled seven vehicle groups down to one car unit and one truck unit.

➤ Trimmed its product portfolio from 89 models in 1994 to 75 by dropping such slow sellers as the Chevy Caprice, Buick Roadmaster, Cadillac Fleetwood, and Buick Skylark. Merged GMC division with Pontiac.

➤ Streamlined product development by appointing one manager to head each vehicle program, replacing a mishmash of chief engineers, manufacturing bosses, and marketing managers.

➤ Cut manufacturing time by 10%, to an average of 30 hours per vehicle, and reduced the U.S. hourly workforce 14%, to 229,000 employees—all since '94. Closed two plants, with two more to shut down in '99.

➤ Needs to reach a new pact with the UAW while spinning off its unionized Delphi parts unit and replacing factories with new ones requiring fewer workers.

➤ Must develop breakthrough car and truck models to halt GM's 20-year slide in U.S. market share. Just 29.2% last year, it was 49% in '67.

➤ Needs to increase GM's sales of trucks, minivans, and SUVs from 47% of total vehicles sales to improve the company's lagging profits per vehicle.

➤ Must improve marketing efforts to lure younger consumers and more aggressively kill off dated, poorly performing models.

DATA: GENERAL MOTORS CORP., HARBOUR & ASSOCIATES, BUSINESS WEEK

HOT SELLERS
Chevy Corvette
Buick Century
Saturn 3-Door Coupe

models and coaxes buyers back into its showrooms, GM faces many more years of cutbacks.

MORE DRAMATIC? For all the problems Wagoner has solved, however, he still needs to do more to boost GM's profitability, which continues to lag the competition'S. Net profit margins for the first half of 1998—before the strike wiped out earnings—fell back to 2.7%, right where they were when Wagoner took over the NAO's in 1994. Meantime, Ford's margins for the period were 6.2% and growing, while Chrysler hit 6.7%. With GM's fourth-quarter margins roaring back to 5.7%, the outlook is brightening as GM snaps back from the effects of the strike. But, as production levels off later this year, it won't be easy to sustain those levels.

GM's critics say the profit lag points to the need for an even more dramatic remake of GM's product lineup. They argue that Wagoner needs to push harder for exciting new cars that will grab consumers. Volkswagen can point to its cute new Beetle, Ford has its lucrative Expedition SUVs, and Chrysler its pulse-pounding Dodge Viper. But even GM's brand-new Silverado, for which Wagoner has high expectations, is boxy and conservative compared with the competition. Says Merrill Lynch & Co. analyst Nicholas Lobaccaro: "The only way to truly fix this company is through a product renaissance."

With Smith focusing on strategy and trade issues, that job now falls squarely on Wagoner. But little in his background, or his makeup, suggests he's likely to push for more radical change. A consensus-builder who methodically works his way through complex problems, Wagoner is the latest in a long line of GM insiders to get a shot at fixing GM. The quintessential company man, he has worked for GM since he graduated from Harvard business school in 1977, joining the auto company as an analyst in its New York treasurer's office.

During those 22 years, he has earned a reputation as a demanding boss, one who combines self-deprecating humor with a competitive streak honed during years of cutthroat basketball games. But he is also a conciliatory team player able to bring warring GM factions together. In a stint as CFO of GM Europe a decade ago, for instance, Wagoner was able to get GM's notoriously turf-conscious Swiss, German, and British units working smoothly together. "He does what's best for the company, not what's best for him personally," says Robert J. Eaton, now DaimlerChrysler co-chairman and the former head of GM Europe. "He's a very apolitical guy."

He has also come far from his roots in finance. As he moved quickly through a series of fast-track jobs in the U. S., Canada, and Latin America early in his career, co-workers remember

RICK WAGONER

BORN 1953

EDUCATION Duke University, B.A. economics, 1975. Harvard, MBA, 1977

FIRST GM JOB Financial analyst at the New York Office

CURRENT JOB President of GM.

WHAT HIS JOB IS LIKE "Juggling while running on a treadmill."

CLAIM TO FAME Fixed GM's ailing Brazilian operations in the early '90s. Later, as CFO of GM, he overhauled the company's balance sheet. He also played a pivotal role in streamlining operations, helping to halt multibillion-dollar losses.

OFFICE DECOR Duke jersey of Detroit Pistons star—and now Chevy pitchman—Grant Hill. A Duke banner signed by GM factory workers. A size XXL pair of boxer shorts emblazoned with GM slogan "Plan to Win."

FIRST CAR A silver 1973 Camaro purchased with money from summer jobs.

WHAT HE DRIVES NOW 1999 Chevy Surburban jumbo SUV.

FAVORITE MOTIVATIONAL TOOL Awarding Twinkies, which he dispenses for any job well done. "If you tasted one today and then tasted it next year, it would taste exactly the same."

FAMILY Married, and has three sons, ages 15, 13, and 8.

FAVORITE HANGOUT Sidelines of middle-school football games, where he coaches his eldest son's team.

that he gamely learned the ins and outs of every aspect of the business. DaimlerChrysler Senior Vice-President Gary L. Henson, who worked at GM's Vauxhall Motors Ltd. in Britain in the 1980s, recalls being teamed with the young finance whiz

HOPEFULS
Chevy Silverado
Cadillac Escalade
Oldsmobile Intrigue

at a manufacturing workshop. Their task was to boost efficiency in the "cut-and-sew" area where seat covers were stitched together. He was amazed to see Wagoner plunge into the nitty-gritty of the shop floor. Marvels Henson: "He was up half the night, rearranging sewing machines."

It wasn't until 1991, however, that Wagoner got a chance to prove his mettle on the operations side. Taking over as head of Brazilian operations, he found them in chaos when he arrived in São Paulo. Wagoner showed that he had matured into far more than a number-cruncher. He was among the first in the auto industry to realize that Brazilians were no longer willing to accept decades-old models from Europe and the U. S. Employing the lean manufacturing techniques he had learned in Europe, he quickly built less expensive Brazilian versions of new Opel-designed cars and U.S.-engineered pickup trucks. "Rick got the whole product lineup modernized, well ahead of the competition," says Mark T. Hogan, the GM manager who ran things after Wagoner. "He read the tea leaves early on."

Wagoner's successes didn't go unnoticed back in Detroit, where—on the heels of 1991's $8 billion domestic auto loss—a boardroom coup had put Smith in charge. Just 16 months after he arrived in São Paulo, Smith named the then 39-year-old Wagoner CFO of the entire corporation. "He did a great job in Europe" and "really charged up that operation" in Brazil, says Smith. "He showed great leadership skills."

Wagoner became a member of the powerful inner circle that Smith brought in to perform triage on GM's battered domestic operations. With losses running $16 million a day, it was GM's darkest hour. As CFO, Wagoner made important contributions early on. One of his biggest: engineering a $6 billion contribution of EDS-backed stock to trim the company's gaping $24 billion pension deficit. He also restored the auto maker's credibility on Wall Street by replacing fancy accounting practices with a more conservative approach.

CONCILIATORY. Wagoner's talent as a peacemaker also helped GM weather its crisis. When GM purchasing czar José Ignacio "Inaki" López de Arriortúa bolted for Volkswagen in 1993, for instance, Smith charged Wagoner with making López' $4 billion in price cuts stick. The challenge: López had left behind a trail of enraged suppliers, who were upset by his tearing up of contracts and other high-handed tactics. Wagoner took a conciliatory approach—but gave back few of López' price cuts. Instead, he sought cooperation and listened to suppliers. "People felt more like participating voluntarily," recalls Kenneth L. Way, chairman of seatmaker Lear Corp. Smith was so impressed by Wagoner's handling of both finance and purchasing that he chose Wagoner to succeed him in running GM's North American auto unit in 1994.

Ever since, Wagoner has been working doggedly to reinvent the way GM designs, builds, and sells its cars. A crucial step has been revamping GM's problem-ridden manufacturing techniques, especially the all-critical changeover process from an old model to a new one. Once an industry laughingstock because of the months it took for model changeovers, GM's recent launches, notably last year's kickoff of the Grand Am sedan and the Silverado pickup truck, have been far smoother.

Drawing on his international experience, Wagoner has also worked to get more leverage out of GM's global expertise. He ordered his Michigan engineers to begin cooperating with their international counterparts to share platforms, engines, transmissions, and other key components. The move will allow GM to make Saturn, Chevy, and Pontiac models from the same chassis it uses to build Opels in Europe. And the number of platforms GM uses globally should drop from 22 today to 14 by 2005, holding out the promise of billions of dollars a year in savings.

At the same time, Wagoner recast GM's archaic product-development system along lines favored by Toyota Motor Corp. and other carmakers. Doing away with a mishmash of chief engineers and marketers who used to jostle for control at each stage, Wagoner shifted responsibility for each truck and car platform to a single executive. Today, these managers oversee a model's development from the early stages of design until it rolls off the assembly line. They also have profit-and-loss responsibility for their vehicles—another first at GM.

Given the strong results the shift has produced, it's easy to see why Smale counts it as one of Wagoner's biggest accomplishments. The head of the full-size pickup program, for instance, has mobilized his team to design the pickup with 25% fewer parts. That, in turn, has enabled factory workers to assemble Silverados 10% faster than previous models.

WAGONER PINS HIS HOPES ON FULL-SIZE PICKUPS LAUNCHED LAST FALL—SUCH AS THE SILVERADO

TOUGH DEMANDS. Indeed, as many of Wagoner's core organizational, engineering, and manufacturing reforms come together in the new generation of vehicles, nowhere is progress clearer than in GM's improving outlook in the highly profitable truck market. GM recently announced it would crank out 977,000 of its brand-new Chevy Silverado and GMC Sierra pickups this year, a 34% leap from the 727,000 built in 1998. Even compared with 1997, a year with far less labor strife, truck production will jump a healthy 11%. Better still, Wagoner expects premium features for which consumers are willing to pay more to add a full 2% to net profits on the new trucks. All told, Wasserstein Perella & Co. analyst Scott Merlis estimates GM's aftertax pickup-truck profits could soar by $1 billion in 1999.

There's more where that came from. GM will launch four new sport-utilities into the red-hot market for full-size SUVS late this year: the Chevy and GMC Suburbans, the Chevy Tahoe, and the GMC Yukon. With all based on the Silverado chassis, analysts figure the $6 billion in revenues from these SUVS will haul in similar profit increases.

Having focused much of his early energy on GM's core manufacturing and design difficulties, Wagoner has more recently turned to another perennial GM problem—spiraling warranty costs. And in the process, the usually gregarious manager has also proved he can be tough when he needs to be. Eighteen months ago, with warranty costs totaling a hefty 5% of net sales, Wagoner summoned senior North American managers to the company's design dome. Reduce warranty costs to 2% by 2001, to save $1 billion, or look for another job, he ordered. So far, GM has hit its interim targets, says Hogan, who now runs North American small-car operations: "He absolutely demanded it."

Wagoner is also learning how to deal with the thorny labor issues that have beset him and Smith for years. Long a hard-liner, Wagoner's efforts to increase productivity and assign more work to outside suppliers helped provoke 13 strikes, at a cost of more than $4 billion, over the past three years. As recently as last Memorial Day, Wagoner fueled the fire by ordering dies removed from a Flint factory that was about to start making critical truck parts.

DUDS

Cadillac Catera
Chevy Camaro
Chevy Lumina

It was a huge and costly mistake. Infuriated workers immediately brought all of GM to a screeching halt in a strike that would ultimately shave $2 billion off of '98 profits for little gain. "Just add that to the list of the other million things where we probably made the wrong call," Wagoner concedes now.

Since then, however, Wagoner has softened his approach. He recently consulted with top United Auto Workers leaders before naming new labor head Gary Cowger, whose years on the factory floor had earned the union's respect. "They were looking for someone who could work well with the union," says UAW President Stephen P. Yokich. And Wagoner now participates far more frequently in meetings and phone calls with union leaders. "We're opening up the dialogue a lot more," he says.

That sort of cooperation is having an impact. Company and union officials are close to resolving union objections to GM's plans to replace older factories with newer plants that use just half as many workers. As part of the deal, the two sides are hashing out details of GM's proposal to assign work to outside suppliers, who would build entire sections of cars. To gain union support, GM is offering to back UAW efforts to unionize supplier plants. Even so, by unloading fixed costs such as factories and parts inventories to suppliers, Wagoner figures he can cut overall costs well below current levels.

Wagoner is also counting on closer union ties to smooth the way for GM's spin-off of Delphi, its $28.5 billion parts unit. GM plans a $1.5 billion initial public offering in early February and expects to divest the remainder of Delphi to its stockholders later this year (box, "Delphi Pushes a Peace Program"). Keeping the peace will be key: Wagoner needs the Delphi spin-off to give another big boost to the efforts to reduce costs. Until now, he has been hampered by GM's obligation to buy Delphi parts, even when outside suppliers were cheaper or could handle more of the assembly task.

It all sounds promising. But will it be enough? Many experts believe Wagoner has just taken the initial steps in the uphill climb to revive GM. And his accomplishments may simply not be enough, according to some large investors. "The feeling is that these guys are not in a hurry," says Timothy M. Ghriskey, manager of the Dreyfus Fund, a big GM shareholder. "GM has a lot of catching up to do."

Here's why: Compared with the other big auto companies, GM still lags in almost every category. The biggest problem remains weak profit margins, even though GM's average profits per vehicle skyrocketed in the fourth quarter. Burnham Securities analyst David B. Healy estimates that GM made roughly $1,300 on each vehicle, corrected for the post-strike buildup and unusually low rebates. Though well above the roughly $874 GM made in 1998's first quarter, it's still much less than the estimated $1,872 Ford pulled in or the $2,266 Chrysler made. The new truck and SUV models, moreover, may not be enough to compensate for the less than stellar performance of GM's extensive car lineup. Overall mid-size car sales dropped 15% last year from 1995, the year before GM began revamping them. And GM's share of that segment slid from 35% to 29%, according to *Ward's Automotive Report.* "What have they put out, other than the Corvette, that created any buzz?" asks Wesley R. Brown, an analyst at Nextrend Inc., a Thousand Oaks (Calif.) auto consulting firm. "There's no emotion or passion surrounding any of their vehicles."

Many critics are urging Wagoner to scrap poorly performing models. GM has too many models—and too many facilities to produce them—for all of them to thrive. Indeed, the snazziest new models may simply be cannibalizing GM, rather than snatching share from rivals. Strong selling cars, like the Chevy Malibu or Buick Century, steal sales from older models. Sales of the bread-and-butter Chevy Lumina, for instance, plunged 22% last year, as many Chevy customers switched to the Malibu. And some new models have fizzled, pulling in far fewer sales than the older models they have replaced. Sales of the redesigned Olds Cutlass, at 53,000 last year, are down 59% from the 1995 sales of the Ciera, the car that it replaced.

Wagoner has made some moves in the right direction. To help clear the way for new models, he pulled the plug in 1994 on GM's three large, rear-wheel-drive cars—the Chevy Caprice, Buick Roadmaster, and Cadillac Fleetwood. It wasn't an easy move. "These are agonizing decisions," he says. But, in truth, he will need to make many more such painful choices in the near future or risk tying up resources in building poor performers that could be better employed building trucks and SUVS.

In the meantime, GM's much-ballyhooed brand-management efforts to tackle the problem of overlapping, look-alike models have not yet panned out.

SO FAR, THE NEW PACKAGE-GOODS BRANDING BROUGHT IN BY ZARRELLA HAS NOT PANNED OUT

Wagoner has been relying heavily on Ronald L. Zarrella, hired four years ago from Bausch & Lomb Inc. as marketing chief, to introduce packaged-goods-style brand management for cars. GM is building 10 midsize models from just three platforms, for example, with each model tweaked to appeal to different consumers. The Century, for instance, is a traditional bench-seat Buick with a floaty ride, while the Buick Regal, based on the same chassis, has zippier handling and bucket seats. The Pontiac Grand Prix has muscle and sporty styling, while the sleeker Olds Intrigue that rolls off the same assembly line aims directly at import-driving baby boomers.

The problem facing Zarrella, who succeeded Wagoner as head of the NAO in October, is that consumers aren't really buying into the branding strategy. Sales of the redesigned Grand Prix were down 7% in 1998 while Regal, Century, and Intrigue sales haven't surpassed pre-brand-management levels. Even stand-out cars that should sell well don't because of the negative baggage of some GM brands. The appealing Intrigue offers an object lesson. "If that car carried the Toyota name, instead of Oldsmobile, it would be the hands-down best-seller in the category," says ING Barings Furman Selz analyst Maryann Keller. But GM sold only a disappointing 91,000 Intrigues last year. Says auto consultant John Wolkonowicz: "They're proving they can't sell Oldsmobiles, no matter how wonderful they make them."

Indeed, no amount of brand management can overcome a fundamental truth: Many of GM's brands still appeal primarily to older buyers. Even GM's most aggressive attempts to lure well-heeled baby boomers have backfired badly. Cadillac's $35,000 Catera, for instance, which was supposed to set a hipper, younger tone for GM's flagship division, needs $1,000 rebates to move a paltry 25,000 cars a year. And the average age of a Catera buyer remains 53.

"OLD MAN." Even in those segments where GM is making strong progress, Wagoner needs to do more—and soon. Despite recent big gains in truck and SUV production, such vehicles still ac-

DELPHI PUSHES A PEACE PROGRAM

When executives from GM's Delphi Automotive Systems unit hit the road on Jan. 25 to drum up investors for next month's initial public offering, they'll have help from some surprising allies. Union leaders, including some who forced the shutdown of General Motors Corp.'s auto unit just two years ago, are rallying to the cause of spinning off the parts giant. "I should go out and promote my team," says Harold W. "Nick" Nichols, chief negotiator for 14,500 Delphi workers represented by the International Union of Electronic, Electrical, Salaried, Machine, & Furniture Workers (IUE).

That's a remarkable shift, but Nichols and other union leaders figure that if they can help make Delphi a winner, they'll have more leverage at the bargaining table in the future. Even the more militant United Auto Workers (UAW), with its 46,000 Delphi members, isn't likely to throw a wrench into the spin-off plans. Although top leaders oppose the spin-off, some plant-level union leaders realize that cooperation may be the only way to save their jobs. Says Gary Hill, president of Local 696 at GM's Dayton brake factory, long a trouble spot for GM labor relations: "There's too much riding on the line for 'He said, she said.' "

Now Chief Executive J. T. Battenberg III is keeping his fingers crossed that labor peace lasts. "We are trying to build a future together," he says. Small wonder. With some on Wall Street fearful that a renewed strike threat could scare away investors, bad news on the labor front could depress Delphi's stock. In the first phase of the spin-off, GM hopes to raise more than $1.5 billion by selling 17.7% of Delphi for 15 to 18 a share. The rest will be divested by late 1999.

MORE DISCLOSURE To ensure he has plenty of maneuvring room, Battenberg wants to negotiate a national labor agreement separate from the one GM will negotiate with its unions later this summer. Delphi's unions will likely fight that plan, but Battenberg hopes to win them over by disclosing more financial information to them than GM typically would. What they'll see isn't pretty: Delphi reported earnings before restructuring charges of just $370 million last year, on sales down 9%, to $28.5 billion.

Battenberg figures that as they pore over the numbers together, labor leaders will help him push through cost-cutting programs and more flexible work rules. Ultimately, though, he will also need wage cuts that the union now opposes. If all goes according to plan, Battenberg will be able to boost efficiency and make Delphi more competitive with nonunion suppliers.

Merely getting out from under the GM structure should go a long way. For starters, Delphi will be better positioned to win business from rival auto makers. Delphi now gets about 65% of revenues from GM's North American unit and another 16% from GM abroad. Battenberg wants to get North America down to 50%.

Still, Delphi has a rough road ahead. It will be hard pressed to compete against nonunion shops, whose workers earn about one-third the pay and benefits of Delphi's unionized employees. With a GM supply contract that guarantees Delphi the right to match the lowest bid on any GM contract until 2002, Delphi will have a couple of years before it truly has to fly on its own. But after that, GM will be free to take its business elsewhere. "Delphi has been in the GM cocoon so long, the risk is that they'll find the real world pretty cold out there," says Burnham Securities analyst David B. Healy. True enough, but it hasn't been too hot within GM lately, either.

By Joann Muller in Detroit

counted for only 47% of GM's sales in 1998, compared with 71% at Chrysler and 61% at Ford. "The truck trend went much faster than our people ever expected," concedes Wagoner. Playing catch-up won't be easy. Japanese carmakers have solid hits with models such as Toyota's RAV4, Honda Motor Co.'s CR-V, and Subaru's Forester. And while crossovers from Ford and Chrysler will arrive next year, GM's versions—such as the models Wagoner introduced at the auto show—are at least two years away.

For all GM's continuing problems, Wagoner appears supremely self-assured—and some insiders find him even a bit complacent. Says one senior GM manager: "Rick is an old young man at GM." He rejects suggestions that he needs to do more to spark sales, because he sees evidence that they are already on the upswing. While he admits GM's lineup could use more flair Wagoner is confident the organization now has "the passion, intensity, and thoughtfulness" to deliver that.

That hardly sounds like the radical steps many in the auto industry prescribe for GM. The consensus is that Wagoner needs to move quickly to kill more car models, close or merge marketing divisions, and rescue standouts like Saturn by giving it more models to sell. "They've got to bite the bullet," says Wolkonowicz. "What's wrong with letting Buick die?" Wagoner doesn't see it that way, though he won't make any promises about keeping divisions or models that don't earn their way. "Nobody's future is guaranteed," he says. Wagoner and his team have declared that 1999 will be the year that the auto maker reverses its 20-year decline in market share. For that to happen, many of the models he's banking on—including a much-anticipated Saturn compact sedan and a reinvented Chevy Impala—will have to do well.

Wagoner remains confident that he can pull it off. "You kind of get a gut feeling that you're on the right track," he says. If he succeeds over the next couple of years, Wagoner will likely have earned himself the CEO job. If he doesn't, the GM board will be under increasing pressure to look outside the company for its next leader. Although Smale says no such move was contemplated when Wagoner was named president, the stakes get higher from here on out. With GM's biggest problems—shrinking market share and underperforming profits still looming large, Rick Wagoner's toughest job still lies ahead.

By Kathleen Kerwin, with Joann Muller in Detroit

Unit 5

Unit Selections

41. **Why Sizzler Fizzled: As Competition Heated Up, Chain's Concept Went Stale,** Glenn Collins
42. **Whirlwind on the Web,** *Business Week*
43. **The New VIP Rooms,** Lisa Gubernick
44. **Lack of Shopping Carts Impact Sales at Traditional Department Stores,** Joseph B. Cahill
45. **The Deal Is Done. Now the Work Begins,** Claudia H. Deutsch
46. **The Balanced Scorecard—Measures That Drive Performance,** Robert S. Kaplan and David P. Norton
47. **Cendant: Who's to Blame?** *Business Week*
48. **A Bit of Barnum on Broadway; Livent Drew in a New Team Despite Juggling Expenses,** Melody Petersen and Geraldine Fabrikant
49. **The Lesson from Barings' Straits,** *Business Week*
50. **How One Firm Tracks Ethics Electronically,** Michael J. McCarthy

Key Points to Consider

❖ Once determined, an organization must design the appropriate organizational form and have the necessary resources to turn a strategy into a reality.

❖ Accounting measures give a narrow perspective of organizational performance. Crucial elements such as customer and employee satisfaction are not reflected.

❖ Because so many activities are entrusted to individual employees, firms need to design a mechanism to monitor ethical conduct.

DUSHKIN ONLINE Links

www.dushkin.com/online/

29. **Murray G. Bacon Center for Ethics in Business**
http://www.public.iastate.edu/~BACON_CENTER/ homepage.html
30. **Center for Strategic Management**
http://www.csmweb.com/body_index.html
31. **Competitive Intelligence Guide**
http://www.fuld.com/index.html
32. **MELNET**
http://www.bradford.ac.uk/acad/mancen/melnet/index0.html

These sites are annotated on pages 4 and 5.

Implementing, Measuring, and Controlling Strategy

Organizations may propose new strategies or changes in existing strategies, but until they are put into operation, they are only concepts. Once a strategic choice has been formulated, the task of management is to make it work. Formulating a strategic plan is an intellectual process for management. Implementing it is an operational process. Good strategies, well implemented, produce successful outcomes. Poor strategies, poorly implemented, lead to disasters. A good strategy poorly implemented alerts rival forces to an opportunity. A poor strategy that is well implemented gives an organization a chance to adapt it and to enjoy some possible success.

In his seminal work *Strategy and Structure,*[1] Alfred D. Chandler Jr. provided the model that would become the building block of strategic management. Studying the significant changes in strategies by several organizations, Chandler identified a four-step process. First, companies changed their strategies to improve their competitive positions. When the strategies were introduced, the organizational structure that had been in place to serve the old strategy no longer functioned effectively, and company efficiency decreased measurably. In response, the organization was forced to change the structure of the firm. With the new, more appropriate form, the firms achieved high levels of productivity and profitability. The most famous example is the move by General Motors and other large firms to decentralize management. This new organizational form allowed long-range strategic decisions to be made at the corporate level, while authority and responsibility for business level strategies rested with the middle managers.

Companies that intend to compete as price leaders need structures and management that support strict cost controls and highly efficient manufacturing and distributional systems. Conversely, those who offer a differentiated, premium-priced product need structures that promote quick response, innovation, and loyal customer and distributor networks.

As we examine information age companies, it is quickly apparent that tall, autocratic structures cannot serve modern knowledge-based operations. Changes in workers' philosophies and ethics mandate a totally revised set of rules, procedures, and policies. Many "new economy" organizations refuse to consider having organizational charts. Significant changes in physical resources are often required to carry out the strategies of e-commerce and Internet companies. Centralization becomes meaningless when thousands of workers can be joined electronically from offices all over the globe.

When an organization commits to a new strategy, or when it decides to continue its existing one, it needs to measure the progress or the success to determine if, indeed, it is going in the right direction. In the strategic management sense, control does not imply exertion of power so much as it does monitoring and evaluating a strategy. It entails measuring the firm's performance in relation to its goals and missions and in relation to its competitive environment.

While many measures test qualitative outcomes such as employee satisfaction, customer response rates, and public relations, the majority of measures still remain financial and statistical. Budgets, income statements, and balance sheets reduce the strategic plan or the results of a strategy to a relatively cold and concise set of ratios. These ratios are then compared to previous years' performance and to industry standards.

Unfortunately, these ratios only tell part of the story. Equally disturbing is the way in which financial measures can be manipulated and distorted. More comprehensive measures such as return on value added have been developed to capture a richer description of the firm's performance. Despite what appear to be strict controls, the increased access that employees have to information often provides some with ample means to circumvent the system.

Several events suggest that the measurement of strategies will change greatly and will have a substantial impact on how strategies are chosen. Stricter rules of disclosure exist in the United States than in most other industrialized countries. As globalization increases through added mergers of international companies, information previously kept proprietary will become public knowledge. Policies and procedures that vary between and among countries will need to be harmonized.

A country that has a controlled press will learn quickly that a free-market economy is not possible without full knowledge of prices and transactions and that any attempt to influence or limit access will not allow that process to go forward.

Increased autonomy at every level suggests that controls need to address the social and ethical issues of a firm and of its employees. Changing values of employees, and changing demands by the organization, suggest reexamining traditional control and measurement techniques. A new set of employee-management relations has emerged in regard to new technologies such as e-mail and working at home. Knowledge-based systems must be based on trust if they are to be effective. Control measures need to measure what is important, to reward rather than punish, to enable rather than to command.

1. Chandler, Alfred D., Jr., *Strategy and Structures: Chapters in the History of the Industrial Enterprise,* M.I.T. Press, Cambridge, MA: 1990.

WHY SIZZLER FIZZLED AS COMPETITION HEATED UP, CHAIN'S CONCEPT WENT STALE

Glenn Collins, ***New York Times Service***

Woe unto the restaurant chain that fails to give Americans exactly what they want, at the moment they want it, and at just the price they want to pay.

These days, even as eating out continues to increase in popularity, restaurant companies are scrambling for customers in an ever more competitive environment.

Moderate-priced restaurants—the Denny's and Red Lobsters—are trying to keep up with tastes so fickle that only a few years ago red meat was spurned as a controlled substance, but it is now prized as a profitable menu item. At the same time these midlevel chains are being pummeled from below by fast-food outlets and squashed from above by slightly classier restaurants.

A victim of these changing tastes: Sizzler International Inc., the nationwide steakhouse chain, which filed for bankruptcy protection.

Although Sizzler called this a restructuring, "I'd call it a little bit more like something Jason would do in the Friday the 13th movies," said Bill Carlino, a senior editor at Nation's Restaurant News.

Why did Sizzler fizzle? "Sizzler got old, got banged up, didn't respond until it was too late," Carlino said. "And when they did, it was the wrong strategy."

Although older independents like Miami Beach's Joe's Stone Crab or Peter Luger's in New York City have had long runs and remain popular, "the life cycle for chain-restaurant concepts has gotten briefer," said Ron Paul, president of Technomic Inc., a Chicago-based restaurant consultant. "People are always looking for the new kid on the block."

Squeezed out by rivals, some fast-food chains provide menus nearly as broad as Sizzler's for a dollar or two less, while slightly more formal family restaurants offer sit-down dining for a dollar or two more. Sizzler got caught in the middle, unable to find just the right formula.

Customers edged away. "There are so many new places to go," said K. M. Woo, who used to be a more frequent patron but still eats about once a week in a Sizzler near his home in Tuckahoe, N.Y., and has also sampled Sizzlers in New Mexico and Texas.

Initially, adding salad bars and buffets was seen as a panacea for restaurants like Sizzler trying to slake customers' craving for variety. They also seemed the perfect answer to Americans' schizophrenic desire to eat healthier while consuming a prodigious amount of food—"gut-fill," as restaurant managers term it.

But buffet food takes a lot of labor to prepare and keep fresh all day, and brings much lower profits than entrees like steak. The expanse of buffet stations cuts down on seating capacity. And the foray by Sizzler into grazing muddied its bring-the-whole-family-down-to-the-steakhouse image.

Others suffering

Sizzler is hardly suffering alone. Shoney's, another midlevel chain, is also caught in a squeeze, with profit margins steadily eroding. Mexican-themed chains like Chi-Chi's and El Torito, both units of Family Restaurants Inc., are struggling.

Even some of Sizzler's more upscale steakhouse rivals, like Steak & Ale, are stagnant as they try to respond to the success of brash new competitors like Outback Steakhouse and Lone Star Steakhouse & Saloons.

What works? One model is Red Lobster, the nation's largest casual dining chain. Red Lobster, a unit of Darden Restaurants, has never abandoned its focus on seafood but has kept in tune with the tastes of middle-class Americans with design changes like a "wharfside" look, and it has remained competitive through aggressive price promotions.

"They have gone through three or four major transformations," said Paul, the consultant. "Without such changes, they would be doomed."

And Denny's, against long odds, has rebounded after a shakeup designed to end racial discrimination practiced at some of its restaurants. "They've never lost their focus as a broad-menu, midscale coffee shop," Paul said. Denny's is a unit of Flagstar Cos.

A look at Sizzler's up-and-down story gives a taste of the risks at this level of the restaurant game.

Appetite for red meat

Sizzler and other steakhouse chains were gored by the decline in demand for red meat more than a decade ago, when, as Paul put it, "Dad was told he can't have steak three or four nights a week any more."

For a while Sizzler ignored the trend, but then, faced with declining sales, it began a dizzying series of special menus, salad bars and buffet extravaganzas that confused customers.

The switch backfired, though, because Sizzler was not designed to make money on buffet items. The Sizzlers, originally configured as steakhouses, don't have room for 100-item food bars and can't generate the high volume that makes buffets profitable.

About five years ago, meanwhile, red meat started coming back into favor, and it is now "a major growth sector in the restaurant industry, if you think of the high-end chains like Morton's, and casual-dining chains like Outback and Lone Star," said David Leibowitz, a managing director of Burnham Securities who follows the restaurant industry.

That didn't help Sizzler, though, because "with the resurgence of interest in red meat, people decided that if they won't have it often, they'd rather do it right, with a better piece of steak," Paul said. So customers would pay a bit more elsewhere.

Indeed, Sizzler's woes signal trouble for a whole class of restaurants, a $3.4 billion group that those in the trade dub variously "family steakhouses," "grill-buffets" or "value steakhouses."

All in all, Sizzler, after 39 years, looked stale. "A new concept is only good for two or three years before you have to revitalize it in one fashion or another," Leibowitz said. "If people think of your restaurants as stale, your faithful patrons will become cleverly disguised as empty seats."

The Chapter 11 filing

That's the predicament Sizzler faced in filing June 3 for Chapter 11 protection, a move that analysts say it used as a way to get out of 136 unprofitable restaurant leases. This is a tactic previously used by retail chains.

The West Los Angeles-based Sizzler, which started in 1957 in a glorified trailer in Culver City, Calif., said it would take a $108.9 million charge against earnings, or $3.92 a share, resulting in a loss for the fiscal year.

It will be left in the United States with 85 company-owned units and 235 franchised restaurants, as well as 136 restaurants internationally. At least five restaurants in South Florida will remain open.

Sizzler's hope for the future is the more upmarket Sizzler American Grills, which feature table service, menus, and higher-quality food, implicitly acknowledging that the chain's offerings no longer measure up to what diners expect. The company hopes to convert all its restaurants to the format at an average cost of $130,000 apiece.

Kevin Perkins, Sizzler's president and chief executive, said the restructuring and Chapter 11 filing had returned the company to operating profitability. Indeed, Leibowitz said, it "will hasten the rollout of the Sizzler American Grills."

A RECIPE FOR DECLINE

Sizzler recently filed for bankruptcy protection largely because its menu and dining atmosphere couldn't keep up with new competition and the changing tastes of consumers. What went wrong?

BUFFETS: Many Sizzler restaurants were not designed for buffets, which require a lot of space and high turnover to be profitable. From a marketing perspective, buffets also de-emphasized Sizzler's image as a steakhouse, diminishing the restaurant's distinctiveness.

DECOR: Some of Sizzler's restaurants have a dated look, while many competitors have created atmospheres that are appealing and modern.

SERVICE: Sizzler, like similar restaurants, is being squeezed between fast-food chains that offer speed and value and family-dining chains that offer table service. Sizzler's cafeteria-style service has less appeal.

QUALITY OF FOOD: Sizzler sells cheaper meats than its competitors. But consumers are increasingly selective about quality when they eat red meat.

SOURCE: New York Times Service

WHIRLWIND ON THE WEB

Computer maker Dell is showing the world how to run a business in the Cyber Age

Michael S. Dell eases his Mercedes 500SL down the driveway of his $10 million mountaintop estate. Bundled against the cold in a sweater and ski parka, he guns the car as he pulls onto State Highway 1. He's in a rush, weaving the silver two-seater in and out of the early morning commuters as he heads for his office, a gleaming complex jutting up from the prairie lands of Round Rock, Tex., just north of Austin.

Fifteen minutes later, Dell reaches the center of his fast-rising computer empire. Today's first stop: the team responsible for making Dell Computer Corp. an Internet phenom, selling $1 million worth of computers a day on its Web site. Dell tosses off his parka and plows into a discussion on how to pump up sales even more. He wants Web pages tailored for corporate customers to order online. And he's impatient for a new feature that dashes a digital confirmation to customers within five minutes of placing an order—his way of reassuring buyers. Says Dell: "The Internet is one of the things I'm most excited about in our business."

For good reason. In just six months, Dell has gone from nowhere in cyberspace to being the No. 1 PC retailer on the Web—with sales growing 20% each month. For the Texas computer maker, electronic commerce is the perfect extension of the company's direct-sales business. Corporations and techno-savvy customers that were willing to buy over the phone are the first ones dialing in to purchase on the Web. "The Internet," says Dell, "is the ultimate direct model."

Suddenly, Dell looks like the right company at the right time. After years of skeptics predicting that the direct-sales approach, like mail-order clothing, would never amount to more than 15% of the market, Dell is cashing in on an altogether different scenario. Direct buyers now account for nearly a third of the PC business, up from 15% six years ago. Throw in an increasingly wired population that is just a mouse click away from buying over the Net, and direct marketers—Dell, Gateway 2000, and Micron Electronics—are sitting pretty.

HOT STOCK. But none are as well-positioned as Dell. In the past three years, it has been on a *jihad* to make its manufacturing and assembly process as fast and fine-tuned as Dell's Mercedes. Today, a custom order placed at 9 a.m. on a Monday can be on a delivery truck by 9 p.m. Tuesday. What's more, this speed has allowed Dell to slash inventories and keep parts costs down so low it can underprice its rivals by 10% to 15%.

> "Speed is everything in this business. We're setting the pace for the industry"
>
> MICHAEL DELL, chairman and CEO, Dell Computer Corp.

The result: Dell is now one of hightech's best growth engines. Last year, unit sales in the U. S. jumped 71%— more than five times the industry's 13.6% growth rate. That pushed revenues up 47%, to $7.8 billion, and, combined with Dell's low-cost style of doing business, sent profits skyrocketing 91%, to $518 million. The surge is expected to continue this year with sales hitting $10.2 billion. That could catapult Dell, which took root in a Texas college dorm room in 1984, from the No. 5 PC maker to No. 3, ahead of Packard Bell NEC, and Apple Computer.

For investors, owning Dell shares has been like putting hellum in their portfolios. The stock nearly quadrupled in 1996 and ran as high as $76 in February. With the selloff in high tech, Dell now trades at $67.50, up 27% this year—a greater rise than IBM, Compaq, Hewlett-Packard, Cisco Systems, even Intel and Microsoft. Dell's 23% return on equity last quarter was nearly triple that of PC king Compaq (at 7.9%).

What's Dell's secret? How has the computer maker managed to defy the naysayers and turn a classically low-margin mail-order operation into a high-profit, high-service business that's the envy of the industry? In a word: speed. Dell has long been a model of just-in-time manufacturing, but now it has upped the ante by applying the same brutal time standard to its supply chain— insisting, for example, that the bulk of its components be warehoused within 15 minutes of a Dell factory. Dell also has seized on the ultimate in low-cost, fast-paced business—electronic commerce. The combination puts Dell in the vanguard of manufacturers in any industry. "If you're good at both, you get a multiplier effect," says Robert E. MacAvoy, president of Easton Consultants, a Stamford, Conn. management consulting firm. "That is Dell."

The company calls it "velocity," squeezing time out of every step in the process—from the moment an order is taken to collecting the cash. Especially the cash. Dell converts the average sale to cash in less than 24 hours, by tapping credit cards and electronic payment. By contrast, industry giant Compaq Computer Corp., which sells primarily through dealers, takes 35 days, and even mail-order rival Gateway 2000 takes 16.4 days. "Speed is everything in this business," says Dell, whose 15% stake in the company is now worth $1.8 billion. "We're setting the pace for the industry." Think of it as Dellocity, a pace so fast that even whirlwind Silicon Valley has taken notice. "I have bruises on my back from Mr. Michael [Dell] when we can't keep up with them," says Intel CEO Andrew S. Grove.

That has rivals itching to do the same. PC makers, such as IBM, Compaq, and Hewlett-Packard are trying to imitate Dell with their own schemes to slash production time and boost service. IBM, for example, no longer assembles PCs for most of its corporate customers. Instead, computer dealers, such as MicroAge Inc., do the work. And in June, Compaq will begin rolling out its own Internet connection, allowing customers to manage everything from ordering a machine to scheduling software updates online. "If copying is the sincerest form of flattery, Dell's getting a lot of flattery right now," says Robertson, Stephens & Co. PC analyst Dan Niles.

Still, competitors have a ways to go to beat Dell at its own game. Take computer production. While machines from Compaq and IBM can languish on dealer shelves for two months, Dell doesn't start ordering components and assembling computers until an order is booked. That may sound like no biggie, but the price of PC parts can fall rapidly in just a few months. By ordering right before assembly, Dell figures. his parts, on average, are 60 days newer than those in an IBM or Compaq machine sold at the same time. That can translate into a 6% profit advantage in components alone.

Dell doesn't stop there. It has also found a way to get most suppliers to keep components warehoused just minutes from Dell's factories in Austin, Limerick, Ireland, and Penang, Malaysia In part, Dell has done this by reducing its number of suppliers to those that will cooperate with its warehousing plan. Dell now buys its components from just 47 companies, down from 204 companies in 1992.

MEXICAN PIPELINE. Keeping the flow of parts running smoothiy requires precise coordination. For this, Dell has turned to outside help. In the U. S., for example, Caliber Logistics Inc., a specialist in setting up efficient supply chains, manages a warehouse 15 minutes from Dell's Austin assembly plant. Suppliers restock the warehouse and manage their own inventories, while Caliber whisks the parts to Dell as needed. The best part: Dell doesn't get billed for the components until they leave the warehouse.

So far, the system is a time killer. STB Systems Inc., a maker of video graphics cards, stocks three weeks worth of its products in warehouses near Dell plants. The Richardson (Tex.) company also supplies Pc makers such as IBM, Compaq, and Gateway, but none are as streamlined as Dell. Were Compaq to suddenly need a rush supply, it could take 12 to 18 hours. IBM and Gateway, he says, could take two days. "Dell is different in that their inventory is minutes away—not hours or days," says STB procurement director Rick Spencer.

For high-cost items, such as the main circuit board—the heart of a computer—Dell has cut more time by switching to regional suppliers. Dell used to order in bulk from one supplier as a way to get discounts. No more. Last year, it went to three regional subcontractors instead of a single manufacturer for all. What it lost in discounts, it more than made up for in time. Now, Dell's Austin plant gets circuit boards trucked in

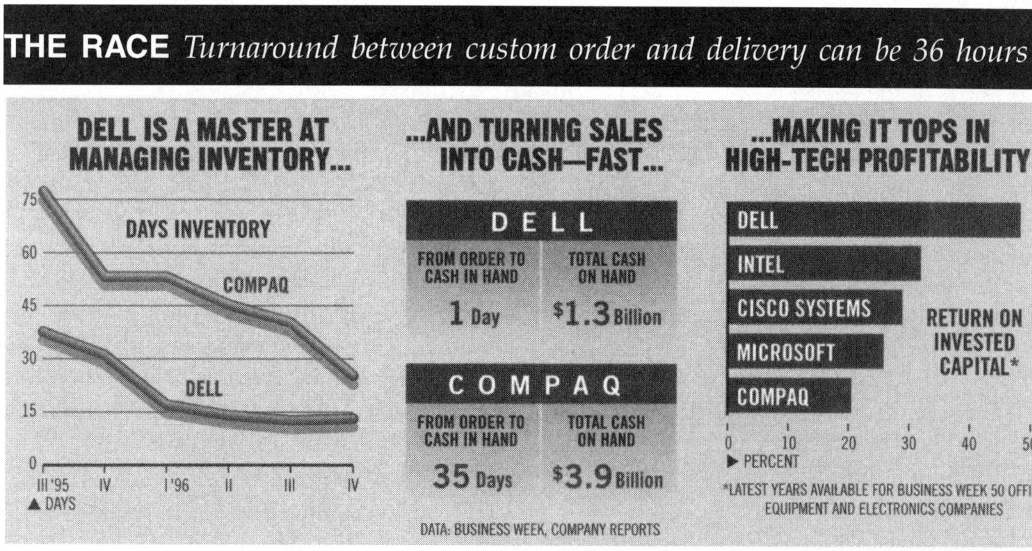

from Mexico in 15 hours, instead of 22 days by boat from its previous Indian supplier.

And then there's monitors. This year, Dell stopped accepting deliveries of video displays for its PCs. Instead, when a machine is ready to be shipped from any of its factories, Dell sends an E-mail message to a shipper, such as United Parcel Service. The shipper pulls a computer monitor from supplier stocks and schedules it to arrive with the PC. By no longer shipping monitors first to Dell and then on to buyers, Dell saves some $30 per display in freight costs.

where in the world they're needed—something the previous supplier, IBM, had failed to do several times. This helped Eastman slash its annual PC costs by $5 million a year, and made Dell its exclusive PC supplier. "Dell has done some wonderful things in customizing these machines," says Eastman's director of computing services, Charlie Oliver.

Today, the Dell machine is firing on all cylinders. In addition to being a PC juggernaut, Dell is moving fast into the $10 billion network server business. Dell's server business, while contributing just 6% of its total revenues, soared 300% last quarter.

"We spent 15 months educating [our] people about return on invested capital"

TOM MEREDITH, senior vice-president and CFO, Dell Computer Corp.

Such rethinking of operations lets Dell operate more efficiently than any other computer company. Its total inventories amount to 13 days of sales, vs. 25 days for Compaq. If this sounds like much ado about nothing, consider this: For every new dollar of capital investment last quarter, Dell shareholders got $1.54 back in profits, compared with 59¢ for Compaq and 47¢ for IBM.

BOLD PROMISE. One of Dell's tricks for managing inventories is shaping demand. In telephone sales, it can daily alter its suggested configurations to guide customers to PCs with widely available parts. As many as two-thirds of the telephone buyers accept the recommended configuration. And for big corporate buyers, who account for nearly 60% of sales, it holds annual "technology briefings" in which Dell offers its view of what key technologies are coming—and picks customers' brains on their needs, too.

It's paying off. At Eastman Chemical Co., Dell snared a contract for 10,000 PCs by guaranteeing all its machines would have the same parts and software regardless of when and In notebook PCs, Dell has become the sixth-largest seller in the $40 billion market.

Now, Dell is working on ways to combine its PC knowhow with better networking service. Through a partnership with network equipment maker 3Com Corp., Dell is trying to slash the 60 to 90 days required to test computer and networking configurations to just two weeks. Instead of each running independent tests of the same gear, Dell will deliver to 3Com each new computer so that 3Com can test compatibility with its networking devices. "There's a big advantage to getting product quickly to market with Dell," says 3Com CEO Eric H. Benhamou. "They know more directly what the customer wants."

Rivals are simply impressed. "At one time, we said only so many customers are willing to buy direct," says Larry Chang, controller for HP's PC business. "But it's increasing. Dell has proven us wrong," In an effort to catch Dell, HP started building business PCS to a customer's specification.

GRIM DAYS. It wasn't that long ago that the PC cognoscenti were predicting Michael Dell and his mail order model would hit the wall. It certainly came close. In the first six months of 1993, Dell had a $65 million loss from inventory writedowns and an industrywide price war started by Compaq.

But the close call was transformed into a lesson on the dangers of growth at all costs. Dell wised up and recruited operations-savvy managers from Motorola, Sun Microsystems, and Western Digital. Financial teams fanned out to talk with employees about new metrics for running the business—minimizing inventories and increasing return on capital. Today, the financial nitty-gritty is deeply ingrained in Dell's 10,350 employees. The marketing department calculates the return on investment for each mailing; purchasing managers figure the cost of unsold inventory each day. "We spent 15 months educating people about return on invested capital, convincing them they could impact our future," says Chief Financial Officer Thomas J. Meredith.

One way to get more bang for the buck: selling PCS over the Web, where Dell has a crew of only 30 people in contrast to the 700 reps that take orders over the phone. In coming months, Dell plans to make this even more attractive by creating custom home pages for its biggest buyers, including Eastman Chemical, Monsanto, and Wells Fargo. By midyear, Dell plans to deliver E-commerce set-ups to 75 companies. Their employees will be able to order a PC and automatically receive the corporate price.

For Dell, the online world promises even greater speed and cost savings. With Dell racing past rivals like Sunday drivers on the Information Highway, there may be a new pace for manufacturers in the Age of the Internet: Dell-ocity.

By Gary McWilliams
in Round Rock, Tex.

At the Movies

The New VIP Rooms

This may be the biggest revolution in films since talkies: Theaters are adding luxury screening rooms, with club chairs and waiters—yours for a few dollars more than a regular ticket. ***Lisa Gubernick*** *reports from the cineplex.*

IT'S FRIDAY NIGHT in Chicago, and Vince Ashby and his wife Cheryl are ready for a night on the town. She's aglow in her blue cocktail dress and high-heeled boots; he sports a navy blazer and spit-polished black loafers. "I really look forward to heading out for a fancy evening," he says.

Their dining room of choice is subtly lit by glowing torchieres. Waiters are bistro-mod in their black and white, mandarin-collared shirts. The Ashbys order deep-dish spinach pizza and Caesar salad, accompanied by a 1997 Hunter Ashby Merlot. In lieu of dessert: a $48 bottle of Taittinger Brut.

You might think this is one of the Windy City's sleek new eateries. But this "restaurant" is part of General Cinema's eight-month-old Premium Cinema, a 70-seat theater fit for a studio czar. After dinner, patrons retreat to an adjacent room of reclining leather seats, cocktail tables and carpeted walls to settle in for the film. "I've seen pictures of private screening rooms," says Mr. Ashby, a software engineer. "But this is the first time I've really experienced one."

So how did they get in? The screening room is part of the local cineplex, and all they did is buy a ticket. In one of the biggest revolutions in cinema since talkies, theater companies are opening such VIP-style screening rooms in cineplexes across the country. For a few dollars more than the price of a regular ticket, status-seeking moviegoers can now order from waiters, use private bathrooms and generally avoid mixing with hoi polloi next door.

In the next six months, GC Co.'s General Cinema Theatres Inc. is planning to open five more high-end screens: three in Baltimore and two in Milwaukee.

Loews Cineplex Entertainment Corp.'s Canadian unit has opened VIP rooms in Toronto and plans three more soon; its U.S. subsdiary expects to open several more in the next year. United Artists Theatres Circuit Inc. is overhauling one of the balconies in its spanking new 14-plex in New York City, for what President and Chief Executive Kurt Hall is calling a "club level," which he plans to open early next year.

Another pillar of American democracy has fallen. It used to be that everyone had to wait in the same movie lines, buy the same tickets and fight their way into the same seats. Now these major theater chains have discovered affordable snobbery—the same principle that drives consumers to spend $3 for a cup of coffee or pay extra to fly business class instead of coach. "I like being served," says Debbie Johnston, a human-resources executive who recently bought a VIP movie ticket in Toronto, "and I like being away from the hordes."

Why the push to posh? Partly because theater owners have overbuilt. During the past four years, the number of new movie screens in the U.S. has increased 19%—from 26,689 in 1994 to 31,865 in 1997. But the number of moviegoers is growing more slowly. Over the same period, ticket sales grew 8%, to 1.39 billion last year. Ticket sales increased just 4% in 1997 from 1996.

As screens multiply, theater owners are desperate for ways to distinguish them. "For this growth to make sense, we must increase our customer base," says Ken Prue, senior vice president of marketing for Loews' Canadian unit, Cineplex Odeon Corp. With tiered-stadium seating and top-flight sound systems becoming de rigueur, one way to attract new moviegoers is to offer them extra amenities.

The VIP treatment also plays right into a larger social trend: the democratization of status. These days, everybody wants to be special, especially when they're part of a mass audience. Whether it's watching sports from the box seats, rather than the bleachers, or ponying up a 78% premium for VIP tickets offered at Broadway's Ford Theater (which include access to a private cocktail lounge and restrooms), it's all a way to express the affluence that has drastically altered the American landscape.

"Status is no longer a part of nobility," says Paul Schervish, director of the Social Welfare Research Institute at Boston College. "Privilege is the province of those who can pay for it."

While most status symbols remain out of reach for most people, VIP movie tickets are affordable—at least occasionally—to the middle class. "For Mr. and Mrs. Joe Average, it's a great way to hang out with the upper crust, without taking out a second mortgage on your home," says Cineplex Odeon's Mr. Prue. And, occasionally, even real VIPs actually show up: At the Premium Cinema screening room, located just outside of Chicago, in Lombard, Ill., Rep. Henry Hyde recently watched "City of Angels," and R. Kelly, a top rhythm-and-blues singer, caught the film "Blade."

"When you're at one of these places, there's no way to know who's splurging and who isn't," says Prof. Schervish. "It's a place where the hoi polloi can be mistaken for the truly affluent."

At the Premium Cinema, service is attentive, not effusive. After moviegoers cruise to the front of the main parking lot and drop off their cars with the uniformed valet, a concierge checks their coats, then escorts them to the restaurant, which is adjacent to the screening room. No rushing to finish dinner before show time; waiters bring unfinished meals to tables inside the theater, shortly before the movie starts.

But there are catches. Meals begun in the cafe often don't transfer well into the screening room. "No matter how efficiently they do it, the food still gets cold, and it does take away from the

The VIP Experience

Now . . .

Looking for a cinema with snob appeal? Here's where you can go now for the VIP experience:

General Cinemas: Premium Cinema

Where: Chicago area (Lombard, Ill.)
Ticket price: $15
Cool Features: Valet parking and separate entrance. Stadium seating with leather reclining chairs. Waiters in black-and-white uniforms serve until movie starts. Fresh flowers in bathroom separate from main theater. Full bar and free popcorn.

Cineplex Odeon: VIP Cinema

Where: Toronto
Ticket price: $8.25 to $12 (Canadian)
Cool Features: Special VIP concierge directs you to your seat. Velvet reclining chairs and seat-side coffee tables. Waiters wear Buck Rogers-style headsets. Separate bathroom. Small club lounge offers free local calls.

Coming Soon . . .

Here are some VIP theaters coming soon to a cineplex near you:

United Artists Theatres: Club Level

Where: New York—Opening: Early 1999
Ticket price: Not available.
Cool Features: Reclining chairs and seat-side coffee tables. Waiter service.

Virgin Cinemas: Premier Screen

Where: Pasadena, Calif.—Opening: End of 1999
Where: New York and Honolulu—Opening: Summer 2000
Ticket price: $12
Cool Features: Free appetizers (pizza, quiche, crudites). Private bar. Waiter service. Seats modeled after those in Virgin Airlines Upper Class, complete with side lever for reclining. Reserved seating.

Loews Cineplex United States

Where: Elizabeth, N.J.; Boston; Pittsburgh—Opening: By year end 1999
Ticket price: Not available.
Cool Features: Designed by architect-to-the-stars David Rockwell. Separate VIP bar. Waiter service.

General Cinemas: Premium Cinema

Where: Baltimore area (Owings Mills, Md.)—Opening: February 1999
Milwaukee area (Wauwatosa, Wis.)—Opening: May 1999
Ticket price: Not available.
Cool Features: Generally the same as those in General Cinemas' existing theater in Chicago (see above).

Cineplex Odeon: VIP Cinema

Where: Vancouver, Quebec City, Toronto (second location)—Opening: December 1999
Ticket price: Not available.
Cool Features: Generally the same as those at Cineplex's existing Toronto location, but VIP area will be in theaters' balconies instead of separate rooms.

meal," says Mr. Ashby, the Chicago software engineer. Still, the quality of the food is less important, he says, than "the whole experience."

In fact, even watching the movie seems to be of almost secondary importance to the experience of feeling like a mini-mogul. The champagne-drinking Mr. Ashby wanted to see "Vampires," but it wasn't playing at the Premium Room, so he and his wife ended up at "Living Out Loud," the saga of a newly single woman. "It's supposed to be a real chick movie," he says, "but after a couple of glasses of 'Tatt,' I won't care."

In Toronto, Cineplex Odeon's VIP rooms don't serve dinner or liquor, just standard concession fare (unless, of course, they're rented out for private parties). But the main attraction is the same: being far from the madding crowd.

Ms. Johnston, the Toronto human-resources executive, and her husband Bob, a data processor, are regulars. On a recent Sunday afternoon, they arrive about 20 minutes before show time for "Pleasantville." The box-office attendant directs them past the main entrance to a special customer-service desk, where a black-vested concierge escorts them up a small flight of stairs. They have the choice of going directly into the 36-seat theater, one of four screening rooms, and settling into one of the overstuffed velvet seats—or else relaxing in a private lounge, appointed with leather club seats.

There are other perks: Screening-room patrons have their own bathroom, all brushed steel and slate. Waiters in high-tech headsets take orders for popcorn, espresso and soda, filling orders before the movie begins. "I don't like lines," says Ms. Johnston. Adds Mr. Johnston: "If you're going out on the town, hey, you want to kick up your heels and enjoy. It's not that much more expensive." Here, VIP tickets cost up to 12 Canadian dollars (or US$7.80), depending on the time—$3 more than sitting in the regular theater.

Inside the VIP rooms, seats are 22 inches wide, compared with 19 inches in the standard cinema next door. And these chairs aren't in tightly set rows. Each has plenty of elbow room—as well as its own set of armrests and faux-burl coffee table.

Not everyone is enthralled by the new configurations. "It makes it really hard to hold hands during the movie," says Esther Springs, a Toronto public-relations executive who came to the VIP room to see "The X Files" last summer with her husband. Another drawback: "The small screen [about a third smaller than those at the rest of the cinema] isn't really very good for action pictures," she says.

Still, she returned with her 11-year-old daughter and 12-year-old son to see "The Mighty." "My daughter really pushed us to come," says Ms. Springs. "She heard about the theater from her friends."

While VIP rooms might appeal for special occasions, some patrons think the price is too steep for most nights. "I don't want to spend $15 a ticket if I'm just going with my family," says Chris Kochan, waiting to see a movie with her sister and brother-in-law. Same story for Craig Smith, who was going to see "The

The Modern Movie Theater

Competition is forcing theater companies to upgrade movie houses for the first time in decades, but some improvements add more to your viewing pleasure than others. In the past year alone, more than 3,000 screens have been built or upgraded, at a total cost of close to $2 billion, says William Kartozian, president of the National Association of Theater Owners. Here are some of the latest bells and whistles:

Stadium-style seating: Most new theater chains build their seats in tiers, with each row 12 inches to 18 inches higher than the one in front. The result: more leg room and better sight lines. **AMC Entertainment** Inc. and **Edwards Theatre Circuit** Inc. both claim to be the first theater chain to have developed this innovation in the mid-1990s. So who really invented the concept? "Actually, it was the Romans," says Don Barton, Edwards' vice president and general sales manager.

Love Seats: AMC and other chains now feature seats with arms that retract, allowing moviegoers to snuggle with their dates or comfort an anxious child. At AMC, the seats are 3 to 5 inches wider than older chairs, and their backs are higher. The newest versions tilt so you can lean back during the scary parts. At **Regal Cinemas** Inc., arms are padded so that they comfortably fill the gap between seats when flipped up.

Wall-to-wall screens: Think Cinerama, the next generation. Instead of being hung on the wall, some movie screens are literally built into the auditorium, curving with the wall. The effect is to enlarge the image and envelop the viewer so that he sees no wall "frame" around the film.

Sound improvements: The alphabet soup of new digital technologies—SDDS, DTS, Dolby Digital—make movies sound richer. The differences among them are fairly technical, but the theater must be equipped to use the system in question. If not, the audio track will play in simple stereo. One change is truly audible to moviegoers: more speakers. At **Carmike Cinemas** Inc.'s new 500-seat auditorium in Savannah, Ga., for example, there are 31 speakers and 14 amplifiers—at a cost of $38,000. Fifteen years ago, top cinema sound systems typically had no more than 13 speakers and four amplifiers.

Beyond Milk Duds: General Cinema is rolling out a high-speed oven that cooks a deep-dish personal pizza from Pizzeria Uno in 70 seconds flat; 15 of the chain's newest theaters have Starbucks "Cafes." In Southern California, Edwards is testing specialty coffees and its own pizzas. Loews Cineplex and Regal Cinemas have coffee bars that are separate from the regular concession stand. Sony is taking its food offerings to the next level: 10 theaters have full kitchens offering everything from popcorn shrimp to "Nachos Grande"—with vegetables and real cheese, not the usual liquefied processed stuff.

Lobby luxuries: ATMs are already de rigueur. Miniature golf is next. That's right, you can now practice your putt at five of Regal Cinemas' 402 theaters, including those in Chesapeake, Va., and Victor, N.Y. Those theaters also have a "Stop and Play" area for the under-six set, featuring climb-through tubes, bouncing balls and dress-up clothes. Baby sitters aren't provided, but you can bring your own, and drop the little one off for a couple hours while you catch a grown-up-appropriate flick. For adults, Regal Cinemas now offers "The Escape"—full bar, pool tables and a simulated roller-coaster ride, but it's available only in Fort Lauderdale, Fla., and there are no plans to expand.

Waterboy" with a group of 20 friends. The luxury room, he says, "is the kind of place I'd go for a date."

While both General Cinema in Chicago and Cineplex Odeon in Toronto have separate theaters for the premium crowd, upcoming plans are to mimic luxury suites at sports stadiums. United Artists and Cineplex Odeon's current plans for expanding its VIP service include exclusive balcony sections with separate audio systems so that moviegoers can get the big-screen experience—and theater owners won't have to rent an extra print.

The big unresolved issue for these new theaters is whether movie distributors will be paid extra to reflect the higher ticket prices. Generally, theater exhibitors keep about 30% of the ticket take for the first week of a film's run, with that percentage increasing the longer a film plays. At Cineplex Odeon, the split with the distributors remains the same for their higher-priced VIP tickets—even though the price covers additional labor costs for the concierges and waiters.

Luxury theaters got their start a couple of years ago in Britain when Virgin Cinemas Ltd. of the Virgin Entertainment Group, opened its first Premier Screen—recliner chairs, free popcorn and crudites, for GBP 10 to GBP 12 ($16 to $20) a ticket, or about double the cost of a standard show. There are now 10 Premier Screens, and Virgin says it plans to open its first in the U.S. next year. Last year, Village Roadshow Ltd. of Melbourne, Australia, opened its first Gold Class Screens there, charging up to 25 Australian dollars (US$15.25) a seat, about 40% more than their regular price. Warner Lusomundo Sociedade Iberica de Cinemas Lda., a Portuguese joint venture with media giant Time Warner Inc., opened its first luxury cinema in Portugal in mid-October.

Analysts say screening rooms are too small to solve the industry's overbuilding ills, but they can help the bottom line without adding huge overhead. "At the end of the day, most seats in a movie theater are empty 80% of the time," says Christopher Dixon, a PaineWebber analyst. "While the margins these new theaters get probably won't add significantly to the bottom line, anything they can do to differentiate a product and drive traffic is a good thing."

Regardless of whether these new theaters are filling their owners' coffers, they are certainly fattening waiters' wallets. "Tips can be much better than at my last job," says Adam Smith, who works the night shift in Chicago and says he recently was tipped more than $100 on a $400 tab. "I do much better at some movies than others," he adds. "Action pictures like 'The Big Hit' don't work so well, but 'Gone With the Wind' really scored. It's the romances where I get really big tips—those are the ones where guys bring dates they are trying to impress."

Lack of Shopping Carts Impact Sales at Traditional Department Stores

Humble shopping cart rolls up retail sales. As old-fashioned as they seem, buggies are perfectly suited for the way people shop today

JOSEPH B. CAHILL

A month from now, as Santa Claus crawls back up the last chimney and heads home, the retail world will begin its annual post-mortem: How did discounters once again manage to trounce traditional department stores?

Was it sophisticated pricing, the latest in-store design, or cutting-edge inventory management?

Actually, after 20 years of growing discounter dominance, a simpler explanation rolls into view: the shopping cart.

So far this year, the six leading discount chains, led by Wal-Mart Stores Inc., have chalked up robust sales increases of 5 per cent or more for stores open at least one year. And each of those chains offers customers the luxury of a shopping cart. Meanwhile, the six leading department store companies, led by Sears Roebuck & Co., don't provide carts. Their year-to-date same-store sales increases have all been less than 5 per cent.

"It's incredible, the impact of a shopping cart," says Britt Beemer, chairman of America's Research Group Inc., a market research firm. His studies show that in mass-market retail stores, the average shopper with a cart buys 7.2 items, while the customer without a cart buys 6.1 items.

As old-fashioned as they seem, carts are perfectly suited for the way people shop today: they're time-pressed and buy more in fewer trips. Mothers struggling to corral children love them. The growing ranks of senior citizens lean on carts for support and appreciate not having to carry their purchases.

Carts empower an impulse. At any given moment, the typical middle class family is mulling the purchase of five to eight big-ticket items, such as a VCR or microwave oven, Mr. Beemer says. "Carts will double the sales of bulky items," he says. "If you walk by a VCR and you have your daughter in tow and some other items in your hands, you'll say, 'I'll get it next time.' "

Carts also make many of the newer retailing strategies work. From "category killers" such as Home Depot Inc. to mass-merchandisers such as Dayton Hudson Corp.'s Target Stores to discount clubs such as Costco Wholesale Corp., stores are getting bigger, carrying a wider array of goods and pushing prices lower. These stores need customers to stay longer, cruise through the whole store, and load up.

Invented in the 1930s by an Oklahoma City grocer named Sylvan Goldman, carts were essential before supermarkets could succeed. Mr. Goldman's design became a multipurpose fixture up and down American society.

So, why would any sane retailer deny its customers a cart? Some, it seems, are just too classy to have stainless steel contraptions junking up their stores. "I'm not sure I could see someone buying a $2,000 suit and hanging it over a cart," says Carolyn Biggs, executive vice-president and director of stores for the Saks Fifth Avenue unit of Saks Inc.

For department stores that compete directly with discounters, operating in uncarted territory is risky business. At a Sears store on the West Side of Chicago, shoppers carry purchases in white plastic bags emblazoned with the Sears logo. The handle: mere cut-outs near the top of the bag. Filled with heavy pur-

From the *Wall Street Journal,* November 24, 1999. Republished by permission of Dow Jones, Inc. via Copyright Clearance Center, Inc.

chases, the bag sags and stretches, the plastic around the handle narrowing to a taut, sharp edge. Moving from department to department, shoppers add another bag with each purchase.

Belatedly, the message is getting through. Sears and Montgomery Ward & Co. are both testing carts—little ones—in some stores. Montgomery Ward thinks carts may encourage customers to browse the entire store and buy things from more than one department. "We want to promote cross-shopping and we wanted to give the customer a vehicle," says William Bass, vice-president of store operations.

These carts bear little resemblance to grocery carts. The baskets are commercial-grade black nylon, with mesh sides and a solid bottom. The tubular black steel frame won't snag apparel or gouge fixtures. Pulling the front of the basket back over the handlebar converts it into a child's stroller with a bag for purchases in back.

For Sears, this use of new technology is hush-hush. "We are embarked on a pilot program that includes the use of shopping carts in selected stores," a spokeswoman confirms. But she won't say where or when. How about why? A survey suggested, she confides, that "customers might appreciate shopping carts."

The boom in discount retailing makes for good times in the cart business. Rehrig International Inc. of Richmond, Va., makes plastic carts and says sales have doubled in the past four years to more than 500,000 carts a year. Unarco Industries Inc., a unit of Chicago conglomerate Marmon Group, controlled by the Pritzker family, sells about 600,000 carts a year.

Unarco is the successor to Folding Carrier Co., the cart company founded by the shopping cart inventor, Mr. Goldman. He dreamed up his invention after noticing that his grocery customers headed to the cashier as soon as their handbasket was full. One night in the office, his eyes fell upon a folding chair. Add wheels and a basket, he thought. It wasn't quite that easy: The first prototype folded up rolling over a matchstick and lost its wheels when it hit a bump.

But Mr. Goldman kept on, and in 1937 advertised the carts in newspapers: "Basket juggling is a lost art at your Standard Food Stores." One of his early models is enshrined at the Smithsonian Institution. And a 1978 biography, by Terry Wilson, seemed to know something about the future of retailing. Its title: "The Cart That Changed the World."

The Deal Is Done. Now the Work Begins.

By CLAUDIA H. DEUTSCH

David Hadfield still winces when he recalls the 1989 merger of Coopers & Lybrand and some international operations of Deloitte, Haskins & Sells.

"We figured they're both accounting firms, they trade in the same markets, so of course their cultures would be the same," said Mr. Hadfield, who was a consultant with Deloitte at the time. "We couldn't have been more wrong."

Deloitte, he explained, was far more free-spirited than the control-minded Coopers. And it took three years of employee defections and financial bleeding—and finally a new management team—to get the firm past its culture clashes.

So last year, when Coopers and Price Waterhouse merged to form the $15.3 billion megafirm PricewaterhouseCoopers, they made sure to avoid the same nightmare. Ten months before the deal was completed, each firm assigned four executives to a merger integration team, which in turn named Mr. Hadfield as its global transition director.

"If no one has full-time responsibility for making a merger work," he explained, "you'll mess up what could have been a perfectly good deal."

There is nothing new about the idea that a merger or acquisition can give rise to cultural conflicts, to quarrels over pay systems, to information systems that don't communicate with each other and to various other problems. Indeed, researchers routinely say that anywhere from one-half to three-quarters of mergers never provide the low costs, added market share or other benefits that management promised shareholders—or that they take much longer than expected to do so.

But until recently, corporations acted as if the only way to better those odds was to look more closely at whether a potential partner's markets and products really meshed with their own, and then to negotiate harder if the deal still made sense.

Now, though, they are also training their magnifying glasses on all the possible glitches that could come after the deal is done—and seeking ways to prevent them.

"We've walked away from companies with autocratic leaders because their employees wouldn't fit in with our team culture," said Ammar Hanafi, director of business development for Cisco Systems, the maker of computer networking equipment. "We even walked away from one that had fancy artwork on its walls, because we doubted it would fit into our culture of frugality."

Cisco, based in San Jose, Calif., has acquired 32 companies since its founding 13 years ago—two of them just last week. It has 15 full-time people dedicated not only to making mergers work, but also to steering management away from marriages that might be undermined by issues of company culture.

As deal-making continues its rampant transformation of corporate America, the concept of in-house merger managers keeps gaining converts.

Allied Signal, General Electric and Lucent Technologies all now have specialists dedicated to the integration of merged companies. In February, AT&T—busy digesting Tele-Communications Inc. and setting up joint ventures with British Telecom and Time Warner—promoted Harold W. Burlingame, its executive vice president of human resources, to the new position of executive vice president of merger and joint venture integration.

"What's changed is that companies are paying as much formal attention to post-deal integration as they pay to the pre-deal part of mergers," said Bruce A. Pasternack, a senior vice president at Booz, Allen & Hamilton, the consulting firm.

Consultants say the list of such companies grows daily. "Lack of attention to cultures and systems has caused a tremendous number of deals to blow up, and that's shown companies that slapping functions together is not the same as integrating them," said Mark N. Clemente, president of Clemente Greenspan & Company, a management consulting firm.

Recent history has been rife with learning opportunities. Accounting irregularities take only part of the blame, for example, for the implosion of the Cendant Corporation, the

Practicing the Steps Even Before the Dance

There is no cookie-cutter approach to merging two companies successfully into one.

Companies that buy other businesses only once in a while usually create a full-time but temporary integration team for any new purchase; the team is disbanded once the acquired company is sufficiently acclimated. Companies like the specialty chemicals maker Hercules Inc., which buy and merge at a steady but not heady pace, often assign a high-level executive to oversee the integration of a new company, giving him or her access to staff support. And corporations like Lucent Technologies or Cisco Systems, which make acquisitions often, tend to have permanent teams whose sole job is to integrate the new companies into their operations.

"If you don't have the same people doing it, then every deal acts as a shock to your whole system," said Ammar Hanafi, Cisco's director of business development, who coordinates integration efforts both before and after acquisitions.

Differences aside, more and more companies are planning for integration even as they research deals. Well before an acquisition is closed, both companies are deciding whose compensation programs will survive, which offices or plants will close, which executives will run the combined business units or be primary contacts for customers, and how the integration process will be communicated to employees. They are ferreting out potential culture clashes and designing training programs to combat them.

In sum, they are creating detailed implementation plans, complete with milestones, for making the merger work and fast. "Having a permanent integration team shaves months off the integration process," said Patricia Russo, the executive vice president who oversees Lucent's merger integration group.

$14 billion company created when HES and CUC International joined forces in late 1997. Most business experts also implicate the mismatch in styles between the controlling and numbers- oriented Henry Silverman, HFS's chief, and the strategy-minded, people-oriented Walter Forbes, the head of CUC.

At AT&T, a good part of Mr. Burlingame's new job is to insure that the company does not repeat with TCI the mistakes it made when it acquired the NCR Corporation in 1991 and McCaw Cellular in 1994.

In both of those cases, AT&T let efforts to coordinate sales pitches, product development and client contacts simmer on a back burner. AT&T never made money on NCR, which it eventually spun off to shareholders. And while AT&T's cellular business eventually prospered after the acquisition of McCaw, Mr. Burlingame believes the company took far too long to absorb its purchase. "We lost a chance to blow the competition out of the water," he said.

There are many reasons that merger integration has emerged as a discipline, with its own dedicated personnel. Corporations have whittled away at headquarters staffs, and the support people who survived—and might be logical candidates for merger duties—rarely have much slack in their schedules. Moreover, top executives recognize that unless they hold individuals accountable for shepherding an acquired company, integration issues could fall by the wayside.

The number of mergers and acquisitions is at a dizzying high. Last year, the Securities Data/Thomson Financial Company, a research firm, counted more than 23,000 deals worldwide, worth $2.5 trillion; the pace this year is even faster, with $840 billion in deals reaching fruition worldwide in the first quarter alone.

Lucent, the big telecommunications equipment maker, has bought 18 companies in its less than three years of existence. Tyco International, an industrial conglomerate, has bought 110 companies since L. Dennis Kozlowski became chief executive six years ago.

"For many companies, mergers have moved from occasional event to a routine, frequent part of doing business," noted Jim E. Fishbein, a vice president of Rath & Strong, the consulting arm of the Aon Corporation.

The deal frenzy has driven prices for acquisitions sky-high, making shareholders unforgiving of deals that do not add to earnings immediately. So the ability to integrate a new company quickly—and wring out some costs in the process—has become a major factor in how a merged company's stock performs.

"Companies have to come full-steam out of the gate to justify the premiums on deals," said Ronald Ashkenas, managing partner of Robert H. Schaffer & Associates, a consulting firm in Stamford, Conn.

Hercules Inc. certainly knows that. Last July, when it announced its purchase of BetzDearborn, another company in the specialty chemicals business, for $2.4 billion in cash and $700 million in assumed debt, it promised investors that by the end of 2000, it would achieve $125 million in synergies—merger-speak for cost savings.

Well before the deal was completed in October, Hercules assigned executives from the two companies to integration teams. Vincent J. Corbo, president of Hercules, presided over the teams, sending each to a different unit to find potential cost cuts and devise schedules for achieving them. He also set up an "integration program office," with a full-time head responsible for seeing that the timetables were met.

Mr. Corbo says the merged company is ahead of schedule on reducing costs. But it is still suffering the types of culture clashes that led to the abrupt departure of William R.

Cook, Betz's former chief executive, shortly after the companies merged.

"We knew that at Hercules decisions are made analytically, while Betz was managed more intuitively," Mr. Corbo said. "But it made sense to get the people in place and the cost synergies planned for before we tried to merge the cultures."

In fact, companies that make frequent acquisitions have found that, after a while, they can handle cost-cutting and personnel issues almost by rote. Their merger integration specialists are high on the learning curve when it comes to disposing of excess real estate, melding pension plans, coordinating accounting systems or handling other important but typical merger chores. Spared of having to reinvent the wheel in those areas, they have more time to study the cultural and market issues that make each merger unique.

"It's a lot speedier if the same people handle the myriad things that are similar in acquisitions and the business units concentrate on melding products, markets and cultures," said Patricia F. Russo, the executive vice president who oversees Lucent's merger integration group.

Gary P. Yeaw, who last year became the first director of human resources for mergers and acquisitions at Allied Signal, the industrial conglomerate, agreed. "You want to customize every integration, but you don't want to start from scratch each time," he said.

Internet technology has made it easier to build banks of institutional memory and advice. About two years ago, General Electric pulled together separate teams from human resources, finance and more than a dozen other corporate functions and set them to interviewing G.E. people who had been involved in some of the hundreds of deals that the company has done in the last few years.

A result is an elaborate site on G.E.'s internal computer network, sorted by subjects like culture or compensation, so that people responsible for those issues can quickly find anecdotes gleaned from past deals, names of G.E. contacts and even tips on how to choose the right leader for an integration team. "The Web page's contents, printed out, would fill enough file folders to line an office wall," said Gary M. Reiner, chief information officer for G.E. "The intranet is the first viable medium for sharing best practices."

For those who have been wounded by past mergers, remembering the worst practices is even more important.

In hindsight, Mr. Burlingame of AT&T concedes that the whole notion behind the NCR deal—that the communications and computing worlds were themselves merging—was flawed. But he believes AT&T exacerbated the problems by not coordinating goals with NCR early on.

"The two companies retained different visions," Mr. Burlingame recalled. "AT&T figured it could build on NCR's customer base to sell full-service networks, but NCR just wanted to use our brand name to sell their hardware."

Now, Mr. Burlingame is already trying to insure that cable employees from TCI and their telephone counterparts from AT&T travel the same road from Day One. High on his list are training programs aimed at keeping TCI employees, who have concentrated on serving local markets, from working at cross-purposes with AT&T employees, who are trying to expand national markets.

With Mr. Burlingame so new in his job, he might do well to pick up some tips from Mr. Hadfield at PricewaterhouseCoopers. Since July, Mr. Hadfield has designed employee-retention programs, redeployed some partners to new posts, sent other partners for merger-related training, dispatched people to explain the merger to clients, streamlined purchasing and otherwise cut costs—and made sure that the firm's 150,000 employees are up to date on the integration process.

Mr. Hadfield, who expects his assignment to last through this year, credits the integration program for the company's success in retaining nearly all of the 9,000 partners who had been most important to the two firms before they merged.

Unlike PricewaterhouseCoopers, EPS Solutions Inc.—also born of a merger of accounting and consulting firms—has no legacy of failure to guard against. But its integration challenge is perhaps the most dire around.

The company, based in Costa Mesa, Calif., was formed on Dec. 14 from the merger of 36 smaller firms. Overnight, 35 former entrepreneurs were playing second or third fiddle to one large organization. And 1,344 employees who had worked for tiny companies were working for a middle-sized one that now plans to go public.

Long before the December D-Day, Christopher P. Massey, the prime mover behind the new company and now its chief executive, met with the other business heads to form integration teams that, as soon as the deal was final, would visit every office to answer questions. They charged one person with integrating all the computer systems. They hammered out a stock option and benefits plan.

When the deal was done, the executives were ready with a 30-page booklet that detailed compensation plans and career opportunities. It addressed frankly the culture shocks that might be ahead but also devoted considerable ink to the benefits of combining client bases and cash flows.

"We wanted employees, from Day One, to be able to go home and prove to their spouses that there was a lot of security," Mr. Massey said. "And we needed to prove to ourselves that we really could turn all those different firms into a single company with a single culture."

He had better prove it fast. EPS closed six more acquisitions last month.

The Balanced Scorecard—Measures that Drive Performance

Robert S. Kaplan and David P. Norton

What you measure is what you get. Senior executives understand that their organization's measurement system strongly affects the behavior of managers and employees. Executives also understand that traditional financial accounting measures like return-on-investment and earnings-per-share can give misleading signals for continuous improvement and innovation—activities today's competitive environment demands. The traditional financial performance measures worked well for the industrial era, but they are out of step with the skills and competencies companies are trying to master today.

As managers and academic researchers have tried to remedy the inadequacies of current performance measurement systems, some have focused on making financial measures more relevant. Others have said, "Forget the financial measures. Improve operational measures like cycle time and defect rates; the financial results will follow." But managers should not have to choose between financial and operational measures. In observing and working with many companies, we have found that senior executives do not rely on one set of measures to the exclusion of the other. They realize that no single measure can provide a clear performance target or focus attention on the critical areas of the business. Managers want a balanced presentation of both financial and operational measures.

During a year-long research project with 12 companies at the leading edge of performance measurement, we devised a "balanced scorecard"—a set of measures that gives top managers a fast but comprehensive view of the business. The balanced scorecard includes financial measures that tell the results of actions already taken. And it complements the financial measures with operational measures on customer satisfaction, internal processes, and the organization's innovation and improvement activities—operational measures that are the drivers of future financial performance.

Robert S. Kaplan is the Arthur Lowes Dickinson Professor of Accounting at the Harvard Business School. David P. Norton is president of Nolan, Norton & Company. Inc., a Massachusetts-based information technology consulting firm he cofounded.

Think of the balanced scorecard as the dials and indicators in an airplane cockpit. For the complex task of navigating and flying an airplane, pilots need detailed information about many aspects of the flight. They need information on fuel, air speed, altitude, bearing, destination, and other indicators that summarize the current and predicted environment. Reliance on one instrument can be fatal. Similarly, the complexity of managing an organization today requires that managers be able to view performance in several areas simultaneously.

The balanced scorecard allows managers to look at the business from four important perspectives. (See the exhibit "The Balanced Scorecard Links Performance Measures.") It provides answers to four basic questions:

- How do customers see us? (customer perspective)
- What must we excel at? (internal perspective)
- Can we continue to improve and create value? (innovation and learning perspective)
- How do we look to shareholders? (financial perspective)

While giving senior managers information from four different perspectives, the balanced scorecard minimizes information overload by limiting the number of measures used. Companies rarely suffer from having too few measures. More commonly, they keep adding new measures whenever an employee or a consultant makes a worthwhile suggestion. One manager described the proliferation of new measures at his company as its "kill another tree program." The balanced scorecard forces managers to focus on the handful of measures that are most critical.

Several companies have already adopted the balanced scorecard. Their early experiences using the scorecard have demonstrated that it meets several managerial needs. First, the scorecard brings together, in a single management report, many of the seemingly disparate elements of a company's competitive agenda: becoming customer oriented, shortening response time, improving quality, emphasizing teamwork, reducing new product launch times, and managing for the long term.

Second, the scorecard guards against suboptimization. By forcing senior managers to consider all the important operational measures together, the balanced scorecard lets them see whether improvement in one area may have been achieved at the expense of another. Even the best objective can be achieved badly. Companies can reduce time to market, for example, in two very different ways: by improving the management of new product introductions or by releasing only products that are incrementally different from existing products. Spending on setups can be cut either by reducing setup times or by increasing batch sizes. Similarly, production output and first-pass yields can rise, but the increases may be due to a shift in the product mix to more standard, easy-to-produce but lower-margin products.

We will illustrate how companies can create their own balanced scorecard with the experiences of one semiconductor company—let's call it Electronic Circuits Inc. ECI saw the scorecard as a way to clarify, simplify, and then operationalize the vision at the top of the organization. The ECI scorecard was designed to focus the attention of its top executives on a short list of critical indicators of current and future performance.

Customer Perspective: How Do Customers See Us?

Many companies today have a corporate mission that focuses on the customer. "To be number one in delivering value to customers" is a typical mission statement. How a company is performing from its customers' perspective

The Balanced Scorecard Links Performance Measures

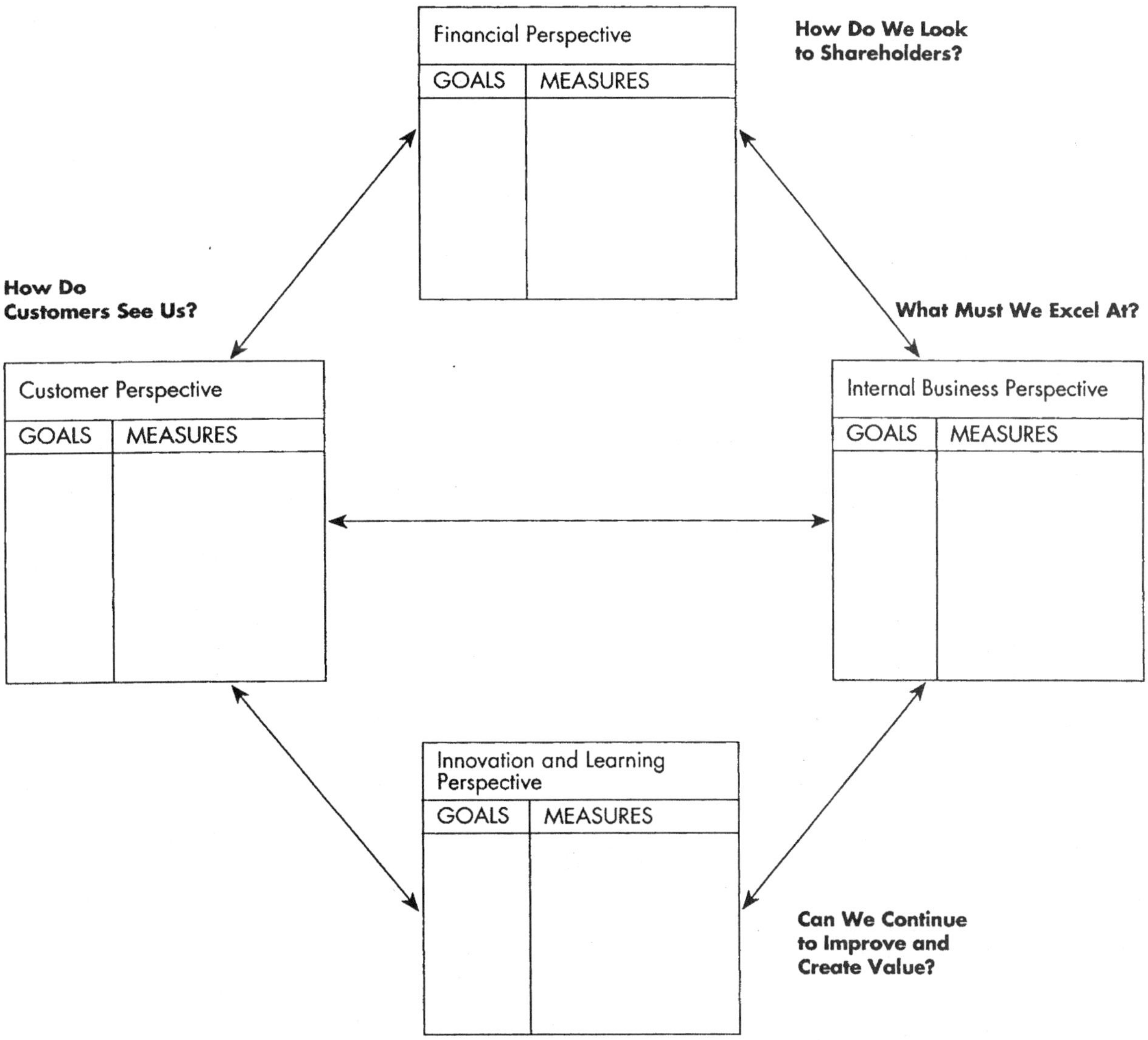

has become, therefore, a priority for top management. The balanced scorecard demands that managers translate their general mission statement on customer service into specific measures that reflect the factors that really matter to customers.

Customers' concerns tend to fall into four categories: time, quality, performance and service, and cost. Lead time measures the time required for the company to meet its customers' needs. For existing products, lead time can be measured from the time the company receives an order to the time it actually delivers the product or service to the customer. For new products, lead time represents the time to market, or how long it takes to bring a new product from the product definition stage to the start of shipments. Quality measures the defect level of incoming products as perceived and measured by the customer. Quality could also measure on-time delivery, the accuracy of the company's delivery forecasts. The combination of performance and service measures how the company's products or services contribute to creating value for its customers.

To put the balanced scorecard to work, companies should articulate goals for time, quality, and performance and service and then translate these goals into specific measures. Senior managers at ECI, for example, established general goals for customer performance: get standard products to market sooner, improve customers' time to market, become customers' supplier of choice through partnerships with them, and develop innovative products tailored to customer needs. The managers translated these general goals into four specific goals and identified an appropriate measure for each. (*See the exhibit* "ECI's Balanced Business Scorecard.")

To track the specific goal of providing a continuous stream of attractive solutions, ECI measured the percent of sales from new products and the percent of sales from proprietary products. That information was available internally. But certain other measures forced the company to get data from outside. To assess whether the company was achieving its goal of providing reliable, responsive supply, ECI turned to its customers. When it found that each customer defined "reliable, responsive supply" differently, ECI created a database of the factors as defined by each of its major customers. The shift to external measures of performance with customers led ECI to redefine "on time" so it matched customers' expectations. Some customers defined "on-time" as any shipment that arrived within five days of scheduled delivery, others used a nine-day window. ECI itself had been using a seven-day window, which meant that the company was not satisfying some of its customers and overachieving at others. ECI also asked its top ten customers to rank the company as a supplier overall.

Depending on customers' evaluations to define some of a company's performance measures forces that company to view its performance though customers' eyes. Some companies hire third parties to perform anonymous customer surveys, resulting in a customer-driven report card. The J.D. Powers quality survey, for example, has become the standard of performance for the automobile industry, while the Department of Transportation's measurement of on-time arrivals and lost baggage provides external standards for airlines. Bench-marking procedures are yet another technique companies use to compare their performance against competitors' best practice. Many companies have introduced "best of breed" comparison programs: the company looks to one industry to find, say, the best distribution system, to another industry for the lowest cost payroll process, and then forms a composite of those best practices to set objectives for its own performance.

In addition to measures of time, quality, and performance and service, companies must remain sensitive to the cost of their products. But customers see price as only one component of the cost they incur when dealing with their suppliers. Other supplier-driven costs range from ordering, scheduling delivery, and paying for the materials, to receiving, inspecting, handling, and storing the materials; to the scrap, rework, and obsolescence caused by the materials, and schedule disruptions (expediting and value of lost output) from incorrect deliveries. An excellent supplier may charge a higher unit price for products than other vendors but nonetheless be a lower cost supplier because it can deliver defect-free products in exactly the right quantities at exactly the right time directly to the production process and can minimize, though electronic data interchange, the administrative hassles of ordering, invoicing, and paying for materials.

Other Measures for the Customer's Perspective

A computer manufacturer wanted to be the competitive leader in customer satisfaction, so it measured competitive rankings.The company got the rankings through an outside organization hired to talk directly with customers. The company also wanted to do a better job of solving customers' problems by creating more partnerships with other suppliers. It measured the percentage of revenue from third-party relationships.

The customers of a producer of very expensive medical equipment demanded high reliability. The company developed two customer-based metrics for its operations: equipment up-time percentage and mean-time response to a service call.

A semiconductor company asked each major customer to rank the company against comparable suppliers on efforts to improve quality, delivery time, and price performance. When the manufacturer discovered that it ranked in the middle, managers made improvements that moved the company to the top of customers' rankings.

Internal Business Perspective: What Must We Excel at?

Customer-based measures are important, but they must be translated into measures of what the company must do internally to meet its customers' expectations. After all, excellent customer performance derives from processes, decisions, and actions occurring throughout an organization. Managers need to focus on those critical internal operations that enable them to satisfy customer needs. The second part of the balanced scorecard gives managers that internal perspective.

The internal measures for the balanced scorecard should stem from the business processes that have the greatest impact on customer satisfaction— factors that affect cycle time, quality, employee skills, and productivity, for example. Companies should also attempt to identify and measure their company's core competencies, the critical technologies needed to ensure continued market leadership. Companies should decide what processes and competencies they must excel at and specify measures for each.

Managers at ECI determined that submicron technology capability was critical to its market position. They also decided that they had to focus on manufacturing excellence, design productivity, and new product introduction. The company developed operational measures for each of these four internal business goals.

To achieve goals on cycle time, quality, productivity, and cost, managers must devise measures that are influenced by employees' actions. Since much of the action takes place at the department and workstation levels, managers need to decompose overall cycle time, quality, product, and cost measures to local levels. That way, the measures link top management's judgment about key internal processes and competencies to the actions taken by individuals that affect overall corporate objectives. This linkage ensures that employees at lower-levels in the organization have clear targets for actions, decisions, and improvement activities that will contribute to the company's overall mission.

Information systems play an invaluable role in helping managers disaggregate the summary measures. When an unexpected signal appears on the balanced scorecard, executives can query their information system to find the source of the trouble. If the aggregate measure for on-time delivery is poor, for example, executives with a good information system can quickly look behind the aggregate measure until they can identify late deliveries, day by day, by a particular plant to an individual customer.

If the information system is unresponsive, however, it can be the Achilles' heel of performance measurement. Managers at ECI are currently limited by the absence of such an operational information system. Their greatest concern is that the scorecard information is not timely; reports are generally a week behind the company's routine management meetings, and the measures have yet to be linked to measures for managers and employees at lower levels of the organization. The company is in the process of developing a more responsive information system to eliminate this constraint.

Innovation and Learning Perspective: Can We Continue to Improve and Create Value?

The customer-based and internal business process measures on the balanced scorecard identify the parameters that the company considers most important for competitive success. But the targets for success keep changing. Intense global competition requires that companies make continual improvements to their *existing* products and processes and have the ability to introduce entirely new products with expanded capabilities.

A company's ability to innovate, improve, and learn ties directly to the company's value. That is, only through the ability to launch new products, create more value for customers, and improve operating efficiencies continually can a company penetrate new markets and increase revenues and margins—in short, grow and thereby increase shareholder value.

ECI's innovation measures focus on the company's ability to develop and introduce standard products rapidly, products that the company expects will form the bulk of its future sales. Its manufacturing improvement measure focuses on new products; the goal is to achieve stability in the manufacturing of new products rather than to improve manufacturing of existing products. Like many other

Other Measures for the Internal Business Perspective

One company recognized that the success of its TQM program depended on all its employees internalizing and acting on the program's messages. The company performed a monthly survey of 600 randomly selected employees to determine if they were aware of TQM, had changed their behavior because of it, believed the outcome was favorable, or had become missionaries to others.

Hewlett-Packard uses a metric called break-even time (BET) to measure the effectiveness of its product development cycle. BET measures the time required for all the accumulated expenses in the product and process development cycle (including equipment acquisition) to be recovered by the product's contribution margin (the selling price less manufacturing, delivery, and selling expenses).

A major office products manufacturer, wanting to respond rapidly to changes in the marketplace, set out to reduce cycle time by 50%. Lower levels of the organization aimed to radically cut the times required to process customer orders, order and receive materials from suppliers, move materials and products between plants, produce and assemble products, and deliver products to customers.

ECI's Balanced Business Scorecard

Financial Perspective

GOALS	MEASURES
Survive	Cash flow
Succeed	Quarterly sales growth and operating income by division
Prosper	Increased market share and ROE

Customer Perspective

GOALS	MEASURES
New products	Percent of sales from new products
	Percent of sales from proprietary products
Responsive supply	On-time delivery (defined by customer)
Preferred supplier	Share of key accounts' purchases
	Ranking by key accounts
Customer partnership	Number of cooperative engineering efforts

Internal Business Perspective

GOALS	MEASURES
Technology capability	Manufacturing geometry vs. competition
Manufacturing excellence	Cycle time Unit cost Yield
Design productivity	Silicon efficiency Engineering efficiency
New product introduction	Actual introduction schedule vs. plan

Innovation and Learning Perspective

GOALS	MEASURES
Technology leadership	Time to develop next generation
Manufacturing learning	Process time to maturity
Product focus	Percent of products that equal 80% sales
Time to market	New product introduction vs. competition

companies, ECI uses the percent of sales from new products as one of its innovation and improvement measures. If sales from new products are trending downward, managers can explore whether problems have arisen in new product design or new product introduction.

In addition to measures on product and process innovation, some companies overlay specific improvement goals for their existing processes. For example, Analog Devices, a Massachusetts-based manufacturer of specialized semiconductors, expects managers to improve their customer and internal business process performance continuously. The company estimates specific rates of improvement for on-time delivery, cycle time, defect rate, and yield.

Other companies, like Milliken & Co., require that managers make improvements within a specific time period. Milliken did not want its "associates" (Milliken's word for employees) to rest on their laurels after winning the Baldrige Award. Chairman and CEO Roger Milliken asked each plant to implement a "ten-four" improvement

How One Company Used a Daily Financial Report to Improve Quality*

In the 1980s, a chemicals company became committed to a total quality management program and began to make extensive measurements of employee participation, statistical process control, and key quality indicators. Using computerized controls and remote data entry systems, the plant monitored more than 30,000 observations of its production processes every four hours. The department managers and operating personnel who now had access to massive amounts of real-time operational data found their monthly financial reports to be irrelevant.

But one enterprising department manager saw things differently. He created a daily income statement. Each day, he estimated the value of the output from the production process using estimated market prices and subtracted the expenses of raw materials, energy, and capital consumed in the production process. To approximate the cost of producing out-of-conformance product, he cut the revenues from off-spec output by 50% to 100%.

The daily financial report gave operators powerful feedback and motivation and guided their quality and productivity efforts. The department head understood that it is not always possible to improve quality, reduce energy consumption, and increase throughput simultaneously; tradeoffs are usually necessary. He wanted the daily financial statement to guide those tradeoffs. The difference between the input consumed and output produced indicated the success or failure of the employees' efforts on the previous day. The operators were empowered to make decisions that might improve quality, increase productivity, and reduce consumption of energy and materials.

That feedback and empowerment had visible results. When, for example, a hydrogen compressor failed, a supervisor on the midnight shift ordered an emergency repair crew into action. Previously, such a failure of a noncritical component would have been reported in the shift log, where the department manager arriving for work the following morning would have to discover it. The midnight shift supervisor knew the cost of losing the hydrogen gas and made the decision that the cost of expediting the repairs would be repaid several times over by the output produced by having the compressor back on line before morning.

The department proceeded to set quality and output records. Over time, the department manager became concerned that employees would lose interest in continually improving operations. He tightened the parameters for in-spec production and reset the prices to reflect a 25% premium for output containing only negligible fractions of impurities. The operators continued to improve the production process.

The success of the daily financial report hinged on the manager's ability to establish a financial penalty for what had previously been an intangible variable: the quality of. output. With this innovation, it was easy to see where process improvements and capital investments could generate the highest returns.

*Source: "Texas Eastman Company," by Robert S. Kaplan, Harvard Business School Case No. 9-190-039.

program: measures of process defects, missed deliveries, and scrap were to be reduced by a factor of ten over the next four years. These targets emphasize the role for continuous improvement in customer satisfaction and internal business processes.

Financial Perspective: How Do We Look to Shareholders?

Financial performance measures indicate whether the company's strategy, implementation, and execution are contributing to bottom-line improvement. Typical financial goals have to do with profitability, growth, and shareholder value. ECI stated its financial goals simply: to survive, to succeed, and to prosper. Survival was measured by cash flow, success by quarterly sales growth and operating income by division, and prosperity by increased market share by segment and return on equity.

But given today's business environment, should senior managers even look at the business from a financial perspective? Should they pay attention to short-term financial measures like quarterly sales and operating income? Many have criticized financial measures because of their well-documented inadequacies, their backward-looking focus, and their inability to reflect contemporary value-creating actions. Shareholder value analysis (SVA), which forecasts future cash flows and discounts them back to a rough estimate of current value, is an attempt to make financial analysis more forward looking. But SVA still is based on cash flow rather than on the activities and processes that drive cash flow.

Some critics go much further in their indictment of financial measures. They argue that the terms of competition have changed and that traditional financial measures do not improve customer satisfaction, quality, cycle time, and employee motivation. In their view, financial performance is the result of operational actions, and financial success should be the logical consequence of doing the fundamentals well. In other words, companies should stop navigating by financial measures. By making fundamental improvements in their operations, the financial numbers will take care of themselves, the argument goes.

Assertions that financial measures are unnecessary are incorrect for at least two reasons. A well-designed financial control system can actually enhance rather than inhibit an organization's total quality management program. (See the insert, "How One Company Used a Daily Financial Report to Improve Quality.") More important, however, the alleged linkage between improved operating performance and financial success is actually quite tenuous and uncertain. Let us demonstrate rather than argue this point.

Over the three-year period between 1987 and 1990, a NYSE electronics company made an order-of-magnitude improvement in quality and on-time delivery performance. Outgoing defect rate dropped from 500 parts per million to 50, on-time delivery improved from 70% to 96% and yield jumped from 26% to 51%. Did these breakthrough improvements in quality, productivity, and customer service provide substantial benefits to the company? Unfortunately not. During the same three-year period, the company's financial results showed little improvement, and its stock price plummeted to one-third of its July 1987 value. The considerable improvements in manufacturing capabilities had not been translated into increased profitability. Slow releases of new products and a failure to expand marketing to new and perhaps more demanding customers prevented the company from realizing the benefits of its manufacturing achievements. The operational achievements were real, but the company had failed to capitalize on them.

The disparity between improved operational performance and disappointing financial measures creates frustration for senior executives. This frustration is often vented at nameless Wall Street analysts who allegedly cannot see past quarterly blips in financial performance to the underlying long-term values these executives sincerely believe they are creating in their organizations. But the hard truth is that if improved performance fails to be reflected in the bottom line, executives should reexamine the basic assumptions of their strategy and mission. Not all long-term strategies are profitable strategies.

Measures of customer satisfaction, internal business performance, and innovation and improvement are derived from the company's particular view of the world and its perspective on key success factors. But that view is not necessarily correct. Even an excellent set of balanced scorecard measures does not guarantee a winning strategy. The balanced scorecard can only translate a company's strategy into specific measurable objectives. A failure to convert improved operational performance, as measured in the scorecard, into improved financial performance should send executives back to their drawing boards to rethink the company's strategy or its implementation plans.

As one example, disappointing financial measures sometimes occur because companies don't follow up their operational improvements with another round of actions. Quality and cycle-time improvements can create excess capacity. Managers should be prepared to either put the excess capacity to work or else get rid of it. The excess capacity must be either used by boosting revenues or eliminated by reducing expenses if operational improvements are to be brought down to the bottom line.

As companies improve their quality and response time, they eliminate the need to build, inspect, and rework out-of-conformance products or to reschedule and expedite delayed orders. Eliminating these tasks means that some of the people who perform them are no longer needed. Companies are understandably reluctant to lay off employees, especially since the employees may have been the source of the ideas that produced the higher quality and reduced cycle time. Layoffs are a poor reward for past improvement and can damage the morale of remaining workers, curtailing further improvement. But companies will not realize all the financial benefits of their improvements until their employees and facilities are working to capacity—or the companies confront the pain of downsizing to eliminate the expenses of the newly created excess capacity.

If executives fully understood the consequences of their quality and cycle-time improvement programs, they might be more aggressive about using the newly created capacity. To capitalize on this self-created new capacity, however, companies must expand sales to existing customers, market existing products to entirely new customers (who are now accessible because of the improved quality and delivery performance), and increase the flow of new products to the market. These actions can generate added revenues with only modest increases in operating expenses. If marketing and sales and R&D do not generate the increased volume, the operating improvements will stand as excess capacity, redundancy, and untapped capabilities. Periodic financial statements remind executives that improved quality, response time, productivity, or new products benefit the company only when they are translated into improved sales and market share, reduced operating expenses, or higher asset turnover.

Ideally, companies should specify how improvements in quality, cycle time, quoted lead times, delivery, and new product introduction will lead to higher market share, operating margins, and asset turnover or to reduced operating expenses. The challenge is to learn how to make such explicit linkage between operations and finance. Exploring the complex dynamics will likely require simulation and cost modeling.

Measures that Move Companies Forward

As companies have applied the balanced scorecard, we have begun to recognize that the scorecard represents a fundamental change in the underlying assumptions about performance measurement. As the controllers and finance vice presidents involved in the research project took the concept back to their organizations, the project participants found that they could not implement the balanced scorecard without the involvement of the senior managers who have the most complete picture of the company's vision and priorities. This was revealing because most existing performance measurement systems have been designed and overseen by financial experts. Rarely do controllers need to have senior managers so heavily involved.

Probably because traditional measurement systems have sprung from the finance function, the systems have a control bias. That is, traditional performance measurement systems specify the particular actions they want employees to take and then measure to see whether the employees have in fact taken those actions. In that way, the systems try to control behavior. Such measurement systems fit with the engineering mentality of the Industrial Age.

The balanced scorecard, on the other hand, is well suited to the kind of organization many companies are trying to become. The scorecard puts strategy and vision, not control, at the center. It establishes goals but assumes that people will adopt whatever behaviors and take whatever actions are necessary to arrive at those goals. The measures are designed to pull people toward the overall vision. Senior managers may know what the end result should be, but they cannot tell employees exactly how to achieve that result, if only because the conditions in which employees operate are constantly changing.

This new approach to performance measurement is consistent with the initiatives under way in many companies: cross-functional integration, customer-supplier partnerships, global scale, continuous improvement, and team rather than individual accountability. By combining the financial, customer, internal process and innovation, and organizational learning perspectives, the balanced scorecard helps managers understand, at least implicitly, many interrelationships. This understanding can help managers transcend traditional notions about functional barriers and ultimately lead to improved decision making and problem solving. The balanced scorecard keeps companies looking—and moving—forward instead of backward.

CENDANT: WHO'S TO BLAME?

A loose accounting culture may lie at the core of the debacle

In all the hoopla over questions about former Cendant Corp. Chairman Walter A. Forbes's travel expenses, it's easy to lose sight of one telling detail: Cendant officials can find only a limited number of Forbes's expense reports and so can't verify how a substantial amount of those funds were spent. Forbes, who resigned on July 28 as investor anger rose over the company's accounting scandal, is now under fire for more than $1 million in expenses for which he was reimbursed.

While the expenses may in fact prove legitimate, the incident provides a glimpse into the loose financial controls of CUC International Inc., which Forbes merged with Henry R. Silverman's franchise giant, HFS Inc., last year to form Cendant. The continued battle over CUC's accounting also shows how deep the animosity within Cendant remains.

Today, four months after the scandal first broke, people close to Silverman says he still exudes a deep sense of personal outrage. Now, the question is whether Forbes, the man many hold accountable for the problems, will keep his nearly $50 million severance package. If Cendant's accounting investigation finds significant expense irregularities, he may be forced to give that up.

COLLEGIAL ATMOSPHERE. Forbes has repeatedly denied all knowledge of accounting shenanigans within CUC businesses. He maintains his expenses were appropriately billed to the company and has promised to provide a full accounting. He declined to comment on CUC's controls until an investigation by Cendant's audit committee is complete. Silverman also declined to comment on the controls.

QUESTIONS OF CONTROL

Sources close to Cendant say loose financial oversight may have contributed to questionable accounting at CUC International.

- A marginalized audit team—based hundreds of miles from the company's Stamford (Conn.) main office—wasn't focused on verifying accounting practices.
- Inadequate accounting software required most revenues and expenses to be manually entered when preparing financial statements.

CUC was long known for its collegial and informal atmosphere. But four individuals close to Cendant and its board, who all declined to be quoted, say that relaxed culture also had a downside: They say CUC's financial controls were lax and insufficient for a company of its size. At the root of the accounting problems, claim the sources: CUC's financial oversight did not mature as its business grew into an enterprise with sales in excess of $2 billion. The lingering question, some of those sources say, is whether the loose controls at CUC were a function of the company's fast growth, or whether they were left intentionally weak to hide questionable accounting.

Intentional or not, the price of CUC's laxity is staggering: Cendant says that 60% of CUC's net income for 1997 simply did not exist. The ongoing investigation has shown that the effect on Cendant was to inflate its net income before charges in 1997 by up to $250 million. The Securities & Exchange Commission and U. S. Attorney's office in Newark, N.J., are investigating, Cendant says.

While there is no evidence Forbes had a role in what Cendant has described as fraud, he appears not to have put adequate checks and balances in place at the booming CUC. For one thing, CUC's internal auditors were based in Nashville, far from the company's main Stamford (Conn.) office. And one of the sources close to Cendant says much of that group's work focused on examining operational questions such as how to improve the efficiency of certain businesses, rather than verifying CUC's books and accounting practices.

One source familiar with CUC's accounting denies the auditors' distance was a problem, because they regularly met alone with the CUC board's audit committee and outside auditors Ernst & Young, and they had the freedom to look into what they wanted.

However, outside experts say that such an arrangement could have undermined their role as financial watchdogs. "Internal auditors should be at headquarters, where they are close to the board and top executives," says Alvin H. Carley, an accounting professor at the Wharton School. "And their first priority should be financial matters."

At the same time, CUC's accounting systems were far from cutting-edge. According to one person familiar with a July 27 briefing conducted for the benefit of Cendant's audit committee by Arthur Andersen & Co., which was hired to examine the accounting mess, CUC had not invested in the kind of highly automated accounting system used by many large companies, including HFS.

With those automated systems, revenue that should be recognized over a given 12-month period, for example, would automatically be coded to hit the income statement under that schedule. But at CUC, the accounting department worked off software that required most revenues and expenses to be manually entered when preparing financial statements. 'That's a big job to do manually," says Jack Ciesielski, publisher of the *Analyst's Accounting Observer.* "In theory you can do it right, but you have to have a lot of checks and balances. Why wouldn't you want to automate something this important?"

It is not clear whether such issues were flagged by Ernst & Young. Ernst & Young says its audits of CUC's financials were done in keeping with professional standards but adds that auditors may not be able to find fraud. Given the magnitude of the apparent fraud, it's not surprising that the firm declined to comment on CUC's controls, saying it may be named as a defendant in litigation surrounding Cendant.

The former CEO says the $1 million-plus in private jet and hotel expenses that he incurred was "justified"

FORBES: HIS SEVERANCE MAY BE IN PERIL

In fact, even after the merger of HFS and CUC, the discovery of CUC's accounting problems may have been delayed by an unusual arrangement. Under the terms struck by Silverman and Forbes, CUC and HFS financial reporting operations were to stay separate for a while. But Silverman's team began raising questions in late February about the quality of information it was getting from Stamford.

Silverman reassigned several CUC financial executives with Forbes's agreement. Shortly after that, Cendant chief accounting officer Scott Forbesno relation to Walterand another executive went to Stamford to meet lower-level accounting managers from the former CUC. Those managers revealed some questionable practices, including accelerated recognition of revenues. The revelations quickly triggered the current investigation.

That inquiry now has also put Walter Forbes's spending under scrutiny. According to one source close to the board, internal auditors from Silverman's team and Arthur Andersen have raised questions about a series of expenses Forbes billed to the company from 1995 through the first quarter of 1998. Cash advances totaling nearly $600,000 were made to him, for example, but Cendant officials have found no formal expense reports to show that the money was used for business. Forbes says that he often spent his own funds on business and that those cash payments were reimbursements. He says he generally filed expense reports weekly, adding, "all my expenses were justified."

JET TURBULENCE. The greatest scrutiny, for now, is on Forbes's use of private planes. Forbes owns shares in two jets for which he personally pays a monthly fee plus per-hour charges. Use of the planes for company business would be billed to CUC. But sources close to Cendant say the hourly charge on trips billed to the company was sometimes as much as twice the market rate for those two jets.

Forbes denies that any charges for the planes were out of proportion. He says the charges factored in the total cost of his share in the jets, and that all travel billed to the company was related to business. Moreover, he says the arrangement was approved by the compensation committee of the CUC board.

More troubling: Forbes wrote a memo last year requesting reimbursement for $596,000 in air travel expenses from 1995 and 1996. According to two sources who have seen the memo, it contains a handwritten note across the bottom indicating that the expense should be charged to the merger reserves related to the HFS deal. Such expenses, Cendant officials confirm, are not likely to be appropriate merger charges. Two sources close to the board say the presence of such an instruction on Forbes's memo raises questions about whether he may have known of some of CUC's improper merger accounting. Forbes says the travel charges were legitimate expenses, that he has not seen the notation on the memo, and that it is not his handwriting. He also says he never directed anyone at CUC to set up any merger reserves.

If Forbes cannot document that the travel and cash advances were proper, Cendant's board may try to reclaim his nearly $50 million severance payout. And Forbes could wind up paying a dramatically higher price for weaknesses at the company he created.

By Amy Barrett in Philadelphia

A Bit of Barnum on Broadway; Livent Drew In a New Team Despite Juggling Expenses

By MELODY PETERSEN and GERALDINE FABRIKANT

Behind the curtain at Livent Inc., the corporate theater producer, the flamboyant impresario Garth H. Drabinsky did not just produce Tony Award-winning Broadway musicals. He also created a brilliant but mythical setting for his business, a world where much of his famously lavish spending was visible on stage but somehow rarely hurt the company's bottom line.

One of Mr. Drabinsky's props was Livent's financial books, which are being investigated by securities regulators. The company's new owners, Michael Ovitz and Roy Furman, say the books appear to have been doctored.

Unlike many musicals that have "angels," or private investors who carefully track how a producer is spending their money, Mr. Drabinsky's shows did not get such scrutiny. Livent, a public company, produced many shows at once, lumping expenses together, and disclosed few details on which ones—if any—were making money.

Other theater executives wondered how long the company could afford extravagances such as a cast of 67 performers for "Showboat" and the dozens of double-page color newspaper ads promoting its shows. One associate of Cameron Mackintosh, the highly regarded producer of "Miss Saigon," "Phantom of the Opera" and "Les Miserables," for example, remembers that Mr. Mackintosh bet him four years ago that Mr. Drabinsky's company would fail. Mr. Mackintosh could not be reached for comment.

Why, then, did Mr. Ovitz, the former talent agent and former president of the Walt Disney Company, put $20 million into Livent, and why did Mr. Furman, a co-founder of the Wall Street firm Furman Selz, agree to put up $2 million and become chairman? Mr. Furman, who sold his firm to ING Group last October, said, "We wanted to be able to look back and say that we were the people who proved to the public that theater was profitable."

"I love theater," he said. "It is very important that theater be done properly." He said that they thought they could change a "financial model that was wrong." Mr. Ovitz declined to comment.

A person close to Livent said that the two men knew before they took control that the company had some financial problems, though they did not anticipate what they call "accounting irregularities." Just last week, Mr. Furman and his new management team announced that they had discovered those irregularities and that they were suspending Mr. Drabinsky and Myron I. Gottlieb, the company's vice president and a co-founder with Mr. Drabinsky.

The company has released few details, but some executives say privately that Mr. Drabinsky kept "a second set of books." They say it appeared that the two men had run out of ways to keep their spending from hurting the company's profits and had inappropriately moved the costs to other accounts.

Mr. Drabinsky and Mr. Gottlieb have denied any wrongdoing and any knowledge of a second set of books. And yesterday, a spokesman for the two questioned why so many accusations were being hurled at them. He said that the new management had been given "ample opportunity during a protracted due diligence process to ask any questions they had."

"Why are concerns being raised now?" the spokesman asked.

But even if the new team had not discovered any irregularities, warning signs that Mr. Drabinsky's high-spending ways would eventually catch up with Livent had been popping up for years. Among them were:

- The company's debt was labeled "junk" last year by Wall Street bond-rating agencies because of worries that the company would not be able to make interest payments that amount to nearly $13 million each year. The company's debt now exceeds $130 million.
- The company, which is based in Toronto, used Canadian accounting standards, which are looser and allow companies to record profits sooner than the rules in the United States. For example, the $29 million loss that Livent reported last year using Canadian accounting would have shown up as $38 million using American standards, according to the company's financial statements.
- Analysts complained about an accounting method that the company adopted in 1996 that in essence allowed Mr. Drabinsky to spend as much as he wanted on a musical for costs such as advertising, costumes and scenery without deducting them immediately from the bottom line. Unlike most other Broadway productions, Livent was able after changing its accounting methods to show a profit on a musical even before ticket sales covered the costs.

"The accounting was aggressive," said David McFadgen, an entertainment industry analyst with Griffiths McBurney & Partners in Montreal. "It just made no sense." Mr. McFadgen has long been critical of the company's financial reporting and recalls how Mr. Drabinsky once yelled at him on the phone for issuing a negative report.

In addition, Livent's vendors had been complaining for years that the company took months to pay its bills. For example, the owners of shoemaking shops and fabric stores in Toronto, where Livent creates most of its musicals, complained about Mr. Drabinsky's slow bill-paying habits to one costume designer who was trying to buy attire for another producer's show.

"Every place I went, they would say, 'You're not with Garth Drabinsky are you?'" said the costume designer, who spoke on the condition of anonymity. "His reputation was the worst." A spokesman for Mr. Drabinsky declined to comment.

What shocked several veteran Broadway producers and executives was the company's high-spending ways. For example, the cast of 67 performers for Livent's revival of "Showboat" was "unprecedented," one Broadway executive said. "And the company was spending massive amounts of money on advertising," this person said, such as double-page color ads in major newspapers, including *The New York Times.*

Some critics also said that given its financial state, the company had spent too much to build theaters—$35 million for the Ford Center for the Performing Arts in Manhattan alone—and to promote shows in a notoriously unpredictable business. They noted that even producers of megahits showed more restraint.

Even Livent's biggest hit before "Showboat" and "Ragtime," the Tony Award-winning "Kiss of the Spider Woman," had reported a loss.

Despite all the financial woes they inherited, Mr. Ovitz and Mr. Furman are said to think that by tightening financial controls, they can turn the company around. One person who knows Mr. Ovitz well said he compared the enterprise to a movie studio that can release several films at a time and let the profits from the blockbusters carry the rest of the company.

And some entertainment executives said privately that the two men might have found the Livent deal appealing because both are at personal crossroads in their careers and both like the entertainment business. Mr. Furman, 59, apparently wanted a new challenge after selling his investment firm. And Mr. Ovitz, once referred to as the most powerful man in Hollywood, has been without a focus since he left Disney. "Where else could Ovitz get control of a highly visible company for $20 million?" asked one industry executive, who spoke on the condition of anonymity.

Mr. Furman is a longtime investor in the entertainment business. Furman Selz had taken large stakes at one time or another in Time Warner, MCA, Carolco, New Line Cinema and others. He has also headed the Film Society of Lincoln Center and is an avid theatergoer.

The two men were so enamored of show business, apparently, that they were willing to set aside Mr. Drabinsky's checkered stewardship of another company, Cineplex Odeon, the movie theater chain, nearly a decade ago. That company was also criticized for its aggressive accounting methods. In 1989, Mr. Drabinsky was ousted in a fierce battle with MCA, one of Cineplex Odeon's largest shareholders.

However, neither Mr. Furman nor Mr. Ovitz had extensive financial experience in the arcane world of live theater. And Mr. Furman had never run a public company. Not only that, for now at least, they must rely on several of the same creative executives who worked for Mr. Drabinsky.

Associates of Mr. Furman and Mr. Ovitz said one main protection they saw for their investment was the value of the real estate: Besides Livent's New York theater, it owns two in Toronto; one in Vancouver, British Columbia, and one in Chicago. A person close to the company estimated their value at up to $200 million, though a theater industry expert, who spoke on the condition of anonymity, gave a lower estimate of about $120 million, not enough to wipe out the company's debt.

Mr. Furman also sees plays as "software" that could generate pay television, pay-per-view and video rights, one of his associates said. But one pay-television executive, who spoke on the condition of anonymity, said there was no recent history of Broadway shows selling to pay TV or pay-per-per view because there was not much interest in buying such projects. Revenues from home-video sales have been slim.

Livent clearly has a long way to go. It has said it will take additional write-offs that have nothing to do with the accounting irregularities, possibly relating to the North American tour of "Showboat." And despite the near-sellout of "Ragtime" in New York, it is doing relatively mediocre business on tour. Though Livent plans to open "Ragtime" in Chicago in October, its debut in London has been postponed indefinitely. If it does open there, Livent might try to cut costs by taking sets and props from an existing production, a person close to the company said.

In the future, "Ragtime" and other Livent shows will have to lure audiences without the huge advertising budgets for which Mr. Drabinsky was famous. That makes the new owners' bet on which plays to produce and which performers to hire all that more crucial.

Alas, those were the things that Mr. Drabinsky, now gone, did best.

THE LESSON FROM BARINGS' STRAITS

It's a long way from the dreary public-housing complex in the London suburb of Watford, where Nick Leeson grew up as a plasterer's son, to Singapore's exclusive Orchard Road section. The cocksure head of futures trading in Barings PLC's Singapore office, Leeson earned a $1 million bonus last year, drove a Porsche, and sailed his yacht on weekends off Malaysia. But all that came crashing down with the Feb. 25 revelation that Leeson, 28, had piled up $1.3 billion in losses on spoiled derivative deals in Singapore and Osaka.

In one humiliating blow, Leeson's huge trading loss wiped out the blue-blood investment bank's $900 million in capital and prompted the Bank of England to put Barings into bankruptcy. The collapse also sent shivers down the spines of bankers around the globe. "With so much money moving around so quickly, this is the kind of thing all of us worry about)" says First Chicago Corp. CEO Richard L. Thomas. "It's stunning to think that a 233-year-old institution can be brought to its knees overnight."

EYE-POPPING. Stunning, perhaps. But not totally surprising. Over the past year or so, one financial shock after another has hit the front pages and CNN. A common thread runs through them: In the global liquidity boom of the early 1990s, when more than $1.5 trillion in U.S. mutual-fund money flooded the globe, money was so available, markets so ebullient, and profits so rich that simple safeguards and controls went by the board. Now, as interest rates rise and the margin for error narrows, many are paying a high price for inattention. Says New York economist Henry Kaufman: "Whether it's Mexico or Barings, these problems reflect inadequate monitoring and supervision."

By any standard, the list of financial accidents since 1994 is eye-popping. Hedge-fund manager George Soros, for example, dropped $600 million by misjudging the strength of the Japanese yen. Procter & Gamble Co. lost $102 million on leveraged derivatives purchased from Bankers Trust Co. The venerable investment house of Kidder, Peabody & Co. was sold off and dismembered after Joseph Jett allegedly ran up $350 million in paper profits on bogus bond deals. Wealthy Orange County, Calif., went bust when its treasurer made a spectacularly wrong bet on the direction of rates. And Mexico, the darling of emerging markets, had to seek a $53 billion international bailout after its debt-fueled economy ran out of hard cash.

Now, Barings joins the casualty list. Administrators from Ernst & Young are selling off pieces of the firm. The Dutch bank ABN Amro is buyings Barings' corporate finance unit, and Merrill Lynch & Co. and Dresdner Bank may bid for other parts. But long after the disposal is over, regulators and financiers will still be asking whether Barings' situation was unique. Many think not. Warns Bank of England Governor Eddie George: "What happened to Barings could happen to any financial institution in the world." Especially if one individual is given enough leeway to bet the entire store.

SLOSH OF FUNDS. In the easy-money boom, too many securities executives lost the ability or will to scrutinize high-energy traders or guard against unethical salespeople. Too many bankers and CFOs neglected to ask whether they understood the complexity—or the downside—of the highly leveraged derivatives they were using to hedge financial risks. And as an influx of some $300 billion in foreign portfolio money sent stock and bond markets soaring in developing countries, too many investors and fund managers stopped asking basic questions about disclosure, accounting, value, and risk.

Fortunately, the accidents of 1994 and '95 have not brought the financial world to its knees. Even with the Federal Reserve and some European central banks tightening, so many trillions of investment dollars are still sloshing around the globe that it's hard for any one event to disturb the momentum for long. In fact, faced with adversity, the global capital market has done a credible job of making capital flow from the basket cases to the healthy.

The affair has caused soul-searching among financiers worldwide. "If this happened at an institution that's supposed to be high quality, what's going on at lesser investment banks?" asks Henry T.C. Hu, a University of Texas professor and derivatives expert. "Perhaps we've been too complacent, and things aren't as clean as people thought."

Chastened, the world's exchange officials, central bankers, and financiers also want to know how the Barings meltdown happened and how they might prevent another one. What they are learning is nothing short of remarkable. It shouldn't be possible, but a lone trader bought enough futures and options contracts in three weeks to amass a $27 billion bet. His local bosses, the exchange regulators in three Asian cities, and Barings' managers in London stayed in the dark.

Leeson's trading-floor peers knew something was up. But they didn't sound the alarm, because Barings had been taking huge positions for years in Nikkei stock-index futures as part of a low-risk arbitrage operation that tried to profit from minute price differences in contracts traded in Singapore and Osaka. Then, around Jan. 26, Leeson mysteriously switched from arb to speculator. He converted all his contracts to buys—most likely in the belief that the destruction caused by the recent Kobe earthquake would stimulate the economy and push up the Nikkei.

When the stock market didn't cooperate, Leeson sold put and call options to raise cash for margin calls and bet that the market would settle into a narrow range. But as the Nikkei continued falling, Leeson is thought to have made one last roll of the dice on Feb. 20.

His losses had accumulated to about $700 million, and the exchanges wanted Barings to put up more cash to cover his deficit. The Bank of England says Leeson then fooled Barings officials in London into writing checks for margin calls, likely by saying the trades were on behalf of a corporate client whose funds would be deposited with Barings in a few days. When he couldn't produce the funds, Leeson fled, leaving behind a note saying: "I'm sorry."

What went wrong is simple: Barings allowed Leeson to wear too many hats. Preliminary investigations discovered that Leeson was both trader and manager, often settling his own trades. That was in violation of Osaka exchange rules and of industry practice, which keeps traders apart from back-office staffers who confirm transactions and write checks. "Leeson was the front office and the back office," says Graham Newall, head of futures trading at Barclays Bank PLC. "You can't stop someone from going berserk, but you can have a system to catch it in 24 hours."

NO RANDOM CHECKS. A Barings source says Leeson was allowed to clear trades because of his previous experience as a settlement clerk at Morgan Stanley & Co. Whatever the reason, critics say Barings clearly lacked the most elemental of security systems to keep track of its traders' activities. For example, Daniel Hodson, CEO of the London International Financial Futures Exchange, believes that Barings lacked informal, back-channel communication links with exchanges, as well as simple random checks of how well its personnel followed rules. And many outside observers say Barings management neglected to investigate why the firm's trading volume was soaring.

To catch such discrepancies, some investment banks, including Merrill Lynch, now have independent risk-management units reporting directly to the CEO. Merrill set its unit up after losing $377 million from unauthorized trading in 1987. But at Barings, says Peter Letley, deputy chairman of HSBC Investment Banking Ltd., "there were no independent controls." That's all the more dangerous when traders are dealing with derivative contracts whose value can fluctuate wildly even on small movements in stock, bond, or currency prices. Says Robert Gumerlock, managing director for risk control at Swiss Bank Corp.: "Derivatives can give you enough leverage to blow yourself up."

Paying too little heed to this reality can be a big problem for all kinds of companies. Abraham M. George, CEO of Multinational Computer Models Inc., helps international corporations manage currency and interest-rate risk. A typical portfolio these days, he notes, may contain a bewildering array of fixed and floating-rate debt, swaps that switch among currencies, options, structured notes, and more. He doubts whether many executives even know if their own treasurers understand the quirky behavior of the instruments in their portfolios. Asks George: "When you have a complex position, do senior managers know what it's worth at any given time?"

LURE OF LUCRE. Investors are asking much the same question of mutual funds, which moved more than $300 billion overseas in the 1990s in search of high returns in emerging markets. It may have been this flood of foreign capital, as much as economic and political reforms, that enabled emerging-market bourses to outperform those in industrial countries by nearly 3 to 1 in the early '90s.

But as markets climbed, many novice fund managers abandoned common sense for the lure of a quick buck. Eagerly acquiring Chilean bank stocks at twice book value or Thai telecom issues with price-earnings ratios of 100, "they understood how to run models, but they didn't really understand whether their earnings estimates were meaningful," says Bruce B. Bee, a veteran global money manager in Denver. So when liquidity started to erode last year, many markets that were high on U.S. cash swiftly returned to more normal valuations.

What should be done about the oversight gap? The solution probably isn't more regulation. The Bank of England is now under fire for missing another major case of deception, having taken heat from the 1991 failure of Bank of Credit & Commerce International (BCCI). But "don't talk to me about rules," snaps central bank chief George. "We've got rules galore. Unfortunately, we've also got criminals."

Some of these will always slip through holes in the system. But as Barings executives found out too late, a far greater willingness to ask tough questions—in good times and bad—might have kept the historic investment bank alive. When the market dishes out discipline, whether because of Mexico's economic misdeeds or Barings' trading scandal, punishment can be swift and severe. By refusing to bail out Barings, the Bank of England made that point crystal clear. Not every failure can be prevented. But a good deal more skepticism would go a long way toward limiting the losses.

How One Firm Tracks Ethics Electronically

By Michael J. McCarthy

BETHESDA, Md.—Lockheed Martin Corp. is turning business ethics into rocket science.

While some companies worry about workers wasting time on the Web, the aerospace giant is aggressively steering them into cyberspace as part of a broad program—born of a bribery scandal—to audit, record and perfect the measurement of employee morals.

Using internal computer programs with names like Merlin and Qwizard, many of Lockheed Martin's 160,000 employees go online these days for step-by-step training on ethics and legal compliance. The system records each time an employee completes one of the sessions, which range from sexual harassment and insider trading to kickbacks and gratuities. Last month, it began alerting managers to employees who haven't yet taken required sessions.

Lockheed Martin's electronic ethics program also closely tracks alleged wrongdoing inside the company. It knows, for example, that it takes 30.4 days on average to complete an internal investigation of ethics violations, and that the company has fired 217 people for them since 1995. In the first six months of this year, 4.8% of its ethics allegations involved conflicts of interest, while 8.9% involved security and misuse of assets.

In short, Lockheed Martin is tackling ethical matters with a scientific precision usually associated with its F-16 fighter jets.

One big reason for these complex ethics metrics: legal defense in case the company faces charges again. Lockheed Corp. did not have such a sophisticated program in place in 1995, when, on the eve of its merger with Martin Marietta Corp., it agreed to pay a $24.8 million fine and plead guilty to conspiring to violate U.S. antibribery laws. Lockheed admitted that it illegally paid $1 million to an Egyptian lawmaker in 1990 for helping sell its C-130 aircraft in that country.

To keep from losing government contracts, Lockheed Martin submitted to a 60-page administrative agreement that amounted to a three-year probationary period. Like clockwork, it was required to turn over to the U.S. Air Force periodic ethics reports, including details of ethical complaints made to its employee hotline and other misconduct allegations.

In its leafy, suburban office park here in the shadow of the federal government, Lockheed Martin hardly wants to jeopardize its contractor status. Fully 70% of its $26.3 billion in sales comes solely from the U.S. government. "If they debar the corporation, that's death for this company," says David T. Clous, vice president for ethics and business conduct.

What's more, the electronic ethics program could win the company lenient treatment should it be indicted in a future case. The decade-old Federal Sentencing Guidelines, which codified fines and penalties for corporate wrongdoing, also established that fines for criminal conduct could be reduced by as much as 95% if a company had concrete internal programs to detect and prevent illegal acts. But if a company couldn't produce a paper trail of proof that it had tried to prevent wrongdoing, fines and penalties could be ratcheted up by 400%.

As part of its drive to stay on the straight and narrow, Lockheed Martin also developed an ethics game, which every single employee, up to Chairman Vance D. Coffman, must play once a year. With cards and tokens, workers spend one-hour sessions packed around tables, considering how to handle ethical quandaries drawn from actual Lockheed Martin cases—from harassment to padded work schedules.

The Ethics Challenge, as it is called, has been a hit—except for one year, when the ethics department revised the game so that it no longer indicated which answers were right or wrong. The idea was to let players debate. But the imprecision drove the company's exacting engineers nuts. "They had a hard time with it," says Brian Sears, an ethics officer for the aeronautics division. The game was revised again, to offer "preferred answers."

Meanwhile, the ethics department went to work developing numerous "interactive" training sessions, on security, software-license compliance and labor charging. The courses, with actors playing out hypothetical cases, were originally produced for CD-ROMs, at a cost of about $150,000 apiece. Clicking along at a workstation, an employee usually takes about 45 minutes to complete a session. A sample question from the kickback-and-gratuity clinic:

A kickback may be in the form of:
A. Cash
B. Gift to a family member
C. Donation to a charity at your request
D. All of these
(The correct answer is D.)

From the sexual-harassment segment:

Which is the best means of addressing harassment when it first occurs?
A. Ignore the harasser
B. Be direct and tell the harasser his or her behavior is unwelcome and offensive

C. Report the harasser to your manager or Human Resources

(The correct answer is B.)

To provide proof that it has been systematically teaching employees the laws appropriate to their divisions and positions, Lockheed Martin also wanted an up-to-the-minute auditing system, which would track who had taken what training session and when. Last year, turning to the power of the Web, it began using its automated Merlin system to instantly track the number of courses taken and by whom.

The company says employees have warmed up to the program, particularly since it went online and workers no longer have to check out CD-ROMs or visit special workstations to meet their training requirements. But Lockheed is realistic. "We never envision people lining up and saying, 'Rah-rah, it's time for compliance training,' " says Tracy Carter Dougherty, director of ethics communication and training.

"Computer-based training can't completely replace personalized training," says Joseph E. Murphy, an ethics and compliance specialist with Compliance Systems Legal Group in Warwick, R.I. But having a system with mandatory clinics and quizzes will help "convince a prosecutor or regulator that the company is trying to prevent and detect problems," he adds.

Indeed, Steven Shaw, the U.S. Air Force deputy general counsel who held a debarment ax over Lockheed Martin until the probationary period ended last year, says he is pleased the company is still keeping close statistical tabs on ethical conduct and compliance training. And noting that the company hasn't been indicted since the Egypt case, he adds, "To me, that says a lot about a company that large. You'll always have people who will make mistakes."

Rocket Science

Lockheed keeps close tabs on how employees are disciplined for ethics violations

	1995	**1999***
Discharge	56	25
Suspension	47	14
Written reprimand	59	51
Oral reprimand	164	146
Other	60	66
Total sanctions	386	302

*Figures to June 30.

Source: Lockheed Martin

Index

A

Abernathy, Bill, 90
accounting, Cendant Corp. and, 216–217
accounts payable, reengineering, 179
Advanced Micro Devices (AMD), 102, 106
alcohol, on eBay, 51
Allen, Bob, 63
AMC Entertainment Inc., 201
America Online Inc. (AOL), 51, 78, 79, 80; impact of merger of Time Warner with, 81–83
American Cyanamid, 111–112
American Express, 40–47, 66
Analog Devices, 103
Andrews, Kenneth, 86
Apple Computer, 66, 124, 125, 126
application-handling processing, reengineering, 175–176
Astra, 25–26
AT&T, 20, 78–80, 82–83, 205, 206, 207
Atlas Door, 144
automotive industry, 127
autonomy, crisis of, and organizational development, 73
aviation industry, in China, 28
Avis, 112
Avon Books, 161

B

balanced scorecard, 208–215
Ballantine, 161
Barings PLC, 221–222
Barrett, Craig R., 102–104, 105, 106, 108
Bartlett, Christopher, 91, 93–94
Bateson, Gregory, 124
Battenberg, J. T., III, 190
Bernstock, Robert F., 172
Bertelli, Patrizio, 114–115
Bettis, Richard, 93
BetzDearborn, 206
biotechnology, pharmaceutical industry and, 130
Bloomberg Financial Markets, 9–10
Bloomberg, Michael, 9–10
Boston Consulting Group, 88
Bower, Joseph, 88
Brazil, Coca-Cola in, 55, 58
break-even time (BET), 211
Brown, Dave, 184
Buffett, Warren E., 50
Burger King, Coca-Cola contract with, 59
Burlingame, Harold W., 205, 207
business ecosystems, 124–132
Butterfield & Butterfield, 52

C

Caliber Logistics Inc., 197
Campbell, Andrew, 91, 93
Carmike Cinemas, 201
Case Technology, 105
Caterpillar, 145
CBS, 82
Cendent Corp., 205, 216–217
CEOs, reasons for failure of, 62–67
Chancellor Media Corp., 79
Chenault, Hortenius, 42
Chenault, Ken, 40–47
China: Coco-Cola in, 58; hotel industry in, 27–29
Christensen, C. Roland, 88
Christensen, Clayton, 8–11
Cineplex Odeon, 200–201, 202
Cisco Systems Inc., 104, 136–137, 205
Coca-Cola, 55–61
Coldwell Banker, 112
collaboration, organizational development and, 74, 75, 76
Columbia/HCA Healthcare, 122
Columbia-Presbyterian Medical Center, 121
Comcast, 78
Compaq, 62, 103, 106
competition, business ecosystems and, 124–132
competitive advantage, 138–150; sustainable, 133–134
conglomerates, diversification and, 87–88
Consolidated Cigar, 112
control, crisis of, and organizational development, 74
Coopers & Lybrand, 205
coordination, organizational development and, 74
COOs, CEOs and, 66
"Copy Exactly," 106
Corbo, Vincent J., 206–207
core competences, diversification and, 92–93
Costco, 155–157
creativity, organizational development and, 73
CUC International, 206, 216–217
customer satisfaction, measures of, and performance, 209–210, 214
Customer Service Supply Chain initiative, at Levi Strauss & Co., 166–167
Cyrix, 102, 106

D

daily financial reports, 213
de Geus, Arie, 134
delegation, organizational development and, 73–74, 75
Dell Computer, 34–35, 196–198
Dell, Michael, 34, 35, 67, 196–198
Deloitte, Haskins & Sells, 205
Delphi Automotive Systems, at General Motors, 190
DeMartini, Paul J., 15–17
department stores, shopping carts and, 203–204
Dialogic, 103
Digital Equipment Corp. (DEC), 10
Digital Research, 125
direction, organizational development and, 73
diversification, 86–96
Donnelly Corporation, 143
Doz, Yves, 93
Drabinski, Garth H., 218–219, 220
Drucker, Peter, 86
DSP Communications, 103, 104
Dunlap, Al, 181
Duracell International Inc., 99–101
Durant, William C., 127

E

Eastman Chemical Co., 198
eBay, 50–54
eBay Great Collections, 52–53
eBayLA, 52
Ebbers, Bernard J., 116–117
Edwards Theatre Circuit Inc., 201
electronic commerce, Jack Welch and, 20
Eli Lilly, 130
environmental regulations, impact of, on gas stations, 15, 16
EPS Solutions Inc., 207
ethics, at Lockheed Martin, 223–224
Ethics Challenge, at Lockheed Martin, 223–224
evolution, organizational development and, 70–77
Excite At Home, 81–82
Exxon Corp., 85–85

F

Federal Express, 135–137
Federal Sentencing Guidelines, 223
firearms, on eBay, 51
Folding Carrier Co., 204
Food Lion, 138–141, 148–149
Forbes, Walter A., 216–217
Ford, Henry, 127
Ford Motor Corp., 127, 175, 179
Formica Corp., 110–113
Fudge, Ann, 46
Furman, Roy, 218, 219–220

G

gas stations, impact of taxes, regulations, and technology on, 15–17
GC Co., 199, 200–201, 202
GE Medical Systems (GEMS), 18, 21, 151, 152–154
Genentech, 150
General Cinemas, 199, 200–201, 202
General Electric, 18–22, 88, 207; use of Six Sigma at, 151–154
General Mills, 90
General Motors, 127, 143, 185–191
General Signal, 90
generator industry, 11
Gerstner, Louis V., 42–43
Ghoshal, Sumantra, 91, 93–94
Gillette Co., 99–101

Glass, David, 35
Goizeuta, Roberto C., 55, 57, 58, 61
Goldman, Sylvan, 203, 204
Golub, Harvey, 40–41, 44, 45
Goold, Michael, 91, 93
Gould, Stephen Jay, 124
Grove, Andrew, 8, 9, 102–103, 105, 106, 107–108
Gucci, 114
Guitierrez, Carlos M., 37–38, 39
Gund, Agnes, 37, 39
Gund, Gordon, 37, 39

H

Haas, Robert, 163–168
Hadfield, David, 205
Hamel, Gary, 92, 134
Haspeslagh, Philippe, 92
Hayes, Bob, 90
health care industry, specialization by hospitals and, 121–123
Healthsouth Corp., 121, 122
Heart Institute, 122
Hercules Inc., 206–207
Hewlett-Packard Company, 97–98, 178–179, 211
HFS Inc., 206, 216–217
Hiner, Glen H., 181–182
Hoch, Orion, 93
Hoeksema, Timothy, 118–119
Honda, 10, 143
hospitals, specialization by, 121–123
hotel industry, in China, 27–29
Hyatt, 27

I

IBM, 10, 92, 124, 126, 127–129
Icahn, Carl, 89
Icarus Paradox (Miller), 140
Independent Grocers Alliance (I.G.A.), 14
information technology, sustainable competitive advantage and, 133–134
Innovator's Dilemma: When New Technologies Cause Great Firms to Fail, The (Christensen), 9–11
insurance application processing, reengineering, 175–176
Intel, 8, 102–109, 128, 129
"intuitive" management, 87
invoiceless processing, 175
Itami, Hiroyuki, 92

I

ITT, 87, 88
Ivester, Doug, 55–61

J

Jager, Durk I., 48–49
Japan, Coca-Cola in, 55, 58
Jemison, David, 92
Johnson, Dorothy A., 37
Johnson, Elmer, 65

K

Kanter, Rosabeth Moss, 91
Kaufthal, Ilan, 111
Kelleher, Herb, 134
Kellogg Co., 37–39
Kellogg, Will Keith, 37
Kessler, Murray, 171, 172
Kiechel, Walter, 92
Kirkland, 157
Kmart, 12
knowledge, information technology and, 134
Kodak, 9, 66
Koontz, Harold, 87
Kroger Company, 12

L

LaMothe, William E., 38, 39
Langbo, Arnold, 38
Langone, Vincent P., 111, 112, 113
leadership, crisis of, and organizational development, 73
leadership development, at General Electric, 22
Leeson, Nick, 221–222
Lenox Hill Hospital, 123
leveraged buyouts, Formica Corp. and, 110–113
Levi Strauss & Co., 163–168
Lexus, 144
Lightspeed, development of, at GE Medical Systems using Six Sigma, 152–154
Litton, 87, 88
Livent Inc., 218–220
Lockheed Martin, 223–224
Loews Cineplex Entertainment Corp. 199, 200
Lotus, 128
love seats, in movie theaters, 201
Lucent Technologies, 10, 206

M

Mannion, Arthur, 10–11
McAllen Heart Center, 121–122
McAllen Medical Center, 121–122
McCoy, James, 12
MCI WorldCom.Inc., 116–117
Medcath Inc., 122
MediaOne Group, 78–79
Methodist Hospital, 122
Mexico: Coca-Cola in, 55, 58–59; Dell and, 197
MGM Studios, 112
Micropro, 125
Microsoft, 10, 78, 80, 82, 127, 128, 129
Midwest Express, 118–120
Miller, Danny, 140
Milliken & Co., 212–213
Mintzberg, Henry, 90
Mobil Corp., 16, 84–85
Motorola, 24
movie theaters, addition of VIP rooms by, 199–202
multibranding, at Levi Strauss & Co., 167–168
Mutual Benefit Life Insurance (MBL), 175–176, 179–180

N

Nanula, Richard, 46
Network Appliances, 107
New York Pain Treatment Program, 123
News Corp., 81
Nintendo, 9
Nokia, 23–24
NordicTrack Inc., 169–170
Nortel Networks, 10
Noto, Lucio, 84, 85

O

Olds, Ransom E., 127
One Source, 13
organizational development, stage of, 70–77
Ovitz, Michael, 218, 219–220
Owens Corning, 181–184

P

paperbacks, 160–162
PassEdge, 106, 109
PepsiCo, 56, 60, 145
personal computer industry, 10; business ecosystems and, 125–129
Pfeiffer, Eckhard, 62
pharmaceutical industry, 129–130
Pickens, T. Boone, 89
Pocket Books, 160–161
Poland, Coca-Cola in, 58
Porter, Michael, 86, 91, 141–142
Portera, Joseph, 156
portfolio management, diversification and, 89
portfolio planning, diversification and, 88–89
Prada, 114–115
Prahalad, C.K., 92, 93
Premium Cinemas, of General Cinemas, 199, 200–201, 202
Price Waterhouse, 205
Procter & Gamble, 48–49, 92
publishing industry, paperbacks and, 160–162

Q

Qantas Airways, 28
QMI (quick market intelligence), 19–20
quality control, 210; Six Sigma at Genenral Electric and, 151–154

R

Raines, Franklin, 46
Rand, A. Barry, 46
Raymond, Lee, 84, 85
Red Lobster, 194–195

red-tape crisis, organizational development and, 74
reengineering, of processes, 174–180
Regal Cinemas, 201
regional auctions, on eBay, 52
Rehrig International Inc., 204
resource allocation, diversification and, 88
restructuring, diversification and, 90–91
revolution, organizational development and, 70–77
Roberts, Roy, 76
Robin Transports, 143
Robinson, James D., III, 41, 66
Rolm, 92
RPS, 135
Russia, Coca-Cola in, 55–56

S

Salick Health Care, 122–123
Sanck Health Center, 121
SAP, at Owens Corning, 183
satellites, 24
SBC Corp., 10
Sculley, John, 66
Sears Roebuck & Co., 203–204
service stations. *See* gas stations
Shangri-La, 27, 28
Shearson Lehman Brothers Capital, 112
shopping carts, department stores and, 203–204
Siboni, Roger, 66
Silverman, Henry R., 216, 217
Simmons Co., 112
Sinegal, Jim, 155–156
Six Sigma, at General Electric, 21, 151–154
Sizzler International Inc., 194–195
Sloan, Alfred P., 127
Smith Frederick W., 135–137
Sonat, 11
Sony Corp., 82
sound systems, in movie theaters, 201
Southwest Airlines, 134
St. Vincent's Hospital, 121
stadium-style seating, at movie theaters, 201
Starwood, 27, 28
STB Systems Inc., 197
stealth attacks, guarding against, 8–11
stock options, at Duracell International, 100
Strauss, Karen, 184
Sun Microsystems, 10
supermarkets, 12–14
Sure Power Corp., 10–11
sustainable competitive advantage, 133–134
Swanson frozen foods, 171–173
SWOT analysis, 140–141, 143

T

Tandy Corporation, 125, 126
taxes, impact of, on gas stations, 15, 16
telecommunications, 23–24
Tele-Communications Inc., 78, 205, 206, 207
Tenet Healthcare Inc., 122
Texas Heart Institute, 122
Texas Instruments, 92
Texas Orthopedic Hospital, 122
Textron, 87–88
3Com Corp., 198
Time Warner, 78, 80; impact of merger of America Online with, 81–83
tobacco, on eBay, 51
TQM (Total Quality Management), 211
Trautwein, Friedrich, 91
Tungsram, 18–19, 21
TV dinners, Swanson frozen foods and, 171–173

U

Unarco Industries Inc., 204
Unicom, 11
United Artists Theatres, 200, 202
United Parcel Service (UPS), 135, 136
Universal Health Services, 121
UPS (United Parcel Service), 135, 136

V

value-based planning, diversification and, 89–90
vending machines, Coca-Cola and, 59
Via, 102
Viacom, 82
VIP rooms, at movie theaters, 199–202
Virgin Cinemas Ltd., 200, 202
Vivonic, 106, 109
Vlasic Foods International, 171–173

W

Wagoner, G. Richard, 185–191
wall-to-wall screens, in movie theaters, 201
Wal-Mart, 12, 34, 35–36, 131–132, 145–148
Walt Disney Corp., 81
Ward, Lloyd, 46
Warner Books, 161
Welch, Jack, 18–22, 65, 66
Whitman, Margaret, 50–54
Whitmore, Kay, 66
Work-Outs, 19, 20, 21

Y

Yahoo!, 83

Z

Zacharius, Walter, 162
Zarrella, Ronald L., 190
Zeien, Alfred M., 100–101
Zeneca, 25–26

AE Article Review Form

We encourage you to photocopy and use this page as a tool to assess how the articles in ***Annual Editions*** expand on the information in your textbook. By reflecting on the articles you will gain enhanced text information. You can also access this useful form on a product's book support Web site at ***http://www.dushkin.com/online/.***

NAME: DATE:

TITLE AND NUMBER OF ARTICLE:

BRIEFLY STATE THE MAIN IDEA OF THIS ARTICLE:

LIST THREE IMPORTANT FACTS THAT THE AUTHOR USES TO SUPPORT THE MAIN IDEA:

WHAT INFORMATION OR IDEAS DISCUSSED IN THIS ARTICLE ARE ALSO DISCUSSED IN YOUR TEXTBOOK OR OTHER READINGS THAT YOU HAVE DONE? LIST THE TEXTBOOK CHAPTERS AND PAGE NUMBERS:

LIST ANY EXAMPLES OF BIAS OR FAULTY REASONING THAT YOU FOUND IN THE ARTICLE:

LIST ANY NEW TERMS/CONCEPTS THAT WERE DISCUSSED IN THE ARTICLE, AND WRITE A SHORT DEFINITION:

We Want Your Advice

ANNUAL EDITIONS revisions depend on two major opinion sources: one is our Advisory Board, listed in the front of this volume, which works with us in scanning the thousands of articles published in the public press each year; the other is you—the person actually using the book. Please help us and the users of the next edition by completing the prepaid article rating form on this page and returning it to us. Thank you for your help!

ANNUAL EDITIONS: Strategic Management 01/02

ARTICLE RATING FORM

Here is an opportunity for you to have direct input into the next revision of this volume. We would like you to rate each of the 50 articles listed below, using the following scale:

1. Excellent: should definitely be retained
2. Above average: should probably be retained
3. Below average: should probably be deleted
4. Poor: should definitely be deleted

Your ratings will play a vital part in the next revision. So please mail this prepaid form to us just as soon as you complete it. Thanks for your help!

RATING	ARTICLE
	1. Danger: Stealth Attack
	2. Supersizing the Supermarkets in a Shift of Power; Discounters and Mergers Alter Balance of Power
	3. Between a Gas Pump and a Hard Place
	4. See Jack. See Jack Run Europe
	5. Nokia: Made in Finland and Sold Just about Everywhere
	6. Zeneca Buying Astra As Europe Consolidates
	7. China Rolls Out the Red Carpet
	8. America's Most Admired Companies
	9. Big Kellogg Shareholders Seek More Snap, Crackle and Pop
	10. The Rise of a Star
	11. New CEO Preaches Rebellionfor P&G's 'Cult'
	12. The Auctioneer: Margaret Whitman, the CEO of eBay, Talks about the Company's Rapid Growth—and Heady Ambitions
	13. Man on the Spot
	14. Why CEOs Fail
	15. Evolution and Revolution As Organizations Grow
	16. The Net-Phone-TV-Cable Monster
	17. You've Got Time Warner—How the Merger Will Affect Other Big Web and Media Players
	18. How 2 Executives Pulled Off the Biggest Merger Ever
	19. Why Diversify? Four Decades of Management Thinking
	20. A Powerhouse of Technology Decides to Split into 2 Units
	21. How Gillette Wowed Wall Street
	22. The New Intel
	23. How Formica Got Burned Out by Buyouts
	24. Prada Goes Shopping
	25. Doc Ebbers' Miracle Diet
	26. Market Place: Midwest Express Profits by Pampering Passengers

RATING	ARTICLE
	27. Specialized Hospitals Taking Over Health-Care Market
	28. Predators and Prey: A New Ecology of Competition
	29. The Changing Art of Becoming Unbeatable
	30. FedEx CEO Smith Bets His Deal with Cisco Will Recast the Future of Shipping
	31. Creating Competitive (Dis)advantage: Learning from Food Lion's Freefall
	32. Six Sigma Enlightenment; Managers Seek Corporate Nirvana through Quality Control
	33. Inside the Cult of Costco
	34. Publishers of Paperbacks Are Facing Sliding Sales
	35. How Levi's Trashed a Great American Brand
	36. How NordicTrack Lost Its Footing
	37. A Makeover for the TV Dinner; Swanson Is Being Upgraded to Restore Market Share
	38. Reengineering Work: Don't Automate, Obliterate
	39. Owens Corning: Back from the Dead
	40. A Close-Up Look at President Rick Wagoner and His Strategy for Reviving GM
	41. Why Sizzler Fizzled: As Competition Heated Up, Chain's Concept Went Stale
	42. Whirlwind on the Web
	43. The New VIP Rooms
	44. Lack of Shopping Carts Impact Sales at Traditional Department Stores
	45. The Deal Is Done. Now the Work Begins
	46. The Balanced Scorecard—Measures That Drive Performance
	47. Cendant: Who's to Blame?
	48. A Bit of Barnum on Broadway; Livent Drew in a New Team Despite Juggling Expenses
	49. The Lesson from Barings' Straits
	50. How One Firm Tracks Ethics Electronically

(Continued on next page)

ANNUAL EDITIONS: STRATEGIC MANAGEMENT 01/02

NO POSTAGE NECESSARY IF MAILED IN THE UNITED STATES

BUSINESS REPLY MAIL
FIRST-CLASS MAIL PERMIT NO. 84 GUILFORD CT

POSTAGE WILL BE PAID BY ADDRESSEE

McGraw-Hill/Dushkin
530 Old Whitfield Street
Guilford, CT 06437-9989

ABOUT YOU

Name ______ Date ______

Are you a teacher? ☐ A student? ☐
Your school's name ______

Department ______

Address ______ City ______ State ______ Zip ______

School telephone # ______

YOUR COMMENTS ARE IMPORTANT TO US !

Please fill in the following information:
For which course did you use this book? ______

Did you use a text with this *ANNUAL EDITION*? ☐ yes ☐ no
What was the title of the text? ______

What are your general reactions to the *Annual Editions* concept? ______

Have you read any particular articles recently that you think should be included in the next edition? ______

Are there any articles you feel should be replaced in the next edition? Why? ______

Are there any World Wide Web sites you feel should be included in the next edition? Please annotate. ______

May we contact you for editorial input? ☐ yes ☐ no
May we quote your comments? ☐ yes ☐ no